The Dragon Wakes

A Cassell BOOK

THE DRAGON
WAKES

CHINA AND THE WEST, 1793–1911

Christopher Hibbert

Harper & Row, Publishers
New York and Evanston

1817

First published in England under the same
title by Longman Group Limited, London

THE DRAGON WAKES: CHINA AND THE WEST,
1793–1911. Copyright © 1970 by
Christopher Hibbert. All rights reserved.
Printed in the United States of America.
No part of this book may be used or
reproduced in any manner whatsoever
without written permission except in the
case of brief quotations embodied in
critical articles and reviews. For information
address Harper & Row, Publishers, Inc.,
49 East 33rd Street, New York, N.Y. 10016.

FIRST U.S. EDITION

LIBRARY OF CONGRESS CATALOG
CARD NUMBER: 75-83600

FOR SUE

Let the Chinese dragon sleep for when she awakes she will astonish the world. Attributed to Napoleon I.

Theoretically, the Chinese communist revolution is a repudiation of the millennial history of China. Communist China has broken decisively with its past, loudly and explicitly disowned its long and splendid history. The recent 'cultural revolution' has emphasized and exaggerated that breach. The deposit of 4000 years has now been repudiated in its totality; everything that is old has been discarded; and all things, we are told, have been made new. But in fact, what has happened? The inheritance of the Kuomintang, of the Chinese Republic, has indeed been rejected, but the older inheritance of the Manchus, of the Chinese Empire, has returned to fill the void.

Today Peking is once again the capital of the Middle Kingdom, Chairman Mao, like the Son of Heaven, is to live for ten thousand years. The Europeans are again outer barbarians, whom the self-sufficient Celestial Empire has no need to know. The usages of international diplomacy, of the comity of nations, have been rejected; and foreign embassies provide the means not of negotiation but of tribute: of the enforced kotow, of the sacked legation, and of periodic humiliation by the officials of a vast, impervious, conformist bureaucracy.

Such is the revenge of history on those who ignore it.

Professor Hugh Trevor-Roper in his Oration Day address at the London School of Economics, 6 December 1968.

Contents

Contents

Illustrations

Illustrations

Grateful acknowledgement is given to the following people for permission to reproduce the illustrations used in this book: Nos 4 and 5, British Museum; No 6 from C. Toogood Downing, *The Fan Qui in China* (1838); Nos 37 and 38 from *Jen-ching hua-pao* (1907) in the Library of The School of Oriental and African Studies; Nos 7, 11 and 12 are reproduced by courtesy of Matheson & Co. Limited; Nos 1, 2, 3, 8, 17, 22, 23, 24, 25, 30, 31, 32, 34, 36, 40, 42, 43, 44, Radio Times Hulton Picture Library; Nos 9, 10, 13, 16, 20, 28, 29, 33, 35, 39, 41, Mansell Collection; Nos 15, 19, 27, National Army Museum; Nos 21 and 26 are from the collection of the Earl of Elgin.

The map was drawn by John Messenger.

Author's Note and Acknowledgements

This is a narrative of the principal events in the troubled history of China's relations with the West during the final years of the Ch'ing dynasty. It has been written in the hope that as well as entertaining those unfamiliar with the story, it may provide some sort of historical background against which the modern Chinese view of the Western powers, and of their own place and importance in the world, may be more easily understood.

I can make not the slightest claim to be an expert Sinologist, and my debt to those who can is naturally very great; it is in some sense indicated by the references to their works which I have cited. I am in particular grateful to Mr Raymond Dawson, University Lecturer in Chinese at Oxford, for having read the manuscript and for having given me much useful advice for its improvement.

I am also particularly indebted to Miss Susan Duncan of the School of Oriental and African Studies in the University of London for her invaluable assistance in reading and translating for me various Chinese sources and for enabling me to see these events more clearly from the Chinese point of view. Except where otherwise stated in the references all the translations from Chinese sources given in the book are hers.

I am most grateful, too, to Mr John Wong of St Antony's College, Oxford, to Mr S. Y. Chiang of Trinity College, Oxford, to Mr P. Hulin and Dr C. I. McMorran of the Oriental Institute, Oxford, to Professor P. G. O'Neill and Mr David Pong of the School of Oriental and African Studies, to Mr G. P. Ferguson of the Hong Kong Students' Office and to Professor Stuart R. Schram of the Contemporary China Institute.

The book is based mainly on printed sources, but I have also consulted and quoted from a number of unpublished authorities and I am extremely grateful to those who have allowed me to do so. I would, therefore, like to thank the Earl of Elgin for free use of the Elgin Manuscripts at Broomhall, Fife, and of the diary kept in China by the eighth Earl of Elgin during his time as special envoy in China in 1856–60; Mr Sean Galvin for the journal kept by William Pitt Amherst, Earl Amherst of Arracan, during his embassy to China in 1816–17; Mr W. E. A. Robinson for the autograph journal of Charles Alfred Newman; Mr W. J. Keswick and Mr Alan Reid for material in the archives of Messrs Matheson & Co. Ltd; the Trustees of the Mitchell Library, Sydney, New South Wales, for the diary of *The Times* correspondent, G. E. Morrison; the editor of *The Times* Archives for the use of a microfilm of this diary and Colonel Peter Fleming who had the microfilm made; Mr R. M. Willcocks for various letters written from China during the Opium War and the Boxer uprising; Mr Gordon J. Weel for the autograph journal of Henry C. Lewis; the Berkshire Record Office for the letters of James Dundas Crawford; and the Buckinghamshire Record Office for the papers of Edward Adolphus Seymour, 12th Duke of Somerset, in the Ramsden Collection.

For drawing my attention to some of these and to other sources I am indebted to Mr B. C. Bloomfield, Deputy Librarian of the School of Oriental and African Studies, Mrs Elizabeth Steele of the Department of Books and Archives at the National Army Museum, Miss E. B. McNeill of the Public Record Office of Northern Ireland, Major A. J. Donald of the Royal Marines Museum, Southsea, Major T. L. Ingram, curator of the Hickleton Papers, Lt-Col. W. B. R. Neave-Hill of the Historical Section, Ministry of Defence Library, Mr W. F. Hammond, Mr John Dineen of the Royal United Services Institution Library, the Assistant Registrar of the National Register of Archives, the Assistant Secretary of the Royal Commission on Historical Manuscripts, Miss Hinda Rose of Messrs Maggs Bros Ltd, Mr Maurice Collis, Mr Charles de Chassiron and Mrs Deane de Chassiron. I am most grateful also to the staffs of the London Library, the British Museum, Messrs Sotheby & Co., Messrs Christie Manson & Woods and Messrs Robson Lowe Ltd.

Author's Note and Acknowledgements

For their assistance in my researches I am extremely grateful to Mrs Joan St George Saunders, Miss Sybil Hay, Miss Christine Ashen, Miss C. A. Willies, Miss Mary Cosh and Miss Caroline Cuthbert.

Finally I would like to thank Mr Hamish Francis for having read the proofs, my wife for having made the index, and my daughter, Kate, for having transcribed various documents for me.

C.H.

I | *Ambassadors Bearing Tribute*

1 | Barbarians from the Western Ocean

As regards the various vassal states, when they come to the Celestial Empire to bring tribute, all their envoys perform the ceremony of the three kneelings and the nine knockings of the head. A Court Letter addressed to Cheng-jui, a Manchu of the Plain White Banner deputed by the Emperor to 'look after the tribute envoy', August 1793.

Every summer when the heat in Peking became unbearable, the Emperor Ch'ien-lung, Son of Heaven, travelled north beyond the Great Wall towards the mountains of Inner Mongolia. Attended by his guards and servants, his musicians, queens and concubines, he was carried to Jehol, to the palace his grandfather, K'ang-hsi, had built in the days before he was born. Here he found peace and contentment.

There were no gardens more beautiful than those at Jehol in the whole of the Celestial Empire. Their name was the Paradise of Countless Trees. Groups of willows drooped their branches by the lotus-covered lake, and shaded the islands and the rock pools where gleaming fish darted in the clear water; walnuts and filberts, medlars and corianders, apples, pears and apricots grew everywhere on the grass slopes. Wherever Ch'ien-lung chose to sit he could contemplate a perfect vista of trees and flowers and water, of streams and rocks, of painted bridges and porcelain lions, of pagodas and pavilions, of the summer-houses of his favourite concubines, of the yellow-tiled roofs of Lamaist temples; and from a hill beside the Temple of Universal Joy he could see far away to the south the parallel roads that led across the Luan he river towards the Great

Wall and Peking, the fair road that was reserved for his own personal use, and the rougher road for the less exalted.[1]*

Ch'ien-lung was standing on this hill between the Hour of the Snake and the Hour of the Horse on the fourth day of the eighth month, the fifty-seventh year of his reign, when a strange sight caught his eye.[2] On the common road, preceded by a hundred mandarins on horseback, was a procession of foreigners in curious uniforms of scarlet, green and gold. Eighteen mounted soldiers led the way, then came a youth with a drum and a man playing a sort of shrill flute which the Emperor was later to learn was called a fife. These were followed by more soldiers in different uniforms, by numerous servants in livery, by more musicians, by several figures in what appeared to be court dress, and finally, in a chariot, by the presumed leader of the deputation who was accompanied by another middle-aged gentleman and a young boy. Sitting on the back of the chariot was a little black boy in a turban.

It was a most unusual spectacle on that road, but not an un-expected one. Several weeks before, the Emperor had been informed of the arrival of the Barbarians from the Western Ocean at Macao. They had come, he was told, bearing gifts and tribute, to con-gratulate him upon his birthday which was to be celebrated on a date known to them as 17 September 1793. They had sailed in several ships from England.[3]

The Emperor had no very clear idea where England was; nor had any of his Ministers. China they knew to be the Middle Kingdom, the centre of the world, as well as the fountain-head of civilization.[4] But all that they knew, or wanted to know, of the countries of Europe was that they were mostly small islands, inhabited by a few Barbarians owing the same kind of allegiance to the Celestial Em-pire as the vassal states of outer Asia, such as Burma, Annam, Korea and Nepal. England, according to one of the few Chinese books to concern itself with such a relatively trivial subject as the Chinese tribute nations, belonged to Holland; the clothing and appearance of the Barbarians who lived there were much like those in all other parts of the Western Ocean. 'The men mostly drink wine,' this authority continued. 'The unmarried women lace up

*Notes and References begin on page 368.

their hips in their desire to be slim. They wear their hair falling loosely over the shoulder, with short clothes and several coats one above the other. When they go out they put on an overcoat over them all. They keep snuff in metallic wire boxes and carry these boxes about with them.'[5]

Holland itself, maintained another work, was a region in the north-west of France whose people were 'all the same as in Portugal'. Indeed, little distinction need be made between the various peoples of the Western Ocean: the Dutch and the English were both *hung-mao fan*, 'red-haired Barbarians'; the French were like the Portuguese and the Italians were like both.[6]

A later authority, which began its history of Europe at the time of the Chinese Shang period (1800 B.C.), at a time when ancient Greece was gradually coming 'under the influence of the Orient', was scarcely more reliable: Europeans were all tall and white, except the dwarfish people of the north-east; they lived mainly on bread, potatoes and fowl or game seasoned with preserves; the upper classes used stone for building, the middle classes brick, the lower classes earth.[7]

All these Barbarians lived by trade, the English mainly by their trade with China, and they were universally coarse, uncivilized, morally and intellectually uncultivated, in every way inferior to the Chinese whose civilization and Empire were already more than two thousand years old by the time of the Emperor Ch'ien-lung.[8]

Ch'ien-lung himself was a man of taste and discernment. His education, rigidly traditional, had been thorough, scrupulous and long; as a boy he had started work on his lessons at five o'clock in the morning and as a ruler he justifiably claimed that he had 'not stopped examining the classics and studying the rites'.[9] He had little interest in Western sciences, but he did not despise the Barbarians' art as some of the Empire's less enlightened mandarins did. He commissioned buildings in the Western style from Jesuit architects and paintings from Jesuit artists; yet to most of his Court and to most of his immediate descendants the foreigners' artefacts were as barbaric as the foreigners themselves. To his grandson it was 'plain that these Barbarians always look upon trade as their chief

3

occupation and [were] wanting in any high purpose'. The official to whom this observation was addressed, agreed: 'At bottom they belong to the class of brutes; it is impossible they should have any high purpose.'[10]

Ideally all foreigners would be required to remain in their own provinces, but the traditions of Chinese courtesy—and the maxim of Confucius who said, 'To have friends coming to one from distant parts, is not this great pleasure?'—imposed upon the Emperor the need to be compassionate in his 'tender cherishing of men from afar' when, in order to share in some measure the benefits of civilization, they passed through the Celestial Empire carrying tribute to the Son of Heaven. Such contacts, however, must be brief, and all intercourse severely limited: it was a crime for a Chinese to teach his language to a foreigner, and the export of all Chinese books was strictly forbidden.

Virtually the only contact between the Chinese and the countries of the West was between Chinese merchants and those few European traders who were tolerated in certain specified ports in the remote south of the Empire. Foreigners were not allowed to live, let alone to carry on business, inside the country; the voyages of Chinese outside Asia were events of the most rare occurrence. There was a Catholic mission at Peking, founded by the Jesuit, Matteo Ricci, in 1601; there were a few Catholic missionaries scattered about the country; periodically a Russian caravan of licensed traders was graciously allowed to make its way to Peking from the north in accordance with a treaty signed after a Russo-Chinese border war in the seventeenth century. But otherwise the only Europeans to be found anywhere in China were the traders on the offshore island of Macao, where the Portuguese had been permitted to establish themselves as a link between East and West in the middle of the sixteenth century; and at Canton, where a monopoly of trade was in the hands of the British-administered East India Company. And even Canton was only available to foreign merchants during the summer months; when winter came they were required to close their stores and counting-houses and sail away to Macao.

Throughout the trading season at Canton they were confined to a small waterfront foreign quarter outside the town, where no foreign women were even allowed; and they were denied direct access to any Chinese official. Business had to be conducted, and all warehouses rented—purchase was forbidden—through a group of Chinese merchants known as the Co-hong. Far from considering that the Barbarians were poorly served at Canton, the Emperor's advisers believed them to be treated as generously as they had any right to expect. Permission to trade could never be demanded as of right; it was granted as a concession. They could see no possible reason why the regulations should in the least be modified. Merchants were, after all, a despised and rather disreputable class; and China was, in any case, happily self-sufficient, without any need of the foreign goods that the Europeans had to sell. She permitted the Barbarians to trade with her only out of compassion, knowing how bleak if not unbearable their lives would be without Chinese goods.

So trade at Canton was not only highly unsatisfactory for the East India Company, it was also emphatically one-sided. It consisted largely of exports—exports of rhubarb, tea and silk, of the cotton fabric from Nanking known in Europe as nankeen, and of growing quantities of fine Chinese porcelain and lacquer-ware for which the rage in England and France for Chinese furniture, Chinese gardens, Chinese architecture and all forms of *Chinoiserie* had created so great a demand.[11] Yet rapidly as Chinese exports from Canton were growing, there was no effective way of increasing demand in China for the European manufactured goods that might otherwise have balanced the trade. Exports, accordingly, had to be paid for in silver. Moreover, any imports that *could* be sold were subject to the most erratically variable customs duties which were imposed by the Canton officials—through the Hong merchants—and which sometimes rose as high as twenty per cent, five times the highest rate fixed by the central government.

Indeed, to trade at all at Canton it was necessary to submit to the most flagrant impositions and to pay constant bribes. There was scarcely an official in Canton who did not make an illicit profit out of the *Fan-qui*, the 'foreign devils'. Even the Emperor's financial representative, known to the British merchants as the Hoppo—a corruption of the Chinese name for the Board of Revenue—was deeply involved. He held his appointment for three years, having paid a great deal of money for it, and he was expected to remit regular sums of money to Peking as well as occasional but generous presents to the mandarins at Court. Nevertheless, by the end of his term of office, it was rarely that a Hoppo had not made a fortune from his share of the harbour and trading dues and from contributions to various funds squeezed out of the Hong merchants.

The customs officials, the interpreters, the pilots who guided the ships up the Pearl River, the compradors who acted as agents in buying supplies for the European business-houses, all pocketed their appropriate bribes and illicit commissions as customary dues.

In desperation the Canton merchants turned for help to the British Government; only by appealing direct to Peking, they considered, could the intolerable restrictions imposed upon the China trade be removed. Thus it was that on that September morning in 1793 the brightly uniformed guards, servants, secretaries and musicians of a British Ambassador could be seen moving slowly up the road to the Emperor's summer palace at Jehol.

*   *   *

The Ambassador was an Irish peer of great tact, probity and accomplishment, Lord Macartney. A graduate of Trinity College, Dublin, Macartney had forsaken the study of law in London to embark upon the Grand Tour, during which he had paid the customary courtesies to Voltaire at Ferney. On his return to England he had enjoyed the friendship of both Lord Holland and Lord Sandwich, and although his original intention was to enter Parliament through the influence of Lord Holland he had decided instead to accept a diplomatic appointment offered him by Lord Sandwich. So, at the age of twenty-seven, he had been knighted and had departed for St Petersburg as envoy-extraordinary to the court of Catherine the Great. He had remained there three years, proving himself a diplomat of uncommon skill, and had subsequently distinguished himself in other appointments, including that of Governor of Madras, where his talents and 'great pecuniary moderation' had earned him the lasting respect of the Court of Directors of the East India Company. During one of his periodic visits to England he had married a daughter of Lord Bute; but the marriage was a childless and, apparently, less than happy one, and Macartney seems to have derived more pleasure from the company of Dr Johnson's circle than from that of his wife. Certainly he had no strong family ties at home, and when the opportunity came to sail to China as England's first Ambassador to the Court at Peking, he was happy enough to go. He embarked at Spithead aboard the sixty-four gun man-of-war, the *Lion*, on 21 September 1792. He was at that time fifty-five years old.

He had advised the Secretary of State to ensure that the embassy was conducted in an appropriately impressive style with a smart military escort, a German band and a suitable number of liveried attendants. And since it was hoped that the embassy would not only achieve a diplomatic success but would also collect useful information about the largely unknown country and people of China, Lord Macartney's suite was further swelled by the inclusion of several experts. As well as two interpreters, obtained after great trouble and expense from a Chinese theological college at Naples, there were two artists—Thomas Hickey, a painter, and William Alexander, a draughtsman—a metallurgist, a botanist, an experimental scientist, a surgeon, a physician who was also a 'natural philosopher', a watchmaker and a mathematical instrument maker. The Comptroller was John Barrow, a hardworking former schoolmaster whose talents and ambition had brought him a long way from his parents' humble home in Lancashire. The Secretary, who was assisted by two Under-Secretaries, was Sir George Staunton, an Irishman like Macartney and for several years a close friend of his.

Macartney had met Staunton while he was serving as Governor of Grenada in the West Indies. At that time Staunton was a doctor who had invested the money he had made from his practice in land and had become one of the islands' leading residents. He had, however, lost all his possessions when Grenada was captured by the French and had later been glad to accept Macartney's offer of employment as his secretary in Madras.

Staunton's young son, a bright, precocious eleven-year-old boy who was to learn a remarkable amount of Chinese on the outward journey from the two interpreters, also accompanied the embassy as page to the Ambassador. Including the military escort and the twenty artillerymen with their six brass cannon, the suite numbered ninety-four men and one boy. Most of them sailed in the *Lion*, the remainder, together with the valuable presents for the Emperor, in a fast East Indiaman, the *Hindostan*.

*　　*　　*

In the cabin of the *Lion*, Macartney, with characteristic tact, had placed a large picture of the Emperor; and on 30 June 1793 when at last the man-of-war and the East Indiaman, followed by two little brigs, the *Jackall* and the *Clarence*, reached the Chinese coast and a pilot came on board the *Lion* with several inquisitive fishermen, they all immediately fell flat on their faces before the portrait and, as Lord Macartney noted in his journal, 'kissed the ground several times with great devotion'.[12]

Three weeks later, after a difficult passage in dark and stormy weather through the China Sea, the convoy reached the Gulf of Chihli and anchors were dropped outside the city of Tengchowfu in the northern province of Shantung. Here for the first time a mandarin of rank came on board the *Lion* to pay his respects to the Ambassador. He was the Governor of Tengchowfu, a pleasant, intelligent man of about thirty-five, with a sharp curiosity about the Englishmen and their mission and an evident desire to help them. He told Macartney he had received instructions from the Court to offer him every hospitality, and to make arrangements for his party to proceed to Peking by road, if they would prefer to do that rather than to go by boat up the Peiho river by way of Tientsin. Macartney said he would prefer the river route; and the next day an experienced pilot came on board to guide the *Lion* to the river's mouth. The Governor also sent Macartney a present of rice, flour, fruit and vegetables, together with eight sheep, eight goats and four bullocks. He hoped that this 'trifling refreshment' would be acceptable to the English gentlemen.[13]

The following morning the convoy weighed anchor and sailed from Tengchowfu into the Gulf of Chihli; and on the last day of July the mouth of the Peiho river was reached. Here two high-ranking mandarins from the Court had been awaiting Lord Macartney's arrival for some days with an enormous number and variety of junks to transport the Englishmen on their river journey, and a store of presents so immense that the Governor of Tengchowfu's gifts did indeed appear 'trifling' by comparison. Meticulously in his journal Lord Macartney recorded them: 120 sheep, 120 hogs, 100 fowls, 100 ducks, 20 bullocks, 14 boxes of Tartar bread, 4,000 melons, 22 boxes of preserved fruit, 22 boxes of dried peaches . . . vegetables, candles, red rice, tea, wine in earthenware jars. 'In truth,' Macartney concluded when he came to the end of his long inventory, 'the hospitality, attention, and respect which we have experienced (so far in China) are such as strangers meet with only in the Eastern parts of the world.'[14]

The presents were brought out to the English ships in seven heavily laden junks by the two important mandarins who had been waiting the embassy's arrival. The mandarins came aboard the *Lion* to present their compliments to the Ambassador. They had been delegated, they told him through an interpreter, to act as his mentors and guides throughout his stay in China. Macartney warmed to them both immediately. One of them was a military mandarin of distinction, the other a civilian. The civilian became known to the officials of the embassy as Chou.[15] Macartney was later to refer to him as a 'man of letters and capacity', a good and faithful friend.[16] Unlike so many mandarins whose lack of interest in anything not Chinese was total, he seemed genuinely and deeply interested in the world beyond the Empire's boundaries.

His superior, known as Wang, was a cheerful good-humoured soldier who had risen to his present position in the army from the ranks. John Barrow, the Embassy's Comptroller, wrote of him that he was 'deservedly a great favourite of every Englishman in the train of the British ambassador'.[17]

Both he and Chou immediately endeared themselves to the English by sitting down to dinner that first night aboard the *Lion* and with engaging determination setting about the task of handling the strange implements with which the foreigners ate. They were soon managing the knives and forks with notable dexterity and relishing the good things on the table. They tasted the European wines one after the other, then tried the gin, the rum, the arrack, the shrub, and, to their obvious satisfaction, the cherry brandy. When they rose to leave they shook hands with the assembled company in the European way, showed their pleasure at the smartness of the guard and the marines who were drawn up on deck to salute their departure, listened to the band with careful attention, and left their hosts with the feeling that their mission had got off to a most auspicious start.[18]

During the next few days, as the junks were loaded with the embassy's luggage and provisions and the presents for the Emperor, this mood of cheerful optimism was maintained. From the decks of the *Lion*, the gentlemen of the embassy watched the Chinese sailors, strong, healthy and cheerful, laughing and singing as they worked in a 'very orderly and well regulated way' on the junks, packing the bags and bales away under the eyes of mandarins who marked each item down on scrolls of paper. All of them had their heads close shaved except on the crown where the strong, black, coarse hair of their pigtails grew in plaits reaching down to their waists; some of them wore bamboo hats with red silk fringes; others worked bareheaded.

The loading of the junks was completed on 4 August, and at nine o'clock the next morning Lord Macartney and his party left the *Lion* and were transported to the river's mouth. On the right bank of the river a guard of honour of soldiers—'not much adapted to military purposes', in John Barrow's opinion—was drawn up by a temporary landing stage on which stood a band to welcome the Ambassador to the Celestial Empire. The Ambassador, however, politely declined the invitation to land extended to him by the friendly mandarins, Chou and Wang, who had prepared a banquet in his honour; and, pleading fatigue and a desire to reach Peking without undue delay, he sailed on towards Tientsin in the comfortable boat, 'resembling the passage-boats on English and Dutch canals', with which the Chinese had provided him.[19]

With excited curiosity he and his companions looked across towards the high river banks and the low, flat, swampy ground, covered with coarse grass and expanses of millet, ten to twelve feet tall, that stretched away into the distance. There were no hedges or fences, boundaries being marked by ditches. Occasionally the stone or brick walls of a rectangular town came into sight, a temple, a pagoda, a tall pyramid of salt bags covered with matting, or a poor-looking village of one-storeyed houses built of mud or half-burned bricks and thatched with straw or rushes, some of them with coloured ribbons and silks dangling from the eaves. Despite the seeming poverty of the countryside, people crowded everywhere, in the fields, along the banks, in an astonishing variety of boats on the river; the men appeared healthy and muscular, the almost naked children cheerful and lively; the women, when glimpsed agilely running out of the Barbarians' sight for modesty's sake, looked weather-beaten but 'not ill-featured', with jet black hair neatly braided on top of their heads and fixed in place with large bodkins.[20]

When darkness fell Sir George Staunton was entranced by the beauty of the scene—the banks illuminated by coloured lanterns, more lanterns swinging from the mastheads of the junks, the lights shining from the cabins of the countless vessels by the river bank, and, now and then, the glowing lamps suspended on high poles beside the gates of a mandarin's country house.[21]

On the morning of 6 August Lord Macartney was informed by a deputation of high-ranking mandarins that the Governor-General of the province of Chihli wished to receive him at the nearby temple of the Sea God to compliment him upon his entrance into the Emperor's dominions and to give him his necessary instructions.

Macartney, with Sir George Staunton, young Staunton and an interpreter, stepped from their junk and walked across a specially erected wooden bridge covered with mats and decorated with scarlet silk to the bamboo palanquins which were waiting for his party on shore. He climbed into a palanquin, sat down on its satin-covered seat, and was carried away at a smart pace by four stout porters to the gates of the temple. Outside the gates there were several red, white and blue tents with pennants flying from each, row upon row of soldiers dressed in blue cotton uniforms laced with red braid and armed with naked sabres, and a troop of cavalry equipped with bows and arrows.

The Governor-General, a dignified and meticulously courteous old man with a benign aspect and a long silver beard, received the Englishmen at the gate and conducted them inside, through painted rooms and spacious courts paved with coloured tiles and decorated with porcelain ornaments, to a conference chamber. Here, after the customary tea had been served in covered cups on oblong saucers, and the formal and elaborate compliments had been paid by each side in turn, the discussion began.

The Emperor, the Governor-General said, was at his summer palace at Jehol in Tartary and would receive the Ambassador there. In the meantime, quarters and store-rooms would be provided for the embassy staff in Peking and elsewhere; during the remainder of the river journey, the junks would be organized in proper procession, each one having a flag and a number of lanterns at her masthead to indicate the rank of her passengers and her proper place in the procession;[22] a hundred or so further mandarins would be allocated to the service of the embassy.

It was impossible, Macartney thought, to describe the ease, politeness and dignity of the Governor-General during the whole conference, the attention he paid to all requests, and the unaffected manner in which he complied with them. 'The whole of his appearance,' Macartney wrote, 'is calm, venerable and dignified. When we returned to our yachts, we found a most magnificent and plentiful dinner prepared for us, which had been sent as a present.'

Nor had Macartney anything but praise for the other, lesser mandarins who were appointed to attend him; their regularity, alertness and despatch appeared 'perfectly wonderful. Indeed, the machinery and authority of the Chinese Government' were 'so organized and so powerful, as almost immediately to surmount every difficulty'.[23]

So gracious and compliant, in fact, had all the mandarins been, from the Governor-General to Wang and Chou and their subordinates, that it seemed reasonable to hope that the embassy's mission would soon be completed in triumph. The only rather disturbing feature—which Macartney thought it prudent to ignore—was that when, to the most deafening noise of gongs and copper drums, the procession of junks continued on its way to Tientsin, the yellow flags flapping at the mastheads of the river fleet were seen to bear, in broad black Chinese characters, this inscription: *The English Ambassador carrying tribute to the Emperor of China.*[24]

A further cloud was cast over the embassy's confidence when the convoy reached Tientsin, one of the largest cities of the Empire. For here Macartney was introduced to Cheng-jui, an important Manchu official, who, since the Governor-General was himself too frail to accompany the embassy to Jehol, was to take his place. Cheng-jui was a vain and obstinate man, ill-tempered and perverse, and Macartney's first interview with him was highly unpropitious. He did not trouble to hide his unfriendly attitude towards the embassy, objecting to various proposals which were made as to its conduct in such a way that Macartney 'could not avoid feeling great disquiet and apprehension from his untoward disposition'.[25]

On their return to the boats, however, the staff of the embassy found yet another magnificent dinner laid out for them, together with personal presents of tea, silk and muslin for each one of them, as well as for all the servants, musicians and soldiers. Then, after dinner the principal mandarins of Tientsin came aboard and were so friendly, talkative and inquisitive, examining with childlike curiosity, though not, it seemed, with undue admiration, the furniture and books and even the clothes of the Europeans, that happier feelings soon prevailed, and hope returned.

The ordinary people of Tientsin, too, displayed a curiosity in the Sea Barbarians that seemed quite as friendly and intense, staring at them for minutes on end, walking out into the Peiho up to their waists, lining the water's edge in their hundreds, rank upon rank, jostling each other on the decks of the multitudinous craft of the river, crowding onto the roofs of the workshops and warehouses, built of a dark blue brick, that extended on each bank as far as the eye could reach.

John Barrow noted that the common people, when they wore anything at all other than a pair of drawers, were dressed in a kind of outlandish uniform of baggy trousers, blue or black cotton smock, large straw hat and thick clumsy shoes which were sometimes also made of straw. The few better dressed men among the crowd wore short, double-breasted silk jackets with high buttoned collars, quilted skirts, black satin boots and velvet caps. Women were rarely to be seen, but when they were they presented a sight even more curious than the men. Beneath short cotton frocks reaching to the knee, they wore wide coloured trousers drawn together below the calf to display a swollen ankle tied round with tasselled ribbons and a tiny stump of a foot. Their toes had been so forcibly compressed in childhood that they grew back underneath the sole, their heels so tightly bandaged that they were all but obliterated; their total length rarely exceeded four or five inches.[26]

The faces and necks of all but the poorest women were covered with white paint, their eyebrows blackened, their lower lips and chins decorated with two vermilion spots. In the knots of black hair that were screwed up on top of their heads, were fixed two long silver or brass bodkins in the form of a flattened cross, as well as large bunches of artificial flowers. Most of the women and, indeed, most girls from the age of eight or nine, had pockets or purses hanging from their clothes in which they carried their pipes and tobacco.[27]

Neither men nor women, the gentlemen of the embassy all agreed, spent much time washing, and apparently they never had a bath. They slept at night in the same clothes they wore by day, and seemed 'unacquainted with the use of soap'. It was a common sight to see men even of the official classes wiping their dirty hands on the capacious sleeves of their gowns, spitting on the floor or 'against the walls like the French'. The richer mandarins blew their noses into square pieces of paper held ready for the purpose by their attendants, but even they made no hesitation in calling for servants to seek about their persons for troublesome vermin 'which, when caught, they very composedly put between their teeth'.[28]

Lord Macartney in the 'Observations on China' he attached to his journal, confirmed that by European standards the behaviour of the Chinese was often disgusting. 'The people, even of the first rank, though so fond of dress as to change it usually several times a day, are yet in their persons and customs frowzy and uncleanly. . . . They wear but little linen and what they do wear is extremely coarse and ill-washed. They seldom have recourse to pocket handkerchiefs, but spit about the rooms without mercy, blow their noses in their fingers, and wipe them with their sleeves, or upon anything near them. The practice is universal, and what is still more abominable, I one day observed a Tartar of distinction call his servant to hunt in his neck for a louse that was troublesome to him.'

At their meals they used no napkins or cutlery but helped themselves with their fingers or with chopsticks which were not too 'cleanly'. They were all 'foul feeders and eaters of garlic and strong-scented vegetables', and they drank 'mutually out of the same cup which, though sometimes rinsed, is never washed nor wiped clean'. They shared their pipes as well as their cups and 'considered it a compliment to offer each other a whiff'.[29]

Nor did the meals themselves make much appeal to the Englishmen's taste. Aeneas Anderson, Lord Macartney's valet, said that to eat their bread, which was not made with yeast, was just like eating dough; and he did not trust their meat as the Chinese were not 'at all particular how the animals were killed, or if they had died from disease'; he once saw some pigs, 'infected with an incurable disorder', thrown overboard, but the Chinese picked them out of the water and ate them with relish. Chinese wine, Anderson added, had a good enough body, but it had 'a sharp and unpleasant taste'. For Staunton even the delicacies of birds' nests and sharks' fins had to be highly spiced to be anything like palatable.[30]

Distasteful as much Chinese food and many Chinese customs appeared to the gentlemen of the embassy, however, nothing they had yet seen in the country, in John Barrow's words, was 'so ill agreeing with the feelings of Englishmen as an instance in the exercise of arbitrary power' which was forced upon their attention two days after leaving Tientsin on their way to Tungchow. The weather was now extremely hot and some of the provisions in the junks were found to be tainted. Immediately the mandarins who were held responsible for this natural misfortune were deprived of their buttons of rank, and their servants were flogged with the stout bamboo canes always held in readiness for the punishment of such negligence.[31]

But although the flogging of servants for the errors of their masters certainly ill agreed with the feelings of an Englishman, it seemed to the Chinese, so Aeneas Anderson said, that when an English soldier was flogged the punishment was carried out with unnecessary severity. One mandarin who witnessed a soldier of the embassy guard being given fifty lashes for buying some of the forbidden Chinese spirit, *sansu*, exclaimed in horror in Anderson's hearing, 'Englishman too much cruel, too much bad'.[32] Certainly it could not be denied that, despite the apparently arbitrary punishments to which they were subject and the seemingly unlimited power of the high officials of the State, the Chinese people obeyed their orders and undertook the most laborious tasks with a compliance that was not merely ready but usually cheerful. No workers, for instance, could be more willing and good-humoured than the men who, now that the junks could no longer sail with the tide, had to drag them upstream by ropes. Their naked backs were burned brown by the sun and permanently bent through the efforts of their labours; mosquitoes, gnats, and gigantic moths buzzed ceaselessly around their sweating shoulders; yet they trudged on, keeping in step to the beating of a gong, as though in perfect contentment, frequently breaking out into song, occasionally stopping for a brief rest and, kicking off their trousers to reveal legs of a surprising paleness in contrast with the dark skin above, plunging gratefully into the cool water.[33]

The countryside beyond the banks up-river from Tientsin was still quite flat, but far more widely cultivated than at the river's mouth. There were large rice fields and expanses of Indian corn as well as millet. Cucumbers, water melons, apples, pears, plums, peaches, and an unusual kind of kidney-bean were noted by those members of the embassy whose duty it was to record such items. Willows grew to an enormous size, though there were scarcely any other trees except the small ones bearing fruit. Villages appeared with astonishing frequency; yet it seemed that by far the greater part of the population of Chihli lived upon the water in an extraordinary variety of vessels, from the smallest of sampans to great junks one hundred and fifty feet long, built in the shape of flat bottomed troughs curved upward at each end with the poop much higher than the prow, and with immensely thick masts rising from the deck to support sails of matting made to fold up like a fan between bamboo poles.

In one day the embassy's junks passed more than six hundred large vessels such as this, each having ten or twelve different families living in separate apartments built upon the deck, so that a group of four of them would constitute a village of at least two hundred people. The river was crammed, too, with countless open barges and merchant vessels on their way to and from Peking, loaded with cotton, wool and copper, rice, silk, salt and tea, and with a puzzling article of commerce, frequently to be seen, that looked like a heap of thick brown crumpets but turned out to be a species of fertilizer made from animal and human excrement, moulded into shape and dried in the sun.

Every few miles a military encampment came into sight; and at every one the soldiers were drawn up to salute the passing boats with colours flying and music blaring. At night these military parades were illuminated by flaring torches and fireworks.[34]

Respectful and welcoming as their reception was, however, all the members of the embassy were refused permission to leave the boats for even the most trivial excursions into the country. Yet the requests were listened to by the mandarins with smiles and nods, with what Macartney called 'the most refined politeness and sly good breeding', and the inevitable refusal was attended 'with so much profession, artifice, and compliment' that the Englishmen 'soon grew reconciled and even amused'.[35]

The attentions of Wang and Chou were as friendly, easy-going and solicitous as they had been since that first convivial evening aboard the *Lion* in the Gulf of Chihli. Almost every day during the slow progress upstream they visited the Ambassador accompanied by the less congenial Cheng-jui whose attitude, so they confided to Macartney in private, they deplored. But when they came aboard his junk on the morning of 15 August their manner was almost as formal as that of Cheng-jui, whose 'settled prejudice' against the embassy was causing Macartney ever deeper concern. The three mandarins had a matter of some delicacy to discuss with the Ambassador; they implied that it was something which could soon be settled; but it was, in fact, a question that was to assume a growing importance during the following weeks.

The subject was adroitly introduced by various references to the different modes of dress that prevailed among different nations. Comparing their own loose clothes with the tight garments of Europeans, they intimated that their own were more convenient for wear at the Chinese Court since they did not interfere with graceful deportment before the Emperor. Would not the knee-buckles and garters which the English wore make it difficult for them to perform the customary salutations before the throne? Macartney hastened to reassure the mandarins: they need have no apprehension on that point for he felt confident that, whatever ceremonies were usual for the Chinese to perform, the Emperor would surely prefer an English Ambassador paying him the same obeisance as would be paid by an Englishman to his own sovereign.

The mandarins seemed reassured; they supposed that the ceremonies in both countries must be virtually the same; but just in case there should be any embarrassment it would be perhaps best to mention now that at the Chinese Court visitors kneeled down upon both knees and made nine prostrations of the head to the ground: it was a customary ceremony that never had been and never could be dispensed with. Lord Macartney replied that at the English Court the ceremony was 'somewhat different'; but, perhaps, it would be better to leave the matter there for the moment; when the embassy arrived in Peking, he would deliver in writing his reply to any confirmed insistence that he should follow the etiquette of the Chinese rather than of the English Court. So the conversation turned away from the question of the kotow to less contentious subjects as the procession of junks approached the suburbs of Tungchow.[36]

At Tungchow the Peiho was no longer navigable, so the rest of the journey to Peking, a distance of about twelve miles, had to be continued overland. The staff of the embassy were lodged in a temple outside the city from which a hundred or so priests had been ejected 'without the least ceremony', and in which, Sir George Staunton noticed with distaste, scorpions and centipedes abounded. Meanwhile, with their customary efficiency, the superintending mandarins organized the transfer of the presents, baggage and stores onto wagons, handcarts and packhorses, and had the more delicate articles packed into padded boxes which, supported on bamboo poles, could be carried on the shoulders of porters. Some of these boxes were so cumbersome that thirty-two porters were required to lift them, and the total number of porters employed in the straggling caravanserai that eventually left Tungchow numbered about three thousand. Behind them followed wagoners and carters, drivers and guards, mandarins and servants, some on horseback, some in sedan chairs, others on foot; then came the Ambassador and his suite, riding in wagons, chairs, small palanquins, or fearfully uncomfortable two-wheeled covered carriages; and last of all rode Wang and Chou and their numerous attendants.

Both sides of the dusty road were lined with spectators, and with people going to and from Peking in all manner of conveyances, including several Chinese ladies in long silken robes, riding with their children in pony-carts or peeping through the gauze-curtained windows of their chairs. To keep away the rougher and more inquisitive of the spectators, a line of soldiers marched in front and along each side of the procession, brandishing long whips which occasionally they brought cracking threateningly to the ground when the crowds grew so thick that the passage of the procession was almost halted.

The English soldiers of the Ambassador's guard, unable to stand the suffocating heat in the closed carriages, got out to walk. The sight of their ruddy complexions, powdered hair and tight clothes struck several of the spectators as being so comical that they immediately burst out laughing. Others, however, seeing how overcome the foreigners were by the heat, pressed back from them and pushed their companions back to give them more room to breathe.

The last few miles of the journey took over two hours, and although they had left Tungchow soon after dawn, the morning was well advanced before the foreigners caught their first glimpse of the walls and towers of Peking through the swirling dust.[37]

*   *   *

Peking was not so much one city as four, each enclosed by walls of an intimidating height. To the south was the Chinese City, to the north the Tartar City and in the middle of the Tartar City were the pink walls of the Imperial City which gave way in its turn to the For-bidden City. The plan of the whole was neat and symmetrical, the straight lines of streets between gate and gate providing an almost gridlike outer covering to the Emperor's secluded palaces within the walls of the Forbidden City.

The foreigners entered through the eastern gate of the Chinese City, passing beneath a towering guard-house whose embrasures were closed by red shutters on which were painted representations of cannon as on the sham portholes of a man-of-war.

Beyond the gate the narrow passage widened into a broad street lined on either side with shops and warehouses painted in a variety of brilliant colours from sky blue to emerald and gold. Before each shop was a tall wooden pillar, higher than the curved sweep of the eaves of the tiled roof, bearing inscriptions in gilt characters—setting forth the nature of the goods to be sold—and decorated from top to bottom with coloured flags, streamers and ribbons. Beneath the pil-lars, selections of the shopkeepers' wares were displayed in heaps, none of the exhibitions making a better show than the huge coffins, twice the size of English coffins, and the gaily decorated funeral biers with their ornamental canopies.

The foreigners had plenty of time to inspect these various articles, for the crush in the streets, as in all the main streets of the city, was appalling, and the procession was reduced to a crawl. The streets were wide enough, but the free passage between the buildings was severely limited both by the piles of wares outside the shops, and by the tents and booths of cobblers and blacksmiths, tinkers and bar-bers, quack doctors, fortune-tellers and auctioneers, who carried on their trade wherever fancy suggested.

Outside the tents and shops and the numerous tea-houses, crowds of people haggled, wrangled and bartered, laughed at the comedians and acrobats, gazed at the conjurors and mountebanks, were shouted at by vegetable sellers endeavouring to force their wheelbarrows and handcarts through the throng, by servants pushing their mistresses about in wheelbarrows, by the drivers of troops of dromedaries laden with coals from Tartary.

The noise seemed deafening even to those Englishmen used to the racket of a London street-market on a Saturday night. The wailing lamentations of a funeral procession, the bawling of fruit sellers, the squalling music of a band conducting a bride to her husband, the discordant twanging of the barbers' tweezers like the jarring of a cracked Jew's harp, appeared never to disturb the complacent serenity of the mandarins who glided along in the midst of their retinues beneath umbrellas, painted lanterns and the various insignia of their rank and station; but to the Europeans in their uncomfortable and suffocatingly hot carriages they were scarcely supportable. The temperature in the carriages was 96° that day, the dust choking, the stench in the streets 'intolerably offensive'.

None of the streets was paved, and only the side lanes, leading off the main streets that linked together the nine gates of the city, were watered. In these quiet lanes the leading mandarins lived in large houses whose blank walls facing the street hid the courtyards, gardens and buildings beyond from common view. Only the biggest shops, in fact, had windows in their front walls; all the houses in the city, most of which were of but one storey, showed no more to the street than a door, a painted wall, a roof, and a sort of terrace protected by a railing or wall on which were placed pots of flowers or shrubs or miniature trees. This gave to the city, in European eyes, a monotonous appearance that the varied colours of the buildings, and the splendid varnished and gilded archways erected over the main crossroads, did little to enliven.

A stranger to Peking 'will immediately perceive', John Barrow observed, 'that every street is laid out in the same manner, and every house built upon the same plan; and that their architecture is void of taste, grandeur, beauty, solidity or convenience'. Moreover, in Peking, there were even fewer women to be seen than there were in other Chinese cities. Occasionally a Tartar woman could be seen walking in the street or riding a horse, but the Chinese women were strictly confined to their houses. The young girls, who were sometimes glimpsed standing at the doors of their houses and puffing at their bamboo-stemmed pipes, retired immediately at the approach of men.

Barrow, who was becoming more and more convinced that Montesquieu's morose view of China was a good deal closer to the truth than Voltaire's beguiling dream, found much else to complain of besides. The city, for instance, had no sewers; and, while nothing was thrown out into the streets, this was because it was the custom of each family to keep a large earthenware jar into which was collected everything that could be used as manure. When the jar was full its contents were sold and transported, in the small boxed carts that supplied the inhabitants of Peking with their vegetables, to the outlying gardens where the vegetables were grown. The carts leaked all over the road and left upon them a smell that continued 'without intermission for many miles'. Barrow found almost equally nauseous the water from the city's wells which, even when boiled and used for strong tea, was still as 'disgusting' as ever.

Although they did not discover all its defects until later, Barrow and his companions were profoundly thankful when, after a painfully slow two hours' progress from the eastern to the western gate, they emerged from Peking and came out onto the road to Yüanming Yüan where, in the grounds of the Imperial palace, accommodation had been prepared for them.[38]

It had been arranged that those presents too delicate to be transported up to Jehol would be unpacked at Yüan-ming Yüan and exhibited there, in the presence chamber of the palace, to await the Emperor's return.

The presence chamber was a fine room with a chequered marble floor, a ceiling 'painted with circles, squares and polygons, whimsically disposed', and, on a raised dais, flanked by spreading fans of Argus pheasants' tails, the throne on which the Emperor was to sit to inspect the English King's gifts.

On one side of the throne was exhibited a magnificent terrestrial globe, on the other an equally splendid celestial one. From the ceiling were suspended several exquisite crystal chandeliers; and at various well chosen places on the marble floor were placed numerous beautiful clocks, Derbyshire porcelain vases and figures, a barometer, a planetarium and an extraordinarily intricate orrery. The whole assemblage, Lord Macartney prided himself, was 'of such ingenuity, utility and beauty' that he doubted whether another apartment in the whole world contained a collection to rival it.[39]

Certainly the Chinese who visited the room—despite a natural propensity to the belief that nothing that came from outside the Empire was really worthy of comparison with its own products—seemed suitably impressed. To be sure, the surly Cheng-jui deprecated the value of all the presents which he insisted were, in any case, not presents at all but *kung-shou*, tribute; but all other visitors, from the old eunuchs of the palace staff to princes of the Imperial blood, expressed their pleasure and surprise, though some of them may have been disappointed not to find the curiosities which a Chinese newspaper reported the English as having brought: several dwarfs not twelve inches high, an elephant the size of a cat and a horse the size of a mouse, a singing-bird as big as a hen that devoured fifty pounds of charcoal a day, and a magic pillow that instantly transported the sleeper to the land of his dreams without the fatigue of travelling.[40]

Before continuing his journey to Jehol with the remainder of the presents—which included carpets, fowling-pieces, pistols, two 'most elegant' saddles and a collection of portraits of English noblemen and statesmen—Lord Macartney returned for a few days to Peking where he was 'not only comfortably, but most magnificently lodged in a vast palace consisting of eleven courts'. This palace impressed his valet beyond measure. His Lordship's apartment, which was hung with a beautiful paper enriched with gilding, had a private theatre belonging to it; and under the floor was 'a stove with a circular tube' that conveyed warm air to the room above.[41] The palace had been built at a cost of nearly £100,000 by a former Hoppo at Canton.

Here, too, as at Yüan-ming Yüan, a stream of visitors daily came to inspect the Barbarians and their possessions. What seemed to attract the greatest curiosity and attention were Joshua Reynolds's portraits of the King of England and his Queen, which had been placed opposite the state canopy in the grand saloon, and the embassy's band which gave a concert in the palace every evening. Indeed, so struck was the mandarin in charge of the Emperor's orchestra with both the music and the instruments that, having attended every concert, he asked permission to send some artists to make exact drawings of the clarinets, bassoons, French horns and flutes, so that he could have similar instruments manufactured in China.[42] Lord Macartney felt obliged to ask the mandarin to accept all the instruments as a gift, but the offer was politely declined. And so, at six o'clock on the morning of 2 September, when the journey to Jehol was resumed, the band was able to continue as part of the company.

The journey up into the mountains was a difficult one over a road which, though it was good as far as the Great Wall, thereafter became rough and stony. But the distance was covered at a comfortable pace, at an average of no more than nineteen miles a day, and Lord Macartney later referred to the ride as 'very pleasant'.He travelled in a neat English post-chaise drawn by four little Tartar horses, and for company had the bright young George Staunton whose father, suffering from gout, was carried in a palanquin. Every night the travellers were lodged and entertained in a wing of one of the numerous palaces of the Emperor that were sited at short distances from each other all along the road between Peking and Jehol; and at Jehol itself they found prepared for them another palace which Lord Macartney judged both 'spacious and convenient'.

The Ambassador had enjoyed his journey; from his well-sprung post-chaise he had been able to admire the 'uncommon picturesque beauty' of the mountains of rock and the deep valleys watered by clear winding streams; he had taken off time to examine at his leisure the Great Wall, that 'most stupendous work of human hands'; and, each evening, he had been able to admire the loveliness of the Emperor's parks and gardens, every one a work of art subtly and gracefully contrived: the Chinese gardener was, indeed, the painter of nature.[43]

Macartney's pleasure was increased on his arrival at Jehol, by a settled compromise over the matter of the kotow. While at Peking he had written his promised paper on the subject, affirming in it his desire to do whatever would be most agreeable to the Emperor but explaining that, being the representative of the first monarch of the Western world, his own sovereign's dignity must be the measure of his conduct. He had proposed, therefore, that he should conform to the etiquette of the Chinese Court, provided that a person of equal rank to his own should perform the same ceremony before a portrait of the King of England. This paper was translated into Chinese for him by a French missionary, but so afraid was every person in China of 'intermeddling in any state matter without the special authority of Government', that the missionary refused to allow his version to appear at Court in case his handwriting were recognized. Young Staunton, therefore, who could now write Chinese characters with 'great neatness and celerity', copied the missionary's translation which was then handed to the mandarins accompanying the embassy.

Cheng-jui immediately expressed his disapproval; but Wang and Chou—who some days before had pressed Macartney most earnestly to perform the ceremony, demonstrating how easy it was, and begging him to follow their example—were now delighted that he had given way so far. They offered to go through a rehearsal of the whole procedure on the spot; but Macartney thought it better to await the approval of the Emperor's Ministers.[44]

This, however, was not forthcoming. Cheng-jui had already been instructed in a Court Letter to inform Lord Macartney tactfully 'that as regards the various vassal states, when they come to the Celestial Empire to bring tribute and to be granted an audience, their envoys perform the ceremony of the three kneelings and the nine knockings of the head. . . . Naturally [the English Ambassador] should obey the regulations of the Celestial Empire.'[45]

So at Jehol the whole tiresome discussion started again. How did the Ambassador pay homage to his own sovereign? By kneeling on one knee and kissing His Majesty's hand. Would he pay such homage to the Emperor? Assuredly. But, then, it was not the custom in China to kiss the Emperor's hand; the Ambassador could surely omit that part of the ceremony and kneel on both knees instead? He had already given his answer on that subject: he would kneel on one knee every time it was usual for the Chinese to prostrate themselves.

'Well then the ceremony of kissing the Emperor's hand must be omitted.'

'As you please, but remember it is your doing, and according to your proposal; it is but half the ceremony, and you see I am willing to perform the whole one.'[46]

There the discussion ended. But it was now clear to the mandarins at Court that the English were sadly backward; indeed they were, a Court Letter complained, 'ignorant barbarians, totally uninformed as to the proper ceremonies'; it was not worth 'treating them with too much courtesy'. Ho-shen, Ch'ien-lung's chief Minister, emphasized that the Emperor was 'extremely displeased' at their 'unwarranted haughtiness'.[47]

Lord Macartney well understood how important the ceremonial of the kotow must have been in the mandarins' eyes. He wrote of the ordinary ceremonies of demeanour that were daily to be observed when one Chinese met another: 'They consist'—even when Wang and Chou met of a morning, though they saw each other every day, they consisted—'of various evolutions of the body, in elevating and inclining the head, in bending or stiffening the knee, in joining their hands together and then disengaging them, and these manoeuvres, with a hundred others, they consider as the highest perfection of good breeding and deportment, and look upon other nations, who are not expert in this polite discipline, as little better than barbarians.'[48]

Nevertheless, Macartney, determined not to demean the honour of his own sovereign, refused to give way; and on 11 September he was informed of the Emperor's decision: on account of the very great distance which the embassy had been sent and of the value of the presents, some of the Chinese customs ('which had hitherto been invariably performed') would now be relaxed. An audience would be granted three days later on the occasion of the Grand Festival at Court.

2 | The Son of Heaven

*He is a very fine old Gentleman, still healthy
and vigorous, not having the appearance of a
man of more than sixty.* Lord Macartney,
September 1793.

The Emperor Ch'ien-lung was eighty-three years old. The fourth
son of the Emperor Yung-cheng, he had succeeded to the throne in
1736. Less than a century before, his Manchu ancestors from Tartary, taking advantage of the troubles of the declining Ming dynasty,
had invaded China from the north, and, proclaiming the new Ch'ing
dynasty, had entered Peking in June 1644. The conquering Manchus
had soon established themselves in power, maintaining their rule by
traditional Chinese methods, accepting Confucianism, but imposing
upon the people a foreign Manchu army and foreign Manchu ways.

They had forced the men of China to shave their heads and wear
pigtails; they had changed the official dress of the country from the
kimono-like gown of the Mings to the Tartar dress with its side
fastenings and high collar; they had imposed a social barrier between themselves and the Chinese which had been partially broken
down by the end of the eighteenth century but which was still
marked. Manchu and Chinese are now indistinguishable; but in
Ch'ien-lung's time the differences between the races were unmistakable even to foreigners. Lord Macartney emphasized in an
appendix to his journal that there were 'two distinct nations in
China'; their appearance was virtually the same but their characters
differed essentially: the Tartar was a member of a privileged élite.
Macartney noticed, for instance, that when on his journey to Jehol a
Manchu mandarin from Court paid him a visit, Wang 'though
decorated with the same button and of the same military rank,
would scarcely venture to sit down in his presence'.[1]

In the long reign of Ch'ien-lung's grandfather, K'ang-hsi (1662–1723), and in his own day, China had enjoyed an era of prosperity and had greatly extended her frontiers. Turkestan and Ili were subjected; the Burmese reduced to suzerainty; the Gurkhas driven out of Tibet. By the time of Macartney's mission the Chinese Empire was larger than it had ever been in the whole of its history, stretching from the Siberian forests beside the Amur River in the north to the tropical mountains of the south; and the Emperor, for all his years, was still its undoubted and autocratic master, the mighty head of a dynasty whose rule had long since been accepted by the Chinese, officials and peasants alike, whose monarcho-bureaucratic system of government had remained in its essentials unchanged since China had been unified under her first Imperial dynasty, the Ch'in—from whom she derived her name—in the third century B.C.

Ch'ien-lung was less intimidating than he had been in his fiery middle age; he left many decisions now to his favourite Minister, the handsome, intelligent, and immensely rich Ho-shen, who had started his career at Court as a guard at the palace gate. But he was as shrewd, as strong-willed, as impatient of criticism as ever. None of his many sons was permitted to share his power; it was he who dominated both the Grand Secretariat and the Grand Council.

These two organizations were in effect the central government, the bodies through which the Emperor dealt with the problems and requests of local officials whose memorials to the throne kept the Court informed of what was happening in the eighteen provinces of the Empire. The Grand Secretariat was responsible for administrative matters and provided the Emperor with draft replies to the memorials of the local officials. The Grand Council, composed of five or six councillors chosen from amongst the Grand Secretaries, was a higher authority dealing with important matters of state and memorials of national concern. Various Boards in Peking, such as the Board of Revenue, the Board of War and the Board of Works, roughly corresponded to the ministries of a European government.

According to Confucian theory an Emperor's role should be inactive rather than positive. But a strong Emperor, by manipulating official institutions and bypassing the bureaucracy, could impose his will on policy.[2] And this the Emperor Ch'ien-lung had done. He had also made his power felt by the local bureaucrats who governed the provinces in his name.

Below the governor-generals or viceroys, who were usually responsible for two provinces, and the governors, who were responsible for one, there were eight ranks of officials each of whom was entitled to wear a coloured button on his cap as well as a particular costume, rising in sumptuousness with the rank, with distinguishing badges on the front and back of his gown—from an embroidered white crane for the first rank to a quail for the eighth.[3]

Their responsibility was considerable—a district magistrate of the seventh rank was often responsible for an area with a population of a quarter of a million people—but their pay was extremely low, so that the almost formalized system of extortion known as the squeeze had become so commonplace as to be unremarkable.[4]

Theoretically any respectable male citizen of the Empire could become an official by passing the necessary examinations, but since these examinations involved years of study and a detailed knowledge of the Chinese classics it was not often that a man from a poor home succeeded in rising to the status of a mandarin. There were a few officials of peasant origin, though; and in his novel *Ju-lin Wai-shih* (*An Unofficial History of the Literati*), Wu Ching-tzu writes of an examination held at Canton in the eighteenth century and of 'the candidates crowding in. There were young and old, handsome and homely, smart and shabby men among them. The last candidate to enter was thin and sallow, had a grizzled beard and was wearing an old felt hat. . . . He was shivering with cold as he took his paper and went to his cell. Chou Chin [the examining Commissioner] made a mental note of this before sealing up their doors.' Later he reads the poor man's paper with much admiration, takes up his brush and carefully draws three circles on it, marking it as first. So, by a few strokes of a brush, the ragged peasant is set upon the road to becoming a revered mandarin.[5]

It was extremely rare, however, that a peasant aspired to the responsibilities of power, even had he felt capable of passing the examinations. To most of China's three hundred million people,[6] four-fifths of whom lived by farming, the mandarin was a remote figure who was rarely seen beyond the high walls and closed gates of his town house, where he lived with his wives and concubines, his children and his numerous servants. The sharply contrasting lot of the peasant who could afford but one wife and no concubine, who was dominated by his father in the same way that he dominated his own children and his wife, was hard and unchanging; and for many life was spent in permanent fear of starvation.

'Not a year passes in which a terrific number of persons do not perish of famine in some part or other of China,' wrote the Abbé Huc, who knew the China of the early nineteenth century as well as any foreigner of his time; 'and the multitude of those who live merely from day to day is incalculable. . . . Many fall down fainting by the wayside, and die before they can reach the place where they had hoped to find help. You see their bodies lying in the fields, and at the roadside, and you pass without taking much notice of them— so familiar is the horrid spectacle.'[7]

The ordinary citizen of the towns shared with the country peasant a total disinclination to meddle with affairs of government, except when he was 'under the influence of some revolutionary movement'. The Abbé Huc, who found the Chinese 'a delightfully quiet people to deal with', described a conversation he once had with some fellow-travellers in an inn about the likely heir to the throne. He tried to involve the other customers, but they would not be drawn. 'To all our piquant suggestions,' the Abbé said, 'they replied only by shaking their heads, puffing out whiffs of smoke, and taking great gulps of tea.'

One of them eventually stood up, laid his hands, 'in a manner quite paternal', on the Abbé's shoulders and said, 'Listen my friend! Why should you fatigue your head by all these vain surmises? The Mandarins have to attend to affairs of State. . . . But don't let us torment ourselves about what does not concern us. . . .'

'This is very conformable to reason,' cried the rest of the company; and thereupon pointed out to the Abbé and the others that their tea was getting cold and their pipes were out.[8]

The Emperor himself, now that he was an old man, did not

fatigue his head with matters that could safely be left to others. Relying on Ho-shen—who was a Grand Councillor, President of the Board of Revenue as well as the father-in-law of one of the Emperor's daughters—and on other trusted Ministers to relieve him of all humdrum work, he declined to overtax his strength by any unnecessary preoccupation with business.

He rose every morning at three o'clock and, borne by sixteen attendants on a high palanquin and surrounded by guards, standards, umbrellas and musicians, he was carried to his private pagoda to worship Buddha.[9] An hour or so, before breakfast at seven, was devoted to his papers; then he would go for a walk in the palace garden with his women or eunuchs before a meeting with Ho-shen which preceded a reception held for the other Grand Councillors and Secretaries. Dinner at three o'clock was followed by a visit to the theatre or some other diversion, and then a time was spent reading or writing poetry with elegant strokes of a brush dipped in vermilion ink. He very rarely went to bed later than seven o'clock. A eunuch remained on duty throughout the night to conduct to him any of his queens or concubines for whom he might feel disposed to call.[10]

He had a hundred concubines, and eight queens, several of whom had borne him children. He had also had four sons by the Empress who was dead.[11] He had seventeen sons in all and numerous grandchildren; and many of these were present when Ch'ien-lung graciously received the English ambassador in his huge pavilion in the park at Jehol soon after dawn on the day of the Grand Festival.

*   *   *

Lord Macartney had dressed for the occasion in rich, mulberry-coloured, embroidered velvet and his mantle of the Order of the Bath with collar, diamond badge and diamond star. Sir George Staunton was quite as resplendent; over his velvet court dress he wore the full and flowing scarlet silk robes of a Doctor of Law in the University of Oxford, complete with academical cap.[12]

After waiting for a considerable time, Staunton heard the sound of musical instruments heralding the Emperor's approach, then 'a number of persons busied in proclaiming aloud his virtues and his

31

power';[13] and at a sign from a nearby mandarin who officiously pulled at Macartney's sleeve, he and the Ambassador both fell on one knee, bending their heads low, as the Chinese prostrated themselves on the ground around them.[14]

As soon as the Emperor ascended his throne, Lord Macartney was conducted to the pavilion where the reception was to be held; he walked up the side steps towards the throne and, kneeling down, held up in both hands, a large gold box encrusted with diamonds containing a letter from the King of England. Ch'ien-lung accepted the box and handed it to his chief Minister who placed it on a cushion; he then presented the Ambassador with a sceptre carved from jade to give to the King in return.

During the 'sumptuous banquet' which followed these presentations, the Emperor sent the Ambassador's party several dishes from his own table together with goblets of warm rice wine which Staunton thought 'not unlike Madeira of an inferior quality'; and he extended his courtesy so far as to invite Lord Macartney and Sir George Staunton to join him in a cup of wine which he gave to each of them with his own hands. They drank it in his presence and Macartney found it 'very pleasant and comfortable, the morning being cold and raw'.

The Emperor then graciously addressed a few remarks to the Ambassador, asking him how old the King of England was and expressing the wish that he might live to as great an age as himself. Macartney returned to his table thinking how 'affable, dignified and condescending' the manner of the Emperor had been. 'He is a very fine old gentleman,' he noted in his journal, 'still healthy and vigorous, not having the appearance of a man of more than sixty.' Staunton noted how 'firm and erect' he was.

'The order and regularity in serving and removing the dinner was wonderfully exact,' Macartney added, 'and every function of the ceremony performed with such silence and solemnity as in some measure to resemble the celebration of a religious mystery. . . . The commanding feature of the ceremony was that calm dignity, that sober pomp of Asiatic greatness, which European refinements have not yet attained.'

Macartney flattered himself that although there were nine other ambassadors present that day, all of them from vassal states of the Orient, their appearance was not very splendid compared with his own.[15]

Indeed, Macartney felt he had good cause to hope now that his mission might soon prove successful; and during the next few days the Emperor displayed further signs of his affability and condescension, raising the embassy's hopes still further.

He gave orders for the Ambassador's suite to be conducted over the Imperial park at Jehol, an instance of uncommon favour which Lord Macartney, a connoisseur of gardens, greatly appreciated, enjoying in the course of a few hours 'such vicissitudes of rural delight' as he did not conceive could be felt out of England, and leading him to remark that if he had not known that 'Capability' Brown had never been to China he would have sworn that he had drawn his happiest ideas from the enchanting gardens at Jehol.[16]

The Ambassador and his suite were also invited to the Emperor's birthday celebrations on 17 September when, as 'the great band both vocal and instrumental struck up with all their power of harmony' and the eunuchs sang a 'slow solemn hymn' very clearly, the entire Court prostrated themselves before a screen behind which His Majesty, invisible throughout the day, sat enthroned. During the performance, on a signal being given, the prostrations were 'nine times repeated', according to Staunton's count. 'All the persons present prostrated themselves nine times, except the Ambassador and his suite who made a profound obeisance.'[17]

A further invitation was issued the next day when a series of plays, both tragedies and comedies, masques and pantomimes were performed at Court. These were followed by exhibitions of wrestling, tumbling, dancing, acrobatics, conjuring, juggling, and, finally, by a display of fireworks, throughout which the Emperor sent to the foreigners a variety of refreshments, though they had dined but a short time before.

Staunton could not make head or tail of the plays, except parts of the pantomime, but he described the conjurors—'operating with their hands so slightly, and distracting the attention so completely as to deceive the sense of sight'—with the fascination of one who had never seen such performers before. Macartney also thought the theatrical performances were wretched, the tumbling, rope-dancing and juggling not at all comparable to Sadler's Wells, and the fireworks inferior to those of Batavia where he had stayed on his outward voyage; but it had to be confessed that there was something 'grand and imposing in the general effect that resulted from the whole spectacle, the Emperor himself being seated in front upon his throne, and all his great men and officers attending in their robes of ceremony, and stationed at each side of him, some standing, some sitting, some kneeling, and the guards and standard-bearers behind them in incalculable numbers. A dead silence was rigidly observed, not a syllable articulated nor even a laugh exploded during the whole performance.'

Before the performance began the Emperor had again showed his affability by summoning Lord Macartney and Sir George Staunton to attend him. He told them, 'with great condescension of manner', not to be surprised at seeing a man of his age at the theatre: this was a special occasion; 'considering the extent of his dominions and the number of his subjects', he could usually spare but little time for such amusements. He ended this short homily by presenting the Ambassador with a box of old japan containing some pieces of agate, and a little book written and painted by his own hand. He desired the Ambassador to give these small presents to the King of England as a token of his friendship, adding that the box had been in the possession of his family for eight hundred years.

Agreeable as his manner was, however, when Macartney endeavoured by the turn of his reply to lead him towards the subject of the embassy, it soon appeared that the Emperor was not disposed to enter into it.[18]

Nor did Macartney find Ho-shen any more forthcoming. The two men behaved towards each other with unfailing courtesy; Ho-shen went so far as to consult the embassy's physician, Dr Hugh Gillan, about his rheumatism and his rupture, and when Gillan explained the nature of his hernia and the method of its cure, the great Minister, so Gillan said, 'seemed quite lost in astonishment. He conversed again with his physicians and at last desired the interpreter to tell' the English doctor that his ideas and all that he had said 'were so extraordinary that it appeared to them as if they had come from the inhabitant of another planet'.[19]

Ho-shen appeared lost in astonishment for a second time when Lord Macartney remarked, during his ride round the Imperial gardens and park, that they 'were a work worthy of the genius of the great K'ang-hsi'. How was it possible, Ho-shen wanted to know, that an Englishman should know that these gardens had been made by the great K'ang-hsi, his present Majesty's grandfather? Macartney replied in his artfully ingratiating way that as the English were a wise and learned nation, and acquainted with the history of all countries, it was not to be wondered at that they should be particularly well informed of the history of the Chinese, whose fame extended to the most distant parts of the world.

It seemed to Macartney a natural compliment, but Ho-shen did not appear to take it as such. 'I suspect that at bottom he rather wonders at our curiosity than esteems us for our knowledge,' Macartney recorded. 'Possibly he may consider it as impertinent towards them and useless to ourselves.' It was true that Ho-shen 'displayed all the good breeding and politeness of an experienced courtier', but Macartney could not help feeling that in his heart he did not approve of the embassy's intentions.[20]

Other senior mandarins seemed to share Ho-shen's disapproval. The Emperor's second favourite Minister, the young Grand Councillor Fu-ch'ang-an, was always polite and gracious; but his elder brother, the great general Fu-k'ang-an who had led the successful army that had driven the Gurkhas from Tibet, was thoroughly suspicious of the Englishmen's motives and behaved towards them in a manner which Macartney could only describe as 'formal and repulsive'. Well aware of his connections and influence, the Ambassador did all he could to placate the general, flattering him upon his great reputation as a warrior and inviting him to watch the arms drill of the embassy's guards. But Fu-k'ang-an declined this invitation 'with great coldness and a mixture of unreasonable vanity', though Macartney had his doubts whether the general had ever seen a firelock in his life.

The Ambassador made allowances, however. Fu-k'ang-an had once been the Emperor's Viceroy at Canton where, perhaps, he had had unfortunate experiences with the Europeans in general and the English in particular: 'He may have remarked (for he is certainly a man of capacity) and felt, with regret and indignation, that superiority, which wherever Englishmen go, they cannot conceal from the most indifferent observer.'

Macartney also made allowances for the displeasing fact that whenever any gentlemen of the embassy made a little innocent excursion into the country, they were always followed by a number of mandarins and soldiers, showing that despite all the pains that had been taken to gain the friendship and confidence of the Chinese, the 'same strange jealousy' prevailed towards the English which the Chinese government had always shown to other foreigners. But then, the reason for this, perhaps, was that the mandarins were apprehensive that, from the novelty of the Englishmen's appearance and the singularity of their dress, they might be subjected to rude curiosity, and that some disturbance would arise for which they would be held responsible, it being a maxim of the Chinese Government never to excuse an official for any accident that might happen in his department.[21]

So, after all, the Ambassador continued to hope, things might turn out well. He could not now suppose that he would be able to gain all the important ends of the embassy, which were to negotiate a treaty of commerce and establish a resident Minister at the Chinese Court, to extend British trade in China by opening new ports, and to reform the organization of the existing port at Canton, to obtain a strip of coastland or an island north of Canton where British merchants could carry on trade throughout the year and where they might live under the protection of British justice.[22] But some of these objects might yet be obtained. All attempts at discussing them had been foiled at Jehol, but there might be further opportunities when the Emperor returned to Yüan-ming Yüan and inspected the presents awaiting his pleasure at the Summer Palace.

*   *   *

John Barrow, who had been left behind at Yüan-ming Yüan in charge of these presents, had not enjoyed himself in the Ambassador's absence. First of all he and his assistants had been offered quarters which he considered 'fitter for hogs than for human creatures', consisting of three or four hovels in a small court. 'Each room was about twelve feet square, the walls completely naked, the ceiling broken in, the rushes that held the plaster hanging down and strewed on the floor, the lattice work of the windows partially covered with broken paper, the doors consisting of old bamboo screens, the floor covered with dust; and there was not the least furniture in any of them, except an old table and two or three chairs in the one which was intended for the dining-room.'

Barrow complained to the mandarin who had been appointed to attend him. The mandarin replied that they were the apartments of one of their *ta-gin* (great men) but as they did not meet with his approval, he would conduct him to others in Peking. These were somewhat larger, though 'miserable, dirty' and 'wholly unfurnished'. But on being assured that they were the property of one of the Emperor's Ministers who lodged in them when his office required him to be in residence close to his master, Barrow felt precluded from further complaint.[23]

He had no such inhibitions when writing the book he published on his return from China; and in this he made clear not only his own disgust at the accommodation offered him at Yüan-ming Yüan and Peking but also his poor opinion of the Emperor's palace itself. The buildings that composed the palace could not, in his opinion, come as anything other than a woeful disappointment to those who had read descriptions of them in the accounts of missionaries. They were painted, gilded and varnished well enough, but they were all modelled after the form of a tent with immense roofs swooping over a single storey. As for the lodgings of the Grand Councillors, the Secretaries and Ministers, the wretched apartments of the state officers at the court of Versailles at the time of the French monarchy were princely in comparison. The lodgings at Yüan-ming Yüan had no glass in the windows, no stoves or fireplaces, no chandeliers or looking-glasses, no bookcases, prints or paintings; they had bamboo fibre screens instead of doors, and instead of curtained beds, wooden benches or brickwork platforms covered with a few mats and hard pillows. Aeneas Anderson endorsed these strictures. The palace, in his view, was extraordinarily neglected. The smell of the stagnant pools in the garden 'infiltrated through all the apartments' which were 'infested with scorpions, mosquitoes and centipedes'.[24]

A kind of pitiful disgust overcame Barrow when he went on to describe the lonely meals a Minister was obliged to take in his solitary cell during his attendance at Court. Not only had he no table linen or napkin, he did not even have knives, forks or spoons: 'A pair of small sticks or the quills of a porcupine are the only substitute for these convenient articles. Placing the bowl under the chin, with these he throws the rice into his mouth and takes up the pieces of meat in his soup.'

Away from Court, so Barrow had occasion to observe on his travels, the mandarin was better served at table and ate an enormous amount at every meal, dipping eagerly into the extraordinary variety of dishes and sauce bowls on the table, drinking a great deal of tea, and ending the meal with pastries and fruit, and cups of a spirituous liquor like whiskey, which they drank almost boiling hot. Several sorts of food were particularly valued for their supposed aphrodisiac qualities—not only the fins of sharks and swallows' nests from the coasts of Cochin China and Cambodia, but also the sinewy parts of the stag, and various species of sea-plants and seaweed which were dried or pickled, made into soup or, mixed with sugar and orange juice, into jelly.

The rich had need of such aphrodisiacs, Barrow supposed, for 'every great officer of state has his harem consisting of six, eight or ten women, according to his circumstances and his inclination for the sex'. But although he might have several wives and numerous concubines, he rarely had a house which any European gentleman would consider elegant or even comfortable. Most of the best residences in Peking comprised a collection of tent-shaped buildings standing on raised stone terraces and arranged in a series of tiled courts surrounded by a high wall. Roofed colonnades of red wooden pillars formed galleries between each building and the next, and between the courts. Most of the rooms were exposed to the rafters of the roof; the floors were laid with bricks or clay; the windows were of oiled paper, silk gauze or pearl shell; holes in the ground covered with stones served as fireplaces from which the heat was conveyed through flues beneath the floor or inside the lime-washed walls; what little furniture the rooms contained was neither elegant nor comfortable. 'There is not a water-closet nor a decent place of retirement in all China,' Barrow concluded. 'Sometimes a stick is placed over a hole in a corner, but in general they make use of large earthen jars with narrow tops. In the great house we occupied was a walled inclosure, with a row of small square holes of brickwork sunk in the ground.'

Nor in any part of the vast empire were there any decent inns. On the road to Peking, Staunton had discovered a village inn, 'nothing like an English inn', yet 'clean and cool and every sort of refreshment was provided'.[25] But all Barrow had been able to find were mean, bare-walled hovels where a traveller might procure a cup of tea and permission to pass the night. The great mandarins, when obliged to travel by road rather than by canal or river in their private junks, passed the night in temples, turning the priests out of their quarters and occupying even the holy precincts as dining-rooms and bedrooms.

Shocked as he was by this profane use of sacred ground, Barrow was even more outraged by the ribaldry and obscenity tolerated on the Chinese stage. Bad enough, he thought, were the comic pieces in which the low jests always obtained from the audience the greatest share of applause, and in which the dialogue was conducted in a kind of monotonous recitative interrupted at intervals by the shrill harsh music of wind instruments, by deafening gongs, kettle-drums and songs. Far worse, though, were the tragedies. In one of these, which apparently was a great favourite, a woman murders her husband by striking him on the head with a hatchet; he appears on stage with a large gash above the eyes out of which issues a prodigious effusion of blood; he reels about for a time, bemoaning his lamentable fate in a song, till exhausted by loss of blood, he falls and dies. The woman is seized, brought before a magistrate, and condemned to be flayed alive. The sentence is executed; and in the next act the victim returns to the stage not only naked but painted so as to appear completely excoriated. In this condition 'the character sings or, more properly speaking, whines nearly half an hour on the stage to excite the compassion of three infernal spirits who sit in judgement on her future destiny'. The character of the woman was played by a eunuch.

Eunuchs, indeed, appear to have been the bane of Barrow's life at Yüan-ming Yüan. Every time he attempted to take a walk in the palace gardens he was stopped by several of them who indicated that he should return to his quarters; whenever he had cause to visit the presence chamber to see the arrangements of the Emperor's presents, eunuchs crowded round him, interfering and inquisitive. They served not only as palace guards, gardeners and custodians of the concubines, but as protectors of the Emperor's numerous grandchildren who attended a royal school in the palace grounds and who were unceremoniously pushed about from playroom to classroom by their fussy shepherds.

They never appeared without their faces being entirely painted, Sir George Staunton said, and without their gaudy dresses being tricked out with all manner of trinkets and tassels. Many of them were fine figures of men, though all traces of their manhood had been removed by the surgeon's knife to fit them for the Emperor's service, and Staunton could not but remark on the continuing strangeness of hearing a strong man over six foot tall speak with the voice of a little girl.

Barrow managed to escape the unwelcome attentions of the eunuchs on his excursions into Peking; but there he had other things to complain of. He had to admit that the Imperial City, which he had not seen on his first painful journey through the capital, was rather fine. It was enclosed by a twenty-foot high wall of polished bricks with a roof of varnished yellow tiles, and contained, as well as the palaces, the gaily coloured offices of the government and the houses of the Court's officials. Its grounds, ornamented with streams, lakes, artificial hills, rocks and groves, exhibited the 'happiest imitation of nature'.

Barrow could also find a few words of praise for the efficiency of the Peking police, whose sentry boxes could be found at every cross roads, whose guard houses were always well-manned and whose nightly practice it was to patrol the streets crying the hour, like London watchmen, and giving notice of their watchfulness by striking upon tubes of bamboo.

One of the regular morning duties of the police, however, gave Barrow occasion to make a more characteristic observation upon the appearance and manners of the capital. It was, he said, tacitly considered part of their job to employ certain persons to go their rounds at an early hour with carts picking up the bodies of babies which had been thrown out into the streets during the night. No inquiries were made; the bodies were taken to a common pit outside the city walls and there indiscriminately tipped in. A Roman Catholic missionary told Barrow that he and his colleagues took it in turns to attend this pit of a morning, to pick out the most 'lively' of the bodies and to take them away to the mission as 'future proselytes', and to baptize those others not yet dead but with less chance of survival. 'When I mention that dogs and swine are let loose in all the narrow streets of the capital,' Barrow added, 'the reader may conceive what will sometimes necessarily happen to the exposed infants, before the police carts can pick them up.' He calculated that every year nearly nine thousand babies were thus exposed to death in Peking alone; and he once saw a little corpse floating down a river 'among the boats, and the people seemed to take no more notice of it than if it had been a dog; this, indeed, would in all probability have attracted their attention, dogs being an article of food commonly used by them'.

Barrow was almost equally shocked by the Chinese passion for gambling which led them not merely to use cocks for fighting but to train quails 'for the same cruel purpose of butchering each other', and even to breed insects for battle: 'These little creatures are fed and kept apart in bamboo cages; and the custom of making them devour each other is so common that, during the summer months, scarcely a boy is seen without his cage and his grasshoppers.'[26]

Out of sympathy as were Barrow and his colleagues with so many aspects of Chinese life, it soon became clear upon the Emperor's return from Jehol that the Chinese themselves were quite as antipathetic towards the whole purpose of the embassy's mission.

3 | Failure of a Mission

We have never valued ingenious articles, nor do we have the slightest need of your country's manufactures. The Emperor Ch'ien-lung, October 1793.

The Emperor came back from Jehol on 30 September; and Macartney, notified that it was the usual compliment to meet him on the road, rose at four o'clock in the morning to be in position at six. The road, on which thousands of soldiers had been working for weeks, was immaculately neat, level and watered, and decorated with painted lanterns hanging from rows of poles. On each side of it, as far as the eye could reach, stood several thousands of mandarins in their official robes, Tartar cavalry and pikemen, standard and shield bearers, musicians and Court functionaries. The approach of the Emperor was announced by a blast of the trumpet, followed by the music of an orchestra; and as he came into sight, preceded by squadrons of cavalry armed with bows and arrows, and borne aloft on a palanquin with glass windows, all his subjects prostrated themselves before him, the Englishmen coming out of the tent that had been provided for them and sinking to one knee.[1]

The next day the Emperor inspected the presents, examining most of them with attention, though showing little interest in the scientific instruments. Courteous and affable as ever, he told the Tartar prince who accompanied him to assure the English through their interpreter that the accounts he had received of their good conduct at Yüan-ming Yüan had given him great pleasure, and he himself had ordered presents—rolls of silk and pieces of silver cast in the form of Tartar shoes—to be given to them as proofs of his entire satisfaction. Sir George Staunton, watching Ch'ien-lung on this occasion, persuaded himself that he seemed interested in the presents, 'indeed, much gratified by the sight of most of them'.[2]

It was the last time that he, or anyone else in the embassy, saw the Emperor, for his Ministers had now made it unmistakably clear to Lord Macartney that no further purpose would be served by his staying in China. They told him that the forthcoming New Year celebrations would be nothing more than a repetition of those he had already witnessed at Jehol; they warned him how much foreigners were liable to suffer from the cold winters of Peking, particularly those who were subject to rheumatism as they had heard to their regret that the Ambassador was. Parrying this strong hint by replying that he was accustomed to cold climates and had, in any case, taken precautions to guard against their ill effects in Peking, Macartney endeavoured once more to open negotiations with Ho-shen. But Ho-shen seemed concerned only with the Ambassador's health and the coming cold weather; and on returning to his rooms Macartney was informed that the Emperor's reply to the King's letter had, in fact, already been written.

On 3 October this reply, reverentially placed upon a yellow silk chair and accompanied by sixteen mandarins and their attendants, was borne to the palace where the English Ambassador was staying. Macartney wrote to Ho-shen setting out the principal requests which he had been commissioned to make and which he had hoped to be able to discuss with him in person. The written answer to these requests was handed over to Macartney on the morning fixed for his departure from Peking at a ceremony attended by Ho-shen and several other leading mandarins all dressed in their robes of ceremony. Ho-shen had what Macartney described as 'a smile of affected affability on his countenance during the greater part of the time'; but the general, Fu-k'ang-an, looked 'confoundedly sour', while Cheng-jui throughout the abortive negotiations preserved 'the same vinegar aspect without relaxation'.[3]

Before the Ambassador took his leave, a junior mandarin was called forward and required to sit down while the Emperor's reply to Macartney's requests, rolled up in a bamboo tube, was tied to his back with yellow ribbons. When the tube was secure the mandarin rose, mounted his horse and rode away to deliver the letter to the Ambassador once he and his suite were well away on their return journey.[4]

* * *

The journey began at noon on 7 October. The slow-moving cavalcade and its attendant porters retraced their steps by road to Tungchow where junks awaited the travellers for their voyage down river to Tientsin. At Tientsin, instead of following the Peiho river to the Gulf of Chihli where they had disembarked from their ships in the summer, they travelled south down the Grand Canal towards the Yellow River.

For the first few days the weather was generally cold and the sky gloomy, the landscape flat and rather dreary with few trees or shrubs. The waterway meandered now this way, now that between the cotton plantations, the willows and Palma Christi, and the burial places of the dead—brick and stone tombs of every shape and size, and, scattered around them, big coloured coffins lying above ground, tied round with ropes, their interment delayed until the time was propitious and a suitable place indicated by a sign from heaven. But by the beginning of November, as the convoy of junks approached Soochow in the Lower Yangtze Valley, the countryside became 'wonderfully beautiful and rich'. The land was cultivated with the utmost care and neatness, and abounded with everything that could be imagined 'to render life convenient and delicious'. Mulberry, tallow, and camphor trees, planes and sycamores, poplars and quaking asps, grew in profusion along the banks, and between them and the mountains in the distance the landscape seemed to be 'one continued village' surrounded by rich well-tended land. The numbers of people everywhere to be seen were 'prodigious'; the crowds of children could 'only be compared to bees rushing from their hives at the time of swarming'.[5]

Soochow itself was known as the Paradise of China. Renowned for its silk since the foundation of the Song dynasty in 960, it was a prosperous, well-built town which Staunton remembered well for the numbers of pretty women he saw in the streets wearing earrings and black satin bejewelled hats. South of the town the Grand Canal passes the beautiful Lake of Tai hu on which Staunton saw scores of neat pleasure boats each rowed by prostitutes who entertained their customers in little bamboo cabins.[6]

Whenever a walled city like Soochow was reached, the myriads of its inhabitants who poured out to see the foreigners sail by 'quite astonished' Macartney, accustomed though he was to the immensity of the Chinese population. At each city the military garrison would turn out, too, with colours flying and band playing. Some of the soldiers were armed with matchlocks—of which, Anderson thought, they seemed rather nervous—others with halberds, lances, swords, and bows and arrows. Their uniforms were expensive and highly coloured, some red, some yellow, others white, buff or blue; but the Englishmen were forced to conclude that the soldiers had a slovenly, unmilitary air and that their quilted boots and long skirts made them look inactive and effeminate. Their heads were covered with shallow straw hats, tied under the chin and decorated with plumes of camel hair; from one side of their belts hung a pipe and tobacco pouch, from the other a fan.[7]

The ten-week journey, through Hangchow, Nanch'ang, Kanchoufu and Shaochoufu to Canton, by canal and river, was 'free of any disturbing incident', except when the junks were launched into the stream of the Yellow River where the rapidly rolling torrent made the crossing from one bank to the other an operation of some danger.

To ensure a safe crossing, a sacrifice to the river god was made in each vessel before it was attempted. In a few boats a pig was slaughtered, but in most a cock. The cock's head was wrung off and thrown into the river, while the body, spouting blood and dropping feathers, was dabbed on the mast, the deck, the anchor and the doors of the cabins. At the same time cups of wine, oil and salt were placed on the forecastle; and as the junk approached the most rapid part of the stream, the captain took up the cups one by one to the sound of drum beats and threw their contents into the river. Then, while the junk was being swept along in the rapid current, lengths of tin foil were burned, crackers and squibs were let off, and the drum was beaten harder and louder than ever.

Our fleet consisted of about thirty sail,' the Comptroller remembered, 'and from each vessel there proceeded, on its launching
into the stream, such a din of gongs and crackers and such volumes
of smoke from the burnt offerings, that the deity of the river must
have been in a very surly humour if he was not pleased with such a
multitude of oblations. The safe arrival on the opposite bank of the
whole squadron was a proof of his having accepted the homage, and
accordingly he was again addressed by a volley of crackers.'[8]

The gentlemen of the embassy enjoyed their return journey to
Canton, though there were times when Barrow felt outraged by the
unaccountably cruel behaviour of the Chinese to each other, or
sharply scornful of their strange customs. He could not but view
with disdain the country people's habit of running after the servants
and soldiers whenever they had occasion to leave the junks, pursuing
them to their places of retirement with receptacles to collect manure
for their fields. Even the barbers, of whom there were several in
every village because of the universal Chinese custom of shaving the
head, always carried bags with them in which they collected the
spoils of their razor which were also used as manure. Nor could
Barrow help but be appalled by the indifference with which most of
the rich regarded the sufferings of the poor. It was not so much that
while the rich man gloried in his corpulence a poorer peasant appeared to subsist on a diet of 'a little boiled rice or millet with a few
vegetables fried in rancid oil', and on tea, boiled again and again
until all its flavour had gone; it was not so much that the rich man
after his heavy meal slept in the middle of the day, fanned by
servants, while the peasant laboured in the fields, sometimes harnes-
sing his wife to the plough like an ox; nor was it so much that millions of peasants lived in hovels divided into two rooms by pieces of
matting, with virtually no furniture so that they had to eat squat-
ting on the floor. What was far worse than the condition of the poor
was their ill-treatment by those in power.

When, for example, extra trackers were required to drag the
junks against a heavy stream, peasants from the villages were pressed
into the service, being paid the equivalent of sixpence a day with
nothing towards the expense of getting home again—often a journey

47

of several days—when they were no longer required. And through-out their service they were kept hard at work by soldiers who lashed at them with enormous whips, with as little compunction as though they had been a team of cattle. Once one of the junks ran aground in the middle of a piercingly cold night; the crew were ordered over-board by the supervising mandarin and struggled in the icy water to get her off. At sunrise, despite all their endeavours, they had failed to do so. The mandarin then gave orders for them all, together with their captain, to be flogged; this was 'accordingly done in the most unmerciful manner'.[9]

Some days later a horrifying incident provided an example of the effects of a 'barbarous law' which held a man responsible for the death of a person who had died in his presence.

The incident occurred at a point on the Grand Canal where several people had crowded on top of an old wrecked junk to watch the English embassy pass. Under their weight the wreck collapsed, tumbling all of them into the stream. Although several boats were passing at the time, none of their occupants appeared to pay the least attention to the screams of the victims or the frantic struggles of the young boys clinging to floating pieces of the wreck. One boat-man was observed busily trying to catch the hat of a drowning man on the end of his boathook. The crew of the junks excused them-selves from complying with the Englishmen's urgent requests that they should heave to, by replying that they were going too fast.[10]

Distressed as they were by such scenes as these, the embassy had no cause to complain of their treatment by the mandarins appointed to attend them on their journey. Indeed, on occasions, the mandarins were unnecessarily concerned for their welfare, as when a group of Englishmen taking a stroll by the river bank before dinner were roughly seen back to their junk by a few soldiers of the Chinese guard. The officer in charge of the soldiers was given forty strokes of the bamboo; and one soldier, who had been particularly insolent, had his ears bored through with wire and his hands bound to them for several days.

In general, however, the proof of attention shown to the embassy by the mandarins was as welcome as it was generous. Knowing that

Englishmen liked milk with their tea, they arranged for two fine cows to be placed on board an accompanying barge. And whenever a banquet was provided by the governors, intendants, prefects or magistrates of the provinces through which the embassy passed, great trouble was taken to prepare the feast in what was understood to be the European style. Instead of stewing small morsels of meat with rice or vegetables, hogs were roasted whole as well as quarters of mutton, geese, ducks and fowl; and if the manner in which they were prepared, being generally glazed over with oil and burnt, was scarcely one which would have found favour with the cooks at the Beefsteak Club, the consideration of it having been attempted at all was much appreciated.[11]

The mandarins, Wang and Chou, were still with the embassy and their friendliness and courtesy were more marked than ever, now that the purposes of the mission seemed not to have been fulfilled. Both had occasion to consult Dr Gillan after having spent a night out at Hangchow. Gillan diagnosed gonorrhoea which, to their astonished delight, he was soon able to cure with a series of injections. They anxiously requested a stock of the marvellous English medicines, Gillan reported, 'with written directions how to use them for future contingencies, both of which requests were readily granted to them'.[12] So intimate, in fact, had Wang and Chou become with the embassy staff by the end of the journey that John Barrow was invited to accompany them to a party given by a friend of theirs aboard a hired yacht. The young girls there were richly dressed, their cheeks, lips and chins rouged like dolls, the rest of their faces and their necks being painted white. Barrow was welcomed by a cup of hot wine from each of the girls who first sipped from it by way of pledging him. During supper, at which the number and variety of dishes exceeded anything Barrow had known in China before, the girls played on the flute and sang; afterwards, they all enjoyed a 'most convivial evening free from any reserve or constraint'. But on leaving Barrow was earnestly enjoined by Wang not to say anything about what he had seen, since their fellow mandarins might condemn him and Chou for allowing a Barbarian to witness such a 'relaxation from good morals'.[13]

Wang and Chou were all the more friendly and relaxed with Barrow and his colleagues since the vinegary Cheng-jui did not accompany the embassy on its return journey, his place being taken as far as Hangchow by Sung-yun, a Mongol Grand Councillor whom Macartney found a most agreeable companion, conducting himself 'on all occasions in the most friendly and gentleman-like manner'. Both he and Ch'ang-lin, the newly appointed Viceroy of Canton who took Sung-yun's place after Hangchow, seemed genuinely distressed that so little encouragement had been given to the English at Court and, at the same time, sincerely hopeful that 'greater indulgence and favour were intended to be shown [to them at Canton] than they had ever experienced before'.

Macartney got on quite as well with the new Viceroy as he had done with the Grand Councillor. His appearance, Macartney thought when he first met him, was 'much to his advantage'; he was 'perfectly well bred . . . candid and gentleman-like'. This favourable impression was confirmed on closer acquaintance: 'He improves upon us', Macartney wrote in his journal on 12 November, 'every time we see him.'[14]

It seemed all the stranger to the Ambassador, therefore, that he had been bustled out of Peking with so little ceremony. 'How are we to reconcile the conduct of the Chinese Government towards us?' he wondered. 'They receive us with the highest distinction . . . express themselves greatly pleased with so splendid an embassy, commend our conduct and cajole us with compliments. Yet, in less than a couple of months, they plainly discover that they wish us to be gone, refuse our requests . . . precipitate our departure, and dismiss us dissatisfied; yet no sooner have we taken leave of them than we find ourselves treated with more studied attention, more marked distinction, and less constraint than before. I must endeavour to unravel this mystery if I can.'[15]

Upon their arrival at Canton the members of the embassy were treated with the same unfailing respect by the mandarins. Indeed, they were welcomed into Canton with such pomp and splendour, received by the Viceroy, the Hoppo and the other great officials of the place with such marked courtesy, and entertained at a banquet

of such magnificence that the people of Canton were astonished to
see the Barbarians greeted in such a way, for they themselves were
accustomed to treating them with scant regard, even with contempt.[16] As soon as the embassy had entered Kwangtung province in
which Canton was situated relations with the Chinese people had got
steadily worse. Previously, if often annoyingly inquisitive, they had
always been smiling and friendly. But in Kwangtung they had all
run out of their houses shouting '*Fan-qui! Fan-qui!* Foreign devils,
imps!'[17]

Now, perhaps, Macartney hoped, all this would change. Certainly
the Viceroy, as he wished the embassy farewell on 8 January, seemed
earnestly to hope that it would. So did Wang and Chou who, as the
Lion prepared to sail down the Canton river between the forts where
thousands of soldiers stood to salute the English ships, broke down
in tears.[18]

But little did change. The Viceroy issued two proclamations aimed
at improving the lot of the English merchants at Canton; but the
proclamations were not enforced, and the Viceroy was soon replaced.
The Hoppo continued to act in the same way that he had always
acted. The Emperor's Ministers maintained 'the vanity, conceit and
pretensions' that Macartney had condemned in his journal, per-
sisting in a confident belief in their own superiority, in a refusal to
recognize that in the view of their European contemporaries it was
they, in their wilful ignorance of modern arts and sciences, who
were now beginning to be considered, after centuries of enviable
civilization, a semi-barbarous people.

Macartney, in fact, had been set an impossible task. The Chinese
had never wanted anything to do with Europeans; and since the outbreak of the French Revolution, of which the great mandarins had
heard alarming reports, their repugnance had been increased by fear,
a fear itself intensified by the knowledge that some of the Barbarian
nations—distinctions were irrelevant—were setting up military posts
and trading stations in India and other parts of south-east Asia.

There was more reason than ever now for keeping the Barbarians
at bay and in their proper place as vassal subjects allowed to trade
only on certain and strictly controlled terms. The fundamental,

deep-rooted and inflexible conservatism of the ruling class of China, both Manchu and Chinese, turned their backs resolutely on any ideas from the West which might upset the age-old and impeccable traditions of China or disturb the superiority of those rich families of officials and landowners whose sons were enabled by long schooling to pass the literary examinations that allowed them to become officials themselves. These mandarins refused to accept that their system of government was capable of improvement, that anything coming from the Western Ocean was worthy of their regard, that the Chinese Empire had need of either trade with Europeans or of such modern gadgets as Lord Macartney's mission had brought as tribute to the Emperor. If the powerful sixty-four gun man-of-war, the *Lion*, or any of the extraordinarily intricate inventions, astronomical instruments, brass howitzers, models of cities and dockyards, that had been transported to China as presents for the Emperor aroused either the curiosity or admiration of his Ministers, they carefully concealed their impressions.

James Dinwiddie, who had accompanied the embassy as a scientific adviser and astronomer, had hoped that the fine planetarium and gigantic lenses would at least impress the Chinese with the 'ingenuity and learning' of the British, but few of them seemed in the least interested.[19] On being shown the workings of an air pump which was presented to him, the Emperor remarked that he supposed such things were 'good enough to amuse children'.[20] Lord Macartney, having seen the 'rough and disagreeable machine' in which the Emperor was transported to Peking, believed he could not fail to be delighted with the 'elegant easy carriages' presented to him at Jehol. But the mandarins expressed their astonishment and shock to Staunton that 'so elevated a seat was destined for the coachman', that 'it should be proposed to place any man in a situation *above* the Emperor'.[21] He never even used the carriages, and years later the British Consul at Amoy found them neglected, in an outhouse of the Summer Palace.[22]

In his edict to George III, the Emperor acknowledged receipt of the 'local products' which had been presented to him as 'tribute articles' and which the appropriate department of State had been 'specially ordered to receive'. But the Celestial Empire had 'never valued ingenious articles' and had not 'the slightest need' of England's manufactures. 'Therefore, O King, as regards your request to send someone to remain at the capital,' this special edict continued, 'apart from not being in harmony with the regulations of the Celestial Empire, such a course, we feel very strongly, would be of no advantage to your country.' Sending the envoys to 'kotow and to present congratulations and also to present the local products' was recognized as a demonstration of sincerity, humility and of loyalty to one who ruled all the countries 'within the four seas' (that is to say who ruled the world); but how could the King of England expect the regulations of the Celestial Empire to be altered 'because of the request of one man?' It was right and proper that men of the Western Ocean should 'look up with admiration to the Empire and desire to study its culture'; but the request for a subject of England —a man whose speech would not be understood and whose dress would be different in style—to reside there to look after trade did not 'conform to the Empire's ceremonial system and definitely [could] not be done . . . . Hence we have issued these detailed instructions,' the reproval concluded, 'and have commanded your tribute envoys to return safely home. You, O King, should simply act in conformity with our wishes by strengthening your loyalty and swearing perpetual obedience so as to ensure that your country may share the blessings of peace.'[23]

So the 'chief and assistant envoys' were dismissed in a document which had, in fact, already been written in draft before their arrival in the Gulf of Chihli. At a cost of £78,000 to the East India Company they had acquired some knowledge of the northern coastline of China and of the navigational hazards of the Yellow Sea; they had learned something, too, of China, her rulers and her people; and that was all. They returned to England with a few mementoes and curios, with the silks and jade, the little books and crystal slippers that had been given to them, sharing Lord Macartney's conviction that 'nothing could be more fallacious than to judge of China by any European standard'.[24] The problems of the China trade were as far from solution as ever.

4 | Lord Amherst and the Kotow

As there is only one sun, there is only one Ch'ia-ching Emperor; he is the universal sovereign and all must pay him homage.
Ho-shih-t'ai, September 1816.

Writing to the Spanish agent in Macao, Jean Joseph de Grammont, a French Jesuit missionary in Peking, expressed the opinion that the failure of Lord Macartney's mission was due largely to his being 'ignorant of the manners, customs and etiquette of this Court', and to his having 'refused to go through the usual ceremony of Kotowing to the Emperor'.[1]

Such an opinion had also been expressed to the Dutch agent; and it was the Dutch who now tried to take advantage of the lesson given to the English. If satisfactory trading arrangements could be made by kotowing to the Emperor, why then, the Commissaries General in the Dutch East Indies decided, their Ambassadors would kotow. They appointed Isaac Titsingh their Envoy and André Everard van Braam his Minister Plenipotentiary.

These two Ambassadors arrived at Canton a few months after Macartney's departure and immediately demonstrated their readiness to conform to Chinese etiquette by kotowing in a temple before the Emperor's name suspended on a banner above the altar. They performed the same ceremony several times upon their arrival in Peking at the beginning of 1795; but despite their practice they were less than adept when the time came to make their obeisances before the Emperor himself, and, while bowing his head to the ground, van Braam's wig fell off at which Ch'ien-lung could not restrain his laughter.

Van Braam and Titsingh appear to have prostrated themselves no

54

less than thirty times during the thirty-seven days they spent in Peking, not only before the Emperor but also in token of their gratitude for presents—silks, purses and ribbons for the King of Holland, dried grapes for themselves—which came to them from the Emperor's hand. They even went so far as to kneel before Ho-shen when he granted them an interview at which no business was discussed.

For the Dutch the whole mission, in fact, was one long humiliation. The Ambassadors were invited to various Court entertainments, at one of which they were privileged to watch the Emperor and his chief Ministers being pushed over the ice by mandarins in sledges supported by the figures of dragons. But van Braam could not enjoy himself. He was lodged in what he called 'a kind of stable'; he was nearly always cold and permanently exhausted, being required to get up so early in the morning. Once he attended the Emperor on a procession to a temple and had to wait three hours, between three and six o'clock in the morning, with the temperature standing at 16° below freezing point. When he was rewarded with food from the Emperor's table, 'the meat consisted of small pieces of ribs and shoulder blades,' he recorded in his journal, 'with not half an inch of lean meat on them, and four or five bones from the back or legs of a sheep (obviously) already chewed. Brought on a dirty plate, it was intended as a mark of honour that the bones could have been those His Imperial Majesty had begun to pick.'[2]

Van Braam and Titsingh left Peking having achieved nothing; and it was several years before a further serious attempt was made by any of the trading nations of the West to try to come to terms with the Emperor. The Tsar Alexander I sent an envoy in 1805, the eleventh attempt that the Russians had made to improve the conditions of their trade, but on reaching Urga in Mongolia the envoy had become involved in protracted discussions over the manner in which he would make his salutations to the Emperor and after four months' negotiation he was curtly dismissed.[3] Despite the Dutch and Russian failures, however, neither the merchants at Canton nor the British government were content to let matters rest where the failure of Lord Macartney's mission had left them; and on the death of the old Emperor Ch'ien-lung in 1799 hope was revived that a satisfactory trade agreement might be negotiated.

* * *

The new Emperor was Chia-ch'ing. He was the fifth son of Ch'ien-lung and his mother was a concubine; but primogeniture did not govern the laws of inheritance, nor had the status of the mother— unless she came from the two lowest ranks of concubines—any influence upon the Emperor's choice of successor.

Chia-ch'ing had early recommended himself to his father as a handsome boy, a dutiful, obedient son, and a promising pupil. In the Imperial schoolhouse he had listened attentively to his teachers, had mastered Chinese and Manchu, learned mathematics and carefully studied the Chinese classics; he had been taught to write with ease and grace, to paint, and to compose essays and verse in the approved manner. In the park he had been urged to perfect his skill as a horseman and an archer. In 1789 he was created Admiral Prince of the First Order and soon raised above all his brothers. He was granted a palace of his own, a chamberlain, a herald and an escort of Tiger Halberdiers and Leopard Tail Archers.

In 1796, in order that his reign should not be longer than that of his grandfather, the great K'ang-hsi, Ch'ien-lung abdicated, adopting the title of Supremely Exalted Sovereign Lord; yet the abdication was far from complete. Even had it been acceptable for a son to wield greater authority than his father, Ch'ien-lung, after reigning autocratically for sixty years, could not bring himself suddenly to abandon power. So, until his father's death, Chia-ch'ing was little more than an emperor in name, taking the place of his father at various tiring ceremonies but having little say in matters of state which still remained in the hands of Ch'ien-lung and of his favoured Minister, Ho-shen.

Chia-ch'ing detested Ho-shen, whose power was so great and whose riches incalculable; and as soon as his father was dead, he set out to destroy him. Within a week a Censor had been found to denounce the evil deeds of the corrupt Minister and of his friend, the general, Fu-k'ang-an, whom Macartney had found so difficult. Both of them were immediately arrested and imprisoned to await trial by their fellow Grand Councillors and the Board of Punishment. Ho-shen's crimes were listed by the Emperor himself in two long edicts; and, having been forced to confess to them under torture, he was condemned to death.

There were six modes of capital punishment: cutting into ten thousand pieces, cutting into eight pieces, beheading, strangling, burning to death and beating to death. But Ho-shen, by Imperial mercy, was allowed to kill himself. General Fu-k'ang-an's death sentence was commuted, but not before he had been conducted to Ho-shen's place of confinement and there forced to witness his friend's suicide.

Having taken Ho-shen's life, the Emperor now helped himself to his possessions, his money, his palaces and treasures. As the President of the Board of Civil Appointments and the head of two other almost equally profitable Boards, Ho-shen had come into possession of nine thousand solid gold sceptres, two thousand three hundred and ninety snuff bottles of cornelian, amber, jade and topaz, one hundred and forty-four sofas of lacquer inlaid with precious stones, one hundred and forty gold and enamel watches, fifty-six pearl necklaces. The inventory of these and other accumulated riches, guarded in Ho-shen's lifetime by over four hundred watchmen, was of extraordinary length and Chia-ch'ing's nature, avaricious, mean and finical, could not but be gratified by its detail.

The new Emperor was an unlikeable man, obstinate and disingenuous. Although both clever and industrious as his father had recognized, he had neither warmth of spirit, nor strength of character. He was quite without his father's affability and panache, while his concern with the ceremonial of the Court was almost obsessional. He issued long edicts concerning the exact places to be taken by officials and princes during the performance of various functions, and once fined his chamberlain half a year's salary for failing to observe a prescribed detail in the regulations concerning dress.[4]

It was a tragedy for China that she had such a ruler at such a time, for the stability of the Empire was now being threatened by rebellions of increasing gravity and significance in the northern and western provinces, where secret societies were springing up like mushrooms and population was growing faster than production. In the east and south, hundreds of miles of coast line were being constantly ravaged by well-organized pirate fleets which the Imperial navy appeared incapable of controlling. There were also growing troubles with the Western Ocean Barbarians, particularly the English whose navy brazenly sailed into Macao in 1802 on the pretext that it might otherwise fall into the hands of the French.

'Didn't these English Barbarians know that they were in the jurisdiction of the Middle Kingdom?' the Emperor indignantly asked in an edict. 'How could the French have any power there to injure them? Had they so much as attempted such a thing, they would have been stopped immediately by Chinese soldiers. The English also plead that their King is anxious to assist us in the suppression of piracy. Do they really imagine our navy amounts to nothing? When our gunboats are massed together on the sea, every sign of piracy disappears. Why should we require outside assistance? All their excuses are irrelevant and absurd.'[5]

The English remained unrepentant; and although they did eventually withdraw their forces from Macao a few years later, in 1808, in collusion with their Portuguese allies, they landed others. Worse still, when the Chinese authorities suspended trade, the English admiral asked for an interview and, on this being properly refused by the Viceroy, the admiral attempted to enforce his outrageous demand by sailing up river to Canton. Compounding their folly, the English roamed over China's seas during their war with the United States of America in 1812, chasing American ships into Macao harbour. Four years later the English were making trouble again, this time by conquering Nepal, a vassal state which China had invaded in 1790 as a punishment for the Gurkha invasion of Tibet and which had thereafter unequivocally acknowledged Chinese sovereignty. It was in the unpropitious year of their conquest of Nepal that the incorrigible English decided to send another embassy to the Chinese Court.

*   *   *

To the English, on the other hand, the time seemed well chosen. The Napoleonic Wars were at last over; and surely now China could not but feel gratified by the friendly overtures of the leading nation of the Western world. Admittedly a letter from George III to Chia-ch'ing wishing him well and informing him of the wicked designs of Napoleon, had received a reply that struck a sadly familiar note: 'Your Majesty's Kingdom is at a remote distance beyond the seas, but is observant of its duties and obedient to our law, beholding from afar the glory of our Empire and respectfully admiring the perfection of our government. . . .'[6]

But, undeterred by former rebuffs, Lord Liverpool's government in London determined to make another effort to negotiate a trade agreement with Peking. To break through a barrier Lord Macartney had failed to penetrate, the British Government selected as their Ambassador Earl Amherst, nephew of the Lord Amherst who had been commander of the British forces in North America during the Seven Years War and chief adviser at headquarters in the American War of Independence. Compared with Macartney, Lord Amherst was an inexperienced diplomat; but his powerful connections and keen interest in foreign affairs recommended themselves to the Government who considered that his lack of any particular knowledge of Chinese affairs would be amply compensated for by the appointment to his staff of George Staunton who had accompanied Macartney to Jehol in 1793 and had now been in China for almost twenty years.

Deciding to make use of the knowledge of Chinese that he had acquired while acting as page to Lord Macartney, George Staunton had returned to Canton in 1798 to become a writer in the East India Company at Canton. Five years later, having inherited his father's title in 1801, he had been appointed a supercargo, an officer in the Company responsible for the care and selling of the cargoes of merchant ships. In 1808 he had taken over the duties of interpreter and by 1816 had become President of the Select Committee. In his leisure hours he had translated and edited the *Ta Tsing Leu Lee, being the Fundamental Laws, and a Selection from the Supplementary Statutes of the Penal Code of China*. Few, if any, Europeans in China knew as much about the country as he did.

Two other employees of the East India Company were also

appointed to Amherst's staff, John Francis Davis, later to become Governor of Hong Kong, and the Rev. Robert Morrison, a Presbyterian missionary who was one of the Company's most expert translators. Also accompanying the mission were Lord Amherst's nephew acting as his page, and Captain Henry Ellis, his secretary, whose *Journal* gives a detailed account of its progress.

At first all went well. The embassy's ships dropped anchor opposite the island of Hong Kong for the purpose of watering; and Ellis was struck both by the 'picturesque situation of the watering place' and the surprised but friendly reception afforded them by the Hong Kong fishermen. He was charmed by the bay at night, the lights of the English ships and the lamps of the fishing boats reflected on the dark rippling waters, the muffled sound of gongs as offerings were given to the fishermen's tutelary gods. He was attracted too by the Chinese people, who seemed at first sight 'active, lively and intelligent, not alarmed at strangers, . . . the dislike of Europeans [being] confined to Canton'.[7]

These favourable impressions were confirmed when the embassy's ships sailed north for the Gulf of Chihli and the Peiho river. The crowds of people who swarmed along the banks to watch the foreigners pass were 'orderly and good-humoured'. They clambered in their hundreds onto junks, they climbed onto the pyramidal stores of salt which became pyramids of men, they waded out into the water packed so tight that they might almost have been screwed together. 'All the salt hills, the decks of the junks, the tops of the houses, the windows, the banks of the river and every rising spot was covered with an immense number of people', William Fanshawe Martin, a volunteer aboard the *Alceste*, recorded in his journal. 'We were rather annoyed by the number of pleasure boats, which flocked round our junk with parties in them, who amused themselves by passing their remarks on us and criticizing our dress.'[8] Yet the Chinese soldiers acting as police had no difficulty in keeping order, only occasionally having to make a threatening gesture with a long stalk of millet to drive back a group of men who were usually permitted to return to their original position once authority had been obediently recognized.

At Tungchow a big scaffolding had been erected opposite the anchorage of the Englishmen's junks, and it was packed from morning to night with people, boys and men and old women, staring at the activity on board, but never once was there the slightest disturbance; and when the Englishmen went ashore to explore the streets, their own inquisitiveness was accepted with good nature. An intrusion through an open door was usually greeted with an invitation to sit down. Captain Ellis could not but complain of the narrow, smelly streets, the dirty and generally ill-clothed inhabitants of Tungchow; but he was delighted by the care that was taken to decorate the blank fronts of the small, single-storey houses with flowering shrubs and dwarf trees in little tubs, with baskets and boxes of flowers, creeping plants and bowers of trellis-work.

Yet, although the journey to Tungchow had been pleasant and comfortable, there had already been hints that the mission might well prove abortive. Chang and Yin, the two mandarins appointed to conduct Amherst to Peking, were agreeable enough. They had come aboard the embassy's ship, the *Alceste*, on 4 August preceded by their enormous red visiting cards, eighteen inches long by six inches wide, and Yin had later introduced to Lord Amherst his eleven-year-old son who had 'readily made acquaintance with young Amherst. This boy, on being presented by his father to the Ambassador, knelt down with much grace and modesty: this is the usual salutation of children to their parents, and of inferiors to superiors.'[9]

It soon became clear, though, that Chang and Yin were far less sympathetic to Lord Amherst's mission than Wang and Chou had been to Lord Macartney's. When Amherst said that he hoped to be able to stay in China as long as the previous embassy, 'no direct answer was returned'; when it was suggested that the Emperor entertained a higher opinion of the English than other European nations, Chang replied that the reason for the Emperor's consideration was that 'the English came from a great distance to manifest their respect'. In a subsequent conversation, the proposition that the embassy might stay in Peking for longer than the six days the Chinese Ministers had planned was 'instantly combated . . . and a return by way of Tientsin was alluded to. In speaking of the presents, they described them as tribute. A remark relating to the incivility of hurrying [the embassy] away after so long a voyage, was met by pointing out the honour conferred upon the embassy by having such great men appointed to attend [it].' When a copy of the letter the Prince Regent had written to the Emperor was shown to Chang and Yin, it was immediately returned: they dared not read it, since it was incorrectly addressed to 'Sir, My Brother'.[10]

Most strained of all were the discussions between the mandarins and the embassy on the subject of the ceremonial to be observed at Court. Careful practice, the mandarins insisted, would be required to secure its being decorously performed; an opportunity to rehearse the full ceremonial would occur at Tientsin where an entertainment was to be given on the command of the Emperor, and at this entertainment the foreigners must conduct themselves as though His Majesty himself were present.

Amherst replied that the gentlemen of the embassy would show the same respect to the Emperor as had been shown in Lord Macartney's time; he would follow Macartney's precedent. Well and good, one of the mandarins said, because Lord Macartney had performed the full kotow as he himself had witnessed. After a deal of increasingly ill-tempered discussion on this point, Amherst agreed to bow at the entertainment as often as the Chinese lowered their heads to the ground. Reluctantly the mandarins agreed to this compromise provided that the English knelt on one knee before bowing. Amherst, persuaded by Staunton that it would be folly to give way, would not commit himself.[11]

The English were, nevertheless, allowed to enter the great hall at Tientsin where a table covered with yellow silk had been placed at one end of the room like an altar; on the table there was a lighted censer. The mandarins arranged themselves reverently before it and were joined by the foreigners. When all were assembled the mandarins sank to their knees. 'At the same instant I uncovered my head, standing erect,' Amherst noted in his diary, minutely recording his movements on this occasion. 'Upon their striking their foreheads to the ground, I made a very low and reverential bow. This was twice repeated. They then rose and I put my hat upon my

head. The same ceremony was repeated a second and third time—
the whole by word of command.'[12]

The ceremony was followed by a play and then by a dinner to
which the foreign guests were 'forced to sit down', in the indignant
words of one of them, 'Tartar fashion cross-legged like our English
Taylors'.[13] After dinner the mandarins displayed their concern at
the unsatisfactory manner of the Englishmen's obeisance. Such a
lack of respect could not be tolerated in the Emperor's presence. On
that occasion, Amherst promised, he would kneel on one knee; the
mandarins wanted him to practise that now and show them exactly
what he intended to do. No, said Amherst, he would kneel for the
Emperor but not for their inspection and approval. Tactfully,
Staunton suggested that Amherst's nephew should demonstrate the
procedure before his uncle; the mandarins expressed their approval
of this, but when the demonstration had been made, they said that
kissing the Emperor's hand would not be permitted. Amherst did not
mind this part of the English procedure being omitted; well, then,
how many times would he kneel down before the Emperor; once
was customary at the English Court but at the Chinese Court he
would certainly bow as often as they prostrated themselves; this
would mean nine bows, and would the boy now show how his uncle
would make them? Feeling increasingly conscious of the absurdity of
the situation, Amherst refused and the discussion then ended.[14]

But after the embassy's departure from Tientsin the talks were
soon resumed, and resumed in an increasingly discordant atmosphere, for the Court, having taken exception to the size of the
embassy—though its numbers were only seventy-five compared
with the ninety-five of Lord Macartney's—ordered the band to be
sent back to the ships, and expressed profound displeasure when it
was learned that the English ships had left the Gulf of Chihli for
Canton without permission. Told that the Emperor refused to dispense with any part of the kotow, Lord Amherst offered to perform
the full ceremony if a mandarin of equal rank with himself kotowed
before a portrait of the Prince Regent. This offer was declined. Then
Amherst agreed to kotow if the Emperor issued an edict declaring
that any Chinese ambassador who might thereafter be sent to the

English Court kotowed there. This was 'impossible'. Finally the Emperor directed the Ambassador to discuss the matter with a mandarin of higher rank than any he had dealt with before, to practise the ceremony in the mandarin's presence and then, if he agreed to perform it in the presence of the Emperor himself, he 'would be admitted to the honour of an audience'.[15]

This important mandarin, Duke Ho-shih-t'ai, brother-in-law of the Emperor, was known to the English as the Koong-yay. He received Amherst with extreme coldness, not asking him to sit down and replying loftily to his repeatedly expressed hope that the ceremony performed before Ch'ien-lung would still be considered adequate now: 'What happened in the fifty-eighth year belonged to that year; the present is the affair of this embassy, and the regulations of the Celestial Empire must be complied with; there is no alternative. . . . As there is only one sun, there is only one Ch'ia-ch'ing Emperor; he is the universal sovereign, and all must pay him homage.'

Amherst once again dared to hope that His Imperial Majesty might be content with the ceremony which had satisfied Ch'ia-ch'ing's father; but the Koong-yay replied, 'his lips quivering with rage', that 'the Ambassador must either comply with the ceremony or be sent back'.[16]

In growing consternation the embassy resumed the journey to Peking, the gate of which they reached about midnight on 28 August. The journey from Tungchow had been a long and uncomfortable one, and Ellis was 'not a little disappointed' when the cavalcade did not enter by the gate, defiling instead along the outside of the wall. He kept an anxious lookout for the next gate; but he was again disappointed when this too was passed and the stream of carriages, carts and Mongolian ponies passed on to take the road to Yüan-ming Yüan which they did not reach until after dawn.

Immediately on arrival, Lord Amherst and his suite were ushered into a small room where numerous mandarins 'of all buttons were waiting; several Princes of the blood distinguished by clear ruby buttons and round flowered badges, were among them: the silence, and a certain air of regularity, marked the immediate presence of the sovereign. The small apartment, much out of repair into which we were huddled,' Captain Ellis added, 'now witnessed a scene I believe unparalleled in the history of diplomacy.'

Lord Amherst was informed by Chang that the Emperor wished to see him, his nephew, and the other members of the embassy immediately. Amherst protested: the date previously suggested was the eighth of the Chinese month; he and his companions had been travelling all night and were not only tired out but were quite unsuitably dressed for an audience; he himself was feeling most unwell. While the argument went on, the small room 'filled with spectators of all ages and ranks,' Ellis continued indignantly, 'who rudely pressed upon us to gratify their brutal curiosity, for such it may be called, as they seemed to regard us rather as wild beasts than mere strangers of the same species as themselves'.

Then the Koong-yay appeared and 'too much agitated to heed ceremony, stood by Lord Amherst, and used every argument to induce him to obey the Emperor's command. . . . All proving ineffectual, with some roughness, but under pretext of friendly violence, he laid hands upon Lord Amherst, to take him from the room; another Mandarin followed his example: His Lordship with great firmness and dignity of manner, shook them off, declaring that nothing but the extremest violence should induce him' to be forced into an audience with the Emperor in his present condition.

At length a message arrived to say that the Emperor dispensed with the Ambassador's attendance and that he had directed his physician to afford his Excellency the medical assistance that his illness might require. So Lord Amherst left the room, climbed back into his carriage and was driven to the residence assigned to him. Here he was informed by the mandarins that the Emperor, incensed by his refusal to attend him according to his commands, had given orders for the embassy's immediate departure.[17]

The return from Peking was even more exhausting and uncomfortable than the journey there. Rain fell in torrents, though this did not deter the spectators from indulging their curiosity by thrusting lanterns into the chairs and carts to get a better view of the foreigners. Captain Ellis 'certainly never felt so irritated' in his life.

'To be exposed to such indecent curiosity while suffering considerable pain from the jolting was too much for the best tempers to bear patiently and produced [in him] something not far removed from frenzy.' He got out of the carriage and attempted to walk but the darkness, the heavy rain, the holes in the road and the apprehension that he might lose the rest of the party induced him to get back into the carriage again.

There were now no soldiers to clear the way, no guides with lanterns to light up the road; and the animosity of the mandarins was amply displayed next morning when a beggar, standing up as Lord Amherst passed by, was instantly ordered to sit down again.[18]

By now Ellis's dislike of China and its 'half-civilized, prejudiced and impracticable people' seems to have become complete. Already he had expressed his boredom with the unchanging landscape of north China, the 'chill of uniformity' that pervaded and deadened it, the monotony of its architecture; he had confirmed Macartney's description of its people as frowzy: the stench arising from them as they had clambered over the decks of the *Alceste* he had likened to that of 'putrefying garlic on a much used blanket'. He had written with distaste of Chinese instrumental music which, 'from its resemblance to the bag-pipes might have been tolerated by Scotchmen, to others it was detestable. Of the same description was the singing.' He had written, too, of his revulsion at witnessing the punishment of face slapping, inflicted 'with a short piece of hide, half an inch thick: the hair of the culprit was twisted till his eyes almost started from their sockets, and on his cheeks, much distended, the blows were struck: his crime was said to be robbing from the baggage-boats: the executioner, and those concerned in the punishment, seemed to delight in his suffering'.

Being a military man, Ellis had accorded the Chinese army particular attention—and particular disdain. The swords, short and well shaped, did not seem bad weapons; nor did their bows and deeply feathered, three-foot-long arrows; but the matchlocks were the worst he had ever seen, while the appearance of the companies of guards, 'dressed in long yellow and black striped garments, covering them literally from head to foot and intending to represent

66

tigers [was] certainly more likely to excite ridicule than terror; defence, from the spread of their shields, would seem their great object'.[19] 'The shields were made of bamboo,' William Fanshawe Martin added, 'on them was painted a Tyger's head. They wore a kind of mask made of the same stuff as their yellow and black striped gown and on the mask was painted the head of a tyger. They were clothed in this manner to frighten their enemies, but the awkward way in which they stood up lounging smoking and fanning themselves moved more for ridicule than to terrify.'[20]

The Emperor had done his best to ensure that his soldiers gave a very different impression from this. They must, he had warned the various local officials through whose territories the English were to pass, 'have all their armour clean and shining and their weapons disposed in a commanding manner to maintain an attitude inspiring both awe and fear'. They must also be alert in their duties of preventing the populace from coming into undesirable contact with the foreigners. For it was the Emperor's desire that the return journey to Canton should afford the members of the embassy as little opportunity as possible of seeing the Chinese people or their country. Orders went out forbidding the people to talk or laugh with the foreigners, prohibiting women and girls from showing their faces. 'On the journey to Peking, the people had been very civil,' William Fanshawe Martin had recorded, 'they frequently invited us into their houses where they gave us tea whatever time of the day it happened to be.'[21] But now there was no such friendliness. A general proclamation issued to the provincial governors commanded that 'the treasurer, the judge and the commander-in-chief of each province should be on its boundary to receive, escort, watch and restrain the English tribute-bearers. Whenever anchoring at a landing place or a change of boats takes place, let there be a strong force in attendance. . . . None of them may land at the places which they pass nor are they allowed secretly to make purchases. If any boatmen dare to buy victuals or other things for them, they shall be immediately seized and severely punished. . . . Decidedly no indulgence shall be shown.'[22]

Through the indulgence of the escorting mandarin, the Englishmen were, as it happened, allowed to land and to go sightseeing. But, for Ellis's part, most of what he saw, he found either ridiculous or unpleasant. There were, for instance, the public vapour-baths, called, or rather miscalled, the baths of fragrant water 'where dirty Chinese may be stewed clean for ten chens, or three farthings: the bath is a small room,' he continued, 'divided into four compartments and paved with coarse marble: the heat is considerable, and as the number admitted into the bath has no limits but the capacity of the area, the stench is excessive; altogether I thought it the most disgusting cleansing apparatus I had ever seen, and worthy of this nasty nation'.[23]

Ellis was delighted when the embassy reached Canton and when, on 7 January 1817, Lord Amherst saw the Viceroy of Canton for the last time to take his leave of him. He was handed a letter from the Emperor, in its silk-lined bamboo tube, and he angered the Chinese by merely making 'a profound bow' on receiving it, instead of performing the prostrations which, it had been suggested the day before, might afford him an opportunity of recovering lost ground in the Emperor's favour. The interview was terminated by 'some unmeaning and formal wishes for the continuance of friendship'; and a few days later Amherst and his suite thankfully stepped aboard the *Alceste*'s barge at the pier head. The crew gave three cheers which the Englishmen found it 'impossible to hear without strong emotions. There was an awful manliness in the sound so opposite to the discordant salutations and ridiculous ceremonies of the nation we were quitting.'[24]

The Emperor's letter which was conveyed to the *Alceste* and thence to the Prince Regent confirmed the pessimism that Ellis had felt on leaving England the year before: 'If you but show the sincerity of your heart and study goodwill,' the Emperor had written, 'one could then say, without the necessity of sending annual representatives to our Court, that you make progress towards civilized transformation. It is to the end that you continue your obedience that I send you this Imperial command.'[25]

*　　*　　*

When accounts of Lord Amherst's treatment at the hands of the Chinese were published in England, the public strongly protested against these 'foolish and costly embassies' which resulted in nothing but insults to His Majesty's representatives. What was the point, asked one writer—who, no doubt, would have been astonished to learn that in 1750 there were probably more books published in Chinese than in all the other languages of the world put together—what was the point in trying to come to any understanding with an ignorant people 'so stupid as not even to comprehend the use of an alphabet'? Surely it would be far better to leave the ignorant, deluded race to their own absurd devices?[26]

The Chinese, for their part, were quite content that the Barbarians should leave them alone and return permanently to their inhospitable islands. One mandarin said as much to a member of Amherst's staff. The Englishman had made some remark about the Emperor's displeasure at the behaviour of the embassy. No such thing, the mandarin retorted, the whole affair was of far too little consequence for the Emperor even to think about it; in fact, he had already quite forgotten it. Inconsistently, the mandarin added that he himself pitied the Englishmen because of the punishments that their King would inflict on them 'for offending the Emperor of the world' and for putting his crown in jeopardy. 'He also said he had a map and could see what a little place our Country was.'[27] As a modern Chinese historian aptly comments, 'Except for creating ill feeling on both sides, nothing was achieved' by Lord Amherst's mission.[28]

II | *Traders in Foreign Dirt*

5 | Merchants and Mandarins

As the port of Canton is the only one at which
the Outer Barbarians are permitted to trade,
on no account can they be permitted to wander
and visit other places in the Middle Kingdom.
Imperial Edict, 1836.

Shortly after Lord Amherst's return to England, the failure of his
mission was emphasized by an Imperial edict which confirmed the
regulations governing trade at Canton and confined the foreign
merchants to the cramped area of their trading stations. These con-
stricted trading stations—warehouses, offices and living quarters—
were known as the European 'factories'. The largest factory, sometimes indeed referred to as 'The Factory', was that of the British
East India Company, which employed far more men than any of its
rivals. The more important of its rivals were the Dutch, the French
and the Americans; the Americans, or 'flowery flag devils' as the
Chinese called them, had sent their first ship to China as early as
1784 and had set up business in Canton in 1802. Smaller factories were run by Danish, Swedish, Spanish, Austrian and Parsee
organizations, though most of these were soon to be put out of
business by their more successful rivals.

The factories were bounded on the south side by the Pearl River
that wound its way down from the city to the Bocca Tigris, the
tiger's mouth—known more usually to the English and Americans
as the Bogue—the narrow channel through which the waters of the
forty-mile-long river flowed out into the Canton estuary. To the
east of the factories was a shallow fetid creek; to the west and north
were the jumbled buildings of the port and suburbs of Canton lying
in the shadow of the city's wall. Seen from the river, beyond the

73

hundreds of junks and sampans lining the waterfront, the factories looked small, for their frontages were extremely narrow—the whole line of them did not extend for much more than a thousand feet— but they all stretched back nearly four hundred feet to the street, Thirteen Factories Street, which separated them from the suburbs to the north. Dividing them into four blocks were three alleys, New China Street, Old China Street and Hog Lane, whose openings were so narrow as scarcely to be discerned between the national flags that flew in a row between the factories and the river.[1]

These alleys, like the open ground separating the long, thin buildings from the river stairs, were crowded with Chinese hawkers and pedlars, beggars and tea-sellers, pimps and mongers, and all the rabble and riff-raff that made a precarious living out of the foreign merchants and the sailors from their ships. Hog Lane was lined with hovels where sailors got drunk on Chinese spirits, doctored to their taste. They were frequently beaten up or robbed or involved in fights that sometimes developed into riots before they could be dragged back to their ships, shouting, struggling, kicking over the heaps of bird-seed laid out for sale in the streets, lurching at any Chinese who came across their path. The spirit most commonly sold to them was a mixture of alcohol, tobacco juice, sugar and arsenic, reputedly aphrodisiac as well as intoxicant; it was fiery and coarse, but not unpalatable, and it was rarely that a shore leave party did not return to the anchorage off Whampoa Island— thirteen miles down river from Canton and the nearest that foreign ships were allowed to approach the factories—without a supply of the forbidden liquor to smuggle aboard.

Old China Street was both wider than Hog Lane and rather more respectable. Its shops sold curios and souvenirs, silks and lacquered ware; but they were dingy places, dark and poky, their fronts closed in by black shutters, their interiors lit by a small skylight or even a hole in the roof. The shopkeepers, though entirely dependent upon foreigners for their custom, seemed not in the least to welcome them, producing the articles they were asked for with sullen slowness, displaying none of that passion for trading which is usually so marked a feature of the Chinese character.

Few Europeans, indeed, took a trip down the Pearl River without realizing at once with what distaste or derision most Cantonese regarded them. Often when a foreign cutter passed by the hundreds of junks which were moored row upon row in lanes of floating houses, the river people, men, women and children, would rush to every aperture, staring, pointing, laughing, shouting insults, signalling in dumb show that they would like to cut the foreign devils' throats. When a group of merchants came out of the factories for a stroll up and down the open ground in front of them, curious observers would squat in rows along the quays, lighting up their pipes and opening their fans, to enjoy a spectacle which seemed never to lose its interest; often they would point in amusement at the *Fan-quis'* absurd clothes and grotesque faces, long-nosed and pale-eyed.[2]

The appearance of the foreigners even struck the better educated classes as strangely displeasing. They reminded one Chinese scholar of the water buffaloes to be seen in the rice fields; he could never distinguish one from another—their faces, like their language, had the sameness of the Gobi desert. Their clothes, so different from the dignity and grace of flowing Chinese drapery, seemed designed to emphasize their jerky, graceless movements. They lifted their feet 'like prancing Manchu ponies', making themselves ridiculous in comparison with mandarins who glided so smoothly over the ground.[3]

The mandarins, of course, had no direct contact with the despised foreigners, leaving it to the Chinese Hong merchants to act as intermediaries. But very occasionally they would deign to attend a formal function in one of the factories, maintaining throughout a perfect dignity and reserve. One day the great Hoppo himself—a mandarin who had recently purchased the lucrative appointment and wanted, so it was believed, to inspect Barbarians at close quarters for fear lest he might be required to answer questions about them during an Imperial audience—was carried aloft by several servants in his palanquin to the factory of the East India Company. Dressed in an elaborately embroidered Court dress, with his mandarin's hat on his head and a long string of beads round his neck, he was accompanied by the Hong merchants and preceded by his footmen who cleared a path for him with long sticks, making sure that all persons on the route were kneeling at their master's approach.

He was helped from his ornate conveyance at the factory door and, surrounded by numerous attendants, his secretary and interpreter, he walked upstairs to the state dining-room where a lavish English breakfast had been prepared for him. Conducted to an armchair at the head of the table, he sat down. The English merchants, standing behind a rail, watched him inspecting, with the most meticulous attention, the contents of the numerous dishes on the table as they were presented to his gaze.

'As each dish was brought successively and held up to his eye,' wrote one of the Englishmen watching him from behind the barrier, 'he examined it very carefully all around as an object of great curiosity, and then languishingly shook his head, as a sign for it to be taken away. Thus he proceeded for a considerable time, until he had looked at every thing on the table, without finding a single article suitable to his delicate stomach. The foreigners all this while were looking on with very different feelings. Their appetites were wonderfully sharpened by viewing so many good things, especially as it was by now their usual time for luncheon. Many of them were witty in their abuse of the old gentleman for his want of taste; and some called him an old fool, and were sorry that they were so situated that they could not show him *how to eat*. However, the Hoppo understood none of these sayings, but quietly proceeded with his examination of the exotic dainties, and when the table had been entirely ransacked, he shook his head once more in sign of disapproval, and then called for a *cup of tea*. The *Fan-quis* could not bear this; the greater number left the room, leaving the prejudiced old Tartar to drink his national beverage by himself.'[4]

Contact between the Hoppo and the foreign merchants was never closer than this. Indeed, this particular Hoppo had shown great condescension in visiting the factory area at all; his predecessors had never been near it, since it was the long recognized duty of the Chinese Hong merchants to prevent there being any direct correspondence or any conversation between the Barbarian traders and the officials of the Emperor, to ensure that no opportunity could ever arise of the traders finding a loophole through which they might gain entry to the Empire.

The Hong merchants, though they were able, like the Hoppo, to make large fortunes out of the European trade, were also forced to pay a high price for their opportunities. They were held entirely responsible for the satisfactory conduct of commercial transactions and for the good behaviour of the merchants involved in them. They were expected, as a notice posted each season in front of the factories warned both them and the foreigners, 'continually to instruct the Barbarians; to repress their natural pride and profligacy, and to insist on their turning their hearts to propriety'. For any misbehaviour on the part of the Barbarians or their servants, they were severely punished by fines or even by being put in chains. They were also liable for regular 'presents' to the Emperor, to the Hoppo, and to various funds, such as the Yellow River fund which was ostensibly raised to meet the cost of flooding but a large proportion of which usually found its way into the purses of the mandarins. Although sometimes exasperated by their manner of conducting business and the unpredictability of their tariffs, the foreign merchants, therefore, felt a certain sympathy for the Hong merchants and were often on friendly terms with them.

An American merchant, William C. Hunter, who came to Canton in 1825 with a cargo of Spanish dollars, furs, lead, scrap iron and quick silver, remembered the leading Hong merchant with affection. He was known to the foreigners as Howqua, all the Chinese merchants being given nicknames ending in 'qua'—corresponding to Mister—and beginning with an attempt to pronounce their real names. Howqua was a small, shrewd, wizened, urbane man, 'a man of marked ability,' in the words of a European who knew him well. 'In any community he would have been a leader. . . . His word was his bond, and in many of his largest transactions was the only one which ever passed between the parties.'[5] He had made an enormous fortune as a Hong merchant, a fortune estimated in the 1830s at over twenty-five million dollars, 'probably the largest mercantile fortune in the world',[6] and one which would have been considerably more had not the Hoppo made such heavy demands upon it.

Hunter described a characteristic conversation he had once had with Howqua in that extraordinary pidgin English in which discussions between the foreigners and the Chinese were habitually carried on.

'Well, Howqua, hav got news today?'

'Hav got too muchee bad news. Hwang Ho (Yellow River) hav spillum too muchee.'

'Man-ta-le (Mandarin) have come see you?'

'He no come see my, he sendee come one piece "chop" (written demand). He come to-mollo. He wanchee my two-lac dollar ($200,000).'

'You pay he how muchee?'

'My pay he fitty, sikky tousand so.'

'But s'pose he no contentee?'

'S'pose he number one no contentee my pay he one lac.'[7]

Despite such demands as this, despite initial payments for their appointments of up to £55,000, many Hong merchants, enjoying the advantages of being the only people from whom the foreigners could buy their goods, lived in as grand a style as Howqua and entertained as generously. Hunter writes of their vast and beautiful houses, the lakes and grottoes and carved stone bridges of their enchanting gardens, the pathways intricately paved with small coloured stones forming the designs of birds, flowers and fish; he describes their sumptuous dinners of birds' nest soup and plovers' eggs, *bêche-de-mer*, sharks' fins and roasted snails, and the liveried servants who escorted the guests home to the factories with lanterns bearing the names of their masters.[8]

So life at Canton had its pleasures for the foreigners. Officially they were forbidden to enter the city, to use a sedan chair or even to go boating on the river; but not all of the regulations governing their behaviour were impossible to evade, while visits to the public gardens on Honan Island were officially permitted three times a month without the payment of bribes.

A trip down the Pearl River, for all the occasional insults and abuse, was a constant delight. With its great coasting junks, and long tiers of salt junks, its rows of countless houseboats and sampans, the Honan Island ferry boats, the lacquered boats of the mandarins, the passenger boats with streamers and lanterns, the barbers' boats and the boats of the rice-sellers and gardeners, the toy-makers, fortune-tellers and jugglers, the little boats rowed by women with one child tied to their backs and another at their breasts, the Pearl River seemed not so much a waterway as a noisy city afloat. Beyond the banks, lined with orange and lemon trees, peaches and lychees, the Canton rice plain stretched far to the distant hills with small villages and walled country houses and tall pagodas rising on every mound; and at Whampoa Island were anchored the graceful, double-decked, delicately rigged East Indiamen, their black and white chequered sides painted and varnished, their figureheads gilded, their tall slender masts towering above the surrounding craft.

Beneath these splendid sailing ships were scores of small sampans, rowed by girls selling fruit, and wash-boats with crews of cheerful, willing washerwomen and seamstresses shouting, 'You savez my? I makee mendee, all same you shirtee last time. Ah, you missee chiefee mate, how you dooa? I savez you long time, when you catchee Whampoa last time. How missee Captinee. I savez him werry wen.'9

As well as the wash-boat girls, there were the girls, in blue trousers and smocks, their plaited hair decorated with ribbons and flowers, who rowed the egg-boats, boats that were almost square and got their name from the circular roofs of matting beneath which the passengers sat. These girls were cheerful and friendly, too, smiling at their passengers with big, white, gleaming teeth.

A young English doctor, arriving in Canton for the first time after a long sea voyage, thought the one who rowed him ashore was exceptionally attractive. As she talked to him in her quick pidgin English he caught hold of her arm. 'Na, na!' she said shrinking back. 'Mandarin see, he squeegee me.' But later she whispered, 'Nightee time come, no man see.'

A few days later Doctor Downing was invited home by a Cantonese tradesman who promised him 'some ladies "all same foot, so so, all same; werry little, can do," at the same time holding his finger and thumb about three inches apart from each other and looking delighted and significant'.

But, as Downing warned, it was considered dangerous for a foreigner to go to one of the floating brothels known as flower boats, the gaudily painted and brightly gilded craft, with rows of flowers in pots on the roof, that were moored along the north bank of the western suburbs. The girls, sitting in silk robes with strings of jewels round their necks, would come out of their apartments at the approach of foreigners, chattering and whispering, laughing and nodding. Yet if a man were to succumb to these temptations, so Downing said, it was likely as not he would never be seen again. Once a rather drunken foreigner jumped on board and was immediately set upon by a gang of eight or ten men; on another occasion a 'poor fellow went on board by himself and insisted on penetrating into the interior. It was ascertained that he had gone in, but he was never heard of afterwards.'[10]

The regulation that no foreign women must ever be allowed in the factories was strictly enforced; and when one fine morning in 1830 some English and American ladies from Macao, tired of their chaste life there, 'popped up in front of the factories', in the words of a French traveller, the mandarins were beside themselves with alarm and indignation. The Viceroy ordered the women to leave forthwith; 'chop' after 'chop' was handed in at the factory doors, warning that unless the order were immediately obeyed the Son of Heaven, hitherto 'so considerate to all beyond the sea', would lose his compassion. To force compliance an official decree suspended trade and commanded all Chinese employees to leave the factories.[11]

Some at least of the merchants were pleased to see the English and American women go. 'What will Canton turn into,' wrote one of them, 'and where will bachelors find rest? Nowhere. Mrs and Miss Low and other ladies are at this moment here! The second day after they arrived several old codgers were seen in immense coats, which had been stowed away in camphor trunks for ten or fifteen years, and with huge cravats on, and with what once were gloves, on their way to make visits!'[12]

Bachelors like the writer of this letter were perfectly content with life in Canton as it was. What better relaxation from a day's money-making could there be than dinner at The Factory? You walked in the cool of the evening through the great outer gate, past the chapel whose spire bore the only visible clock in Canton, up the broad flight of stone steps to the verandah, and thence into the dining-room where the silver on the table glittered in the light of the chandeliers, where Chinese servants in long robes and caps stood behind every chair, and where portraits of George IV and Lord Amherst looked down from the high walls.[13]

Besides, when the winter shipping season was over in March, all the foreigners had to return from Canton to Macao and there were women enough there. The boats set sail to the sound of beating gongs and firecrackers, to the burning of hundreds of strips of red paper as a propitiation to the gods. There were usually about twenty boats in all, providing accommodation for the merchants and their servants and for milch cows and their keepers. The 120-mile voyage down the Pearl River, through the Bogue, and across the Canton estuary took them three or four days.[14]

From the bay, Macao presented an attractive sight. Behind the sweeping promenade, the Praya Grande, that curved by the edge of the sea, the white baroque buildings glittered in the sun. The ground rose sharply from the water front, and above the Praya Grande, on either side of the stepped streets, could be seen churches and convents, houses and shops, the shadowed walls of the Senate House and the trees of the Bishop's garden. The Portuguese had been at Macao since the middle of the sixteenth century; and up till 1685 they had enjoyed a monopoly of the China trade; but the town since then had fallen far from its former greatness, and on closer inspection its splendour was seen to be sadly decayed. Yet so taken by its charms did many merchants become that when it was time for them to retire, they could not bring themselves to return to the cold of Europe.

In the summer season there were numerous parties, dances and fancy-dress balls, musical soirées, fêtes and theatrical performances, receptions in the Portuguese governor's residence and dinners everywhere. There were cricket matches for the English in the field below Fort Monte, horse races on the course south of the boundary that cut off the peninsula on which Macao stood from the Chinese mainland. An entertaining evening could be spent with one or other of the European residents, in particular with George Chinnery, the painter, who had lived in the far east for thirty years and had countless amusing stories to tell of his experiences there. He was 'a monstrous epicure' though he drank nothing but tea, according to Miss Low of the American colony, and towards the end of his life he needed four bearers to carry him about the town. 'He is fascinatingly ugly,' Miss Low went on, 'and what with a habit he has of distorting his features in a most unchristian manner, and with taking snuff, smoking and snorting, were he not so agreeable he would be intolerable.' But so agreeable was he, and so expert was his cook, that invitations to his house were eagerly sought.[15]

A good meal could also be had at Marquick's English hotel; but amongst the chief delights of Macao were the dinners held in the summer residence of the East India Company where, as one young American guest recorded in her journal, 'everything on the table was splendid—a whole service of massive plate. There were about sixty at table. . . . The time passed very pleasantly.'[16]

Some of the guests at these lavish dinners felt constrained to wonder how it was that the merchants, who complained so bitterly of the appalling difficulties of the China trade, contrived to be so very rich.

The answer could have been supplied by a visit to a small island that lies in the Canton estuary between Macao and the island of Hong Kong, Lintin Island.

*   *   *

From the Praya Grande at Macao all that could be seen of the island, twenty miles away to the north east, was the soaring, towerlike mountain from which it derived its name, Lintin, the Solitary Nail. But passengers sailing up the bay to Canton passed near enough the island to discern the masts of armed foreign ships lying at anchor in the open roadstead. Beyond the foreign ships, ranged along the shore, were what appeared to be houseboats; their decks, cleared of masts and rigging, were roofed over and equipped with chimneys and decorated with flower pots. Occasionally other vessels might be seen, Chinese men-of-war junks sailing down towards the roadstead

from the north; and, at their approach, the foreign ships, having un-
loaded their cargoes, would weigh anchor, clap on all sail and dip
away as fast as they could to the south. Yet, it was noticed by those
who had watched this curious performance several times, that the
Chinese junks never caught up with the foreign ships nor ever
opened fire until they had sailed far out of range.[17] For the foreign
ships were clippers from India delivering at Lintin to the receiving
boats and store ships permanently anchored there a commodity
which was contraband in China, but which the Chinese authorities
in Canton were prepared to let in at a price, while appearing vigilant
in their efforts to keep it out. The commodity was opium.

For centuries—at least since the early eighth century when the
opium-producing poppy had been introduced into China by the
Turks and Arabs—opium had been eaten raw as a medicine; but it
was not until the early seventeenth century that, following the
example of the Formosans, the Chinese began to mix it with tobacco
and smoke it. At first demand for it was small, and even by 1750
fewer than four hundred chests, or sixty thousand pounds of the
drug, were imported annually. By the end of the century, however,
as the number of addicts increased, imports had multiplied several
times and as many as two thousand chests were finding their way
into the country each year, most of them from India, the rest—
exported mainly by Americans—from Turkey which, for this reason,
was widely supposed in China to be part of the United States.[18]

By the time of Lord Amherst's mission the number of chests imported each year had risen to three thousand, by 1820 to nearly five
thousand, by 1825 to almost ten thousand. By 1830 the amount,
still rising rapidly year by year, was approaching twenty thousand,
an amount before long to be doubled, trebled and quadrupled.

The trade was spectacularly profitable. It was profitable to the
Cantonese officials who were paid immense bribes to allow it to continue in defiance of the Emperor's commands; it was profitable to
the East India Company on whose estates in Bengal the best opium
was cultivated; it was profitable to the Chinese merchants and
smugglers who purchased the drug at Lintin Island and distributed
it on the mainland. It was, above all, profitable to the British and

American firms in Canton who, since the East India Company was unwilling to become directly involved in an illegal trade that might jeopardize their privileged position, were the main wholesalers.

'There is a great trade in opium here, the Chinese having become excessively addicted to it,' the missionary Robert Morrison wrote to friends in Dublin in 1828. 'And there is only one Christian merchant in Canton who conscientiously declines dealing in the pernicious drug. He is an American. The East India Company, as a body, don't deal in it, but their Captains do. This poison depraves and corrupts the Heathen and yet Christians actuated by the lust of gold smuggle immense quantities of it into China from our Indian Possessions annually.'[19]

A few years after this letter was written, one British firm in Canton, Messrs Jardine and Matheson, were selling six thousand chests a year and making an annual profit from opium alone of £100,000.[20]

By this time a considerable part of the revenue of the East India Company, and hence of the administrators of India, was derived from the opium auction sales in Calcutta; and it had become accepted both by the Company and by the British Government that, since the Indian economy was so heavily reliant on the opium trade, the opium trade must be maintained. Gladstone might well speak of 'this most infamous and atrocious trade', but the prevailing, official view was that the Empire demanded its continuance. 'It does not seem advisable', a Select Committee of the House of Commons reported in 1830, 'to abandon so important a source of revenue as the East India Company's monopoly of opium in Bengal.'[21]

While it was in the interests of the British Empire to keep opium flowing into China, the Government of the Chinese Empire were as anxious to keep it out. As early as 1729 an Imperial edict had forbidden the sale and consumption of the drug; and one of the Emperor Chia-ch'ing's first acts was to repeat his father's prohibition, to declare opium contraband, to outlaw its importation and domestic cultivation. Yet, in spite of his edicts, the number of opium smokers continued to increase; by 1813 the habit had spread to his immediate entourage, many of his eunuchs and even members of the Imperial bodyguard being confirmed addicts. He ordered new and sterner punishments to be inflicted; all officers convicted of opium smoking were to be dismissed from the service, given one hundred strokes of the bamboo, and made to wear the cangue—a heavy wooden collar through which the hands were fastened—for two months.[22]

But by this time opium had become a necessity for unknown thousands of Chinese, as well as a highly profitable business. It did not prove too difficult to suppress poppy growing inside China, for Chinese opium was of a very inferior and unsatisfying kind—it being, of course, impossible for the soil of the Celestial Empire to produce the noxious crops that grew so profusely in less fortunate countries. But it did prove impossible to prevent its importation when so many Chinese officials and merchants were making money out of it, when so many Chinese people—more than two million it was estimated in 1835—were addicted to it, when so many foreigners were exercising their power and cunning to increase demand for it.[23]

The young American, William Hunter, was given his first lesson in how to increase demand soon after his arrival in China in 1837 to join the firm of Russel and Company. Hunter was sent aboard a schooner, the *Rose*, to see how opium was sold by the firm along the South China coast. The *Rose* took on a supply of opium from the store ships at Lintin Island and sailed north for Namoa in the Bay of Swatow. Here a mandarin, reclining comfortably in an armchair beneath a silk umbrella and fanned by various servants, was rowed towards the *Rose* from a Chinese man-of-war junk. Who was this man? asked Hunter, innocent and apprehensive. He was the official in charge of the port, the captain of the *Rose* told him. But was it all right to let him come aboard when there were scores of chests of opium stored below? Oh, perfectly all right, the captain assured him; in fact, it was indispensable; there were 'certain formalities' to be attended to. So the mandarin was helped aboard, made to feel welcome with a cigar and a glass of wine, paid the usual compliments through an interpreter.

Might he enquire, he asked politely, why the American ship had anchored at Namoa when it was well known that all foreign ships might anchor nowhere but Canton? A very proper question: the

Rose had, indeed, been bound for Canton but adverse winds had forced her into Namoa where, it was hoped, she might take on supplies and water. All that was needed in the way of supplies would be provided, the mandarin promised, but the ship must then immediately depart for Canton. Upon saying this he bent down to extract from his boot a red document which he handed to his secretary to read out 'True copy of Imperial edict dated Tao-kuang, 17th year, 6th moon, 4th sun. As the port of Canton is the only one at which the Outer Barbarians are permitted to trade, on no account can they be allowed to wander and visit other places in the Middle Kingdom. His Majesty, however, being ever desirous that his compassion be made manifest even to the least deserving, cannot deny to such as are in distress from lack of food through adverse seas and currents the necessary means of continuing their voyage. When supplied they must not linger but put to sea again immediately.'

The edict was handed back to the mandarin who put it back in his boot and rose to his feet as a signal that his attendants might now leave him. Hunter recorded the conversation between him and the *Rose*'s captain which then ensued:

'His Excellency: "How many chests of foreign mud have you on board?"'

'Captain Forster "About two hundred."'

'His Excellency: "Are they all for Namoa?"'

'Captain Forster: "We want to try the market here."'

'His Excellency: "You are wise. Further up the coast the officers are uncommonly strict. I am informed that at Amoy smugglers have recently been decapitated."'

'Captain Forster: "We have no intention of going to Amoy."'

'His Excellency: "You are wise, I repeat. We can assume then that you are landing your chests here."'

'Captain Forster: "With Your Excellency's permission."'

'His Excellency: "My permission, if I may put it so, depends upon your offer."'

Satisfactory terms were agreed, the money was handed over and the waiting dealers, having observed the mandarin's departure, came aboard to complete the negotiations.[24]

By the time of Hunter's initiation into the mysteries of the opium trade, smuggling along the coast had become a thoroughly organized business. Its potentialities had been recognized several years before, in 1823, by James Matheson, son of a Scottish baronet, and later to become the partner of his fellow Scotsman, William Jardine, in the prosperous firm of Jardine and Matheson.

William Jardine, a forceful, energetic man who provided no chair in his office for visitors so as to impress upon them how little time he had to spare, had started life in the East as a surgeon aboard an East Indiaman, but an aptitude for business had prompted him to forsake medicine for trading, first of all in Bombay and then in Canton where, as a junior partner in one of the leading opium firms, he had proved himself, in the words of a colleague, 'an excellent man of business in this market'. The voluntary retirement of one of his partners and the compulsory retirement of the other, who was considered to have disgraced the respected name of the company by marrying his coloured mistress, had brought the firm under the sole control of Jardine. For two or three years Jardine remained on his own; then, in 1828, the success of the younger James Matheson, who had built up a considerable capital by trading in opium along the coast, induced Jardine to enter into partnership with him and to develop his own coast trade.[25] Messrs Jardine and Matheson were soon the owners of a fleet of rakish clippers, the fastest of which could reach Lintin Island from India in under three weeks instead of the two or three months taken by the old teak ships. These clippers, ensuring that the firm was the first in the market every season, were largely responsible for its early success, a success which was greatly enhanced by the expert help of the man who acted as interpreter during some of the most profitable voyages.

This man was a Prussian missionary, the Rev. Karl Friedrich August Gützlaff, 'a short square figure', in the words of a young Englishman who knew him at this time, 'with clothes that for shape might have been cut in his native Pomerania years ago, a broad trimmed straw hat, his great face beneath with a sinister eye'.[26]

Gützlaff had been born in 1803, the son of a tailor who apprenticed him to a girdler. Disliking the work, Gützlaff contrived to obtain a place at a school for missionaries in Berlin and in 1824 he sailed for Siam where he learned the Fukien dialect from Chinese settlers. Five years later, at Malacca, he married a wealthy English-woman whose early death enabled him to go to China as a missionary on his own account. In China he had soon established a reputation for himself as an assiduous distributor of Bibles, pamphlets and medicaments to the natives, as a linguist of uncommon skill, fluent in Cantonese and other dialects, and as an excellent interpreter aboard the East India Company's ship, *Lord Amherst*, which, in defiance of the Chinese Government's rule forbidding entry to any ports other than Canton, had sailed under a false name up the coast to see what market there might be for goods other than opium.[27]

It had seemed to Jardine and Matheson, then, that Gützlaff would be an ideal man to act as their interpreter. Of course, Jardine said when approaching him, it was the firm's earnest wish that Dr Gützlaff should 'not in any way injure the grand object' he had in view by appearing interested in what by many was considered an immoral traffic. 'Yet such traffic is so absolutely necessary to give any vessel a reasonable chance of defraying her expenses,' Jardine continued, 'that we trust you will have no objection to interpret on every occasion when your services may be requested. . . . The more profitable the expedition, the better we shall be able to place at your disposal a sum that may hereafter be employed in furthering your mission, and for your success in which we feel deeply interested.' Whether or not the expedition was profitable, a Christian magazine that Gützlaff was publishing would be guaranteed for six months, and throughout the voyage there would be constant opportunities for the distribution of Christian tracts. Gützlaff's declared horror of the opium trade proved not to be so strong as his passion for prosely-tizing. 'After much consultation with others,' he afterwards wrote in an account of his voyages which omits to mention the exact nature of his duties, 'and a conflict in my own mind, I embarked on the *Sylph*.'[28]

The expedition was as successful as Jardine and Matheson had hoped; a subsequent one made a profit of over £50,000, and Dr Gützlaff's services, in the opinion of the clipper's captain, would be-come 'invaluable' as trade increased.[29]

Each year trade did increase; and with every case of opium went a supply of Christian propaganda. The ships returned with crates of silver coins to the detriment of the Chinese economy and with charts of coastal waters, ports and harbours to the danger of Chinese security.

6 | The Napier Fizzle

*The great ministers of the Celestial Empire
are not permitted to have private intercourse
by letter with outside Barbarians. If the Barbarian headman throws in private letters, I,
the Viceroy, will not receive them or even
look at them. . . . Even England has its laws;
how much more the Celestial Empire.* Lu
K'un, Viceroy of Kwangtung, July 1834.

Highly profitable as the opium traffic was to all the merchants
involved in it, there was a growing feeling in Canton that renewed
efforts would soon have to be made to persuade the Chinese to open
up the country to the legal importation of the other goods which the
manufacturing nations of the West were producing in such large
quantities. For who could tell how long the illicit traffic would be
permitted to continue? Who could honestly feel satisfied that the
China trade was maintained by means of bribery and corruption?[1]

The ending of the East India Company's monopoly of the China
trade in 1834 seemed to the British a good opportunity to reopen
negotiations with the Chinese Government. The governing body of
the Company, the Select Committee, which had represented the
foreigners in Canton in their dealings with the Hong merchants,
would have to be replaced by a new authority. Ideally this new
authority should be a British diplomat of high rank able to deal
directly with the Chinese officials, bypassing the Co-Hong. The
British community in Canton had long felt it intolerable that, rather
than risk the Chinese putting an end to trade, the Company had
always in the past been prepared to give way in the face of official
pressure—'a jew selling oranges in 'Change Alley would blush at
such baseness'.[2]

The memory of an incident in 1784 continually rankled. In that

year an English sailor, on firing a salute in honour of some guests
who had dined on board his ship, had accidentally killed a Chinese
boatman and wounded two others. The Company had submitted to
Chinese demands that the sailor should be handed over to executioners; and the unfortunate sailor—the last Englishman to be so
abandoned to Chinese justice since that time—had been tried, condemned and strangled.[3] Had not the 'Chinese commerce of Great
Britain been purchased with the blood of the gunner of the *Lady
Hughes*?' a writer, signing himself 'British Merchant', had demanded in an 1833 issue of the *Chinese Repository*, a quarterly
newspaper edited by Protestant missionaries at Canton. 'Had not his
immolation up to this day, remained unavenged? There is the smell
of blood still.'[4]

American merchants became equally heated over the more recent
case of an Italian-born sailor serving aboard the United States ship
Emily in 1821. This sailor, annoyed by a pestering fruit-seller, had
thrown an earthen jar at her and knocked her out of her boat into
the water where she had drowned. His surrender to the Chinese
authorities being refused, American trade was stopped, and it was
not opened again until the unfortunate culprit was handed over to
the Chinese who tried him in an all-Chinese court, found him
guilty and had him strangled.

In the view of most British and many American merchants,
Western commerce could no longer be permitted to remain subject
to caprice when a few gunboats could settle the matter in a few
hours. Open war on China might not be advisable, but the threat of
war could do nothing but good; and if war were to come the outcome of it could not be doubted.

The time was considered propitious for such determined action,
for the Chinese Empire was in a sorry state. There had been devastating floods in 1832, followed by famine in the central provinces
and then by drought; there had been uprisings in Canton province
and in Formosa; the new Emperor, the moody and vacillating reformer Tao-kuang, had felt obliged to address a 'Memorial to
Heaven', excusing himself for presenting such an unusual supplication by the 'extraordinary ills' afflicting the people.[5] The despatch

of a resolute British diplomat to Canton was, therefore, eminently and immediately desirable.

The British Government concurred; and the Foreign Secretary, Lord Palmerston, appointed Lord Napier of Meristoun, a Scottish landowner and a convinced Presbyterian, Chief Superintendent of Trade at Canton. Lord Napier, a sound, religious, forthright and rather unimaginative man who had seen service as a midshipman at Trafalgar and was now in his late forties, was given his instructions on New Year's Eve 1833. He was to go to live at Canton, announcing his arrival 'by letter to the vice-roy', and to look after the interests of the British merchants there, dealing on their behalf with the Chinese authorities. He was to respect the laws and customs of the country, to be moderate, reasonable and circumspect, and not to use menacing language or to seek the help of the Navy 'unless, in extreme cases, the most evident necessity' required it.[6] These instructions, open to interpretation though they were, did not allow Napier the use of that firm hand that had been advocated in Canton; and no sooner had he arrived there than he was made forcibly aware of the strong feelings entertained by many of the British colony and, in particular, by William Jardine, its hard-headed spokesman.

Jardine's forceful personality exercised an unmistakable influence on the early impressions of the new Superintendent of Trade, who was soon convinced that the East India Company had been too soft in the past with the Chinese, allowing them to believe that England 'depended upon them for food and raiment, and that the Emperor was the only monarch of the universe'.[7] As Lord Napier saw it, it was the duty of his mission to throw open—and he had declared his intention of handing down his name to posterity as the man who had succeeded in throwing open—'the wide field of the Chinese Empire to the British Spirit and Industry'.[8]

To the Chinese authorities, on the other hand, Napier's mission was wholly unacceptable from the outset. In the first place, since he was not a merchant, he could not be granted permission to live at Canton, which he had had the effrontery to enter without so much as asking for a pass; in the second place, Chinese regulations did not permit, as had so often been explained to the Barbarians in the past, any direct contact between foreigners connected with trade and the Emperor's provincial delegates. No possible use, therefore, could be served by Lord Napier's appointment.

Lord Napier himself had not been long in Canton before he was given proof of the Chinese attitude towards him. His letter to the Viceroy of Kwangtung and Kwangsi translated into Chinese by the missionary, Robert Morrison, was headed by the character denoting 'Letter' rather than by that meaning 'Petition' which was required as a superscription upon all documents addressed to the Viceroy through the Hong merchants; it was an unalterable rule in the administration of the Empire that every communication must begin with a clear indication of its nature as one addressed to a superior, an equal or a subordinate. The 'Letter' was carried to the city gate by Lord Napier's secretary, J. H. Astell, who was accompanied by a party of foreign merchants. Here there was yet another breach of regulations, for no communication could be presented by more than two persons. At the gate the already controversial document was offered to a mandarin. The mandarin, declining to take it, said that an official of higher rank was on his way. After an hour this official arrived; but he also declined to accept it, as did several other officials who followed him. By now a large crowd had gathered at the gate, and the secretary and the merchants were roundly abused, both by shouts and rude gestures, for their impertinence and ignorance. At length there arrived various Hong merchants, including old Howqua, shrewd, ingratiating, smiling and bowing, with the suggestion that Mr Astell should hand the letter to them, in accordance with traditional custom, and they would take it to the Viceroy. When this offer was refused, two other mandarins came up, both of higher rank than the ones who had come before, and the performance was repeated: the 'Letter' was offered; it was politely declined; it was offered again; it was refused again. After more than three hours the pantomime, eagerly watched by the jeering crowd, was concluded. Astell accepted the impossibility of getting rid of the letter and walked back to The Factory with his companions.[9]

At this fresh instance of Barbarian insubordination, the Viceroy, Lu K'un, a highly competent administrator, immediately wrote to

Peking to give the Emperor the astounding news that Lord Napier had 'actually sent a letter to your Majesty's Minister bearing on its face the forms and style of equality, together with the absurd characters Ta Ying Kuo—"Great Britain". . . . It is plain on the least reflection that in order to distinguish the Chinese from outsiders it is of the utmost importance to maintain dignity and sovereignty.'[10]

In the meantime the Viceroy had to be content with following the customary practice of laying the entire blame upon the Hong merchants and threatening them with dire punishment. So, using characters that described Lord Napier as the Barbarian headman, 'Laboriously Vile',[11] Lu K'un wrote to the Co-Hong to inform them that they were held responsible for his extraordinary conduct, that they must ensure he did not misbehave again: 'If the Barbarian headman throws in private letters, I, the Viceroy, will not receive or look at them. . . . Nations have their laws; it is so everywhere. Even England has its laws; how much more the Celestial Empire! How flaming bright are its great laws and ordinances. More terrible than the awful thunderbolt. Under this whole bright heaven who dares to disobey them. . . . Should the said Laboriously Vile oppose and disobey, it will be because the Hong merchants have mismanaged the affair. In that case I shall be obliged to report against them.'[12]

Two further edicts followed hard upon this one; and by order of these, Laboriously Vile was to be given no opportunity of misbehaving again: he must leave Canton at once, and if he refused to go the Hong merchants would be punished with the utmost severity. 'Say not that you were not forewarned,' they were admonished. 'These are the orders. Tremble hereat! Intensely tremble.'[13]

In Lord Napier's opinion it was not so much the Hong merchants who ought to be trembling as the Viceroy himself and his colleagues. It was time the Chinese were given an ultimatum, he advised the cabinet in London; and if the ultimatum were not complied with, the forts and batteries along the coasts and rivers should be destroyed. 'Three or four frigates or brigs, with a few steady British troops, not Sepoys, would settle the thing in a space of time inconceivably short. . . . Such an undertaking would be worthy the greatness and the power of England.' It would have 'brilliant consequences' not only for the British firms trading in China but for the Americans and other nations as well; and it could be performed 'with a facility unknown even in the capture of a paltry West Indian Island'.[14]

Such advice was much to the taste of Messrs Jardine and Matheson and other firms making large sums from the illegal coast trade in opium; but those whose livelihood depended upon the port of Canton being allowed to remain open were becoming increasingly alarmed by what they took to be Napier's provocation, and they began to protest that the Superintendent of Trade was likely to do their cause more harm than good. Undeterred, Napier continued to urge a bold policy, emphasizing the impossibility of the ludicrously ill-equipped Chinese army standing up to a few good British troops. The batteries at the Bogue were 'contemptible'; there was 'not a man to be seen within them'. What could an army 'of bows, and arrows, and pikes, and shields do against a handful of British veterans?'[15]

On 22 August, however, Lord Napier was given information which led him to hope that force would not be necessary after all. Three mandarins of great authority had arrived in Canton from Peking; they would be calling on him next morning at eleven o'clock.

Two hours before they were due, a party of Chinese arrived at The Factory where the interview was to take place carrying a number of ceremonial chairs. Three of the chairs they arranged in a row facing south, the direction in which authority was traditionally required to face; the other chairs were placed in two rows at right angles to the first row, running along the western and eastern sides of the hall; one of these rows had its back to the portrait of George IV. The three great mandarins, they said, would naturally take the seats facing south, the Hong merchants, the others; no arrangements for seating the English had been made.

Lord Napier was outraged when told of these impertinent arrangements and gave immediate orders for the position of all the chairs to be changed so that none should have its back to the King's picture. He himself would sit in the place of honour, he decided, with a mandarin on each side of him; the third mandarin would sit facing him across a table flanked by his secretary and the assistant Super-intendent, John Francis Davis.

When Howqua arrived at The Factory he was appalled by the way the English had altered the position of the chairs and he begged Lord Napier not to insist upon a disposition that could only cause grievous offence to the dignity of the mandarins, that could only result in the punishment of himself and the other Hong merchants who would be forced to pay crippling fines. Such an arrangement of the seating would, no doubt, be very proper in England, but this was China. Could not Lord Napier give way on this small point for the sake of the Hong merchants whose relations with the foreigners had always been so friendly, and, if not for them, at least for the happy continuance of trade?

No, Lord Napier decidedly could not. He had made up his mind that the interview would be conducted upon his terms, and in no other way could it be conducted. Certainly this was China, but the discussions were to take place in an English factory and in no cir-cumstances could the dignity of England be compromised. Lord Napier's determination was more deeply fixed, and his irritation further increased, as eleven o'clock came and went, half past eleven, twelve o'clock and there was no sign of the mandarins' arrival. By the time they did arrive, at a quarter past one, he was extremely angry, though as he rose to meet them, bowing to them across the table in his full dress uniform, he appeared outwardly controlled.

The mandarins, for their part, were calm, gracious and unhurried. They did not apologize for being late, for officials of their rank could not be late in China: they had arrived some two hours after the time appointed as was the custom when calling upon a lesser personage; had they been calling upon one of higher rank than themselves they would have arrived early; it would have been a break of an age-old tradition if they had arrived at eleven o'clock, the time that the English had appointed. It would also have been an unforgivable breach of traditional courtesy if they had shown any displeasure at the seating arrangements which had been made for them. They sat down, with protestations at the honour accorded them, in the chairs to which they were shown.

Had they not been told, Lord Napier immediately enquired of Howqua, that the time fixed for the visit was eleven o'clock? When Howqua admitted that they had, Lord Napier delivered himself of this rebuke: 'It is an insult to His Britannic Majesty which cannot be overlooked a second time. Whereas on previous occasions you have had only to deal with the servants of a private company of merchants, you must understand henceforth that your communications will be held with the officers appointed by His Britannic Majesty, who are by no means inclined to submit to such indignities.'

The mandarins listened impassively to Dr Morrison's translation. They made no reply. Lord Napier continued: What, might he ask was the purpose of their visit? They had been ordered, the senior of the three replied, to find out why he was in Canton and when he intended to leave it.

He had been sent there, Lord Napier said, as Superintendent of Trade, to manage the commerce of the free merchants in Canton, to take the place of the Select Committee of the East India Company, thus filling an appointment which the Viceroy himself had requested should be filled. As to when he would leave Canton, he would leave when it was convenient for him to do so.

The mandarin politely reminded Lord Napier that what had been requested was not an official whose acceptance required a fundamental alteration in the regulations governing trade in Canton, but a merchant whose status would allow those regulations to continue as before. If the King of England had wanted a change in the regulations, he should have made an appropriate request to the Viceroy which would have been submitted to the Emperor. What he should not have done was to send a representative who assumed privileges that, so far from being granted, had not even been sought.

Although the discussion continued for some time, there was nothing more of any importance that could be said. During the meal that followed the mandarins were as polite as ever; indeed, they were affable; and when they left, full of compliments, their behaviour seemed to imply that they had enjoyed an encounter which would soon, no doubt, be repeated. Lord Napier's subsequent self-congratulatory despatch and his subsequent behaviour showed how little he understood the Chinese character, how deeply he misconceived the effect of his forthright conduct.[16]

Supposing that the mandarins' assumption of complacent superiority was as much resented by the Chinese people as it was by himself, he arranged for a proclamation to be circulated in Canton identifying the interests of foreign merchants with those of 'the thousands of industrious Chinese who must suffer ruin and discomfort through the perversity of their government'.[17]

The Cantonese authorities immediately retorted by a counterblast against the 'lawless foreign slave . . . the Barbarian dog . . . named Laboriously Vile' who was warned that it was 'a capital offence to incite the people against their rulers', that it would be a justifiable act to decapitate him and display his head 'as a warning to traitors'.[18]

A few days after this notice was published a special Edict declared that since there could be no peace while Laboriously Vile remained in China, all commercial transactions between the Chinese and the English were prohibited until the date of his departure. Chinese workers employed by the English were ordered to leave at once; and shopkeepers were forbidden to sell supplies to the English merchants who would be prevented from approaching the city of Canton from the factory area by a strong guard of soldiers.[19]

A copy of this proclamation was fixed to the gate of the English factory and placed under guard of twenty soldiers. Informed of its presence there, Lord Napier came down, ordered it to be removed forthwith, commanded the soldiers to withdraw—which, with threatening shouts and gestures, they did—and then returned to his dinner.[20]

The time had come, he was now persuaded, for a display of British power; and he had at his command the means to display it. The frigate, *Andromache*, in which he had arrived at Macao seven weeks before, had not yet sailed for home, and, with a second frigate, the *Imogene*, which had come from Indian waters to relieve her, was still anchored in the Canton estuary outside the Bogue. Before dinner was finished that evening it was decided that these two frigates should be ordered to enter the Pearl River and sail up to Whampoa Island. If the forts at its mouth opened fire, they were to return the fire, though not to start firing first; after passing the Bogue a guard of marines was to be sent forward to The Factory by cutter. Once this action had been taken Lord Napier felt confident that the Chinese would soon come to heel.[21]

The two frigates weighed anchor in a light breeze soon after midday on 7 September, slowly sailing towards the forts that guarded the entrance of the Bogue on either bank. The Chinese opened fire, first with blanks and then with shot; both frigates returned the fire when the shot began to fall near them; but although the two ships, tacking toilsomely in the gentle wind, presented easy targets, very little damage to either of them was done, for the guns in the forts were fixed solidly in the embrasures, incapable of swivelling to follow the movements of vessels in the river below. The *Andromache* and *Imogene* were only superficially scarred; they got through to Whampoa with two sailors killed and six wounded.[22]

It was a victory of a sort, but for Lord Napier an empty one. He excused his drastic action in ordering the frigates to force a passage of the peaceful river by pleading the danger in which the British merchants and their property stood. He was concerned to 'protect the treasure of the East India Company, the British merchants at Canton, and their property'.[23] Yet there was no real danger: the agents of the East India Company at Macao afterwards reported to the Court of Directors in London that the treasure, still at The Factory at Canton awaiting the closure of accounts, was not in the least at risk and never had been; if they had been asked about bringing up the frigates to Whampoa they would certainly have advised against it. There was not even much inconvenience: supplies were adequate in the European quarter, and the Chinese shopkeepers were quite prepared to ignore the Viceroy's command provided they were reasonably rewarded.

Condemned by some of the merchants for having gone too far, urged on by Jardine and others to go still further, ill with a fever brought on by the humid heat, Lord Napier turned in furious resentment upon the man he took to be responsible for his discomfiture.

'It is a very serious offence to fire upon or otherwise insult the

British flag,' he angrily told the Viceroy; 'I recommend the Viceroy and the Governor to take warning in time; they have opened the preliminaries of war. . . . His Majesty will not permit such folly, wickedness and cruelty, as they have been guilty of since my arrival here, to go unpunished . . . therefore tremble Viceroy Loo, intensely tremble.'[24]

Viceroy Lu K'un had no cause to tremble; he knew that Lord Napier's threats were meaningless, for he had rendered the frigates harmless. He was not only an excellent administrator, he was widely experienced in military matters; after distinguished service as a quartermaster-general in the campaign against the Muslim rebels in 1806, he had been awarded the red coral button and the title of Junior Guardian to the Heir Apparent; and after further distinguishing himself against the Yao rebels of Hunan twenty-five years later, he had been granted the right to wear the coveted double-eyed peacock feather and the hereditary rank of Ch'ing-ch'e tu-yü of the first class. In 1832 he had been appointed Viceroy at Canton in succession to an official who had been exiled to Urumchi for incompetence. Assisted by the provincial commander-in chief, Lu K'un had been strengthening the military defences of Canton and increasing the size of the garrison ever since Lord Napier's arrival. His reaction to the British warships forcing a passage past the Bogue had been immediate and effective.

He had ordered the river between Whampoa Island and Canton to be blocked by sunken barges, by cables and stakes; opposite Whampoa the banks of the river had been protected by the building of stockades and gun emplacements; scores of fireboats had been put into commission and supplied with firewood, straw, saltpetre and sulphur; a flotilla of war junks had been sent to patrol the area; over two thousand troops had been alerted. Laboriously Vile had no alternative but to withdraw.[25]

Fortunately for Napier his now raging fever gave him an excuse to leave Canton without it appearing that he had been forced to do so. Through his doctor he applied for permission to sail to Macao, agreeing at the same time to withdraw the frigates to Lintin Island. He hoped to be allowed to go in the British cutter that had brought the marines to Canton; but this hope was dashed by the Viceroy who insisted that he should go by a Chinese boat.

He did so, and the passage was appallingly slow. For Napier, tormented by the heat, the beating of gongs and the explosion of firecrackers, it was fatal. By the time he rejoined his wife and daughters at Macao he was close to death; and at Macao, on the night of 11 October, when the jangling bells of the Portuguese churches had been stilled at his request, he died.[26]

*   *   *

Lord Napier's provocative policy died with him. In London the sound common sense of the new Foreign Secretary, the Duke of Wellington, brought about a change in the Government's attitude towards the China trade. In Wellington's opinion nothing should be done to upset the existing arrangements which, unsatisfactory though they might be, could well be made much worse; the Napier mission was nothing but a misguided 'attempt to force upon the Chinese authorities at Canton an unaccustomed mode of communication with an authority with whose power and of whose nature they had no knowledge, which commenced its proceedings by an assumption of power hitherto unadmitted'. The true cause of the trouble was the 'pretension' of Lord Napier in 'fixing himself at Canton, without previous permission, and insisting upon direct communication with the Viceroy'. In future the Government ought to seek 'to establish a commercial intercourse between British subjects and China' by the 'conciliatory methods' formerly practised by the experienced gentlemen of the East India Company.[27]

Such an attitude struck James Matheson, now the first president of the British Chamber of Commerce in Canton, as one of 'submissiveness and servility'. Matheson had sailed home with Lady Napier and her daughters to commission a memorial to Lord Napier and to persuade the Government to act decisively. But he found the Duke a 'cold-blooded fellow' and a 'strenuous advocate' of pacification.[28]

Undeterred by such criticisms, the cabinet appointed as the new Superintendent of Trade, Lord Napier's assistant, John Francis

Davis, who had been in China in the service of the East India Company since 1813, had formed one of Lord Amherst's suite in 1816 and had long advocated a policy of remaining 'perfectly quiet', of taking no coercive measures against the local government.[29]

7 | The Offence of Captain Elliot

*The Barbarian headman has omitted the
respectful expression 'Celestial Empire', and
has absurdly used such words as 'your
honourable country', giving expression to his
own puffed-up imagination. . . . Let him not
again offend against the dignity of the Empire.*
The Viceroy, Teng T'ing-chen, in orders to
the Hong merchants, April 1837.

To the Chinese, Napier's actions in flouting their traditional Confucian concepts of law and government, in treating with such disrespect official proclamations which should always be regarded with
veneration, were an outrage they would find it difficult to forgive
and a demonstration of how truly, how irretrievably barbaric the
Barbarians were. To many of the British merchants at Canton, the
entire episode was just the 'Napier fizzle', a proof that unless much
stronger measures were to be adopted, the problems of the China
trade would never be satisfactorily resolved. Headed by Jardine and
Matheson, eighty-five merchants signed a petition to King William
IV beseeching him to despatch to Canton a diplomat with orders to
demand reparations for the insults offered to Lord Napier and the
expansion of trade to other Chinese ports. He should sail in a ship of
the line and be accompanied to Chinese waters by two frigates, three
or four armed light vessels and a steamer.

To John Francis Davis who continued, so he assured London, 'in
a state of absolute silence and acquiescence' at Macao, this petition
seemed the height of folly. It was 'crude and ill-digested', he wrote
on 19 January 1835 to Lord Palmerston, who had now returned to
office as Foreign Secretary; it represented the opinion only of 'a
portion of the English traders at Canton (for some of the most
respectable houses declined signing it)'.[1] Two days later, Davis,

well aware of his unpopularity with most of these traders and of the uselessness of his position, resigned his £6,ooo-a-year appointment in favour of Sir George Robinson, his principal assistant, and sailed home to England.

To the growing dissatisfaction of the Canton traders, Robinson, who was content to be a mere registrar of shipping, continued Davis's quiescent and conciliatory policy which was now as unacceptable in London as in Canton.[2] Its disadvantages were explained to Lord Palmerston by Captain Charles Elliot, R.N. who had been on Lord Napier's staff as Master Attendant, or naval aide, the year before. He had then demonstrated his contempt for Chinese marksmanship by sailing through the Bogue with the *Imogene* and the *Andromache*, and, while the shore batteries blasted away at him, reclining in an arm-chair on the deck of his cutter, sheltered from the sun by a large umbrella.

Elliot was a talented and ambitious man of thirty-four. A son of a former Governor of Madras, and a grandson of the first Earl Minto, he had entered the Royal Navy as a volunteer in 1815. His service had been distinguished, his promotion rapid; he had attained the rank of captain before he was thirty. After 1828 he had been employed by the Colonial Office and the Foreign Office and had become a valuable authority on slavery at the time its abolition was being debated. He had been disappointed to be nominated Master Attendant, with overall responsibility for British shipping in the Pearl River, for he believed himself worthy of a more important position; and he had seen in the widespread criticisms of Sir George Robinson's *laissez faire* policy an opportunity to gain promotion. His proposals of a more forceful stand at Canton led in December 1836 to his appointment by Palmerston as Superintendent of Trade in Robinson's place.[3]

By the time of Robinson's dismissal, the authorities in Canton were congratulating themselves on having successfully subdued the Barbarians' insubordination; and when Elliot applied for permission to move to Canton from Macao, Lu K'un's successor as Viceroy, Teng T'ing-chen, noted with pleasure that the application was not a 'Letter' but in the form of a 'Petition', headed by the required superscription *Pin* and that 'the phraseology and subject matter of the Barbarian's address [were] reverential and acceptable'. Evidently the English had learned their lesson; and permission for Elliot to come to Canton was granted. Elliot, although well aware that the use of the character denoting *Pin* would scarcely be welcomed by Lord Palmerston, was deeply gratified that 'for the first time in the history of our intercourse with Canton the principle [was] most formally admitted that an officer of a foreign sovereign, whose functions [were] purely public, should reside in a city of the Empire'.[4]

But the authorities in Canton did not admit that there had been any change in their views: the Superintendent's title might be different from that of the representative of the East India Company who had formerly carried out his duties; these duties, however, remained the same, as did the responsibilities and limitations of his office. The Viceroy and his colleagues remained as watchful as ever for any signs of seditious conduct on the part of the Superintendent of Trade.

Elliot was not long in giving offence. On the eve of his departure from Macao, he sent the Viceroy a communication which was intended to make it clear that as Superintendent of Trade he was an official, not a merchant. He had been prompted to write the letter by news from Singapore that seventeen Chinese sailors had been rescued from a sinking junk by an English ship, and he expressed the belief that 'the interchange of these charities cannot fail to strengthen the bonds of peace and goodwill between the two nations'.[5]

The Viceroy was appalled by the tone of familiarity underlying these words. How could there possibly be, he demanded of the unfortunate Hong Merchants who had been so remiss as to pass such a document to him, 'what the Barbarian headman is impertinent enough to term "bonds of peace and goodwill" between the Occupant of the Dragon Seat and the small, the petty?' The Superintendent had compounded his error by omitting 'the respectful expression, "Celestial Empire" and [had] absurdly used such expressions as "your honourable country"'. Not only was this 'deplorably disrespectful', but the ideas that animated it were 'ludicrous in the extreme'. The Hong merchants must ensure that no such missive ever reached his hands again; the Superintendent might be excused this once as he was new to the appointment, but he must be made to understand that a second lapse could not be tolerated.[6]

Berated by the Viceroy for his outrageous disrespect, Elliot was at the same time urged by Lord Palmerston, to continue 'on every suitable opportunity, to press for recognition on the part of the Chinese authorities' of his right to receive 'direct from the Viceroy sealed communications addressed to him without the intervention of the Hong merchants'.[7] What Palmerston did not tell Elliot was how he should proceed when the Viceroy not only refused, as refuse he certainly would, to address communications to him direct but also to receive them from him direct. In fact, Elliot was given no very clear instructions at all, being left to maintain as best he could a balance between those British merchants pressing for a firm stand against Chinese pretensions and those who feared that such a stand might mean the loss of privileges already acquired.

His position was made peculiarly difficult by the growing complications of the opium traffic which was now being conducted on a larger scale than ever. The Government seemed to want him to overlook it in the interests of the tea trade, in which the Viceroy himself was deeply involved.

To ingratiate himself with Peking, the Viceroy made a display of his efforts to put down the traffic. He ordered the police to be ruthless in their suppression of Chinese smugglers and in driving their boats out of the river; he demanded that the leading European and American dealers—nine of whom, including Jardine, he named—should be expelled from the country. But when the foreign dealers ignored his demand for their expulsion, he took no steps to enforce it; and when the police were successful in ridding the river of the smugglers' boats, he arranged for a fleet of boats he himself had chartered for the purpose to bring the drug through the Bogue from Lintin Island as before. Occasionally he advertised his zeal in the suppression of a trade from which he was making a fortune by executing a Chinese smuggler or a few coolies discovered rowing a

consignment of opium ashore from a British clipper; and once he
ordered the strangulation of a dealer outside the foreigners' factories to emphasize their indirect responsibility for the victim's
death.[8]

This unfortunate man was conducted by two executioners to the
open ground before the American factory about eleven o'clock on
the morning of 12 December 1835. Here a magistrate, carried to the
place in a sedan chair, ordered a cross to be erected and a tent to be
put up by his servants so that he could watch the strangling in comfort. While these preparations were being made, 'an unusual hub-
bub of something extraordinary about to take place attracted the
attention of some foreigners who were on the Square at the time'.
Amongst these foreigners was William Hunter, the American, who,
when the news had flown from factory to factory and seventy or
eighty foreigners had collected in the square, acted as their spokesman to protest against its use as an execution ground.

'The Mandarin in charge said that the orders he had received
must be carried out,' Hunter remembered, 'that the Square was a
portion of His Majesty's Celestial Empire. He was told that might be
so, but it was leased to us as a recreation ground, and that we *would
not permit* its desecration by a public execution! This was a bold
thing to say. During this short interval the scene was a most extraordinary one. There was the cross, and close to it the victim with a
chain about his neck held by two jailers, all looking on with a quiet
curiosity. The servants of the Mandarin were supplying him with
constantly renewed pipes; his attendants, a few soldiers, and his
chair-bearers, seemed more amused than anything else. There is no
telling what might not have taken place had it not been for a boat's
crew who happened to come from Whampoa that morning.'

These sailors took matters violently in hand by seizing the cross,
smashing it to pieces, and using the bits to lash out at the heads and
shoulders of the executioners and any other Chinese foolhardy
enough to remain within striking distance. They tore down the
magistrate's tent, knocked over his chair and table, his pipes, teapot
and cups, and would have attacked the man himself had not the
merchants interfered to protect him, enabling his chair-bearers to

shuffle him away in the wake of the executioners who had managed in the confusion to drag off the prisoner for strangulation at a more convenient time.

By now a large crowd of Chinese had gathered in the square, and although they seemed 'perfectly inoffensive' the merchants had thought it prudent to withdraw to the factories. But this ignominious retreat before an unarmed rabble was too much for some of the more impetuous of them; they soon rushed out again with sticks, determined to drive the impudent fellows off the ground. The Chinese refused to give way; there were eight thousand of them now, 'the vilest of the population', Hunter thought; and they fought back with sticks and stones, forcing the foreigners once more to seek the shelter of the factories which they barricaded against the jeering, shouting mob.

The police were nowhere to be seen; it appeared that the authorities had abandoned the Foreign Devils to their fate; and their only hope seemed to lie in getting in touch with old Howqua who would surely come to their help once he knew the danger in which they stood. So Hunter and a young fellow-American, Gideon Nye, agreed to climb out onto the roof and to try to reach Howqua's house by clambering across the tiles to Hog Lane and then racing down Factory Street.

Howqua at once despatched a messenger to the prefect of Canton who also acted promptly; and soon after Hunter and Nye had returned to the besieged factories, they heard, to their great relief, the beating of a gong heralding the approach of the prefect and his soldiers. From the balconies of the factories the merchants watched the rabble being dispersed with whips, rushing away from the soldiers in every direction, some of them falling into the river where 'several were drowned, not a boatman offering them the least assistance. Wide open flew the Factory gates,' Hunter concluded his account, 'and in an instant the imprisoned occupants appeared with looks of relief indescribable. The Mandarins passed the night on the ground, chairs were procured for them, officials' lanterns were lighted, and, conscious of the entire safety which we now enjoyed, we all turned in. The next day everything reassumed its normal state of comfort and safety. . . . Approaching the Mandarins in the morning to thank them for their timely assistance (rather a "cool" thing to do, as someone remarked, seeing we had taken the law in our own hands and had driven away the officer of justice the day before!) they received us very courteously, and assured us we had "nothing to fear".'

'This was the most serious of many provocations inflicted by foreigners upon the authorities,' Hunter added later. 'We treated their "chops", their prohibitions, warnings, and threats, as a rule, very cavalierly. . . . We disregarded local orders, as well as those from Peking and really became confident that we should enjoy perpetual impunity so far as the opium trade was concerned. . . . We often spoke of [the Mandarins'] forebearance and wondered at the aid and protection they extended to us; in fact, they considered us more as unruly children.'[9]

It was universally agreed that there would have been no riot at all, had the young and rowdy merchants not provoked it by rushing at the Chinese and beating them with sticks. This was confirmed even by William Jardine who made an entry to that effect in his diary, adding that so secure did the merchants feel under the protection of the Chinese police that when Captain Elliot, who was at Whampoa that evening, sent a hundred armed sailors to the factories, the merchants gave them supper and sent them back.[10]

On Captain Elliot's return from Whampoa he felt it his duty to call the merchants together and warn them that the whole cause of the potentially dangerous affray had been the recent extension of the opium traffic. All restraint seemed to have been thrown aside; British cutters were no longer unloading their cargoes at Lintin Island, but were actually bringing them past the Bogue into the Pearl River. This, he announced, must stop immediately, and he issued orders accordingly.[11]

But Elliot knew how little he could really do to control the opium traffic. He understood well enough that this could only be done if the British Government decided that it should be done, and if the Chinese Government found local officials with the character to get it done. Elliot felt convinced that the day was not far off now when the

Chinese would act; and when they did act, the consequences could be disastrous. They might well act against the opium traffic by stopping all trade; this the British would regard as a hostile act, and war might result.

It would be called an opium war because opium happened to be the article of commerce that had caused it. But the war would not really be fought over opium; it would be fought over trade, the urgent desire of a capitalist, industrial, progressive country to force a Confucian, agricultural and stagnant one to trade with it, to accept the manufactured goods it had to sell.

'Had there been any alternative to opium, say molasses or rice,' wrote Hsin-pao Chang, 'the conflict might have been called the Molasses War or the Rice War. The only difference would have been a matter of time: in the hypothetical case, the major article of import being harmless, the lethargic Chinese would not have been alarmed into action so soon. The war could have been postponed, but not avoided.'[12]

The war, as it happened, was precipitated by the appointment on 31 December of a High Commissioner at Canton, with plenipotentiary powers and the supreme command of Canton's naval forces. The High Commissioner was required to 'investigate port affairs'[13]; but what he was really intended to do—and what the foreign merchants soon learned he intended to do—was to find a method of suppressing the opium trade.

Above: Chinese soldiers paraded on the banks of the Peiho river in honour of the British embassy travelling to Peking. August 1793. *Left:* George, 1st Earl Macartney (1737–1806). Leader of the British embassy to the Emperor of China in 1792–3

Sir George Staunton (1737–1801). Secretary to the British embassy

Above: The Emperor Ch'ien-lung (1711–1799) being carried in procession to th[e] Imperial audience tent at Jehol. September 1793. *Below:* 'The Reception of th[e] Diplomatique and his Suite at the Court of Pekin.' A prophetic cartoon by Jam[es] Gillray published on 14 September 1792, a week before Lord Macartney embarke[d] aboard the *Lion* at Spithead.

The Hoppo, the Emperor's representative at Canton, declining to eat breakfast at the East India Company's factory

Chinnery's portrait of the leading Chinese merchant in Canton, known to the foreigners as Howqua

William Pitt Amherst, Earl Amherst of Arracan (1773–1857). Leader of the British embassy to the Emperor of China in 1816

The Emperor Tao-kuang receiving civil and military mandarins in his palace in the Forbidden City, Peking

The gardens of the Imperial Palace at Peking

Ningpo, one of the five Chinese ports opened to British trade and residence under the terms of the Treaty of Nanking

Yeh Ming-ch'en, Imperial Commissioner at Canton in the 1850's

Sir John Bowring (1792–1872), appointed Governor of Hong Kong and Chief Superintendent of trade in China in 1854

James Bruce, 8th Earl of Elgin (1811-63), appointed British Envoy to China in 1857

Above: French troops attacking the bridge at Pa-li-ch'iao south of Peking. September 1860. *Left:* Charles Guillaume Marie Appollinaire Antoine Cousin Montauban, Comte de Palikao (1796–1878), commander of the French army in China 1859–60

Right: Harry Parkes (1828-85), acting-Consul at Canton and interpreter for the British Army, demanding the surrender of the Taku forts, August 1860. *Below:* A skirmish with Tartar cavalry in the campaign of 1860

8 | The Opium Destroyed

*I now give you my assurance that we mean to
cut off this harmful drug for ever. What it is
here forbidden to consume, your dependencies
must be forbidden to manufacture. . . . You
will be showing that you understand the principles of Heaven by respectful obedience to our
commands.* Commissioner Lin Tse-hsü to
Queen Victoria, March 1839.

The appointment of the High Commissioner followed one of those
long debates from time to time conducted in China by means of
memorials submitted to the throne by various statesmen and
officials.

The Emperor Tao-kuang, having reformed his Court and dismissed the most turbulent of his concubines and comedians, had
turned his attention to the opium issue and had invited memorials
on the subject. The invitation had led to a number of contradictory
suggestions being made to him. He was advised that 'opium is
nothing less than a flowing poison; that it leads to extravagant expenditure is a small evil, but as it utterly ruins the minds and
morals of the people, it is a dreadful calamity'. He was warned that
its continued use would ruin the Empire's economy, for farmers
would use their savings to buy it instead of improving their farms,
merchants would spend their profits on it instead of extending their
businesses. He was reminded of the official report that laid the
blame for the failure of the weakened troops who were sent to fight
the Yao rebels in 1832 on the habitual smoking of opium. He was
urged to expel all foreign ships from Lintin and to seize their
cargoes, to place a ban on the export of tea and rhubarb, to keep this
ban in force until the Barbarians, begging for their lives, promised
not to bring in any more opium, and then, before lifting the ban, to

execute several dozen of their leaders and a few hundred Chinese collaborators. He was exhorted—and this advice at least was acted upon—to order the beheading of convicted wholesale brokers, the strangulation of opium-den keepers, of officials who accepted bribes, and of addicts who were still smoking opium after being allowed a period of eighteen months to break themselves of the habit.

One of the earliest memorials was presented by Hsü Nai-chi, sub-director of the Court of Sacrificial Worship, who recommended that since the traffic in opium was impossible to control, the drug should be legalized. The Emperor, refraining from making any comments himself, as was the usual custom, forwarded the memorial to Canton for the comments of the local officials there. Before their views had been formulated, however, Hsü Nai-chi's memorial had been strongly condemned by several other memorialists, including Lin Tsê-hsü, Governor-General of Hupei and Hunan, who submitted three memorials in the summer of 1838 recommending that the measures he had adopted in his own provinces in central China should be applied throughout the Empire. Lin insisted that the traffic could be brought to an end if an amnesty, during which smokers could surrender their pipes and supplies without fear of prosecution, were to be followed by the severest of punishments, including the death penalty, being visited upon all subsequent offenders.[1]

Two months after the third of his memorials was received at Court, Lin was summoned to Peking where he was granted the special privilege of being allowed to ride a horse in the Forbidden City, and had no less than nineteen interviews with the emotional Emperor during one of which, so it was reported, His Majesty broke down and wept and said, 'How alas can I die and go to the shades of my Imperial fathers and ancestors, until these dire evils are removed!'[2]

Satisfied that Lin could help him to remove the evils if anyone could, the Emperor chose him as the instrument of his will.

Lin Tsê-hsü was at this time in his early fifties. The second of the three sons of a poor scholar from the province of Fukien, he had gained such high marks in all his examinations that a brilliant career had been foreseen for him at an early age. The promise had been soon fulfilled, and his rise to a governor-generalship had been rapid. He 'had a dignified air', according to a foreign observer who saw him for the first time in the year of his appointment as High Commissioner, 'rather a harsh or firm expression, was a large, corpulent man, with heavy black moustache and long beard'.[3] Another European who knew him at this time described 'a fine intelligent forehead and a rather pleasing expression of countenance, enlivened by small dark piercing eyes. He possesses a voice, strong, clear and sonorous. In dress he is plain while in his manners he can be courteous, but is more generally rather abrupt.'[4]

Lin left Peking for Canton carried in a litter by twenty bearers and accompanied by an outrider, six guards, a cook, two kitchenmen and the drivers of the two large carts in which his luggage was packed. His pass required him to remember that his status as a traveller was not as high as that of an official of similar rank making a journey in his own province; he was to be content with the ordinary fare at Government rest-houses, never demanding anything expensive like fried swallows' nests; his attendants and servants were strictly forbidden to receive any gratuities on the journey; he must pay for the expense of his litter-bearers and for the hiring of all boats.

He kept a diary during the journey and on the first day of the nineteenth year of the Emperor Tao-kuang (14 February 1839) recorded that at dawn he reverently set out an incense-altar aboard the ship in which he was sailing down the Grand Canal, kotowed in the direction of the Palace at Peking and wished the Emperor a Happy New Year. Then he bowed to the shades of his ancestors and made offerings. In the early morning there was a violent north wind, but by the Hour of the Snake (9 a.m.) it calmed down a little and he was able to continue his journey to Nan-ch'ang.

At Nan-ch'ang heavy snow began to fall, covering the banks of the river and settling on the ice-coated gunwhales of the ship which made but slow progress down the Canal because of the head wind and the number of grain-transport boats anchored along both shores. Soon after passing Kan-chou on the Kan River the ship had to be abandoned, for the waterway was so shallow and winding that the trackers could no longer haul it along. Lin and his attendants, his escort, servants, bearers and luggage were transferred into a number of small boats which took them as far as Nan-an. Beyond Nan-an the river was no longer navigable and the journey had to be continued overland, across the high Mei-ling pass and down to Nan-hsiung in the province of Kwangtung. He did not reach Canton until 10 March.[5]

It was a Sunday. He was brought ashore seated in a large official boat, surrounded by mandarins, and followed by numerous smaller boats, flags streaming from their masts, their sides painted with gold characters on a black ground to indicate the ranks of their occupants. The crews of all the boats were dressed in new uniforms, red trimmed with white, and wore conical rattan hats of the same colours. The soldiers lining the banks and the walls of the forts also wore new uniforms. Both shores of the river, every door and window, every place where a man could stand and watch was crammed with faces. But there was no noise; throughout the ceremony of welcome a respectful and universal silence was maintained.[6]

Immediately after moving into the Yüeh-hua Academy at Canton, where rooms had been prepared for him as his head-quarters, Lin set to work with a will. He was full of confidence: a modern Chinese historian says of him that he 'was a tremendously self-confident and arrogant man'. He had no real experience of handling 'Barbarians', but he recklessly announced, 'I am intimately acquainted with the wily ways of the Barbarian from my sojourn in Fukien.'[7]

First of all Lin prepared a long report for the Emperor, notifying him of his arrival, giving accounts of his interviews with the Viceroy and other local officials, expressing his satisfaction that strong measures against both Chinese and foreign transgressors had already been put into effect when his appointment was announced, and finding cause for hope in the successful outcome of his mission in the fact that 'the foreign merchant Jardine', the sly and cunning ringleader of the opium smugglers, had fled from Canton and taken ship to England on hearing that Commissioner Lin's first act would be to arrest him—though, in fact, Jardine had sailed for home, rich in retirement, to continue his partner's work in attempting to persuade the Government to pursue a more bellicose policy in China. At the hour of the Rat, late on the night of 12 March, Lin bowed to his completed report and despatched it to Peking by relay post.

Lin now turned his attention to gaining the cooperation of the Cantonese people in concluding the task which the Emperor had entrusted to him. He wrote an address to the school-teachers requiring them to report to the authorities any students who smoked or sold opium and, to form the students into groups of five, in accordance with a time-honoured Chinese system, with a leader responsible for the behaviour of the rest. He wrote to the sailors employed on the patrol ships urging them not to smoke and to hand over the whole of the cargoes they captured, not just a proportion as they usually did. He wrote to the Hong merchants warning them that there was a large amount of evidence as to their complicity with the foreign smugglers, whose ships they certified as free from contraband on entering the river when they well knew that the opium they carried had already been disposed of, and threatening them that if they persisted in their evil ways he would solicit the Imperial death warrant and 'select for execution one or two of the most unworthy'. Lin also wrote to the 'gentlemen, merchants, soldiers and peasants of Canton', reminding them that no province had such a bad reputation for opium smoking and dealing as Kwangtung, and informing them that although reforms had been attempted in the past, this time the authorities were determined to persevere until the task was finished.

He decided that he must also write to Queen Victoria pointing out to her: 'The Way of Heaven is fairness to all: it does not suffer us to harm others in order to benefit ourselves. . . . I am told that in your own country opium smoking is forbidden under severe penalties. This means that you are aware of how harmful it is. But better than to forbid the smoking of it would be to forbid the sale of it and, better still, to forbid the production of it, which is the only way of cleansing the contamination at its source. So long as you do not take it yourselves, but continue to make it and tempt the people of China to buy it, you will be showing yourselves careful of your own lives, but careless of the lives of other people, indifferent in your greed for gain to the harm you do to others; such conduct is repugnant to human feeling and at variance with the Way of Heaven. . . . I now give you my assurance that we mean to cut off this harmful drug for ever. What it is here forbidden to consume, your dependencies must be forbidden to manufacture, and what has already been manufactured Your Majesty must immediately search out and throw to the bottom of the sea, and never again allow such a poison to exist. . . . You will be showing that you understand the principles of Heaven . . . by respectful obedience to our commands. . . .'

The letter went on to inform the Queen that all opium discovered in China was being destroyed and that any foreign ships that arrived in China in future with the forbidden drug on board would be set fire to, so that all the rest of the cargo would inevitably be destroyed as well. The English would therefore not only fail to make a profit but ruin themselves into the bargain. 'Our Heavenly Court,' Lin concluded, 'would not have won the allegiance of innumerable lands did not it wield superhuman power. Do not say that you have not been warned in time. On receiving this Your Majesty will be so good to report to me immediately on the steps that have been taken at each of your ports.'[8]

In addressing, through the Co-hong, the foreign merchants themselves, Lin's tone was less exhortatory but quite as stern. He required them to remember that it was only through the kind favour of the Emperor that they were permitted to trade in China at all. China, as had so often been emphasized in the past, had no need of foreign goods whereas foreigners could not survive without either the tea or rhubarb which were so essential to the maintenance of their health.[9] A stoppage of all trade would, therefore, harm the foreigners greatly but the Chinese not at all.

Yet even worse consequences than the stoppage of trade would follow upon the foreigners' refusal to comply with these present demands. They were aware of the dire penalties imposed upon the Chinese who transgressed the laws against opium; they would do well to remember that the laws applied just as much to foreigners.

Lin's demands were these: they must hand over all the opium they had aboard their ships and sign declarations that they would never bring opium to China again. They were given three days in which to comply with these orders.

*   *   *

The foreign merchants, particularly the English merchants, had not taken the news of the Commissioner's intended reforms too seriously. All Chinese officials were more of a joke than anything else; they all made a great fuss, but they all had their price. To be sure, even before Lin's arrival, the campaign against opium had been getting disturbingly intense. By early December 1838 it was estimated that two thousand offenders, smokers as well as dealers and brokers, had been imprisoned and there was at least one execution every day. It was undeniable that since Lin's arrival the crusade was being waged more seriously than ever: in sixteen weeks the new Commissioner had put five times as many people in prison and confiscated seven times as many opium pipes as the previous authorities had done in three years; it was becoming impossible to sell opium in Canton on almost any terms at all. But it would all soon blow over. Anyway, what could old Lin possibly do against the foreign traders? He could not get his way by stopping trade, for the trading season was virtually over; he could not get his hands on the stocks of opium which were either at Lintin Island or on clippers sailing up the coast. As for his threat to submit Englishmen to Chinese justice, why that was just laughable.

But on 19 March Commissioner Lin showed that he was not like other officials: he meant exactly what he said. He issued an order forbidding any foreigner to leave Canton for Macao. Their self-confident complacency disturbed by news of this, the merchants sent an urgent message to Captain Elliot.

At six o'clock on the evening of 24 March when Elliot, wearing his naval uniform, had managed to get through to Canton in the fast gig of the only ship of war then in Chinese waters, a new crisis had been reached. An English sea captain, drunk after a dinner held to celebrate the Queen's birthday, 'thought fit solely for his amusement to fire ball shot on a Chinese frigate moored near his ship. He fired nine shots one after the other.'[10]

Lin's growing anger with the Barbarians was further inflamed by this. He reacted to the merchants' request for time to think the matter over by shutting the customs office, closing the river by patrols of junks, and parading troops in the suburbs. Moreover, he sent the Hong merchant Howqua, together with his colleague, Mowqua, to the factories to tell the foreigners that he was not a man to trifle with, that the opium must be immediately delivered up. As they reported his words, Mowqua was trembling and even the normally placid Howqua was more disturbed than the merchants had ever seen him. If the opium were not handed over, Mowqua said, assuredly both of them would be strangled.

Some of the merchants, notably James Matheson, refused to believe that any harm would come to either of them; they had obviously been sent to arouse the foreigners' sympathy. But most of them refused to risk the old men's lives by taking any chances; they had grown fond of them over the years, they were a familiar and endearing part of the Canton scene. So it was decided that a generous amount of opium, well over £100,000 worth, including a good deal belonging to the Hong merchants, should be given up to the Commissioner, 'under solemn protests by the community', in the hope that that would satisfy him.

It certainly did not satisfy him. He soundly berated Howqua and Mowqua for believing he might be content with so small a fraction; he had asked for all the opium, and all of it he would have. The two merchants were sent back to the factories with the demand that 'the Barbarian Dent', the senior partner of Dent & Co. and, now that William Jardine had retired, the senior British merchant in Canton, should present himself before him at once. Dent had no less than six thousand chests, Lin insisted, and he would force them out of him.

Lancelot Dent was a good-natured and easygoing man who got on well with the Chinese; he had opposed Lord Napier's unequivocal stand and had strongly disapproved of William Jardine's ideas and methods. Believing that no harm could possibly come to him, he agreed to go into the city and see the Commissioner. But his colleagues said they would not hear of such a thing unless he first obtained a safe-conduct which Howqua and Mowqua were accordingly sent back to collect.

The unhappy pair returned next morning not only without a safe-conduct but with chains round their necks, the buttons torn from their caps. They bore the sad news that Howqua's son and another of the Hong merchants had been imprisoned, and they repeated the Commissioner's demand for Dent's appearance at the Yüeh-hua Academy. Again Dent agreed to go, but again he was dissuaded by the others who feared that he might be tortured, and that once he had given way and handed over his stocks, they would all be forced to do the same.

Howqua and Mowqua pleaded that they dared not go back without him, and eventually, to their profound relief, one of his younger partners agreed to go instead of him. This, however, was far from acceptable to Lin. If Dent did not come into the city himself, his partner was warned, he would be dragged there forcibly from his house. This was the situation when Elliot arrived from Macao.

He saw it as a very 'dismal' one; he spoke of the possible necessity of withdrawing all the British merchants to Macao and of the time having come for the use of force. Dismissing the belief of some of the merchants that a compromise might yet be reached, he forbade Dent to make a visit to the city that had been planned for Monday morning. Commissioner Lin retaliated by giving orders for the withdrawal of all Chinese servants and compradors from the factories, for the cutting off of food and water supplies, and for the blockading of the factories by junks in the river and by soldiers on shore.

The Chinese employees received their orders to leave the factories at about eight o'clock in the evening, and within a few minutes hundreds of them could be seen scurrying across the square with their belongings 'as if they were running from a plague'. Within half an hour all of them had gone; and immediately after their departure further steps were taken to make the blockade of the area more secure than ever. New China Street was barricaded with wooden bars and guarded by a strong force of police; another strong guard was stationed in Old China Street; all the other streets were bricked up.

That night and on subsequent nights the factories were guarded by five hundred men armed with pikes, spears and sticks; the ground in front of the buildings was patrolled by guards in special uniform beating gongs and blowing horns; the streets behind were lined with soldiers whose officers moved into the Consoo House, the merchants' council chamber. In the river the junks were joined by tea-boats and chop-boats filled with soldiers, armed with match-locks, bows and arrows, and equipped with gongs and conch shells with which they maintained a fearful noise all night.

Yet the blockading of the factories—though not before attempted on this grand scale—was, at least, something to which the merchants were accustomed and which some of them even enjoyed. 'We made light of it,' wrote one of them, 'and laughed rather than groaned over the efforts to roast a capon, to boil an egg or a potato. We could all clean knives, sweep the floors, and even manage to fill the lamps. But there were mysteries which we could not divine; our chef, Mr Green, after a vain attempt to boil rice—which, when prepared, resembled a tough mass of glue—proved a most wretched cook, and took to polishing the silver, but abandoned that and finally swept the floor.'[11]

The Chinese responsible for guarding the merchants carried out their duties with the greatest friendliness and good humour, occasionally laughing at their plight, shouting cheerful instructions on how to cook, wash a shirt or clean a floor, looking on with amusement as the younger ones played cricket and leapfrog and raced each other up the flagpoles. Sometimes a merchant, recognizing a former servant in the crowds of guards, would rush up to him holding up a jacket that needed mending and insisting, with assumed severity, that it 'must be mended instanter'. Sometimes a group of young Europeans would rush up to the barriers pretending to be determined to escape, threatening to force their way up Old China Street, and the Chinese, momentarily alarmed, obviously unwilling to use their weapons, would shout at them, 'Hae Yaw, how can do? No good talksee so!'

The Hong merchants and their servants had little difficulty in getting through to the factories to provide their foreign friends with supplies of food to augment the already adequate stocks.

* * *

Despite the cheerfulness of the merchants in his charge and the ineffectiveness of the good-humoured blockade, Elliot now came to the conclusion that he must give way to the Commissioner's demands. Concerned, so he announced, for the safety and liberty of the foreigners detained in Canton, he required all British subjects to surrender to him every chest of opium under their control, guaranteeing on behalf of the Government—which was, by his action, obliged to acknowledge its recognition of the illegal trade and its power to control it—an indemnity for all stocks surrendered.

The British merchants were happy enough to comply. It had been almost impossible to sell opium of late; now they were relieved of the efforts of finding customers and, at the same time, assured of a good price for the new crop. Some of them were surprised by Elliot's sudden surrender. They had not felt themselves in any danger. Elliot himself, indeed, on the day after he agreed to hand over the opium told Captain Marquis, the commander of the ships at Whampoa, that he was 'without apprehension as to the safety of life and property'.[12] Yet he surrendered over 20,000 chests, worth nearly three million pounds, the whole amount, so he was assured, of the British stocks. The Hong merchants were as astonished as the foreigners; one of them asked Matheson 'What for he pay so large? No wantee so much. Six, seven tousand so would be enough.'[13] But the British had no cause for complaint; and some of them, eager to profit from Elliot's promise of compensation, quickly repacked their opium so that it filled more chests.

Nor had Commissioner Lin any cause for complaint. Accepting the offer and giving instructions for the landing of the opium on the island of Chuenpi at the mouth of the Bogue, he signified his pleasure at the 'real sincerity and faithfulness' displayed by the English whom he asked to persuade the Americans, French and Dutch merchants to follow their good example. Sending them a present of food, he also asked the Emperor's approval of a reward of five catties (6½ lbs) of tea for each person who surrendered a chest 'to reward his sense of obedience and to strengthen his determination to repent and improve himself'. When a message from the Emperor arrived with a present for him of roebuck flesh—the Chinese name of which also means 'promotion assured'—together with a scroll bearing the legends 'Good luck' and 'Long life', Lin recorded in his diary how he 'respectfully burnt incense and kotowed nine times'.[14]

* * *

On 10 April Commissioner Lin, writing despatches on the way, was rowed down river to the island of Chuenpi at the entrance to the Bogue, passing at Whampoa the fully loaded British tea clippers whose crews, kept waiting there for their papers until the opium had been handed over, shook their fists at him. But he glided by without interruption and was soon established at Chuenpi in a large wooden pavilion from which he could watch the collection of the drug and record the number of chests received.

He thought it as well to write to the Emperor offering to send all the opium to Peking: he was anxious that there should be no grounds for the suspicion that he might not have destroyed the drug but sold it secretly at some vast profit. At first it was decided in Peking that the opium should be despatched north, as Lin suggested; but later this order was rescinded because of the difficulties of transportation and the dangers of some of the cases being lost or stolen on the journey. The Commissioner was instructed to destroy it locally.

Lin, in fact, had been planning to do this while waiting for a reply to his letter. He rejected the idea of burning it, for the residue could still have been used as an inferior but none the less usable drug; and he decided to have it thrown by coolies into deep trenches filled with water. Other coolies, standing in the water, would churn it up with sticks, then decompose the mixture by adding salt and lime to it. The most trusted of his subordinates would supervise the operation, stripping and searching the coolies after each day's work, and ensuring that the residual sludge was drained off safely into the creek.[15]

As an apology for polluting the Canton estuary, Lin decided to make a sacrifice of a pig and a sheep, 'together with clear wine and diverse dainties', to the Spirit of the Southern Sea who was advised to tell all the creatures of the ocean to move away for a time to avoid being contaminated.[16]

The sacrifice was duly made early on the morning of 1 June; and on 3 June the destruction of the opium began. A fortnight later C. W. King, a partner in the American firm of Olyphant & Co.— the one important firm in China that resolutely refused to deal in opium—was permitted to witness the procedure with a few companions, including the first American missionary to China, Elijah Coleman Bridgman, founder and editor of the *Chinese Repository*.

King and Bridgman were much impressed by the efficiency with which the operations were conducted. The area in which the trenches had been dug was enclosed by a bamboo fence and closely watched and guarded by overseers. No one could enter the enclosure without a ticket and without being submitted to a search on his way out; one coolie discovered trying to get out with a few ounces of opium was immediately beheaded on the spot.

After watching the operations for some time, King and his party were conducted to the Commissioner's pavilion where, so Lin recorded in his diary, 'they saluted me in the foreign way by touching their hats. One of my staff then conveyed to them suitable instructions and warnings, and after they had been given a present of things to eat, they retired.'

An English account of the interview which appeared in the *Canton Press* was more detailed. Lin, who was surrounded by an astonishing number of mandarins in summer silks, satin boots and straw hats, appeared to the Americans as 'bland and vivacious, without a trace of the fanatic's sternness with which he was credited. He looked young for his age [54], was short, rather stout, with a full round face, a slender black beard and a keen black eye. . . . Once he laughed outright when Mr King, on being asked which of the Chinese [Hong merchants] was the most honest, found himself unable to name one.'[17] Later he frowned when told about the steamships now in use as gunboats in the British Navy.[18]

Some time before, Lin had comforted himself in a memorial to the Throne with the belief that the British Navy's power was much overrated. In fact, England's warships were very unwieldy, 'successful only on the outer seas'; they were no match for Chinese craft closer in shore. As to the said Barbarians' soldiers, they did not know how to use fists and swords; also their legs were so firmly bound with cloth that they had no freedom of movement. Should they land, it was apparent they could do little harm: what was called their power could be controlled without difficulty.[19]

Other officials assured the Emperor that the English Barbarians were 'an insignificant and detestable race', too poor 'to contribute to the expenses' of an army as far from their home as China was. Their warships, though waterproof, were not fireproof; and when once set alight by firecraft it would be the simplest matter in the world to cannonade them from the shore batteries, 'displaying the celestial terror and so exterminating them without the loss of a single life'. As for their soldiers, if they should ever get ashore, they were buttoned up so tight that once they fell over they could never get up again.[20] How could such enemies withstand the might of the Empire, the Chinese soldiers of the Green Standard Army, the 230,000 men of the Manchu Army?

Although many officials continued for years to cling to these purblind views of the relative merits of Britain's and China's naval and military strength, Lin, at least, was gradually being forced to amend them, just as his subscription to the ancient Chinese belief that the English nation would die of constipation if not regularly supplied with Chinese rhubarb was dispelled by the knowledge of how little rhubarb was actually exported from Canton. But he still clung to other misconceptions about the Barbarians which stood in the way of any satisfactory settlement with them. He believed that the British Government did not fully support the opium traders, and that if strong measures were used against them there would be no repercussions from the authorities in that far away country from which they came. He believed also that the best way to deal with the English was alternately to threaten and cajole them, bully them and then reward them for giving way; and he felt quite sure that any reasonable Englishman would surely recognize China's right, its customary right hallowed by centuries of observance, to punish foreigners living in China who did not obey the laws of China.

To Captain Elliot, on the contrary, the Commissioner's imprisonment of British citizens with a view to forcing them to obey his commands was nothing less than an act of piracy for which compensation must be paid. It was, so he wrote to Palmerston, 'the most shameless violence which one nation has ever yet dared to perpetrate against another'. It was not that Elliot approved in any way of the opium trade; he considered it, in fact, 'a trade which every friend to humanity must deplore', a trade 'discreditable to the character of the Christian nations, under whose flag it is carried on'; but he felt it to be his bounden duty to protect all European and American traders, whether or not they were engaged in the opium traffic, from what he took to be the 'acts of aggression of the Chinese government'. He was determined that no further opportunity should be given to the Chinese to act aggressively again. He advised sixteen leading opium traders, including Dent and Matheson, whom the Chinese had required to sign bonds never to return to Canton, to give the required undertakings; and then, on 24 May, he himself left Canton with all the Europeans recently detained there.

Having got those for whose safety he felt responsible safely away from the clutches of the Chinese, he let fly at Palmerston a fresh outburst of condemnation of Commissioner Lin, the 'rash man' who was 'hastening on in a career of violence' which would react upon the Chinese Empire in a 'terrible manner'. He urged the Government on to 'powerful intervention'.[21]

It was, however, Commissioner Lin who was again the first to intervene. For while Captain Elliot continued to express his disapproval of the opium trade, while Lin himself, having destroyed 2,613,879 lb of opium, was assuring the Emperor that now that the Barbarians' capital was laid waste they 'probably would not dare' to commit the same crimes again, the traffic continued at a faster rate than ever. The price, as the dealers had foreseen, had risen to a new peak of a thousand dollars a chest, and strenuous efforts were being made to fill the urgent demand. Clippers were racing for India to collect fresh supplies. From his new headquarters in Manila, where William Jardine's nephew had been sent before the crisis began, Matheson was reorganizing the coastal trade; other firms were carrying on as brisk a business as they had ever done in Canton from Lintin and Macao.

As soon as Lin became aware of this widespread resumption of the traffic, he determined to stamp it out with measures as ruthless as those he had adopted in March; and at the beginning of July an incident occurred on the Kowloon side of the Hong Kong anchorage that gave him his opportunity.

Lin recorded the event in his diary under the date 12 July as though its importance did not at first occur to him: 'Sudden changes from fine to rain. Wrote a poem using the same rhymes as the Governor-General in a poem of his. Heard that at Kowloon Point sailors from a foreign ship beat up some Chinese peasants and killed one of them. Sent a deputy to make inquiries.'[22]

What had happened was that some British and American seamen while wandering drunkenly through a village near their anchorage had provoked an argument with the local people in a wine shop. The argument had erupted into a fight; the fight had resulted in the death of one Lin Wei-hsi. Realizing at once how the situation might be exploited by that 'rash man', Commissioner Lin, Captain Elliot hurried to Hong Kong, paid £300 compensation to Lin Wei-hsi's family, £25 to other villagers, and a *douceur* of £125 to the mandarins.

9 | The Flag Insulted

> *What does anybody here know of China. Even those Europeans who have been in that Empire are almost as ignorant of it as the rest of us. Everything is covered by a veil, through which a glimpse of what is within may occasionally be caught, a glimpse just sufficient to set the imagination at work and more likely to mislead than to inform.* Thomas Babington Macaulay, Secretary of State for War, in the House of Commons, April 1840.

For the next few weeks neither the entries in Lin's diary nor his day-to-day activities gave any indication that he considered the incident at Kowloon to be as serious as did Captain Elliot. On 14 July he recorded 'a fine day; wrote couplets on fans'. On 31 July he noted how torrential were the rains that had caused waist-deep floods in the market-place, and he made a list of the scholars appointed as examiners for the forthcoming Provincial Examinations. He held an examination himself of the students attending the Canton academies, setting them subjects for essays and themes for poems; he supervised the destruction of opium pipes and of opium that had been seized north of Canton. But little other than his request for a translation of Emeric de Vattel's *Law of Nations* indicated that he was considering the problem and the opportunity presented by the murder of Lin Wei-hsi.[1]

Emeric de Vattel was quite categoric that *'les étrangers qui tombent en faute doivent être punis suivant les lois du pays'*. Yet Commissioner Lin's demand that the foreigners should hand over the murderer to the Chinese for execution seemed wholly unreasonable to Captain Elliot since he could not discover who the murderer was. Several sailors had been involved, many blows had been struck; a trial of six of the troublemakers had resulted in the jury acquitting one and in the sentencing of the other five to imprisonment and fines.

'If the principle that a life is not to be paid for with a life,' Lin protested on 17 August in reply to a refusal by Elliot to hand over a victim, 'what is it going to lead to? If an Englishman kills an Englishman or if some other national, say a Chinese, does so, am I to believe that Elliot would not demand a life to pay for a life? If Elliot really maintains that, after going twice to the scene of the murder and spending day after day investigating the crime, he still does not know who committed it, then all I can say is, a wooden dummy would have done better, and it is absurd to go on calling himself an official.'[2]

Five days later Elliot was upbraided again, this time not only for protecting Lin Wei-hsi's murderer but also for allowing the opium trade to revive. If the culprit were not surrendered to Chinese justice and if all the fresh opium were not given up for destruction, the whole might of the Empire would be arrayed against him.

Already Lin had taken steps to punish the English by ordering all their supplies at Macao to be cut off; now he decided to make a long-proposed visit to Macao and to take with him the Governor-General and several hundred troops.

Captain Elliot felt that he had no alternative but to advise the British merchants and their families in his care to leave Macao and to seek refuge aboard the ships of the merchant fleet at Hong Kong. There were no ships of the Royal Navy at that time in Chinese waters; the Portuguese, unwilling to offend the Chinese, were not prepared to offer their protection to the British; so that if Commissioner Lin marched across the barrier with troops and occupied Macao, the British would be at his mercy.

Certainly many of the European residents were thoroughly alarmed, too frightened to go out into the streets at night. There was a terrifying affray in the bay on the night of 25 August when the British schooner, the *Black Joke*, was plundered by pirates disguised as soldiers. The captain of the schooner, Mark Moss, was savagely attacked by the pirates, his left ear was cut off and stuffed into his mouth; and all his Lascar crew with one exception were killed and thrown overboard.

The artist, George Chinnery, confessed that he was in a 'state of anxiety beyond expression', that he dared not move out of his house until the time came to leave. 'To be away is everything to me,' he told James Matheson. 'I should like to paint a few good pictures (at least try at it) before I'm put to the sword. Rely on it, something serious if not dreadful is coming.'[3]

Chinnery and his compatriots, on board a little fleet of small boats, schooners and lorchas, sailed from Macao on 26 August; and Lin reported to the Emperor that although they had, no doubt, a certain stock of dried provisions they would 'very soon find themselves without the heavy, greasy meat dishes' for which they had such a passion and need. Moreover, the mere fact that they would be prevented from going ashore and getting fresh water was 'enough by itself to give power of life and death over them'.[4]

With these thoughts in mind, Lin entered Macao soon after dawn on 3 September, being met at the barrier by the Portuguese Governor and a guard of honour comprising a hundred Portuguese soldiers who, 'dressed up in their foreign uniforms' and 'playing Barbarian music' marched in front of the Commissioner's sedan. Lin stopped at the temple of the God of War to burn incense; he gave presents of silks, fans, tea and sugar-candy to the Portuguese officials, and of beer, mutton, noodles, wine and pieces of silver to their soldiers; he burned incense before the image of the Queen of Heaven at the Niang-ma Tower; and then was carried down the whole length of the Praya Grande.

'The Barbarians are fond of architecture. They build their houses with one room on top of another, sometimes as many as three storeys,' he noticed. 'The carved doors and green windows look like gold and jade. To-day the men and women alike were all in the streets or leaning out of the windows to see me pass. Unfortunately foreign clothes are no match for foreign houses.'

This was Lin's first sight of Europeans in the mass, and he found them grotesque, the men tightly encased from head to toe in short serge jackets and long, close-fitting trousers. 'They look like actors,' he thought, 'playing the parts of foxes, hares and other such animals on the stage. . . . Their hair is very curly, but they keep it short, not leaving more than an inch or two of curl. They have heavy beards, much of which they shave, leaving one curly tuft, which at first sight creates a surprising effect. Indeed, they really do look like devils; and when the people of these parts call them "devils" it is no mere empty term of abuse. They also have devil-slaves, called black devils, who come from the country of the Moors and are used by the foreigners to wait upon them. They are blacker than lacquer, and were this colour from the time of their birth. The foreign women part their hair in the middle, and sometimes even have two partings. . . . Their dresses are cut low, exposing their chests, and they wear a double layer of skirt. Marriages are arranged by the young people themselves. . . .'[5]

It was clear that Lin was in a contented and self-confident mood in Macao. His promotion to the governor-generalship of Kiangsu, Anhwei and Kiangsi in the Lower Yangtze valley, one of the most desirable of all posts to which a mandarin could aspire, had come through; and only the day before he had received instructions to proceed to Nanking as soon as his present mission was accomplished. He had issued a proclamation calling upon the people of Kowloon and Hong Kong to intercept and cut off all supplies from the English, and to resist any attempt by them to get ashore for water or food.

He could not but hope that the foreigners, unable to subsist at Hong Kong, would soon either return to Canton, submitting to all the proper regulations of the Canton authorities and carrying on a legitimate trade to the benefit of the Emperor's finances, or they would sail for home, thus removing an evil influence from the Middle Kingdom. But neither of these hopes was to be realized. Instead, two days after Lin's visit to Macao, on 4 September 1839, the first shots in what was to become known as the Opium War were fired at Kowloon.

*   *   *

A 28-gun frigate of the Royal Navy, H.M.S. *Volage*, commanded by Captain Smith, had arrived at Hong Kong from India in response to a request for protection despatched to the Governor-General by Captain Elliot. Smith and Elliot, accompanied by Dr Gützlaff as interpreter, had sailed over to Kowloon from Hong Kong to ask for supplies for the families aboard the merchant fleet. They had come up against a line of men-of-war junks riding at anchor beneath a fully manned battery. Gützlaff's eloquent requests, mingled with impassioned pleas on behalf of the hungry and thirsty women and children lying helpless in the boats behind him, and with warnings about the might of British arms, resulted at first in his being directed down the line of junks from one commander to the next and then in his turn being threatened with a taste of the cannon balls from the batteries ashore. A subsequent attempt to obtain supplies further up the coast was equally unsuccessful when the police prevented the villagers from making any sales.

By now, as Elliot later admitted to Palmerston, his 'feelings of irritation' betrayed him into a measure which 'under less trying circumstances' it would be difficult indeed to vindicate. He gave Captain Smith, who was only too pleased to obey him, orders to open fire on the junks. The engagement was soon over. The Chinese craft, though they returned the fire with spirit and had far more guns than the enemy with which to do so, were soon all severely damaged; while so incompetent were their gunners that they inflicted scarcely any damage at all. 'The Junks' fire, Thank God! was not enough depressed,' a young English sailor told his brother. 'We hove the vessel in stays on their starboard Beam . . . and gave them three such Broadsides that it made every Rope in the vessel grin again.—We loaded with Grape the fourth time, and gave them Gun for Gun.—The shrieking on board was dreadful . . . this is the first day I ever shed human blood, and I hope it will be the last.'[6]

Out-gunned and out-manoeuvred, the Chinese were saved only by the setting sun and by Elliot who, having now overcome his 'feelings of irritation', refused Smith permission to finish them off in the morning.

While the British went ashore to buy the supplies previously denied them, Commissioner Lin—following the traditional usage of Chinese officials in such circumstances and accepting the extravagant claims of the local commander—reported to Peking that 'a victory over superior forces' had been obtained. The Emperor, who had warned his servant 'against timidity', noted in the margin of the report in his special vermilion ink, 'You and your colleagues will never get into trouble with me for taking too high-handed a line. My only fear is lest you should show weakness and hesitation.'[7] He waited for further good reports from Canton. They were not long in coming; they told of an engagement at the mouth of the Pearl River in which the foreigners were once again taught a severe lesson.

The trouble had started here over Captain Elliot's order forbidding British ships to sail up to Canton, and Commissioner Lin's contradictory insistence that they were free to do so provided they undertook, by a signed bond, that they were not trading in opium and agreed to submit themselves to Chinese justice if discovered doing so. Lin considered these bonds to be of supreme importance, for by signing them the foreigners would recognize the Chinese rights of jurisdiction over them and abandon their own claims to extraterritoriality which were at the root of so many disputes. As Lin told the Emperor, 'the Barbarians take their promises very seriously; they never break an agreement or even fail to keep an appointment. A bond, as they look at it, is a very serious matter and is rarely given. It is not as in China where bonds are so liberally used that their effect has become doubtful. The more reluctant they are to give the bonds, the more sure we are of the dependability of their bonds, and the more we should strive to acquire them.'[8]

Lin accounted it a triumph, therefore, when the master of a British merchantman, the *Thomas Coutts,* carrying a cargo of cotton, rattan and pepper from Bombay, agreed to sign the bond and, in defiance of Captain Elliot's prohibition, sailed through the Bogue to Canton.

'It would be difficult to point to a more reckless transaction,' Elliot angrily complained to Palmerston, 'or to one more injurious in its results.'[9] But to Lin, of course, the master of the *Thomas Coutts* was a 'model foreigner'. 'With what frankness and correctness' he had behaved! If *he* had no hesitation in signing the bond, this must mean that those who would not sign it had sinister reasons for their refusal. Lin wrote to Elliot threatening to arrest him if he persisted in his obstinacy: all the British ships must either enter the Pearl River on the same conditions as the *Thomas Coutts* or depart from Chinese waters within three days. Also, Elliot must either surrender the murderer of Lin Wei-hsi or submit to all the sailors involved, as well as himself, being tried by a Chinese court. The punishment for disobeying these commands would be the annihilation of the English fleet.

On receipt of this ultimatum, Elliot wrote immediately to Captain Smith of the *Volage* requiring him, 'in this grave conjuncture menacing the liberty, lives and properties of the Queen's subjects', to escort the merchant ships to a more secure anchorage at T'ung-ku Bay, near the island of Chuenpi and to take the *Volage* and the *Hyacinth*, a smaller frigate that had recently come into Chinese waters, to the Bogue. Here he was to make 'a moderate but firm address' in his own name to Commissioner Lin and to Admiral Kuan, the officer in command of the large force of men-of-war junks and fireboats now assembled in the mouth of the river.

Glad of the opportunity of taking a firm line, Captain Smith left Kowloon at once, beating up the estuary in face of a strong wind. He arrived at Chuenpi on 2 November when a letter, addressed to Commissioner Lin, was despatched to Admiral Kuan's flagship requiring that the proclamation threatening to annihilate the English if the bonds were not signed should be withdrawn. The letter was returned unopened. A second letter was then sent, demanding the withdrawal into the river of the Chinese fleet, and adding that it would be 'well so to do'. To this Admiral Kuan replied, 'At this moment all that I, the Admiral, want is the murderous Barbarian who killed Lin Wei-hsi. As soon as the time is named when he will be given up, my ships will return into the Bogue. Otherwise, by no means whatsoever shall I accede. This is my answer.'[10]

Reluctant to fire the opening shot, Captain Elliot, who had joined Smith aboard the *Volage*, pondered the possibility of despatching yet another letter to the Admiral; but Smith, eager for further action after the exciting taste of it at Kowloon, advised strongly against it:

the Chinese were clearly bent on drastic action; they might attempt to board an English ship to seize by force a sailor whom they could execute for the murder of Lin Wei-hsi; they might even try to sink or burn the English fleet. If they were not driven back into the Bogue, they would endanger the lives of all the British families aboard the merchantmen. To sail away as though they were frightened of the Chinese would be an insult to the traditions of the Royal Navy. This was not the time to regret that the views of the Government were not known; London was thousands of miles away; it was up to the men on the spot to act on their own responsibility.[11]

Elliot gave way; the signal to engage was hoisted; and the *Volage*, followed by the *Hyacinth*, bore suddenly northwards across the front of the anchored Chinese fleet, their guns blazing. Within three quarters of an hour, four men-of-war junks had been sunk and the rest so badly damaged that there could have been no possibility of their withdrawing into the river had not Elliot reminded Smith that this had been the whole purpose of the action. So, with one sailor wounded aboard the British ships, and with only some slight damage to their rigging, the fight was broken off. The *Hyacinth* was ordered not to sink the waterlogged flagship on whose deck the valiant Admiral Kuan had been seen through the smoke, sword in hand before the mast, engaging Her Majesty's ships in handsome style, 'manifesting a resolution of behaviour', as Elliot put it, 'honourably enhanced by the hopelessness of his efforts'.

Lin reported the Admiral's heroic behaviour to the Emperor and his successful efforts in forcing the English warships to retire. Captain Elliot, for his part, although he had no cause to misrepresent the course of the engagement, was apprehensive as to his own Government's reaction to his having started it. He explained Captain Smith's arguments in some detail, adding almost apologetically, 'I could only offer Captain Smith the expression of my concurrence in his own sentiments'.[12]

*   *   *

An apology was scarcely necessary. It was not, of course, that public opinion in England approved of the opium traffic. There was a general agreement that Gladstone may well have been right to term it a 'most infamous and atrocious trade'. As the *Edinburgh Review* more temperately expressed it, 'The importation of Indian opium into China has increased in an extraordinary manner. . . . We cannot make this statement without some feelings of regret, since a contraband trade in this drug, carried on with great obstinacy, is naturally calculated to increase the dislike of the Chinese Government towards the strangers engaged in it.'

But then, the English comforted themselves with the thought that it was perhaps unreasonable to worry too much about the spread of opium addiction in China when there was the problem of alcoholism at home. Even the *Quarterly Review* strongly doubted that 'the evils of opium were worse than those of gin and whisky'.

This was certainly the view of those involved in the trade in China. The American, William Hunter, who admitted that all the foreign merchants were 'equally implicated'—the American firm of Olyphant and Co. being the one notable exception—protested that after a personal experience of forty years he had 'rarely, if ever' seen 'anyone physically or mentally' injured by smoking. 'As compared with the use of spirituous liquors in the United States and England, and the evil consequences of it, that of opium was infinitesimal.'[13]

Hunter's views on opium were widely shared. Opium was far less harmful than alcohol, protested the Canton merchants, soothing rather than inflaming in its effects, infinitely less pernicious, one English writer insisted, than the 'vile liquor made of rice'; the evils of the trade were grossly exaggerated by those who knew nothing of it.[14]

In England strenuous efforts were made to satisfy the public that the Canton merchants were engaged in a perfectly harmless and honest traffic. After all, it was pointed out, the Chinese were smoking opium long before Europeans came to Canton, and they would not now give it up just because the foreign merchants declined to supply it. Was it not openly smoked at the Chinese Court? And did not the places where it was smoked elsewhere in China have the 'merit of retirement from the public eye' as compared with the garish gin-palaces of London? In any case, it was not as if it were a poison; it was a balm which Heaven in its mercy had bestowed upon the human race. 'What blame can attach to a physician should his patient take two or three times more than the quantity of laudanum he has prescribed?' asked a pamphleteer in an open letter to Lord Palmerston. 'And if the same reasoning be applied to the smoker of the drug, who prefers it to wine or spirituous liquor, why should the seller be blamed if, instead of three pipes a day, he smokes six or twelve?'[15]

This complacently disingenuous argument did not, of course, find universal support. It was certainly true that, used occasionally and moderately, opium was not a dangerous drug; that many moderate smokers found it comfortingly relaxing; some, when they first began to smoke it, found it mildly and pleasantly aphrodisiac. It was true, too, that some of those who used it regularly showed no ill effects. Dr Downing knew a woman who habitually ate twenty grains a day, remained in excellent health and was the mother of numerous children. But, as Downing warned, she was but an exception to the 'general rule of its highly pernicious effects' when its devotees, many of whom spent half their income on it, found that they could not live without smoking it heavily, and increasingly so. An impaired digestion was followed by lassitude, loss of appetite and the wasting of the addict's strength. The complexion became more and more sallow; gradually the gums separated, and the teeth blackened and decayed. Finally the mind deteriorated, memory and judgement failed; and, in premature old age, the addict was in an almost constant state of trembling with distorted neck and contracted fingers. Withdrawal symptoms were both acutely painful and emotionally exhausting. Most consumers, Downing added, were men between the ages of twenty and fifty-five and of all ranks of society, officials, merchants, labourers and, above all, soldiers. One could not 'wonder, therefore, that the Emperor should feel alarmed, when the very basis of his despotic government is thus assailed'.[16]

But then, the propagandists riposted, it was well known that the corruption of the Chinese Government was itself largely to blame. All classes of people 'from the pampered official to the abject menial continually' flocked to the opium dens, which were 'as plentiful in certain towns in China as gin shops in England. . . . Opium pipes and other apparatus' for smoking were 'publicly exhibited for sale in Canton, both in shops and among the wares of street hawkers.' How could this be unless the officials were not all up to their necks in the traffic themselves, or unless the mandarins were not hand in glove with the smugglers? It had to be admitted that the Chinese authorities were at last taking action against the foreign traders, but (as it was widely reported in articles being published in England at this time) the importation was being stopped only for selfish reasons, to protect the home growth. Commissioner Lin Tse-hsü was one of those mandarins who shared between them 'thousands of acres laid down in poppy-plantations'.[17]

Those better-informed Englishmen who were unwilling to accept this kind of propaganda were far more susceptible to the emotive stories appearing in the Press about the imprisonment of their fellow countrymen in Canton, the threats made against them and their families, the gross insults that had been offered to the flag. If they had known of Commissioner Lin's letters to Queen Victoria they would have felt further outraged. The first of these letters written shortly after his arrival in Canton was apparently never sent, and a later one written after the destruction of the opium stocks seems never to have arrived; but the sentiments they express and the assumptions they make represented the kind of presumptuousness that the English felt to be intolerable.

In the second letter, Queen Victoria, as a tributary sovereign of the Emperor, was instructed to have 'the plant plucked up by the very root', and to visit with condign punishment any criminal who dared to plant another poppy. 'On receipt of this letter,' she was commanded, 'let your reply be speedy, advising us of the measures you propose to adopt. Do not by false embellishments evade or procrastinate. Earnestly reflect hereon. Earnestly obey . . .'[18]

The Foreign Secretary, Lord Palmerston, was peculiarly, not to say notoriously, susceptible to anger at the arrogance that prompted the composition of documents like this. He was also convinced that the Parliamentary Committee of 1832 had been right to recommend that it was 'inadvisable to abandon so important a revenue' as the income derived from the export of opium, and that Parliament had been justified in adopting the Committee's recommendations. He listened, then, with special sympathy to the views expressed to him by the opium merchant William Jardine who, not long after his return to England in 1839, was elected Member of Parliament for Ashburton, and by Jardine's partner, James Matheson, whose publication, *The Present Position and Prospects of the British Trade with China* had been widely read on its appearance in 1836. In this work Matheson had written of the Chinese as a 'truculent, vainglorious people' who ought to be given a very sharp lesson, and he had quoted approvingly the verdict of an acknowledged expert on China that 'we have treated them with too much forebearance; they have all the braggart, as well as all the recreant qualities of cowardice in their nature. If we were to make a decided demonstration of hostility, we should speedily obtain all that we require at their hands. They are uniformly overbearing and insulting to all those who happen to be in their power, but cringing and abject to those who exhibit a determination to resist them.'[19]

Fully in agreement with this view, Lord Palmerston was satisfied, before news reached him of Captain Smith's action against Admiral Kuan's fleet at Chuenpi, that the time was fast approaching when force would have to be used.

To persuade Parliament and the country to endorse such a policy, however, would need considerable political skill. There would be no difficulty in winning support on the grounds that the nation's honour was at stake; but there might well be strong opposition to the notion that the Chinese must be forced to pay compensation for the opium that had been destroyed—and the Chinese *must* be forced to pay, for it would be folly to suppose that the Government could survive unscathed the presentation of a bill for payment by the taxpayer of the huge sum now being demanded by the opium dealers in accordance with Captain Elliot's guarantee to them when they handed their stocks over to Commissioner Lin. It would be unwise, Palmerston therefore decided, to make any statements about a military expedition to China until it had been put into effect.

In the first week of February he wrote to the Governor-General of India with confidential orders for the prompt collection of four thousand troops and sixteen warships which were to be in the Canton estuary, under command of Admiral the Hon. Sir George Elliot, Charles Elliot's cousin, by the end of June. Long before that, of course, the Opposition would discover what was afoot; but Palmerston hoped to be able to avoid having to give any compromising reply.

As early as 12 March a member of the Opposition asked, 'Is there any truth in the report, very generally believed, that war has been declared against China?', to which Lord John Russell, Secretary for the Colonies, made an appropriately inconsequential reply about there being 'no official intelligence amounting to what the Hon. Member has stated, namely a declaration of war'.

Further questions from Sir Robert Peel, Leader of the Opposition, were parried by Palmerston who spoke in the vaguest terms of what might conjecturally be done, and of the 'national interest' forbidding further disclosures at present. A week later the Opposition demanded to know more; the newspapers were full of unconfirmed reports; urgent preparations were now known to be under way in India.

Under pressure, Lord John Russell admitted that certain preparations were, indeed, being made; they were to obtain reparations for insults, compensation for loss of 'merchants' property', and security for future trade.

But Peel was not satisfied; he moved a vote of censure; and Palmerston was obliged to hold a debate earlier than he had wanted. He fixed it for 7 April.

The vote was moved by Sir James Graham, Member of Parliament for Pembroke, formerly a prominent advocate of the Reform Bill and soon to be Home Secretary when Peel came to power in 1841. It had been decided by the Opposition that the less said about the opium traffic the better; their party had accepted the recommendations of the 1832 Parliamentary Committee and had not subsequently shown itself unduly concerned with reform. Any protestations now of outraged morality would surely strike a disingenuous note. So Sir James Graham's inordinately long and, in places, profoundly boring speech, which occupies eighteen pages of Hansard, concentrated upon the Government's incompetence in having immediately provoked the Chinese by abandoning the normal methods of communication for 'Palmerston's Pin-point', in having allowed the situation to deteriorate to its present pass, and in having left Captain Elliot without any clear instructions on how to proceed in the difficult circumstances in which the Administration's bungling lack of coherent policy had left him. The Opposition did not doubt—and later in the debate Peel himself emphasized that they did not doubt—that war was now necessary owing to the violent behaviour of the Chinese; but it was clear that its prevaricating conduct of the crisis so far rendered the present Government unworthy of the country's confidence in its ability to wage it.

Two young members of the Opposition refused to accept that war was necessary. To Sidney Herbert, then M.P. for one of the divisions of Wiltshire, it was a 'war without just cause', a war fought to 'maintain a trade resting upon unsound principles, and to justify proceedings which are a disgrace to the British flag'. To Gladstone, who, six years before at the age of twenty-four had been appointed to a junior lordship of the Treasury by Peel, it was an 'iniquitous war' that would leave an ineradicable mark on the country's conscience. 'A war more unjust in its origins,' he said passionately, refusing to limit himself to the prescribed limit of Peel's attack, 'a war more calculated in its progress to cover this country with permanent disgrace, I do not know, and I have not read of.' It was nonsense, Gladstone contended, to speak of the impossibility of controlling the opium traffic, to talk, as the right honourable Member for Edinburgh had talked, of the failure of the six thousand men of the British customs service to prevent the smuggling of brandy and tobacco into England as though that excused the failure of the Government to suppress the smuggling of opium. 'Does he know,' Gladstone asked, 'that the opium smuggled into China comes exclusively from British ports, that it is from Bengal and through Bombay? If that is a fact—and I defy the right honourable gentleman to gainsay it—then we require no preventive service to put down this illegal traffic. We have only to stop the sailings of the smuggling vessels; it is a matter of certainty that if we stopped the exportation of opium from Bengal, and broke up the depot at Lintin, and checked the cultivation of it in Malwa, and put a moral stigma upon it, that we should greatly cripple, if not extinguish, the trade in it.'

To this indignant outburst Palmerston calmly and sardonically replied that he did not find any reference to the uprooting of Bengal opium in the Opposition's motion, and anyway, that if the growing of Bengal opium were to be forbidden the cultivation of the poppy would be transferred to Turkey, Persia, or to one of those Indian states over whose internal administration Britain had no jurisdiction. As for the criticisms of the rareness and brevity of his instructions to Captain Elliot, was it really necessary to keep the House talking for so long about this? 'I gave the Superintendent instructions,' Palmerston said drily, 'and have been blamed because they were not long enough. Gentlemen who make long speeches think, I suppose, that I should write long letters. They imagine that precise instructions contained in a few but significant words are not proportioned to the length that they had to travel; they imagine that when you write to China your letter should be as long as the voyage.' Moreover, what fuller instructions was it suggested that Captain Elliot should have been given? Was it proposed that he should have been ordered to expel every smuggler and drive away every clipper? 'I wonder what the House would have said to me, if I had come down to it with a large naval estimate for a number of cruisers to be employed in the preventive service from the river at Canton to the Yellow Sea for the purpose of preserving the morals of the Chinese people, who were disposed to buy what other people were disposed to sell them.'

Lord Palmerston went on to reassure the House that no international complications need be feared from a war, that bloodshed might in any case not be necessary. He held up a memorial which he said the American merchants in Canton had presented to Congress in January. The memorial referred to Lin as a robber and suggested that if a naval force from England, France and the United States appeared off Canton a satisfactory trade treaty could be signed without the loss of a single life. But the House was scarcely in need of such assurances; the outcome of the debate had already been decided. The motion of censure was defeated by an uncomfortably narrow margin, but the speech made by the young historian, Thomas Babington Macaulay, Secretary of State for War, on the first day of the debate had made it seem impossible that any stout-hearted, patriotic Englishman could vote in any other way.

'What does anybody here know of China?' he asked, admitting his own ignorance. 'Even those Europeans who have been in that Empire are almost as ignorant of it as the rest of us. Everything is covered by a veil, through which a glimpse of what is within may occasionally be caught, a glimpse just sufficient to set the imagination at work and more likely to mislead than to inform.' But what they did know was that the men who built the British Empire had had the sense and spirit to treat all orders that came from home as waste paper; for what was the purpose in obeying long instructions written six months before when the problems they had been designed to resolve had completely changed their nature? Lord Palmerston's instructions were certainly brief but they were entirely adequate. In any event, surely the House ought to be concerned with the present, not with the past; and the present situation demanded that 'this most rightful quarrel' should be prosecuted to a triumphal close, 'that the brave men, to whom is entrusted the task of demanding that reparation which the circumstances of the case require, may fulfil their duties with moderation, but with success, that the name, not only of English valour, but of English mercy, may be established'.

'The place of this country among nations,' cried Macaulay, rising spiritedly to his theme, 'is not so mean that we should trouble ourselves to resist every petty slight, but there is a limit to that forebearance. I was much touched, and I believe others were also, by one passage contained in the dispatch of Captain Elliot, in which he communicated his arrival at the factory at Canton. The moment at which he landed he was surrounded by his countrymen in an agony of despair at their situation, but the first step which he took was to order the flag of Great Britain to be taken from the boat and to be planted in the balcony. This was an act which revived the drooping hopes of those who looked upon him for protection. It was natural that they should look with confidence on the victorious flag which was hoisted over them, which reminded them that they belonged to a country unaccustomed to defeat, to submission or to shame—it reminded them that they belonged to a country which had made the farthest ends of the earth ring with the fame of her exploits in redressing the wrongs of her children; that made the Dey of Algiers humble himself to her insulted Consul; that revenged the horrors of the black hole on the fields of Plassey; that had not degenerated since her great Protector vowed that he would make the name of Englishmen as respected as ever had been the name of Roman citizens . . .'[20]

Two months after these words were spoken, in June 1840, fifteen men-of-war, five armed steamers of the East India Company and 4,000 British, Irish and Indian troops began to assemble off Macao to redress the wrongs of the country's children whose plight Macaulay had so movingly evoked.

10 | The Empire at War

Our military affairs are in the hands of civil officials, who are very likely admirable calligraphists but know nothing of war. Ch'i-shan, Governor-General of Chihli, August 1840.

Over six months had passed at Canton since the *Volage* and the *Hyacinth* had swept aside Admiral Kuan's fleet off Chuenpi. During this time both the legal trade and the opium traffic had been successfully resumed by the foreign merchants. Thanks to the Americans who had remained behind at Canton when the British withdrew to Macao and who were now acting as their agents, Captain Elliot was able to report 'the striking and gratifying fact that the lawful import trade' was being conducted more advantageously than at any time within the past five years. At the same time, although there were occasional fights between the smugglers and Chinese patrol boats, both Dent & Co. and Jardine and Matheson were once more making immense profits out of opium.

Lin Tse-hsü endeavoured to reassure the Emperor that the situation was well within his control. Although there had been only a few outbursts of sporadic firing since the fight at Chuenpi, Lin reported to Peking six fresh victories over the Barbarians, the Six Smashing Blows against the English warships which still appear in Chinese histories of the period. The Emperor, however, was beginning to lose faith in his servant. At the end of January, Lin was informed that his appointment as Special Commissioner was terminated, and that he was to take over from Teng T'ing-chen the governor-generalship of Kwangtung and Kwangsi. Teng was to be found other employment; Lin himself was not to be promoted to the governor-generalship at Kiangsi after all. In the middle of February he received his first sharp rebuke from the Emperor: 'If measures are not taken to root out this evil once and for all, you, Lin Tse-hsü, will be called to account.'

Lin responded to these criticisms by reports on the energetic action he was still taking, on the ever continuing campaign against the smugglers and smokers of opium, on the new batteries that were to be erected at Kowloon and Kuan-yung. He wrote of the military preparations being undertaken, of the punishments inflicted on the authors of the lampoons now being distributed in Canton where the people were complaining that the authorities, by chasing the British out of the factories, had put hundreds of people out of work and undermined the economy of the province. As to the rumours that the British were sending warships to Canton, he declined to give them any credit; the rumours, he assured the Emperor, had been circulated in an attempt to cause alarm; they need not be taken seriously.

He repeated this belief in a reply to a letter dated 26 April from the American consul in Canton who had urged the Chinese authorities to speed up the process by which American ships were searched, granted permission to enter the port and unload their cargoes; if this were not done, thousands of tons of shipping might be trapped in the Pearl River by a blockading British fleet. Lin replied that the delays were occasioned by the necessity to ensure that the American ships were not carrying British goods, that the exclusion of the British had enormously increased the American profits, and that, in any case, to talk of a blockade was ridiculous. How was it possible for the British to blockade a Chinese port?

Even when the British fleet of warships and troop transports did arrive, Lin continued to reassure the Court. There was nothing the warships could do. Admittedly they appeared to be heavily armed, but they probably contained little other than opium.

'It is certain that they will not venture to create disturbances,' he informed the Cantonese people in a public edict. Nevertheless, he thought it was well to issue instructions for the further improvement of the fortifications, and for the enlistment of boatmen and peasants into a militia. The militiamen were urged to act like heroes in defence of the country against the Foreign Devils and were promised rewards, regulated by a nicely balanced scale, for the destruction of their force, ranging from a prize of twenty thousand dollars for a big warship to twenty dollars for a black soldier.[1]

The militia, however, were given no opportunity to display their courage; for, a few days after their arrival off Macao, the British sailed north. Captain Elliot was aboard the fleet carrying a letter to the Emperor which demanded that the local officials at Canton should be punished for their unlawful treatment of himself and other British subjects, and that the opium, surrendered as a ransom for their lives, should either be returned to them or paid for.[2] An attempt was made to deliver this letter under a flag of truce north of the island of Amoy. But, as an unarmed cutter from the *Blonde* 'approached the shore it was observed', wrote Elliot Bingham, first lieutenant of the *Modeste*, 'that a considerable body of troops were drawn up with the apparent intention of preventing a landing; and no sooner had the boat's bow touched the beach than they advanced their weapons and rudely repulsed them, desiring them to be off and refusing to listen to them'.

The next morning a second attempt was made 'to persuade these fool-hardy men to receive Lord Palmerston's letter, but the troops were drawn up as they had been on the previous day, and a vast crowd of spectators assembled'. The interpreter 'displayed a chop, written in large characters, setting out the peaceable intention of the ships, and blaming the conduct of the mandarins which so enraged them that they dashed into the water and made an attempt to seize the boat; but a few strokes of the oars soon put her beyond their reach. [The interpreter] then called to them to know if they would receive the letter; in reply to which they all roared out *no*, accompanied with much abuse.'

As the boat's crew rowed back to their ship, the Chinese soldiers discharged 'two or three arrows and a matchlock at them'. At this, two of the *Blonde*'s thirty-two pound shots were volleyed ashore, sending 'the whole mass, officers, soldiers and spectators flying for their lives, leaving five or six of their number dead upon the beach'.[3]

So the fleet sailed away without having delivered the letter; and when, at the beginning of July, Captain Elliot arrived off Tinghai on Chusan Island, four hundred miles further north, the document was still in his care.

On arrival at Tinghai, Lord Jocelyn, Military Secretary to the China Mission, accompanied by Captain Fletcher of H.M.S. *Wellesley*, went aboard the Chinese admiral's junk which he recognized by 'its more numerous pennons and three tigers' heads painted on the stern'. His orders were to summon the town to surrender within six hours.

The Chinese admiral was ashore at the time, but in the course of half an hour he returned to his junk. As Lord Jocelyn later recorded, 'he was an old man, and bore in his face the marks of opium. . . . We opened the summons, and they read it in our presence, and indeed before the assembled troop: the deep groans and increasing pressure of the people warned us that we were among a hostile multitude . . . the summons addressed to the people stated that no injury was intended to them, but it was against their rulers we had come to make war for their unjust acts. Of this they seemed perfectly aware; but they hated the invading Barbarians more bitterly than their Tartar rulers; and their clenched hands and anxious faces proved to us how false was the idea that we were coming among a people who only waited for the standard of the foreigner to throw off a detested and tyrant yoke . . . they complained of the hardship of being made answerable for wrongs that we had received at Canton, and said, naturally enough, "Those are the people you should make war upon, and not upon us who never injured you; we see your strength, and know that opposition will be madness, but we must perform our duty even if we fall in so doing." '[4]

All night long, by the light of painted lanterns, the people on shore could be seen digging earthworks and placing guns and gingalls[5] in position; and when daylight came soldiers marched out to line the embankments and the wharfs, their brilliantly coloured banners flying in the sunlight. Mandarins riding small but strong-looking horses, or scurrying along on foot between one detachment and the next, were everywhere giving orders and delivering messages of encouragement.

The British men-of-war lay in line with their port broadsides facing the town, two hundred yards from the wharf. At eight o'clock the commander of the fleet, Commodore Sir James Gordon Bremer, gave orders for the signal to prepare for action to be hoisted; but, 'hoping to the last they would repent', he withheld his fire until half-past two in the afternoon when a shot was fired at a martello tower in a commanding position on shore. Immediately the fire was returned by the whole line of junks and by all the guns on shore. 'Then the British shipping opened their broadsides on the town,' Lord Jocelyn continued his account, 'and the crashing of timber, falling houses and groans of men resounded from the shore. The firing continued on our side for nine minutes, but even after it had ceased a few shots were still heard from the unscathed junks.

'When the smoke cleared away a mass of ruin presented itself to the eye, and on the place lately alive with men, none but a few wounded were to be seen, but crowds were visible in the distance flying in all directions. A few were distinguished carrying the wounded from the junks into the town, and our friend [the Chinese admiral] was seen borne from his vessel, having lost his leg. . . .'[6]

After this devastating bombardment, the British troops landed on a deserted beach at Chusan without difficulty, finding 'a few dead bodies, bows and arrows, broken spears and guns remaining the sole occupants of the field'. They were temporarily halted by the deep ditch round the town of Tinghai, the bridge over which had been demolished, and by the town's locked and barricaded gate; but they soon scaled the walls. The ramparts and parapets were strewn with matchlocks, pikes, rockets with arrow heads, and packets of quick-lime which it had been intended should be thrown into the eyes of the Barbarians if they ever reached the base of the walls. In the main street, in front of houses on which the plea, 'Spare our Lives', was placarded, a few trembling inhabitants performed the kotow before the officers of the victorious army. Other frightened people were crowded in the temple, burning incense before the gods; but otherwise the town seemed to be deserted.

'Scarcely a soul was to be seen,' wrote Lieutenant Bingham of the *Modeste*, 'thousands had left the city, but many families remained shut up in their houses.' Not until it had become quite clear that the fighting was ended, did they gradually begin to show themselves, and then 'the rabble speedily commenced a system of plunder; and goods from the deserted houses were carried out of the city night and day'. An appeal that orders should be given to prevent anything passing the gate was at first refused on the grounds that 'the inhabitants ought to come and look after their own affairs'. Only when it appeared likely that the town would soon have been cleared of all provisions were instructions given to stop the robbers at the gates, and prevent them from climbing over the walls. By then Tinghai was in chaos; the Chinese military commander had been carried away mortally wounded; the chief constable had killed himself; and it was not until the forthright Karl Gützlaff was appointed magistrate that order was gradually restored.

A less energetic and more sensitive man than Dr Gützlaff would have been overwhelmed by his task. His office was besieged by people clamouring 'for the recovery of their property, who on getting an order for it, helped themselves most liberally, taking very good care to make up for all previous losses; and rarely, if ever, did the true owner become possessed of what was justly his. Coffins, notwithstanding the order, were allowed to pass, until the notice of the sentries was attracted by the quantities of dead relations, when their curiosity prompted them to examine one of these pretended repositories of the dead, which proved to be full of rolls of silk, crape, and other valuables. . . .

'The coffin-artifice failing, other methods were resorted to by the ever prolific minds of the Chinese. Several met their death from the sentries, while trying to force their way by them. One aged rogue, overladen with plunder, sank in the canal; many received the penalty of their crimes from the people they were attempting to rob. One fellow in particular, was found tied to a post in the market-place, so tightly bound that the blood oozed out from his hands and arms, and his eyes were starting from their sockets. Another was brought to the magistrate's office, who had been thus treated by his captor—a literary graduate—and it was two hours before he recovered the use of his speech. The learned character seemed much astonished, and could not at all understand why he should be accused of cruelty, having, as he stated, merely executed an act of justice.'[7]

The occupying forces behaved with as little respect for private property as the Chinese rabble. Elliot Bingham did not wonder that 'under the temptation excited by hunger, irregularities were committed', or that 'an occasional peasant more venturous than his countrymen, when making for the town with poultry, was eased of it before he arrived at his journey's end'; but other officers spoke more harshly of the behaviour of the British and Indian troops who appropriated silks, fans, porcelain, the tiny fairy-like shoes of Chinese ladies as 'lawful *loot*'.[8]

'While we have been issuing proclamations, talking sweet words,' complained one such officer, 'our soldiers and sailors have been plundering them and forcibly carrying off their poultry and cattle. . . . We are now going to break open all the unoccupied shops and houses and take possession of them for governmental purposes. As they will no longer bring poultry and vegetables to market, we are going to forage their farms. . . . As they will sell us no fish we are going to take measures to prevent them fishing at all. . . .'[9]

The only means whereby a householder could ensure himself immunity from the depredations of the troops was to purchase for an agreed amount of livestock a 'security placard' that could be hung outside his door. But householders who had left the town, having secured such a placard, afterwards returned to find that their homes had been broken open to be used as winter quarters by the troops, and that their possessions had been carted off to the temple to be sold by auction.

When the soldiers were drunk on the pernicious Chinese spirit, *samsu*, their officers found it impossible to control them. 'This Shamshu could not be kept out of reach of the men,' Colonel Wyndham Baker wrote home to his family, 'and its effect on them was of the most dreadful nature and very different from that of the spirits we are used to in England. A man no sooner took a small quantity than he was in a most dreadful state and committing the most horrible atrocities which I am sorry to say are but too common. . . . We have been destroying every drop we can get hold of, and I think in one day I must have destroyed some 20 hogsheads. . . . The Chinese, except as regards the use of opium, are exceedingly temperate in their habits and we cannot account for the immense distilleries which have been discovered here.'[10]

As the weather grew colder in November, more and more doors, window frames and wooden partitions began to disappear from the houses, and the soldiers, accustomed as they had been to an Indian climate, kept up constant roasting fires. 'Many streets entirely disappeared,' a naval officer recorded. 'Reports were made, and orders issued to put a stop to these irregularities, and burning the materials of the houses or their furniture was prohibited; little attention was paid to the order.'[11]

* * *

In reporting to the Emperor upon the 'dastardly crime' of the British in capturing Tinghai and upon the behaviour of the Barbarian troops there, Lin Tse-hsü assured him that he was just about to hold a final inspection of his own troops who should shortly be ready 'to engage in a final battle of annihilation'. But by the time this letter was received the Emperor's disillusionment with Lin was complete.

The despatches that arrived at Peking from Canton had for months been both contradictory and complacent. Promises of final battles of annihilation had been followed by admissions that it was not worth while 'embarking on a combat at sea'; opium smugglers had been reported at one moment to be effectively punished, at the next to be as active as ever; the severe penalties attached to opium offences had been represented as being responsible for a reduced demand, yet the British were reported to be lowering their prices so demand was increasing; although 'a good deal of smoking' still went on, the villainy of the smokers was being gradually broken; it was hoped that the evil would eventually be extirpated.

'You speak of having stopped foreign trade,' the Emperor at last burst out in exasperation, 'yet a moment later admit that it is still going on. You say you have dealt with offenders against the opium laws, yet admit that they are still at large. All this is merely an attempt to put me off with meaningless words. So far from doing any good, you have merely produced a number of fresh complications.

The very thought of it infuriates me. I am anxious to see what you can possibly have to say for yourself!'[12]

The Emperor's exasperation had been greatly increased by his having received, almost at the same time as one of Lin's more negative reports, the letter which had been addressed to the 'Chinese Emperor's minister' by Lord Palmerston, and which Captain Elliot had at last managed to deliver by sailing up to the very mouth of the Peiho River and entrusting it to the care of the Governor-General of Chihli, Ch'i-shan. The letter made it clear that in the view of the British, Commissioner Lin and his friend, Teng T'ing-chen, were largely responsible for the outbreak of hostilities through their having consistently misled the Emperor as to the situation in Canton. The Emperor later denied that Lord Palmerston's accusations had any influence over his decision to dismiss both Teng and Lin from their appointments, but, almost immediately after receiving the letter, he did dismiss them both.

'You have dissembled to us, disguising in your dispatches the true nature of affairs,' the Emperor castigated Lin. 'You are no better than a wooden image. And as we contemplate your grievous failings, we fall prey to anger and melancholy. Your official seals shall be immediately taken from you and with the speed of flames you shall hasten to Peking, where we will see how you may answer our questions. Respect this. The words of the Emperor.'[13]

Lin had made all arrangements to obey this summons to Peking when, within a few hours of his intended departure, he was told to remain at Canton to await the arrival of Ch'i-shan, the Governor-General of Chihli, who would soon be there to conduct an enquiry into his behaviour.

Ch'i-shan was about two years older than Lin and had enjoyed an even more distinguished career. As well as being Governor-General of Chihli, he was a Manchu official of the central government, a man of great power and wealth. He had long been opposed to Lin's methods of dealing with the opium problem, having himself advocated a policy based on the more effective prevention of imports rather than on the severe punishment of offenders. Now that the Barbarians had arrived in his province, the metropolitan province, for the first time since the Amherst mission of 1816 and had come within his own jurisdiction, he had the opportunity of representing to the Emperor his belief that all the troubles at Canton had stemmed from the Barbarians' not unreasonable sense of grievance at Lin Tse-hsü's high-handed actions.

The British, he contended, must be treated with circumspection; they were a reasonable, well-mannered and respectful people if allowed to indulge their curious yet harmless passion for trading; but they could prove troublesome. An envoy he had sent to inspect their fleet at the mouth of the Peiho reported that their steamships could 'fly across the water, without wind or tide, with the current or against it'; their cannon were 'mounted on stone platforms' which could 'be turned in any direction'; their armed forces were in the hands of men trained in their craft whereas the military affairs of the Empire were in the hands of civil officials, who were 'very likely admirable calligraphists but [knew] nothing of war'.[14] It was obviously essential that the Barbarians must be persuaded, with blandishments and promises, to return to Canton.

Ch'i-shan was an ingratiating and persuasive man. The British found him polite and agreeable, a pleasant change from the uncompromising Lin; and by the middle of September he had induced Captain Elliot to go back to Canton where, by what he represented to the British as a happy chance, he himself had been posted, and where they could discuss their differences in a more pleasant and relaxed atmosphere. He was sure, he told them, that 'any false accusations' made against them could soon be 'cleared up'. Commissioner Lin and his colleagues at Canton had failed to interpret 'the temperate and just intentions of the Emperor'; the whole matter would be 'investigated in detail and the culprits severely punished'.[15]

Captain Elliot congratulated himself on having gained a diplomatic advantage. He wrote to James Matheson, 'We have not brought you back a great waving olive branch, but I think we have a twig of the blessed plant in our portfolio. Though gusts may pass over it and thin the leaves, still we indulge the hope that it will take root and grow into a goodly tree.'[16]

Certainly it seemed that the new Commissioner was bent on peace. Soon after his arrival the defence works at Canton were dismantled, the local militia disbanded, and the British were promised a resumption of trade and given hope to expect the payment of an indemnity. After making all these concessions, Ch'i-shan was, therefore, saddened to be met with a reiterated demand not only for the cession of the 'large and properly situated' offshore island mentioned in Lord Palmerston's letter and now specified as Hong Kong, but for the use of two ports other than Canton—Amoy and Foochow in the province of Fukien to the north. When Ch'i-shan prevaricated, knowing that the Emperor would never willingly submit to these demands, the British decided to use a little more force.

Orders were accordingly given to the Navy to capture the forts on either side of the entrance to the Bogue and thereby to open up the Pearl River and the way to Canton to British shipping. This operation was conducted on 7 January 1841. It lasted little more than two hours; a few British sailors were wounded, none mortally; an estimated five hundred Chinese were killed. They had fought bravely, as their opponents agreed, but their weapons were no match for the great guns of the Royal Navy and the far superior firearms and training of the British soldiers.[17] A few days after this operation, at the Lotus Flower Wall, on the banks of the Pearl River downstream from Canton, the outline of what was to become known as the Convention of Chuenpi was agreed between Ch'i-shan and the British negotiators.

Ch'i-shan surrendered to the British demands for an indemnity of six million dollars for the opium seized by Commissioner Lin, for the cession of Hong Kong, and for the re-establishment of the British merchants at Canton. In return the British agreed to withdraw from Tinghai on Chusan Island which they had not, in any case, had any wish to retain, making, as Sir John Francis Davis said, 'a virtue of necessity' in giving up an island where the climate did not suit them and where their forces were being wasted away by disease.[18]

Before the news of this fresh humiliation reached him, the Emperor had been infuriated by reports of the Barbarians' perfidious attack on the Pearl River forts. It was clear that the said Barbarians were 'outrageous and not amenable to reason'. 'We must elucidate their mind on the one hand,' he wrote, 'and prepare for contest on the other. After prolonged negotiation has made them weary and exhausted, we can suddenly attack them, and thereby subdue them.'[19]

But there could be no more negotiations now; the time for action had come; the British must be utterly destroyed. Orders went out for troops from all the provinces of the Empire to gather at Canton, and for the Emperor's cousin, I-shan, who was to assume the title of Rebel-quelling General, to take command of them with Lung-wen and Yang Fang as his two senior officers.

As for Ch'i-shan, when the news of his surrender arrived at Court, he was violently upbraided for a misdemeanour so great that it showed he had 'no conscience'. He was sentenced to undergo the confiscation of all his possessions and to be carried to Peking in chains. At Peking he was tried and sentenced to death; but, having helped himself to his servant's accumulated fortune of £10 million and his 425,000 acres of land, the Emperor allowed him to live on in exile and to survive, like Lin Tse-hsü—now exiled also to the wastes of Turkestan—to return one day to the Imperial service.[20]

Captain Elliot, noting with some satisfaction his opponents' disgrace, was quite content with the arrangements he had made; so were most of the foreign merchants. Trade could now be conducted at Hong Kong without official interference; the indemnity for the opium could be added to the profits made since the confiscation had taken place; and there was nothing in the Convention of Chuenpi to prevent the opium trade continuing.

The Court and Government in England, however, were far from satisfied with Elliot, who had settled for so very much less than he had it in his power to obtain. 'The Chinese business vexes us much, and Palmerston is deeply mortified at it,' the Queen told her uncle, the King of the Belgians. '*All* we wanted might have been got, if it had not been for the unaccountably strange conduct of Charles Elliot . . . who completely disobeyed his instructions and *tried* to get the *lowest* terms he could.'[21]

Palmerston's mortification was indeed acute. 'It seems to me,' he wrote, 'that Captain Elliot is disposed to act upon an erroneous principle in his dealings with the Chinese and to use too much refinement in submitting to their pretensions. . . . After all our naval power is so strong that we can tell the Emperor what *we* mean to hold rather than that *he* should say what he would cede.'[22]

Palmerston strongly reprimanded Elliot for having disobeyed and neglected his instructions, for having 'deliberately abstained' from using the force placed at his disposal, and for having accepted, 'without sufficient necessity', terms which fell far short of those he had been instructed to obtain.

'You were instructed to demand full compensation for the opium which you took upon you two years ago to deliver up,' Palmerston continued. 'To ask Parliament to pay the money was out of the question. You have accepted a sum much smaller than the amount due to the opium holders. You were told to demand payment of the expenses of the expedition, and payment of Hong debts. You do not appear to have done one or the other. You were told to retain [Ting-hai] until the whole of the pecuniary compensation should be paid, but you have agreed to evacuate the island immediately. You have obtained the cession of Hong Kong, a barren Island with hardly a House upon it. . . . Throughout the whole course of your proceedings, you seem to have considered that my Instructions were waste Paper, which you might treat with entire disregard, and that you were at full liberty to deal with the interests of your Country according to your own Fancy! . . . You will no doubt, by the time you have read this far, have anticipated that I could not conclude this letter without saying that under these circumstances it is impossible that you should continue to hold your appointment in China.'[23]

So Elliot was dismissed, as Lin and Ch'i-shan had been dismissed; the British Government repudiated the Convention of Chuenpi, as the Emperor—instructing his new servant, I-shan, to 'extirpate the Barbarians'—also repudiated it; and both sides prepared for a renewal of the fighting.

Hundreds more troops were enlisted at Canton, the volunteers—as a foreign observer had noticed several weeks before—being required to demonstrate their acceptability by lifting up a heavy spar, weighted with pieces of granite, over their heads until their arms were straight. Those who succeeded in raising the weight were marched up to a table for registry, the others being at once rejected. Thousands of wooden crosses were placed on the walls of Canton, for it was supposed the foreign troops would not fire at them for fear of offending their god; and chamber pots, used by women, were collected for hanging from roofs and cornices, the exhibition of female uncleanness being a traditional way of counteracting the powers of witchcraft.[24] Any citizen heard uttering traitorous or despondent sentiments was severely disciplined; one man found guilty of such indiscretions was punished shortly before the British attack—of whose expected repulse he was unpatriotically sceptical—by being led through the streets by a guard of soldiers, his bare back beaten from time to time with a rattan, and a sharply pointed arrow bearing a miniature flag stuck through each ear.[25]

The first blow against the Chinese came at the beginning of March. Captain Elliot, as yet unaware of his dismissal, decided no possible purpose could be served by remaining inactive while the Chinese gathered their strength to attack. So on 2 March orders were given for the fleet to break through the Bogue again and sail down to Whampoa. Soon afterwards, however, to the annoyance of his more militant countrymen, he agreed to a truce and, thereafter, according to a British doctor in Canton, his 'acts became daily more clouded and veiled in obscurity. In private conversation he changed his opinion every few minutes; and as for his public acts, his proclamations [showed] the vacillating nature of his temperament. His sole object seems to have been to re-establish trade; whether on terms honourable or otherwise to Great Britain, it did not appear to matter much to him.'[26]

While Elliot hesitated between force and conciliation, the Chinese continued with their 'acts of provocation'. On the night of 10 May they sent fire rafts against the British ships and later allowed a mob of Cantonese to attack and plunder the factories and to set several of them alight. The American merchants still in their factory were dragged off inside the walls of the city where their protestations that they were not British were rejected with the comment that if that were so they 'ought to speak a different language and wear a different dress'. After nearly two days' imprisonment in the city gaol, they were 'at length turned out,' in the words of the *Chinese Repository*, 'and carried in chairs to the ruined Factories, where they were planted just as if they had been portions of the marble statue which had been destroyed'. Several American sailors and marines were with them, their claims not to be English having been closely investigated by the Chinese who examined them all for the tattoo marks which they believed would have established their English identity.[27]

*   *   *

On 24 May 1841, the British again took the initiative by beginning an assault upon Canton. Although many soldiers had died in the unhealthy camps on Chusan, nearly 2,400 men were available for the attack and a general of 'acknowledged bravery and distinction', Major-General Sir Hugh Gough, had recently arrived from Madras to take command of them. Gough's plan was for one of his regiments, the 26th (Cameronians), to land at the factories and strengthen the position there; and then for the main body of his force to be taken upstream past Canton in the armed paddle-steamer *Nemesis*, and in a long stream of almost eighty boats in tow of her, to the little village of Tsing-poo which stood on the banks of the Pearl River beyond the rice fields to the north-west of the city. Once established there, with a fortified post in a nearby temple, he could advance on the town from the rear, taking the two pairs of forts that guarded its northern gates.[28]

All this General Gough achieved without much difficulty, suffering few casualties except in the regiments exposed to the fire of the Chinese on the city walls. The Chinese 'defenders behaved very well', in the opinion of one of Gough's young officers, 'coming to the brow of the hill, waving their arms and beckoning to us to come on. One man, in particular, attracted great attention by his daring and coolness. He came to the front of the hill, and stood waving a red banner over his head, and though the fire of the cruizers, *Columbine* and *Phlegethon* was excellent, several shot knocking the dust up at his feet, he never flinched from his place, but kept on defying us until he was actually cut in half by a thirty-two pound shot from the *Phlegethon*. Another man took up his flag, and, I believe, shared his fate.'

Later, this same officer recorded, the men of his regiment had to shoot 'a great many Chinese, for they stood pretty well. One man, a white button mandarin, stood behind a tree. I had passed without seeing him, when hearing a scuffle, I turned round, and saw that he had wounded one of my party in the chest with his spear. He then closed with him and got his forage cap off; another man came up and thrust at him with his bayonet, which he wrenched off with the firelock, but was shot by a third.'[29]

But despite the sturdy resistance of the Chinese, by late afternoon General Gough was in a position to take Canton by storm the following day. In the morning, however, while waiting for his heavy guns to come up, he saw a white flag waving above the northern gate.

I-shan, the Rebel-quelling General, had never shown himself as resolute a warrior as his cousin, the Emperor, had hoped he would be. Less concerned with the Barbarians than with the supposed enemies of the Manchu dynasty amongst the Chinese defence volunteers, he had not discouraged the government troops from disarming and murdering any armed civilians to whom they took a dislike. Nor were most of his subordinate officers any more zealous in offering resistance to the Barbarians than he was himself. One of them, who had placed his artillery so far away from the foreign ships that they were well out of range while his own position was accurately bombarded, excused himself on the grounds that they were 'using the sorcery of their evil religion'.[30]

I-shan, following the precedent set by his predecessors at Canton, made claims in his report to the Emperor that bore little relation to the facts, maintaining that the Barbarians had been brought to a sudden standstill before the walls by the apparition of a spirit which had brought them to their senses,[31] and that he had been persuaded to come to terms with them by the people of Canton who, 'weeping and wailing, sending up loud cries to heaven, had choked every pathway and earnestly begged that peaceful arrangements should be entered into'. His action in coming to terms would surely be recognized at Court as a clever diplomatic stroke, for once the British fleet had left the Pearl River, the Chinese would be able to 'renew the fortifications and seek another occasion for attacking and destroying the Barbarians at Hong Kong', thus restoring to the Empire its ancient territory. For the present, therefore, he had been prepared to accept the obligation to pay a ransom of six million dollars to the British in return for their not occupying the town, and to disband its garrison.[32]

If I-shan could pretend to be perfectly satisfied with the terms of the truce, General Gough could certainly not. Elliot, 'whimsical as a shuttlecock', had not merely brought the operations to a sudden halt when they could have been so satisfactorily concluded; he had placed the British troops 'in a most critical situation' with their communications 'constantly threatened' and their camps obliged to maintain a 'continued watchfulness'. For, however much Elliot put his confidence in the Chinese, Gough trusted them not a bit, nor would the British 'be justified in relaxing in the least'.[33]

*　　*　　*

Relieved as the Chinese negotiators were to escape with no worse punishment than the payment of an indemnity for the 'ransom of Canton'—knowing that the Hong merchants rather than the Court or themselves would in any case eventually be forced to find most if not all the money—the patriotic defence volunteers refused to accept what they conceived to be a further humiliation at the hands of the foreigners. They massed threateningly in the hills to the north-east, and Gough was obliged to send the 26th Regiment, supported by the 37th Madras Native Infantry and a battery of rockets, to disperse them.

The Chinese volunteers bravely stood their ground against the rockets, and when the British infantry moved into the attack a sudden fierce thunderstorm, pouring down cascades of water onto their muskets, obliged them to use their bayonets, which were no match for the long spears of the patriots.

At the village of Sanyuan-li a detachment of British troops was separated from the rest of the force and defeated; and although the volunteers were soon afterwards dispersed with what Captain Hall of the paddle-steamer *Nemesis* called 'great loss' and forced to flee 'in confusion', their courage had been temporarily rewarded.[34] They had achieved something that the Tartar soldiers of the Manchus had never yet managed to achieve: they had won a fight against the foreigner. Their triumph was never to be forgotten. Today in China the name of Sanyuan-li is celebrated as the people's first victory over the evils of imperialism.[35]

11 | The Empire in Defeat

On going into the houses, the scenes which there met the eye were horrible. Men, women, and children were found drowned or hung; whole families seemed to have destroyed themselves. Lieutenant Alexander Murray on the occupation of Chapu, May 1842.

While the battle of Sanyuan-li was being fought, Elliot's successor was sailing to China aboard the *Sesostris* with instructions to authorize a far firmer policy than ever Elliot himself had considered, not necessarily to make any demands in the matter of opium which Her Majesty's Government had 'no right' to do, but certainly to ensure that the British plenipotentiary was 'treated by the plenipotentiary of the Emperor of China upon a footing of perfect equality'.[1] The name of this British plenipotentiary was Sir Henry Pottinger.

An Irish administrator who had distinguished himself in India where he had been Governor of Madras, Pottinger arrived in China on 10 August 1841 and immediately made it clear that he was going to stand no nonsense from any Chinaman. 'He is a most popular character with the army and navy,' wrote an English officer, 'his penchant for energetic measures, even of somewhat an indiscriminable nature, finding much greater favour than the vacillations of his predecessor.'[2] In Pottinger's opinion it might well rest 'with the Queen of England to pronounce what ports or portions of the sea coast of China shall be added to Her Majesty's Dominions'.[3]

Less than a fortnight after Pottinger's arrival, General Gough's expeditionary force, now increased in size to 2,700 men by the arrival of the 55th (Westmorland) Regiment at Hong Kong, sailed northwards with the object of taking the war into the very heart of China.

In the first of a series of well-conducted amphibious operations, Amoy was taken on 26 August with the loss of two men killed and fifteen wounded; then, on 1 October, Tinghai was re-occupied with casualties similarly slight. The fall of another port, Chinhai at the mouth of the Ningpo river, soon followed; and on 13 October Ningpo itself was captured. These successive Chinese defeats were due to the general incompetence of the Emperor's troops, not to cowardice. Indeed, British reports agree that the Chinese soldiers usually fought with great bravery. At Amoy, so an Army surgeon wrote in his journal, they ran down the rugged face of the rock, discharging their matchlocks and throwing stones at the invaders.[4] At Tinghai, an artillery officer said, 'the British anticipated no opposition at the landing place as all the batteries were on the other side of the hill and our ships kept up a constant fire on them; at the moment of our boats pulling off for the shore not a Chinaman was visible, but by the time we reached the breach the whole hill was covered with soldiers who poured in a very galling fire on us.'[5]

'The Chinese themselves are a very powerful race,' Colonel Wyndham Baker decided, expressing a widely held opinion. 'They would make such perfect soldiers if taken properly in hand.'[6]

Despite the ease with which Ningpo was taken, Henry Pottinger demanded that it should be sacked; for here some British prisoners of the Chinese, including the widow of a sea-captain, had been savagely ill-treated. The terrible story that the widow and her companions told of their misadventures had been repeated from regiment to regiment throughout the army and had confirmed the soldiers' belief in the cruelty of their enemies.

It appeared that the *Kite*, a vessel of three hundred tons, had grounded on quicksand on its way to Chusan on 15 September the year before. Her master, Mr Noble, had been drowned. Mrs Noble, Lieutenant Douglas, and the chief mate, had managed to escape in a small boat together with two boys. They were seen by the crew of a Chinese fishing-boat who kindly gave them some rice and water and a piece of old matting which they were able to make into a sail. On approaching Chusan they were seen by another boat whose crew agreed to tow them into harbour, but instead, landed them on the banks of a canal where they were handed over to a mandarin and some soldiers.

On being seized the men were severely beaten around the knees to prevent their running away. 'They would have treated Mrs Noble in the same brutal and still more indecent manner,' wrote Elliot Bingham in his indignant account of the affair, 'had it not been for the spirited conduct of Mr Douglas, notwithstanding which she received several blows. Chains were then put around their necks, and they were hurried, or rather dragged to a large city, through the streets of which they were paraded to the hootings and howlings of the assembled savages. They were then taken to a joss-house [temple], where one of the soldiers forcibly wrenched Mrs Noble's wedding-ring from her finger. Lieutenant Douglas's hands were here lashed behind him, and he was in that condition secured to a post. Mrs Noble, the mate, and one boy, were then dragged on about twenty miles further, being exhibited in several towns through which they passed; and no doubt from what afterwards appeared, Mrs Noble was represented as sister to the Queen of the Barbarians.'

They were then imprisoned in another temple for two days, being secured to the walls by chains around their necks; and afterwards, with heavy irons round their legs and arms, they were forced into bamboo cages and carried about as interesting exhibits from town to town. 'The cages were then at length placed in boats, and after proceeding along a canal for three nights and two days, they arrived at Ning-po, never having been permitted to quit their cages for any purpose during that period.

'Lieutenant Douglas and the other boy had been conveyed in a similar manner, but by a different route, thus affording the inhabitants of a greater extent of country a peep at the Barbarians.

'The [Lascar] crew, as it was hoped might be the case, had been taken off the wreck by some Chinese boats, and were also prisoners at this place, Ning-po. Several of these poor fellows died during their imprisonment, from the hardships they had to endure.'[7]

It was as a reprisal for these outrages that Pottinger pressed General Gough to sack Ningpo, an event to which, so he reported to the Foreign Office, he had 'looked forward with considerable satisfaction';[8] but Gough, whose bluff kindliness greatly endeared him to his men, refused to sanction so brutal an action. Before the operations began he had issued strong warnings against looting; and though it had been impossible to enforce these at Amoy, once the town had been ransacked by Chinese plunderers, he was determined to spare Ningpo if he possibly could. With the help of what responsible citizens there remained in the town he established a force of Chinese policemen to protect the possessions of its people.

Such a force was much needed, for although the British troops were prevented from behaving as badly as they felt sure Tartar troops would behave if in occupation of an English port, the ravages they committed were destructive enough. Unoccupied houses were dismantled for firewood; shops were plundered; the town's best bell was seized as a prize and shipped off to Calcutta; the largest temple was used as a barracks for winter quarters, its rooms being divided by wooden partitions hammered into floor and ceiling. 'When I look at this place,' Gough lamented in a letter home, 'I am sick of war.'[9]

'At Ningpo,' Lieutenant Alexander Murray confessed, 'several times we were obliged to have recourse to the plan of taking a few respectable inhabitants and detaining them as hostages, treating them, however, well, until a fresh supply of bullocks was brought in. This is by far the best way of getting supplies in China, instead of sending out foraging parties; for, as soon as the people see a red coat coming, they drive away the cattle and hide them among the trees on the hills. They are also very dextrous in concealing their fowls, stowing them in all sorts of curious places, in baskets covered over with rubbish, or hung up to the ceiling.'[10]

Nor was it only this cavalier treatment of their buildings, livestock and possessions that led the Chinese so strongly to dislike the Barbarians. Quite as objectionable was the contemptuous way in which they treated them personally, pelting them with snowballs, tying their pigtails together or even cutting them off as a punishment, gathering to laugh at them as they carried huge and unwieldy sacks of corn on their heads out of the public building which the military had taken over as a granary.

Stories of the ill-treatment of the people of Ningpo and the other

occupied towns of Chekiang and Fukien, and of the barbaric behaviour of the foreigners, had soon spread all over China and were
much embellished in the telling. At Tinghai, it was said, the chief
English officer had dressed himself in the clothes of the Municipal
God and had given the God his own red uniform to wear instead; at
Ningpo they had destroyed the figure of the Municipal God and had
put their own idols in the temple in its place and went each morning
and evening to worship them; elsewhere they had raped and
plundered, taken away babies from their mothers and forced young
girls into concubinage. 'They carry off young men,' a spy in Tinghai reported, 'shave their heads, paint their bodies with black
lacquer, give them a drug which makes them dumb, and so turn
them into black Devils, using them to carry heavy loads.'[11] Karl
Gützlaff's rough and ready methods as the new magistrate of Ningpo
were described by the poet Hsü Shih-tung:

> *On his dais he sits passive and majestic,*
> *While the mob throngs below.*
> *He has no scribes to assist him,*
> *There are no papers on his desk,*
> *Yet never has the business of the court been*
>   *handled so swiftly as by Kuo Shih-li.*
>
> *From down at the side of the dais*
> *Someone cries out that he has been wronged,*
> *A fellow from who knows where came to his house and*
>   *extorted money from him.*
> *Directly he hears it, Kuo Shih-li, without another word,*
> *Picks up his stick, climbs down from the dais and*
>   *waddles off into the town.*
> *A moment later he reappears, dragging the culprit along,*
> *Ties him up, bares his back, and gives him fifty*
>   *with the lash. . . .*
>
> *Yesterday an old peasant passed down the street*
> *On which his office stands.*
> *When he got home he heaved a sigh; his heart was very sad.*
> *'We once had magistrates of our own, where are they now?'*[12]

Stories of the havoc being wrought by the foreigners in Fukien and
Chekiang reached another poet, Pei Ch'ing-ch'iao, at Soochow. Pei

expressed his indignation in a set of nine poems which he showed to his father, a fanatical military man, all the more fanatical because he had failed as a staff officer actually to get into battle. 'If you feel so strongly about it,' the father said, 'why don't you join the army?' Pei did join the army and his father gave him a sword, telling him that if he did not cut off the foreign chieftain's head with it, he would not be welcomed home again on his return.

The army into which Pei Ch'ing-ch'iao enlisted at Soochow was commanded by a forty-year-old Manchu, I-ching, another cousin of the Emperor but one who was trusted by him to put up a better fight than I-shan had done at Canton. So confident, indeed, was the Emperor in I-ching's talents that he gave him a cornelian snuff-bottle on the back of which was the figure of a horseman who appeared to be the bearer of a despatch announcing victory.

I-ching's main objective was to recapture Ningpo, and he sent Pei there as a spy to find out the strength of the occupying forces. After a long examination Pei was admitted into the town on a wall of which there hung the head of one of his unfortunate predecessors above the admonitory legend: 'This is the head of the Manchu official Lü T'ai-lai who came here to obtain military information.'

Encouraged by Pei's report that the garrison numbered less than three hundred men—its actual strength was rather more than four times this figure—General I-ching instructed the literary men on his staff to compose announcements of victory. 'Thirty of these were sent in,' Pei recorded in his diary, 'and the General arranged them in order of merit. The first place went to Miu Chia-ku who had composed a detailed and vivid account of the exploits of the various heroes.'[13]

The attack on Ningpo was planned for the Hour of the Tiger (between three and five o'clock in the morning) on the twenty-eighth day of the first month (10 March), a 'Tiger' day, 'Tiger' dates being celebrated as propitious for military adventures.

Originally an earlier date had been fixed for the attack, but I-ching was a man who liked to take his time. He had accepted the command, it was said, because he had welcomed the opportunity of visiting the beauty spots of the Lower Yangtze Valley and had certainly spent so long enjoying the company of the singing-girls of Soochow that it was over four months before he had arrived in Chekiang and had managed to get his troops into position for the long-awaited assault on Ningpo.[14]

*   *   *

For weeks the British troops in Ningpo had been expecting the attack. Every day, one of their officers remembered, 'we heard rumours of armies collecting, and orders being given for our utter extermination. Very little credit was given to these reports, for we did not believe that the Chinese would dare to attack us, though the great extent of the walls made the circumstance feasible. The people of Ningpo, on the other hand, seemed certain a great attack was impending; and on the morning of 10 March they began to leave the town, declaring that the English would soon be driven out. The shops were all shut and the market people said they would not be returning to Ningpo next day, drawing their hands across their throats and pointing at the soldiers as they spoke. The beggars who hung about the barracks wandered off, too, promising to come back to beg again if there were any soldiers still alive when the bang-bang was all over.'[15]

'On the evening of that day', said Lieutenant Murray, 'Mr Gutzlaff [director of intelligence at Ningpo as well as magistrate] positively asserted that we should be attacked, that same night. Even under this assurance, none of the guards were reinforced, nor were any preparations made to receive the ̇ enemy. The patrols were merely ordered to keep a sharp look out, and each officer was charged to go out three times during the night. The rest of the force went quietly to bed.'[16]

It was the opinion of another officer, Lieutenant John Ouchterlony, that the fault for this lack of preparedness lay not so much with the army as with Gützlaff who 'did not express himself to the military authorities in a manner sufficiently marked to lead them to suppose that he himself attached credence to the report'. But whether Gützlaff was sufficiently emphatic or not, the army's going quietly to bed that night had little effect on the outcome of the fighting that followed. For the attack was preceded by a whole series of mischances and mistakes that rendered victory for the Chinese impossible to conceive.

An early misfortune had befallen some Chinese volunteers who had joined the army from the Golden River region in Western Szechwan. A number of them had been ordered out on patrol soon after their arrival in camp; they lost their way, wandered back into their own lines where a Chinese officer, misled by their strange speech and the unfamiliar writing on the tablets that they wore suspended from their waists, mistook them for soldiers in the pay of the British and gave orders for them to be attacked. Some were killed, others wounded, the rest bound up and dragged off as prisoners to Chang Ying-yüng, I-ching's commander in the field, an opium addict frequently incapacitated. On learning what had happened to their comrades, the rest of the volunteers mutinied and were not satisfied until the officer responsible had been thrown into prison and thirty of his men had been flogged.

Then there was trouble in the main army when orders came for a general advance towards Ningpo. The country people, frightened that the approaching array would devastate their farms like locusts, ran away before them, carrying off all their livestock and possessions. The indignant, hungry troops, unable to live off the land and ill-supplied by their own commissariat officers, who protested that they had neither money nor transport, threatened to go home unless they were properly fed. They were dissuaded from doing so; but most of the hired civilian porters, struggling with the guns and baggage down the mud-filled roads, absconded before they had carried their loads to the forward camp from which the attack on Ningpo was to be mounted. Unfortunate as these early setbacks were, there were far worse yet to come.

It had been planned that before the attack on the walls was made, the ships in the river would be set alight by fire rafts. But the men whose duty it was to tow the rafts towards the ships dared not approach closer than three miles before setting them alight, so that the English sailors had plenty of time to intercept them, fling grappling hooks at them and drag them in to the bank. Nor could any men be found prepared to approach the foreign ships close enough to throw aboard the monkeys that were supposed to jump about the decks with fire crackers tied to their backs, hurling sparks into the powder magazines.

The land operations were no more efficiently conducted than those in the river. Of the 36,000 troops which were originally intended to hurl themselves against the gates, scarcely more than one-tenth actually did so, thousands not having joined the army by the time appointed, thousands more being kept behind to act as body-guards to I-ching and his multitudinous staff. Moreover the Golden River volunteers, the spearhead of the attack, went into the assault armed only with knives, believing that the General's order forbidding the use of cannon, which he thought would endanger the lives of the people of Ningpo, applied also to the use of matchlocks.

These brave men, so lightly armed, ran towards the gate which the Chinese commander behind them saw to his pleasure was open. Supposing from this that the enemy had fled, he gave orders for all the troops under his command to pour through it. Dashing forwards, so 'mad with excitement' that English observers felt sure that they must have taken 'an immense quantity of opium', they fell into the trap that had been laid for them: mines exploded on every side; and the English, running round the outside of the walls from the northern gate, caught them as they struggled to escape. 'Our soldiers fled precipitately,' wrote the poet Pei Ch'ing-ch'iao. 'But the streets and lanes [of the suburbs outside the western gate] were so narrow and soggy that they could not get away, and our losses were very heavy.'[17]

The losses among those Chinese who did eventually manage to force their way into the town were heavier still. Caught in an enfilading fire from the infantry on either side, they were faced in front by the heavy guns of the artillery which opened up on them from a distance of less than fifty yards. 'The effect was terrific,' according to John Ouchterlony, 'for the street was perfectly straight, and the enemy's rear, not aware of the miserable fate which was being dealt out to their comrades in front, continued to press the mass forward, so as to force fresh victims upon the mound of dead and dying which already barricaded the street. . . . The infantry resumed their firing and such a storm of balls was kept up upon the enemy, that in a short time the street was choked up, and when, for want of a living mark, the men were ordered to advance, their steps fell upon a closely packed mass of dead and dying.'[18]

'The carnage was horrible,' agreed Alexander Murray. 'The dead bodies, indeed, lay piled five or six deep for a considerable distance along the street', blocking it to such a degree that 'the guns were obliged to be left behind; but we moved on, through the suburbs, and about the end of them, fell in with the main body of the Chinese, in full retreat. We pursued them for about six miles, killing many. They never attempted to stand, halting only once to fire some gingalls, and then continuing their flight. It was fortunate for us that they did not know how small our party was; for if they had turned upon us, we should have had little chance. . . . The most extraordinary part of the scene was the coolness with which the country people looked on, crowding the bridges and every spot from which they could see well, in amazing manner. We were obliged to call and make signals to get out of the line of fire, to prevent their being shot, and I can safely say not an unarmed person was touched. The circumstance of their thus assembling showed what confidence they had that we would not injure them; but the little interest they took in their countrymen did not raise them in my estimation. They seemed rather to enjoy their defeat, regarding what was passing as an amusement. . . .'[19]

Many of the British troops, too, regarded the killing of Chinese soldiers as a kind of amusing sport. Another British officer described the plight of a group of Chinese who had got out of Ningpo and were trying to escape across a paddy field. 'Two British sailors and a soldier about fifty yards apart from each other, formed the points of a triangle, in which some six or eight Chinese were running helplessly about over the paddy field, some disarmed, and others with swords in their hands. Our three men were loading and firing at them as cooly as if they were crows, and bayonetting to death those who fell wounded. I endeavoured to stop them but they paid no attention.'[20]

*   *   *

Although the Chinese were repulsed with such ease at Ningpo, when the British troops resumed their offensive in the spring of 1842 they found that their enemy could not always be treated with the contempt displayed by a soldier of the Royal Irish who, disdaining to waste a cartridge on the laughable fellows, and saying that he would show them 'the Tipperary touch', knocked one off the walls of Ningpo with the butt end of his own matchlock and another with the bolt of the door of the cell in which he had been recently confined for drunkenness.[21] Those who shared the Irishman's scornful opinion of the military skills of the Emperor's army had to revise their judgment after coming into conflict with his Tartar troops at Chapu in May.

Chapu lies on the coast, south of Shanghai, on the northern arm of the Bay of Hangchow. It was held by a strong garrison of Tartar troops occupying, with their wives and families, the high northwestern corner of the town from the rest of which they were completely separated by a line of ramparts.

The brave resistance of the three hundred-odd Tartar defenders of a temple at Chapu was judged typical of their fierce tenacity. The inside of the temple was darkened by mats draped over the windows so that any foreign soldier who managed to break in would be at a dangerous disadvantage until his eyes became used to the half-light and he could pick out the loopholes and alcoves where the Tartars sat concealed. The first assault was made by the Royal Irish who were met by so ferocious a fire that it was decided to wait for reinforcements. A second attempt, made by some men of the 49th, was given a similarly savage reception; and their Colonel gave orders that no more attempts should be made until the artillery came up. But Lieutenant-Colonel Tomlinson of the Royal Irish, stung into action by some remarks 'which he considered a reflection either upon his regiment or himself', instantly led a headlong charge and burst in at the door. 'He had hardly got in before he received two balls through his neck,' wrote one of his subalterns. 'He was carried out and expired in about five minutes, sincerely regretted by us all, both as a commanding officer and a friend. Every one who went into the house was either wounded or killed. . . . The doorway was narrow and inside that was a sort of screen from behind which the enemy could fire. The place could not be carried by a rush as many men could not get in at a time. But after the Colonel's death it was almost impossible to prevent the men from trying to get in, for they became quite furious and exposed themselves recklessly. Some rockets having come up, they were fired from the doorway [into the building] to try and set it on fire; but we did not succeed.'

At length the constant hammering by the guns of the artillery, the explosion of a powder bag which rent a hole in the wall, exposing many of the Tartars to musket fire, and the success of some sailors who, on a second attempt, managed to ignite the woodwork of the upper storeys, combined to subdue the defenders' fire. But only when almost all of those inside the Temple had been killed, wounded or forced to drop their matchlocks to beat out the fires caused by the blazing timbers that dropped on their wadded uniforms from above, was their fire silenced completely.

Then, as the smoke began to clear, there was seen sitting down amongst the wounded an old Tartar colonel calmly smoking his pipe; at the approach of the British soldiers, he put down his pipe and tried to cut his throat with his sword.

Near him lay a soldier of the 18th who had been shot dead. 'The Chinese had savagely mutilated him with his own razor which they had taken out of his knapsack,' reported one of his officers, 'cutting his ears and nose, also scooping his eyes out. It is a great proof of their ferocity that they should commit such cruelties amidst the horrors of their own situation, expecting almost immediate death.'[22]

Rather than submit to defeat, many soldiers followed the colonel's example and cut their throats. Their families, too, killed themselves in their hundreds, hanging themselves from the beams of their houses, drowning themselves in wells even though the water was only six inches deep, poisoning themselves until, as John Ouchterlony said, the floors of the houses in the Tartar part of the city were strewn with bodies, 'bloody from the wounds by which their lives had been cut short, or swollen and blackened by the effects of poison'.[23]

'On going into the houses,' young Alexander Murray confirmed, 'the scenes which there met the eye were horrible. Men, women, and children were found drowned or hung; whole families seemed to have destroyed themselves. .... I can imagine the men doing this, for the poor devils are often executed by their own Government for their want of success. But why women should be so resolute seems extraordinary, for many a one being taken out of the water by us in time to save them, attempted to drown themselves again. I have heard Mr Gützlaff say, however, that as we advanced to the north, the Tartar population would always destroy themselves after a defeat.'[24]

Certainly at Chinkiang, the next town which the British attacked and—after the hardest fight they had had so far—captured in their northwards advance, the same scenes were repeated, the Tartar troops who survived the battle killing their families and then themselves, leaving the widows and orphans of those killed in action to drown themselves in shallow ponds and wells. 'It may be said that the Mantchoo race in this city is extinct,' reported General Gough, who took his army away from its putrid smells to occupy the higher, healthier ground outside it. 'I was glad to withdraw the troops from this frightful scene of destruction.'[25]

As before in the other towns, so here at Chinkiang, capture was followed by looting which made Gough 'sick at heart of war and its fearful consequences'.[26]

'The Foreign Devils went around from house to house,' a Chinese witness reported, 'seizing gold and silver and women's headdresses. The clothes they toss to the poor. Rogues from far and near got wind of this, and crowds of them have come to guide foreigners to likely houses. When the foreigners have smashed in the gates and taken what they want, these scoundrels take advantage of the confusion to make off with everything that is left.'[27]

Another Chinese witness recorded in his diary the devices employed by the people of Shanghai in saving their valuables from the foreign troops: 'A man with a large "pot-belly" went out of the city. The Foreign Devils saw him and suspected him of having something hidden in his trousers. They were forcibly taken down and the man was searched. However, all they found was the man's penis. At this the Foreign Devils got into a great rage, but after a while they saw the funny side of it so they just gave him a light beating and released him. Since this incident, anyone concealing anything in his trousers deliberately makes up a large parcel for his back and walks bent like a hunchback, deliberately going very slowly as if in great pain. In this way the Foreign Devils do not stop and question them.

'Another thing, concerning the refuse carriers, or rubbish men as they are called in common parlance. When the foreigners first came, these people still continued to take the rubbish out of the city. The foreigners, not knowing what it was they were carrying, stopped them and searched the containers, so getting their whole bodies covered in the filthy stuff. Now when they see them they give them a wide berth and hurry them on as fast as possible. Since this, people have started wrapping all sorts of things in oiled paper and oiled cloth and covering them over with all sorts of waste, thus getting their valuables out of the town without being questioned by the Foreign Devils.

'Learning from this, some people have put their gold and silver into the bottom of night soil buckets, covering it in filthy water, then adding rice grass, leaves and other vegetation.'[28]

The Barbarians, so this diarist said, were not only guilty of looting in Shanghai: 'On the day the foreigners entered the city all the women and girls who had not already fled, fearing that they would be raped, all hid in empty tombs, long grass, dried-up irrigation ditches and in ruins. Gradually those who could not stand being in hiding took the risk of slipping back into the town at dead of night. Some even shaved off their hair in order to pass as men. A few managed to escape detection but most of them were exposed and raped.'[29]

Even the dogs of Shanghai sensed the evil nature of the Barbarians: 'When a dog sees something unfamiliar it always barks. On the day the Foreign Devils took the city if a dog met them it would prick up its ears and skulk away with its tail between its legs. Not one dog in the whole city dared bark. We have a dog in our household whose barking can be quite dreadful. When the foreigners came and the dog saw what they were like he skulked away to the safety of the stove and would not eat for the whole day. Only after they had gone did he come out. He must have sensed their violent and wicked spirit and not have been able to go anywhere near them.'[30]

* * *

The capture of Chinkiang, at the junction of the Grand Canal and the Yangtze, opened up the road to Nanking, 'the Southern Capital', and thoroughly alarmed the Court. Up till then the Emperor, comforted by reports of how 'the red-bristled Barbarians', though 'wildly careering in the Celestial waters', were being forced from the coasts of the Empire, had refused to consider negotiations. To a General who suggested that the hostilities should be ended he sharply retorted that the request deeply aggravated his anger.[31] But now that the foreigners' ships, under the skilful direction of their admiral, Sir William Parker, were transporting the invading troops down the Yangtze River towards Nanking, he felt compelled to send Commissioners to the British headquarters to negotiate a settlement.

The three Commissioners who received his instructions were Niu Chien, Governor-General of Kiangsu, Anhwei and Kiangsi; I-li-pu, a former Governor-General of these provinces; and Ch'i-ying, a fat and friendly man in his middle sixties, the son of an Imperial clansman.

The negotiations began in an unpromising atmosphere on 8 August when Chang Hsi, I-li-pu's most trusted servant, together with 'a whole train' of companions, came aboard the *Cornwallis* carrying a dispatch from his master and wearing a mandarin's crystal button, to which he was not entitled, so as to lend authority to his visit.[32] In Chang Hsi's own account, Henry Pottinger and his colleagues 'gesticulated and shook their heads' while reading and discussing his master's dispatch, 'each with a smiling face, and sometimes a puzzled frown'.

The dispatch was 'all empty talk', Robert Morrison, the interpreter, eventually complained. 'The situation today is not to be compared to that of previous days.' If their terms were not accepted, he threatened, after taking Nanking the British would advance to take Peking.

'You people usually talk about attacking Peking,' Chang Hsi angrily objected. 'Is it an easy thing to talk about? In the capital city the standing army of Manchu, Mongolian and . . . Chinese troops are calculated to be more than 200,000.' He went on to enumerate the further military resources of the Empire, rising in increasing passion to this theme. When Morrison said that, all the same, the British military action *would* continue if satisfactory terms were not agreed, he cried out 'Wherever you go, you attack cities and kill and injure our people; does it not make Heaven angry?'

Chang felt 'a hundred turmoils in his belly and extremely distressed', and after further argument he 'burst into a rage and beat the table and shouted: "If you are too haughty and overbearing, I am only afraid that Heaven above us will not forgive you, and naturally you will face the disaster of destruction! . . . You people are born in a form unlike human beings, and what you are doing is unlike what human beings care to do. How can you say it is not mean? You kill people everywhere, plunder goods, and act like rascals; that is very disgraceful; how can you say it is not like bandits? You alien Barbarians invade our China, your small country attacks our Celestial Court; how can you say you are not rebellious?" Hsi beat the desk, spat on the floor, and denounced them in their cabin; the Barbarians looked very angry. When the Indian Barbarians outside the window heard the noise, they took out their swords and barred the door of the cabin and took off the ladder hung up at the edge of the ship. . . . The Barbarian chief Pottinger said, "If you have something to say, let us discuss it calmly; it is not necessary to be angry." Chang laughed sardonically. . . .'

The discussion then did grow more calm; and, as Chang 'argued with them back and forth, from early morning until evening', the British agreed 'to hold up the bombing of the city temporarily' until a satisfactory Chinese reply was received.

On their way back to the city, Chang's companions congratulated him upon the spirited way in which he had stood up to the Barbarians. One of them, who admitted he was so afraid himself aboard the ship that he could not open his mouth, told him, 'Your words were like the running of a river; you answered all questions as soon as you were asked, you talked endlessly like running water, and eventually you had so many arguments, and angry denunciations. How quick was your wit; it really made us happy, and it is, indeed, the most delightful thing in ancient and modern times. . . . But I am afraid the three high authorities may not humbly follow your tactics.'[33]

The speaker was right. The three Commissioners were wholly disinclined to follow Chang's example. They reported to the Emperor that the time had come to 'take advantage of the present occasion, to ease the situation by soothing the Barbarians', who would otherwise run over the country 'like beasts, doing anything they like'.[34]

On 20 August the Commissioners went aboard the *Cornwallis* for the first time. A fourteen-year-old English boy who was studying Chinese in Robert Morrison's office was introduced to them, whereupon Ch'i-ying, so the boy recorded, 'seeing that I was a regular "red-haired Barbarian" took a bit of a fancy to me. I tried to talk as much as possible, but could only stammer out a few words, while I could not understand Kiying in the least, who speaks the northern mandarin very broadly. . . . I rather like Kiying's appearance, for he has a fine manly honest countenance, with pleasantness in his looks; but I cannot say the same of Eleepo [I-li-pu] or Niu-Kien, for they look dull and heavy, with coarse features, which seemed to show that they were takers of opium.'[35]

The three men were shown round the ship which they seemed surprised to learn was by no means one of the largest in the British Navy. 'His Excellency Niu Chien,' so Chang Hsi said, 'had thought that the paddle-wheel of the steamer was turned by oxen, and he had frequently asked Hsi about it; Hsi told him the truth, but Niu had not been able to decide whether to believe it or not; now he sighed and believed it.'[36]

A week later Niu and his two colleagues returned to the *Cornwallis* for the signing of the treaty. Unfortunately, on this occasion, I-li-pu was very ill and had to be carried up the side of the ship in a chair and laid on a sofa on deck. His servant, Chang Hsi, was to blame; for on being sent to one of the British steamers for some medicine which a ship's doctor had recommended to his master, he got extremely drunk in the gunroom and lost the instructions. I-li-pu had consequently taken in one gulp an amount intended to last for three days. He managed to sign the treaty, however, drawing the characters wearily between those of Niu Chien and Ch'i-ying.

Ch'i-ying clearly evinced 'deep consciousness of fallen power', in the words of an English observer[37]; and both he and Niu Chien were 'much alarmed' and 'suddenly changed countenance', when, to celebrate the end of the war, the guns of the *Cornwallis* fired a twenty-one gun salute. But when they took their leave soon afterwards, 'each party seemed satisfied and pleased with the other'.[38]

* * *

The Treaty of Nanking, which thus ended the first Anglo-Chinese War on 29 August 1842, was the beginning of a series of humiliating treaties imposed on China by force.

In accordance with its terms Amoy, Foochow, Ningpo and Shanghai, which with the addition of Canton made up the five 'treaty ports', were all to be opened to British trade. The cession of Hong Kong was confirmed. An indemnity of twenty-one million dollars was to be paid; the regulation that all business must be conducted through the Hong merchants was rescinded, and an official British representative was to be accepted in China.[39] Although part of the indemnity was allocated to the payment of compensation for the opium destroyed by Commissioner Lin, and although Pottinger endeavoured to persuade the Chinese to legalize future traffic in the drug—disingenuously arguing that the prohibition of the cultivation of the poppy in India 'would merely throw the market into other hands' and that the problem rested entirely with the Chinese who would not smoke it if they were virtuous and whose officials would not let it in if they were incorruptible[40]—there was, in fact, no mention of the opium trade in the entire treaty.[41]

III | *Rebels and Innocents*

12 | 'The True Lord of China'

Our Heavenly King has received the Divine Commission to exterminate the Manchus, to exterminate all idolaters generally, and to possess the Empire as its True Sovereign. . . . We command the services of all and we take everything. All who resist us are rebels and idolatrous demons, and we kill them without sparing. Proclamation of the Taipings, October 1851.

Scarcely had the Treaty of Nanking been signed than the other trading nations of the West entered into negotiations with the humiliated Chinese Government in an effort to obtain for themselves some of the advantages that the war had won for Britain. Anxious that these other nations should not obtain any greater advantages than those for which they had fought, the British inserted into the supplementary Treaty of the Bogue—a treaty signed in July 1843 providing that British nationals should be subject to their own laws and the jurisdiction of their own consuls—a clause that recognized Britain as the 'most-favoured' nation, entitled to any right any other country might succeed in obtaining for itself. They were wise to do so, for the next year both the United States and France, Britain's two principal rivals in the China trade, signed treaties with China; and soon Belgium, Sweden, Norway and Russia had all followed their example. The American agreement, the Treaty of Wang-hsia, which gained for the United States most of the concessions already granted to the British, also included an important clause guaranteeing toleration for their Protestant missionaries. This toleration, afterwards extended to the Protestant missionaries of other countries, introduced a new and potentially dangerous factor into China's relations with the West.[1]

For the moment, however, it was the almost limitless opportunities for trade opened up by the Treaty of Nanking that preoccupied the British. In their first excitement at these opportunities, British merchants—wholly ignorant of social conditions in China and totally unaware of how little the Chinese had to spend on any foreign goods other than the opium which was now sold in greater quantities than ever—poured into the country a variety of goods that the people had neither the inclination nor the means to buy, from pianos made in London to knives and forks manufactured in Sheffield. But if it proved impossible to dispose of such commodities, other goods—in particular, Lancashire cottons—did find a ready market, adding to the general unrest in the country by putting many local industries out of business. It was true that the value of Chinese exports was now rapidly increasing, that in 1844 over seventy million pounds of tea was being exported from Canton and Shanghai, that in the seven years between 1843 and 1850 silk exports increased by over a thousand per cent; but so long as there were over five hundred ships selling opium in Canton alone, there was no possibility of the balance of trade turning in favour of the Chinese.

The economic problems of China in the years following the war were aggravated by a series of natural disasters that brought widespread flooding and famine. The Yellow River, the bane of poor Howqua's life at Canton, broke its dykes three times between 1841 and 1843, inundating tens of thousands of acres and killing millions of people. The Lower Yangtze also broke its banks in 1849 and caused the worst floods that had been experienced in the area for a hundred years. By then other provinces had been devastated by storm and drought, epidemic and pest. Moreover the population of the country, which had risen to about 350 million in the past century, was growing far faster than were the cultivated areas of the country.

Nor was it only the poorer classes who were becoming more and more discontented. The decrease in the land tax—the Government's main source of income—caused by the flooding of the Yellow River and the Yangtze, had led to new sources of revenue being devised, the substitution of heavy fines for other forms of punishment and the sale of civil offices, the one device increasing the numbers of criminals left at large to prey upon the community, the other arousing the hostility of the official classes and scholars who feared for the loss of their ancient privileges.[2]

To the growing animosity of the Chinese towards the Manchu dynasty was added the deep sense of humiliation occasioned by the recent war, the defeat of China by a small force of foreign troops. 'The British War with China of 1841-42 was most injurious to the peace of the country,' wrote Thomas Taylor Meadows, an interpreter long resident in China and a recognized expert on its affairs, 'because the power of the Government had for long depended greatly on prestige; because large districts had been brought to ruin; and because the calling out of bands of local militia had taught the people their power. It is well known that, previous to the war, the appearance of the insignia of a Mandarin, accompanied by a few lictors armed with whips, could disperse the most turbulent crowd in Canton, the most turbulent city in the Empire; and, by a long established rule, the people were denied the possession of firearms. But during the war arms were so generally distributed that loose characters of all kinds got possession of them, while at the same time respect for the Government had been destroyed by the manner in which its immense pretensions had been broken through by the despised Barbarians.'[3]

The atmosphere of the country was, in fact, ideally suited to the outbreak of rebellion. It was with difficulty, and at enormous expense, that the Government had crushed the various uprisings which had been so disturbing a feature of the last years of the Emperor Ch'ien-lung and of the reign of his son; but serious as these rebellions had been, they were to seem of little consequence when compared with the revolt that broke out in the first year of the reign of Tao-kuang's successor, Hsien-feng, the nineteen-year-old prince who was raised to the Dragon Throne on his father's death in February 1850. This was the revolt of the Taipings, fellow members, with the 'Younger Brother of Jesus Christ', of the Society of God Worshippers.

*   *   *

The Taipings owed their origins to Hung Hsiu-ch'uan, one of the five children of a Hakka farmer who lived in a village near Canton. The Hakkas ('guest settlers') had originally come from North China and had begun to form their own communities in the southern provinces of Kwangtung and Kwangsi as early as the fourth century; but they had remained isolated and aloof, retaining their own customs, speaking their own dialect, determinedly segregate, at odds with both their southern Chinese neighbours and the Manchu government.

Hung's father was a respected man in his own Hakka community and, though by no means prosperous, he had hopes that his bright young son would make his mark in the world beyond the fields of the village. When Hung was six years old his father paid for him to go to school to study the Confucian classics and, though his family had to make sacrifices to enable him to do so, he remained at school for eight years, thereafter studying on his own. Yet try as he would, he never succeeded in passing the examinations without which his father's ambition for him could never be achieved.

In 1837, while in Canton at the age of twenty-three, making one of his numerous attempts to pass the essential examinations, a stranger pushed a book into his hand as he was walking back from the examination hall to his lodgings. It was a pamphlet in Chinese issued by the Protestant mission in Canton and distributed in the streets by Liang A-fa, the first Chinese convert to Protestantism. Hung seems to have briefly glanced through it, paying little attention to its message; but he did not throw it away.

The next year, so bitterly disappointed at having failed the examinations yet again, he fell seriously ill and in his illness he had a strange vision: he saw himself in a vast palace where there appeared an old man, who handed him a sword telling him to use it to kill devils and to protect his brothers and sisters. There also appeared to him a younger man, known as 'Elder Brother', who went with him when he left the palace to fight the devils.

During the course of this vision Hung became delirious, jumping out of bed and throwing himself around the room as he struck the demons of his fevered imagination. On his recovery he was seen by his family to have undergone a strange transformation, to have become stronger in both body and spirit, with a more self-confident demeanour and a firmer, more imposing gait. He was described by a friend as 'a rather tall man, with oval face and fair complexion, his eyes large and bright, his look piercing and difficult to endure, his voice clear and sonorous—when laughing, the whole house resounded; his hair was black, his beard long and sandy, his strength of body extraordinary, his power of understanding exceptional'.[4]

He left home, became a teacher in a village school—a 'rather severe' teacher who 'kept his pupils in strict order'—and for the next few years, until 1843, nothing remarkable seems to have happened to him. But then a relative, going through his books one day when visiting him, was surprised to find the Christian pamphlet that had been pressed upon him in Canton. His own curiosity in it now aroused apparently for the first time, Hung read it with care; and immediately the meaning of his vision was made plain to him. The old man in the palace was God, the other man there, the 'Elder Brother', was Jesus Christ, he himself was the younger son of God and so the younger brother of Jesus Christ. By putting the sword into his hands, God, the Heavenly Father, had appointed him, Hung Hsiu-ch'uan, His lieutenant on earth with the duty of wiping out all His enemies. These enemies were represented by the idols of false religions; they were incarnate in the evil servants of the Manchu dynasty and in the person of the Manchu Emperor himself.[5]

Obsessed by this new faith, by his idiosyncratic version of Christian teaching, the now passionately dedicated Hung soon made converts amongst his own family and friends who joined him in founding a Society of God Worshippers. One of his friends, Feng Yün-shan, also a Hakka, took the message of the gospel into the troubled province of Kwangsi where another Society of God Worshippers was formed. By the summer of 1847 this branch of the Society had more than three thousand members, all of them devoted to the worship of the Heavenly Father and, therefore, denying the traditional Chinese belief that no one but the Emperor could offer sacrifice to Heaven.

Gradually the Society's beliefs were given a more formal basis by the various theological writings of its founder, by a set of Ten

Commandments similar to those issued on Mount Sinai, by a list of prayers to be said and rituals to be observed on appropriate occasions, and by anathemas promulgated against idols which both Hung Hsiu-ch'uan and Feng Yün-shan had been indefatigable in removing from shrines and temples.

Such iconoclastic behaviour, and the revolutionary doctrines propagated by his converts, brought down upon Feng the anger of a leading mandarin of Kwangsi who had him arrested and tried on a charge of creating public disorders and propounding false doctrines. With Feng in prison and Hung in Canton—where he had gone to seek instruction in the deeper mysteries of Christianity from an American missionary who, doubting his capacity to understand them, refused him the benefit of baptism—two less exalted members of the Society of God Worshippers kept its spirit alive by claiming to have been selected by God and Jesus as their earthly spokesmen. These men, Yang Hsiu-ch'ing and Hsiao Ch'ao-kuei, both charcoal-burners, were recognized as worthy of taking their place in the Society as, next to Hung, its most revered prophets.

In 1851 their importance in the hierarchy was confirmed by their elevation to the rank of Kings, Yang Hsiu-ch'ing being known as the Eastern King, Hsiao Ch'ao-kuei as the Western King. Hung himself was proclaimed the Heavenly King, and his friend Feng, who had done so much proselytizing for the Society of God Worshippers in its early days in Kwangsi, was given the title of the Southern King. There were two other Kings, Wei Ch'ang-hui, the King of the North, and Shih Ta-k'ai, the Assistant King.

These last two, Wei Ch'ang-hui and Shih Ta-k'ai, had both come from prosperous families, the movement having by now attracted a far wider variety of converts than the Hakka peasants, the disgruntled members of other non-Chinese tribes, the poor miners and charcoal burners who had formed its original nucleus. There were landlords and businessmen in it, pawnshop owners and scholars, farmers driven to banditry by rising rents and official corruption, as well as pirates whose ships had been sunk by British warships, Cantonese coolies put out of work by the Opium War, deserters from an increasingly corrupt and demoralized army, beggars, bandits, loafers and former members of various anti-Manchu secret societies like the White Lotus sect and the Triad or Heaven and Earth Society.

It was this growing anti-Manchu nationalist element in the movement, combined with its demands for a complete overthrow of the traditional order prompted by its pseudo-Christian origins, that led to its ambitious declaration of war on the Government, its occupation in the name of God of the mountain town of Yungan, and its proclamation of a new dynasty. Yungan means perpetual peace, so it seemed appropriate to give the new dynasty the name of *T'ai-p'ing t'ien-kuo*, the 'Heavenly Kingdom of Great Peace', a name deemed additionally appropriate since *T'ai-p'ing* was a very ancient expression for a period of happiness and plenty. *T'ai-p'ing* also contains a suggestion of equality, the idea of the equality of all people being one of the movement's fundamental tenets.[6] It was here at Yungan that it was first publicly announced that Hung Hsiu-ch'uan, chosen by God to be the leader of the Taipings, was henceforward to be known as the Heavenly King. 'Our Heavenly King has received the Divine Commission to exterminate the Manchus,' a proclamation announced, 'to exterminate all idolaters generally, and to possess the Empire as its True Sovereign. The Empire and everything in it is his, its mountains and rivers, its broad lands and public treasuries. . . . We command the services of all and we take everything. All who resist us are rebels and idolatrous demons, and we kill them without sparing; but whoever acknowledges our Heavenly King and exerts himself in our service shall have full reward.'[7]

From Yungan the Taipings, now over ten thousand strong, marched into Kwangsi province and then into Hunan. In December 1852 they crossed the Tungt'ing lake, captured Yochow and with a huge fleet of boats supplied by watermen who joined the rebel army, they sailed up the Yangtze to Hanyang which they occupied on the 23rd, and then on to Hankow which fell on the 29th. By this time their numbers had increased more than tenfold, and with this great force they set about besieging Wuchang, the provincial capital of Hupei.

Both Feng Yün-shan, the Southern King, and the Western King,

Hsiao Ch'ao-kuei, the former charcoal-burner, who in every engagement 'had shown himself regardless of personal safety, always fighting in the foremost ranks', had been killed in the earlier operations; but the other charcoal-burner, the Eastern King, Yang Hsiu-ch'ing, had proved himself a military leader of remarkable accomplishment. 'A man of thirty-five,' in the description of a French traveller, 'he is short and pitted with the smallpox, and his scanty moustache stands bristling on his upper lip. He speaks with remarkable facility, and is very accessible to all his subordinates.'[8]

Under command of this tough and resourceful commander, and with the help of the miners who had joined the rebels in the early days of the Society of God Worshippers, the Taipings succeeded in digging a tunnel towards one of the gates of Wuchang, exploding a mine beneath it, and pouring into the town through the breach. An army that had come up to its relief was routed; and the road to Peking lay open.

Many of the rebels wanted to move on to the capital immediately. The young Emperor, Hsien-feng, and his Court had been portrayed in Taiping propaganda as monsters of the most heinous kind, responsible for most if not all the social ills of China, sexual predators and voyeurs of horrid depravity. 'The Manchu demons collect all our pretty girls to be their slaves and concubines,' the rebels had been told. 'Three thousand girls, with powder and pencilled eyebrows, are defiled by dogs! A million rouged faces share pillows with lustful foxes! . . . Whenever there is flood or drought, the Manchus just sit and watch us starve, without the slightest compunction. . . . If we investigate the origins of these Manchu Tartars, we find their ancestor was born from the copulation of a white fox with a red bitch, a union bound to produce a monster!'[9]

The Manchus were, indeed, 'no better than swine or dogs', and the worst of them all was 'that Tartar dog, Hsien-feng'. Anyone who succeeded in cutting off his head was promised a lavish reward. But although there was strong feeling in the rebel army that the time was ripe to kill him and all the other Manchu dogs, although preparations were made by the Court to flee from Peking to Jehol, the Taiping leaders decided to move no further north at the moment.

They turned south instead to the rich, fertile lands of the Lower Yangtze Valley. With a greatly increased army of both men and women, they captured Nanking, the 'Southern Capital', with the same expert ease as they had taken Wuchang, slaughtering its entire Tartar garrison and their families—some 25,000 people in all—and renaming it the 'Heavenly Capital'.

Even more than the British expeditionary force during the Opium War, the Taiping rebels had shown how weak was the Manchu dynasty, how ill-organized and unruly its plundering soldiers. As the Governor of the province of Kwangsi had sadly admitted to the Governor of Hupei, 'Our troops have not a vestige of discipline; retreating is easy to them, advancing difficult; and, though repeatedly exhorted, they always remain as weak and timorous as before. When personally in command I found that the troops—and they were from several different parts of the country—were all equally useless. . . . As for these rebels, they have leaders skilled in the use of troops and they cannot by any means be likened to a disorderly crowd, their regulations and laws being rigorous and clear.'[10]

It was certainly true that the Taiping army was subjected to the most rigid discipline. Troops who retreated in battle or who threatened to desert were immediately killed by their officers. No contact of any sort was allowed on pain of death between the men and the units of women soldiers who accompanied them on their campaigns; no opium, alcohol or tobacco were allowed in the camp. The army was also so well led that the strategy of its commanders, as many other aspects of the movement, was later both studied and emulated by the Communists.

The discipline of the army, its abstinence and the revolutionary ideals that inspired it, were now applied to all those people who fell under the rule of the kind of communistic and theocratic state which the Taipings established. Opium, alcohol and tobacco remained proscribed; so did the shaving of the front part of the head and the wearing of pigtails which the Manchus had introduced into China. Prostitution was outlawed; rape was punished by death; the binding of the feet was forbidden; women were treated as the equals of men, allowed to hold civil appointments and to share in the grants of land which it was intended should be distributed in amounts varying with its quality. And since the Taipings' version of Christianity, though it borrowed a good deal from Confucianism, Taoism and Buddhism, was essentially monotheistic, pictures and idols of Buddha, statues, temples, even Confucian ancestor tablets were rigorously destroyed.[11]

*   *   *

The Christian basis of the movement and the declared belief of its leaders that, as all the peoples of the world were equal, the Chinese were superior to none of them, strongly recommended themselves to the West. And once the rule of the Taipings seemed to have been firmly established at Nanking—with a treasury reputed to contain six times as many taels as the Imperial treasury at Peking[12]—diplomatic and trading missions began to arrive there in the hope of establishing friendly relations with a movement which one day soon might overthrow the Manchu dynasty.

The first mission to arrive was British. It was led by Sir George Bonham, the Governor of Hong Kong, who, accompanied by Thomas Taylor Meadows as his interpreter, arrived at Nanking aboard the steamer *Hermes* at the end of April 1853. On the way Bonham had been given encouragement by a Taiping leader at Chen-chiang who assured him that the 'Taipings would be friendly to the foreigners and would not interfere with commercial relations'. It came as something of a disappointment, therefore, when, on arrival at Nanking, the members of a delegation sent ashore to arrange a meeting between Bonham and the authorities were immediately required by the soldiers who conducted them to the Northern King's house to kneel down before two persons standing on the threshold in yellow silk gowns and hoods. On refusing thus to demean themselves, the British delegates were reluctantly admitted to the house where they were subjected to a lecture by the Northern King, the former businessman, Wei Ch'ang-hui, on the inferiority of all foreign governments to the government of the Taipings. The ruler of the Taipings was the 'True Lord of China'; and the Lord of China, Wei reminded the British delegation, 'is the Lord of the whole world;

he is the second son of God and all people in the whole world must obey and follow him'.

When the interview was turned to the subject of religion, the imperious manner of the Northern King became rather more indulgent. 'He stated that as children and worshippers of one God we were all brethren,' the interpreter, Thomas Taylor Meadows, recorded; 'and after receiving my assurance that such had long been our view, also, inquired if I knew the "Heavenly Rules". I replied that I was most likely acquainted with them, though unable to recognize them under that name; and, after a moment's thought, asked if they were ten in number. He answered eagerly in the affirmative. I then began repeating the substance of the first of the Ten Commandments, but had not proceeded far before he laid his hand on my shoulder in a friendly way, and exclaimed, "The same as ourselves! The same as ourselves!"'[13]

So the first official contact between the Taipings and a Western government, though seeming so very unpromising at the outset, ended amicably enough. Sir George Bonham did not manage to gain an interview with Hung Hsiu-ch'uan, the Heavenly King and Lord of the whole world, but he did succeed in bringing back from Nanking a signed undertaking that foreigners could come into Taiping territory and trade freely there—except, of course, in opium. He expressed it as his opinion that 'more political and commercial advantages [were] likely to be obtained from the insurrectionists, than . . . from the Imperialists'.[14]

Concerned that the British should not obtain any special privileges, the French now decided to send a delegation of their own. Their Jesuit missionaries had already had dealings with the new rulers of Nanking and had cause for strong complaint, since the Taipings did not choose to extend their brotherly affection towards the foreign Protestants to Roman Catholics. Services held in Nanking by the Jesuits for their converts during Holy Week of 1853 had been interrupted by militant Taipings who forbade the congregation to pray on their knees and ordered them to sit down and recite the new prayers for the Heavenly King.

'The Christians replied that they were Catholics and knew no other religion,' wrote one of the French Jesuits, 'whereupon they were told that unless they complied with the instructions within three days, they would all be decapitated.' On Good Friday when the Catholic converts had gathered in their chapel for the adoration of the Cross, suddenly the Taipings came rushing in again, 'shouting and threatening. They broke the crucifix, overturned the altar and insisted on having their own prayer recited'.[15]

By December, however, resentment against the Catholics had cooled, and the French diplomatic representatives were welcomed courteously by the Taiping leaders who stood up to greet them. The meeting was conducted with an 'air of dignity and grandeur', said the priest, Father Clavelin, who acted as the mission's secretary. The blue and richly embroidered robes of the Taiping Ministers deputed to receive them, their fine red laced boots, 'the diadems of chiselled gold on their foreheads, their grave and dignified bearing and a numerous retinue forming the background behind them', all contributed to this grand and dignified atmosphere. 'One of them, speaking for some five or six minutes gave us a short summary of their doctrine,' Father Clavelin continued, 'and did so with incomparable calm, assurance, and dignity. . . . Upon our insisting that we had come with no hostile intent, but rather as friends, the Minister replied at once: "Since you worship the same God as ours and we all have but one Creator, you are not only friends, but brothers as well."'

Father Clavelin had not been favourably impressed by his first sight of Nanking. Many of its houses had been burned by their previous owners, who chose to commit suicide rather than submit to the Taipings; most of the rest looked decrepit; and not a single shop was open. But the people seemed to be well dressed, 'woollen cloth, silk and even satin being quite common', and if it had to be admitted that they crowded round the foreigners with much curiosity, they 'did not display any sign of hostility'. In fact, it could not be denied that the title 'brother' with which the rebels addressed each other was 'to a large extent justified'. A 'sort of family atmosphere' prevailed among them.[16]

The Americans who next came into Taiping territory, on a mis-

sion similar to those of the British and the French, were also agree-
ably struck by the 'most cordial feeling' displayed towards foreigners
by the Chinese people under Taiping rule. 'Few, if any, of the
people had ever seen a foreigner or a foreign vessel before, and their
curiosity and wonder were very great,' they told Thomas Taylor
Meadows after a visit to Wuhu, seventy miles south of Nanking, in
April 1854. 'The greatest deference was shown to those who went
ashore. In several instances respectable men even fell on their knees
in the street before the foreigners and their guides, to testify their
respect.'[17]

'All the people we saw were well-clad, well-fed, and well provided for in every way,' Elijah Bridgman, who accompanied the
American Minister, decided. 'They all seemed content, and in high
spirits, as if sure of success.'[18]

Certainly at this time the eventual success of their cause seemed
assured. An expedition towards Peking under the leadership of the
Eastern King, Yang Hsiu-ch'ing, who had already displayed his
formidable military skill, had been frustrated by the onset of a bitter
winter and by lack of seasoned troops; but a simultaneous campaign
against the cities of Central China had been notably successful, and
the continuing war against the Manchu forces in Kiangsi and Hunan
gave hope of even greater triumphs. There had been a serious set-
back when government forces, trained in both military virtues and
Confucian ethics by the redoubtable scholar-official, Tseng Kuo-fan,
retook the two important cities of Wuchang and Hanyang, a set-
back that resulted in orders being given by the Lord of the whole
world for the decapitation of his defeated generals. But at the port of
Kiukiang, Tseng Kuo-fan's counter-offensive was blocked by the
Assistant King, Shih Ta-k'ai, whose generalship was scarcely less
remarkable than that of the Eastern King.[19]

At the beginning of 1855, Shih Ta'kai managed to regain the
ground that had been lost, extending Taiping control over the whole
of the fertile Lower Yangtze Valley.

But by this time relations between the various Kings, once so
harmonious, were approaching breaking-point. Their leader had
virtually severed all connection with the outside world of war,

revolution and reform. Although the most rigorous controls were imposed, in peace as in war, upon the sexual activities of the people under his rule, he permitted himself the solace of numerous concubines with whom he lived in a vast palace of exotic splendour. The many apartments of this palace, roofed in tiles of green, gold and scarlet, had been built by thousands of workmen on the site of the demolished palace of the Manchu Governor-General, and were surrounded by a long yellow wall, crowned by minarets. On rare occasions, in a palanquin borne by sixty-four attendants, the Heavenly King would come out through one of the gates of the palace into the streets of Nanking, and then, as when any of the other Kings passed through the streets, the ordinary passers-by were required to kneel on pain of immediate decapitation. But most of the time Hung remained within its walls, abandoning himself to the pleasures of his harem, his garden, his pavilions, his religious pronouncements and the embellishment of his legend.

The legend scarcely needed embellishment for, after all, he alone of all people on the earth had been in heaven and had seen God and Jesus Christ; he alone knew from personal experience that God was a benign figure with a golden beard, clothed in a black robe decorated with a dragon design, that He wore a high, brimmed hat and sat on a throne surrounded by His family and court. God had spoken to him and only to him of His problems, of Buddhism and Taoism, the false teachings of the Devil, of Confucius who had had to be given a beating in heaven for misleading the people, and of the demons who continued to inhabit the world despite the flood and the earthly death of His elder son, Jesus. Only he had first-hand knowledge that both God and Jesus had wives—and Jesus's wife had been particularly kind to Hung when her brother-in-law had failed to learn his biblical lessons.

Most of these facts had always been known by the faithful, but now it appeared that Hung had been born out of the belly of God's first wife before heaven and earth existed. He had, therefore, witnessed the creation, had known Abraham, and had seen Jesus descend to earth to be born of a woman as he himself had had to descend to be born of a woman when his turn had come to rule the earth as his father's chosen envoy.[20]

While Hung became more extravagant in his claims, so did Yang Hsiu-ch'ing, the Eastern King, whose gifts of speaking with the tongue of God had first led to his elevation in the Taiping hierarchy. Although he had not actually lived in heaven like Hung, his contact with it through the Holy Ghost gave him the unique ability to communicate the commands of God the Father to the people of the earth. One of these commands, issuing from the Holy Ghost towards the end of 1853, was to the effect that Hung, who had impatiently kicked one of his concubines, was to be punished with forty strokes of the bamboo rod. On Hung's humbly agreeing to submit to this punishment decreed by the divine will, Yang received a further message which permitted a remission of the sentence.

Thus Yang demonstrated his power, and it now became known in Nanking how deep was the rift between the Heavenly King, whose face was so rarely seen beyond the walls of his palace, and his arrogant lieutenant, the Eastern King whose numerous household, staff, attendants and subordinate officers were now the virtual rulers of the Taiping empire. It was also becoming known that there was a strong difference of opinion and mutual dislike between the Eastern King and his colleague, Shih Ta-k'ai, the Assistant King, who did not enjoy the same power; and that Wei Ch'ang-hui, the Northern King, was burning with resentment against both of them. Towards the end of 1856 the jealousies and animosities erupted into violence.

Enraged by Yang, who now claimed to have received a message from the Holy Ghost that he should be raised to the same status as the Heavenly King, Hung sent for Wei Ch'ang-hui and Shih Ta-k'ai both of whom were away from Nanking campaigning with the armies. They were ordered to return to the capital at once. Wei Ch'ang-hui arrived first, and immediately celebrated his return by invading Yang's palace with a squad of his soldiers and killing his rival together with all the numerous members of his household. He then announced that so ashamed was he of his terrible conduct that he would submit to a public scourging in the grounds of the palace of the Heavenly King; all his victim's supporters would be welcome there to witness the punishment. On the day appointed the supporters arrived at the palace gate and, on handing over whatever weapons they happened to have brought with them, were admitted inside. When they had all collected in the enclosed space prepared for the scourging, Wei's soldiers sprang out at them and cut them all to the ground. Later, the rest of Yang's known supporters were all arrested in their homes, and they too were killed.

When Shih Ta-k'ai, the Assistant King, arrived from Wuhan in response to the Heavenly King's summons, he learned that more than twenty thousand people had been slaughtered by the Northern King who was now issuing orders as arrogant and ruthless as any that had formerly come from the palace of the murdered Yang. Shih Ta-k'ai publicly protested; and was instantly warned that any further protest would result in his own murder. Escaping by night by climbing a rope over the city wall, he rejoined his army and marched back to Nanking with forty thousand men, demanding that Wei must be punished for his crimes which by then included the murder of Shih's wife and family.

Before he reached Nanking the punishment had already taken place. Wei and two hundred of his men had been murdered, and Hung was once more in control of his Heavenly Capital. Concerned that he should not lose it to Shih, now greeted by the people as a hero, he promoted two of his incompetent elder brothers to the vacant kingships. Disgusted by the new Kings' meddling in affairs with which they were wholly ill-equipped to deal, Shih left Nanking for his army once more, disillusioned and embittered, mortified by the intrigues and jealousies that were sapping the vitality of the Taiping revolution to which he had dedicated his life.[21]

* * *

The Western powers, too, were becoming disillusioned with the Taipings. Three years before, it had seemed likely that the Manchus would soon be overthrown. In July 1853 the American missionary, Charles Taylor, had noted in his journal, 'The whole Empire is in a ferment of excitement. Disaffection to the existing government is spreading rapidly, and signs of it are manifest in the open resistance to the oppressive demands of the Mandarins in every direction. . . . The feeling is becoming universally prevalent among the people of all classes, that the Empire is destined soon to change hands.'[22]

It had appeared at that time that the Emperor had shared that feeling himself. The *Peking Gazette* published numerous of his almost abject supplications to heaven in which he undertook 'to pray fervently' for the peace of his subjects who were suffering such great calamities, and in which he 'bitterly reproached' his officers for not preventing them. He promised that any rebel who killed his leader would not only be pardoned but also be rewarded with many favours.

'Filled with dread and apprehension,' one such supplication ran, 'I humbly entreat Heaven to pardon my offences and to spare my unhappy people. May all the officers of the Court and the provinces awaken to better feelings in their hearts, and devise ways and means to ward off the calamities which are now afflicting the people. . . . I have frequently reproached myself, and I have prayed to Heaven to forgive my sins, to save my people and not to let them suffer any more on my account. May all future calamities fall upon my head alone!'[23]

By the time news of the wholesale murders in the Heavenly Capital reached Peking, Hsien-feng had regained his nerve; and the foreigners in China, dismayed by what Charles Taylor called the 'wild fanaticism' of the rebels, had begun to doubt the desirability of a change of dynasty, and to welcome reports which indicated that not only was the revolution being contained, but that in many rural areas the people were rising against their Taiping rulers.

In Chekiang province bands of counter-revolutionaries were training in the hills, and near Ningpo one of these bands had ambushed and put to flight a Taiping force, killing or wounding three hundred rebel soldiers. The Taipings soon returned and vengeance 'was savagely complete', in the words of the English missionary, A. E. Moule. 'A town of ten thousand people was burnt down, and the whole of the long, lovely valley, twelve miles in extent, was blasted by fire and the precious trees were cut down. . . . I have myself seen ponds and pools which had been filled not long before with the bodies of women and girls who had drowned themselves to escape from T'ai P'ing hands.'[24]

Protestant missionaries like Moule and Catholic priests such as Father Clavelin—who, on asking how the Taipings treated people who refused to pray with them, was told, 'people who refuse to pray or to renounce idols are put to death'—now alike condemned the violence of the Taipings who were said not merely to destroy all the buildings of Manchu construction in any town they captured, but also on occasions to massacre the entire population of towns that offered them resistance. As Frederick Bruce, the first British Minister in Peking, was later to say, there was little hope now of 'any good ever coming of the rebel movement. They do nothing but burn, murder and destroy.'[25]

At the same time, the foreign merchants anxiously awaited the day when trading conditions could return to normal. It was true that opium was the only commodity placed under a complete embargo; it was true, also, that exports of both tea and silk from the provinces controlled by the Taipings were actually increasing. But trade was completely disrupted in the areas where fighting was still taking place; and who could be certain that the Taipings' social and economic policies might not eventually deprive the merchants of their livelihood altogether?

There was, therefore, a growing demand for foreign intervention against the Taipings on behalf of the Manchu Government. This had always been a possibility, the argument being that if Britain and France came to the help of the Emperor, they would be in a position to demand trading privileges far more favourable than those theoretically granted by the Treaty of Nanking. Sir George Bonham, when on his way to make contact with the Taiping leaders in 1853, had been strongly urged by the British Consul in Shanghai to suggest to London that the British Army should put down the revolt in the Emperor's name. As it happened, after investigating conditions in Nanking and the surrounding rebel-held territories, Bonham had recommended that Britain should maintain a policy of neutrality. And the British Government, about to invade the Crimea, could, in any case, scarcely have been expected to mount an expedition to China as well. But now the Crimean War was over, and demands for British intervention were being made again.

These demands were being considered when news reached London that there had been an incident at Canton of which the repercussions seemed likely to make the Taiping revolution of relatively small concern.

13 | The *Arrow* Affair

The gate of China is Canton, and unless we can subdue the resistance and force an entrance there, I believe the difficulties of obtaining any improved position in China will be almost invincible. Sir John Bowring, Governor of Hong Kong, January 1857.

The hopes entertained by the foreign merchants in Canton that the series of treaties signed at the end of the Opium War would make life much easier for them had soon been disappointed. The Chinese had shown themselves no more prepared to regard foreigners as equals than they had ever done. The treaties were represented as a means of keeping them more strictly in order, or as a demonstration of the Empire's great compassion towards strangers from afar who were, after all, ignorant Barbarians without understanding of the ways of the civilized world.

The transformation of Hong Kong from a charming island of a few scattered fishing villages to a rough-and-tumble trading centre, crowded with Foreign Devils and the riff-raff that they always collected around them, seemed to the Chinese a timely warning of what might happen if the Barbarians were granted any further concessions. By the British Governor's count, there were eighty thousand Chinese living on the small island by the end of 1856. Though some were honest fishermen and boatmen, tradesmen and shopkeepers, though others were trusted servants in the residences of the Governor, the Bishop, the Attorney-General and the houses of all the other colonial officials and merchants who had established themselves there, thousands more were smugglers and opium dealers, trouble-makers and criminals, active members of anti-

Manchu secret societies and Taiping rebels. It was not surprising
that the Europeans and Americans felt exposed to violence there;
that, as the Bishop of Victoria was later to say, they felt 'exposed,
not merely to the ordinary danger of a foreign residence, but to the
cup of the poisoner, the knife of the assassin and the torch of the
midnight incendiary'.[1]

Nor was it only at Hong Kong that the foreigners felt exposed to
these dangers. At the other Treaty Ports, though rarely seriously
molested, they were jostled in the streets and sometimes spat upon;
at Canton, where the right of foreign residence was still denied
despite the Treaty of Nanking, anti-foreign riots were common,
while anti-foreign pamphlets were distributed openly and displayed
upon the walls. The Americans here were particularly liable to
assault, since the weather vane on top of the flagstaff outside their
factory was supposed to have been the cause of more than one outbreak of sickness amongst the Chinese population. In May 1844
there were serious anti-American riots during which a manifesto
was distributed in the streets warning that 'You men of America
may truly dread local extermination'.[2]

Most Cantonese manifestoes, however, were directed against the
detested English: 'We note that you English Barbarians have formed
the habits and developed the nature of wolves, plundering and
seizing things by force. . . . Except for your ships being solid, your
gunfire fierce, and your rockets powerful, what other abilities have
you got? . . . Our hatred is already at white heat. If we do not completely exterminate you pigs and dogs, we will not be manly Chinese
able to support the sky on our heads and stand firmly on the earth.
. . . We are definitely going to kill you, cut your heads off and burn
you to death! We must strip off your skins and eat your flesh, and
then you will know how tough we are. . . . We ought really to use
refined expressions. But since you beasts do not understand written
characters, therefore we use rough, vulgar words to instruct you in
simple terms.'[3]

The Chinese authorities claimed that this violently hostile attitude
of the Cantonese towards the English would alone make it quite impossible for them to allow the foreign merchants to live inside the

walls, even if the Chinese version of the Treaty of Nanking had been capable of the interpretation which the English had put upon their own version. So, despite repeated requests and complaints by succeeding Superintendents of Trade, the merchants were still in 1856 cooped up in the confined area of the waterfront factories, still treated as though the Opium War had never been fought.

The man responsible to the Emperor for keeping the foreigners in their place at this time was Yeh Ming-ch'en. He was Imperial Commissioner at Canton, Viceroy of Kwangtung and Kwangsi, a strong, fat, ugly, intelligent, ill-tempered man with a detestation of foreigners that was almost obsessional. He had demonstrated both his bravery and his cruelty in campaigns against the Taiping rebels, whom he had decapitated in their thousands immediately upon capture. He had proved his cunning and resource in continually refusing to accede to the English demands, regretting that his duties kept him away from his *yamen* on the days suggested for interviews, and refusing to commit himself to an alternative appointment until his astrologer had assured him that the day was auspicious. He pretended to understand that when, in 1849, the Superintendent of Trade—in obedience to the known wishes of the British Government who did not want to go to war over entry into Canton—had written to him to say that the matter of entry rested 'where it was, and must remain in abeyance', what was meant then, and what was still meant now, was that the British were no longer interested in gaining entry at all.[4]

It was, in fact, the universal belief of the foreigners in Canton that Yeh was more of a nuisance than even Commissioner Lin had ever been. They could not but agree with Dr Peter Parker, the American representative in China, whose opinion was that 'in his insane and insufferable conduct towards foreigners' Yeh stood 'alone and pre-eminent'.[5] They also concurred with the opinion of the Governor of Hong Kong who later decided that he was the 'incarnation of ancient Chinese pride, ignorance and unteachableness';[6] and they eagerly awaited the day when he would go so far in his 'insufferable conduct' that an excuse would be given for using force to humble him.

They awaited the day all the more eagerly because there were now in China representatives of foreign governments who were prepared to take the sort of strong line that the poor, lamented Lord Napier had tried to take. There was Dr Peter Parker, Yeh's untiring critic, a former missionary who advocated firm demands for a far greater freedom of trade than the present treaties would have permitted even if fully enforced. There was Monsieur de Bourboulon, the French representative, a small, resolute, peppery man dwarfed by his tall, thin Scottish wife who smoked huge black cigars and could speak three languages with equal facility and had plenty to say in all of them.[7] Above all, there were the two British officials, Harry Parkes, Acting Consul at Canton in the absence of Rutherford Alcock, and Sir John Bowring, Governor of Hong Kong, a post that was now incorporated with the Superintendency of Trade.

Parkes was not yet thirty, but he had lived in China for fifteen years. His mother had died when he was four; his father had been killed in a carriage accident when he was five; his uncle and guardian had died when he was nine. So in 1841 he had been sent out to live with his cousin, Mary, the second of the three English wives of Dr Gützlaff, a former schoolmistress and missionary who helped the boy to learn Chinese, which he had completely mastered before her death in 1849. Already by then he had accompanied Sir Henry Pottinger to Nanking as a very young personal assistant, and had subsequently served in the consulates at most of the ports which the Treaty of Nanking had opened to foreign merchants. During these years—and in particular during his time at Shanghai where the formidable Rutherford Alcock, who was then Consul there, had conducted interviews with the Chinese wearing full dress uniform complete with cocked hat and the several Spanish decorations awarded him when serving as an army surgeon in the Peninsula—Parkes had acquired the conviction that, in dealing with Chinese officials, it was essential never to underestimate the importance their training had taught them to attach to what appeared in Western eyes as trivial matters of detail and form. He had also become convinced that the only way to be certain of reaching a satisfactory settlement with them was to stand one's ground on every particular; to make a concession was to invite a counterproposal; to compromise was to fail.[8]

These views were completely endorsed by Parkes's superior, the Governor of Hong Kong, Sir John Bowring, a man over twice Parkes's age and one whose extraordinary and disarming ugliness contrasted with the young Consul's delicate good looks. Bowring had come to these views through a shorter experience of China. It was not until 1849 that he had arrived in Canton at the age of fifty-seven after a varied career that had taken him from a clerk's stool in Exeter to the editorial chair of the *Westminster Review*, and finally to a seat in the House of Commons. Here he had sat as radical member for Bolton until the depression of 1847 had dissipated his modest fortune, almost entirely invested in iron works in South Wales, and had made it necessary for him to seek more gainful employment.

Bowring had been a close friend of Jeremy Bentham whose collected works he had edited in eleven volumes, and of Richard Cobden with whom he had been a prominent member of the Anti-Corn Law League. He had travelled widely, was an outstanding linguist, had translated Russian, Polish, Spanish, Serbian, Hungarian and Danish poetry, was a Doctor of Laws in the University of Groningen, and had written a hymn. He was a man of high intelligence and no tact, impatient, imprudent and brave.

In the middle of October 1856, a report came to him from Harry Parkes that renewed his anger against the Imperial Commissioner whose tyrannous conduct in the past he had continually deplored. It appeared that on the eighth of the month, the police at Canton had boarded a sailing vessel, the *Arrow*, which was anchored opposite the factories, had pulled down the British ensign from the stern and arrested the entire crew. The ship was owned by a Chinese, but she had been registered in Hong Kong and had a British captain, so that the action of the police was undoubtedly illegal under the terms of the Treaty of the Bogue of 1843.

Bowring learned that Parkes had moved promptly, strongly protesting to the authorities who had blandly replied that they had acted under the suspicion that one of the members of the crew was the father of a pirate and that the others might be involved in the son's nefarious activities. Later Parkes had written to Yeh Ming-ch'en: 'I hasten therefore to lay the case before Your Excellency, confident that your superior judgement will lead you at once to admit that an insult so publicly committed must be equally publicly atoned. I therefore request Your Excellency that the men who have been carried away from the *Arrow* be returned.' They should be returned, Parkes added, in his presence and, if accused of any crime, they could then be conveyed to the British Consulate for examination by himself and by Chinese officials deputed by His Excellency.[9]

In response to this request Yeh had offered to return nine of the twelve men, but the other three were being held on charges of piracy. The *Arrow*, the Imperial Commissioner insisted, had been built in China and was owned by a Chinese; there was therefore no question of her being considered a foreign vessel.[10]

When Bowring read these documents he realized that the opportunity for which he had been waiting might well have come at last. Here now might be his chance to call up the Navy, to force an entry into Canton, and to establish by force the right of foreign residence there. He agreed with Parkes that even if the three men were, in fact, pirates the Chinese police had no right to arrest them; they should have asked the British authorities to do so on their behalf in accordance with the 1843 Treaty. He noticed that the British registration of the *Arrow* had expired, which theoretically weakened his case, but this did not alter the fact that she *had* been registered in Hong Kong and that her British captain had been flying the British flag. He approved of Parkes's action in refusing to accept the return of only nine of the crew: they must all be returned with an official apology, otherwise a police junk would be seized as a reprisal by a British gunboat.

'Cannot we use the opportunity and carry the city question?' he wrote to Parkes after Yeh's refusal to give way had led to the seizure of a junk—a junk, it was later discovered with some embarrassment, that did not belong to the police or indeed to the Chinese Government at all. 'If so I will come up with the whole fleet. I think we have now a stepping stone from which with good management we may move on to important sequences.'[11]

Five days later, on 21 October, Yeh was given an ultimatum. He replied, within an hour of its expiry, by returning all the members of the *Arrow*'s crew. But his failure either to admit that she was a British ship or to apologize was deemed sufficient grounds for instructions being given to Rear-Admiral Sir Michael Seymour to bring the Navy into action.

On 23 October the four Barrier Forts guarding the approaches to Canton five miles downstream from the city were bombarded and taken with four or five Chinese casualties; on the 27th the city wall and Yeh's *yamen* were shelled; on the 29th Admiral Seymour led a party of marines through a breach in the wall and forced his way into the *yamen* from which the Commissioner, protesting that he felt no sense of danger, had been taken away by his staff when the shelling began.

Accompanying the English marines was the United States Consul at Hong Kong, a former militia general named Kinnan who could not abide the thought of the British having all the glory. 'Mr Kinnan did still better than the others,' in the sardonic words of the Comte de Courcy, de Bourboulon's temporary successor. 'While his countrymen . . . ransacked with great haste the Viceroy's rooms and harem, he tried partially to rob the English of the honour of the victory by resolutely planting the flag of the United States on the breach. He forgot that his colleague Mr Perry, who himself was taking part in the looting, had proclaimed, at the beginning of hostilities, the neutrality of that flag. But, as the American merchants say, you must not be too angry with General Kinnan seeing that he was drunk.'[12]

*   *   *

For the next few weeks there were sporadic outbursts of fighting as the Royal Navy tightened its hold on the Pearl River by destroying forts, spiking guns, opening fire on concentrations of war junks and the sides of the breach in the city wall. The Chinese replied by sinking hulks across the channels, sending fire-rafts against the English ships and throwing aboard them 'stinkpots' of powdered sulphur which, when ignited, caused so poisonous a smell that the sailors jumped overboard to escape from the fumes.

In Canton, Commissioner Yeh issued a reward of thirty dollars—
later increased to 100 dollars—for every English head presented to
him, sent Admiral Seymour a letter instructing him to 'consider
maturely' his bounden duty to conform in his actions 'to the
principle given us by heaven', and published proclamations to the
Cantonese people assuring them that he had given voice to their
'unanimous expression of objection' to the English Barbarians'
demands. Repeatedly he announced to the people that he was determined not to grant the foreigners' requests, 'let them carry their
deceits and machinations to what length they will'.[13]

In response to his diatribes against the foreigner, a mob of
Cantonese with blazing torches rushed screaming into the factories
on 15 December and set them alight. A member of the English
Consul's staff was killed in the fire, but Harry Parkes himself had
sailed to see the Governor in Hong Kong a few days before.

Hong Kong was by now a more dangerous place than ever.
Scarcely a day passed without a foreigner being assaulted in the
street; and early in the New Year of 1857, the Governor and his
family, together with several other officials and their wives, nar-
rowly escaped death by poisoning when a Chinese baker put arsenic
in their bread—fortunately for them, far too much arsenic so that
instead of dying in agony they were all immediately sick.

Up till this time Bowring had been comforting himself with the
thought that Yeh would surely soon surrender, and while that hope
remained he did not want to ask for reinforcements. But now that
the Chinese had burned the factories and forced Admiral Seymour
to withdraw his ships from the anchorage there, now that Hong
Kong was becoming so dangerous, and that reports had come in of a
violent mutiny aboard a British steamer on its way there from
Macao—a mutiny during which several Europeans were decapitated
by Chinese sailors wearing the insignia of Commissioner Yeh's
militia—Bowring decided he must ask for help.

On 10 January he wrote to the Governor-General of India for five
thousand troops; and to the Foreign Secretary, Lord Clarendon, he
explained that he had been obliged to ask for them because, although everything that could be hoped for from the naval forces

had been accomplished, it was 'absolutely necessary' for the country's 'final triumph' to take the city of Canton. 'The gate of China is Canton,' he insisted, 'and unless we can subdue the resistance and force an entrance there, I believe the difficulties of obtaining any improved position in China will be almost invincible.'[14]

*　　*　　*

Seven weeks went by before Lord Clarendon received Bowring's letter, and by then he had already spoken in the House of Lords in a debate on Bowring's conduct of the *Arrow* incident.

Immediately on learning of this incident and of the action so far taken at Canton, Clarendon had consulted the Law Officers of the Crown whose verdict was that, although the *Arrow*'s Hong Kong registration had not been renewed by the date in question, the Chinese had still broken the 1843 Treaty. Bowring's seizure of a Chinese junk in reprisal had accordingly been approved.

The Government, led by Palmerston since February 1855, had been considering for a long time a demand for the strict observance of the treaties with China or their complete revision. 'The Time is fast coming,' Palmerston had recently written, 'when we shall be obliged to strike another Blow in China. . . . These half-civilized governments such as those in China, Portugal and Spanish America all require a Dressing every eight or Ten years to keep them in order. Their minds are too shallow to receive an Impression that will last longer than some such Period and warning is of little use. They care little for words and they must not only see the Stick but actually feel it on their Shoulders before they yield.'[15]

It seemed to Palmerston and his colleagues then, as it had seemed to Bowring, that the *Arrow* affair provided a good opportunity to deflate the pretensions of Commissioner Yeh and to gain entry into Canton. It had also seemed a good opportunity to obtain a new treaty which would permit, amongst other things, the appointment of a permanent representative in Peking as *The Times* had suggested in an editorial on 2 January and as Samuel Gregson, Member of Parliament for Lancaster, Chairman of the East India and China Association and one of the leading spokesmen for the politically

influential China merchants, had proposed in a letter to Clarendon
on 6 January.

Several members of the Government had had uneasy qualms
about the action taken. It had long been British policy not to become so deeply involved in China that the country's resources were
dangerously strained; to defend British interests, certainly, but not
to expand them by force. Apart from this, there had been the unpleasant thought, as the Attorney-General had expressed it in
Cabinet, that Bowring's conduct might have been 'somewhat more
high-handed than was absolutely necessary'. But then, it would
never have done to disown Bowring. To do so, as it was later to be
maintained in debate, would be disastrous for the dignity and safety
of the already hard-pressed officers of the consular service in the
East. And, in any case, even if they did disown him, what he had
done would still remain done. So it had been agreed that, although
the Opposition would certainly try to make capital out of their
decision, the Government would not deny Sir John Bowring their
full support.[15]

The Opposition, led by Lord Derby, rose to the challenge with all
the eagerness that the Government had feared. Lord Derby, indeed,
normally a far from zealous Member of the House of Lords, admitting that he was far too busy with his racehorses and his pheasants
to bother with politics, astonished everyone by his energy in organizing his supporters and allies for the attack. On 24 February he
aroused the House to cheers by his condemnation of Bowring's
'utmost arrogance', his 'most offensive assumptions of superiority',
contrasting his 'perfect monomania about getting into Canton' and
his 'menacing, disrespectful and arrogant' language with the 'fore-
bearing, courteous and gentlemanlike' language of the Chinese
officials. He hoped that their Lordships would not 'on any consideration give the sanction of their voice to the shedding of the
blood of unwarlike and innocent people without warrant of law and
without moral justification'.

This theme was hotly pursued by other Members of the Opposition. The aged Lord Lyndhurst, a former and highly respected
Lord Chancellor, declared that Bowring was 'one of the most

mischievous men' he had ever known, demanded to know how the *Arrow* could be a British ship when she was not owned by a British subject, and how a Chinese subject could have rights bestowed upon him against the wishes of the Chinese Government. To Lord Ellenborough, a former Governor-General of India, *Doctor* Bowring, as he disdainfully referred to him, was 'the eternal obstacle to peace'. Lord Malmesbury, once Foreign Secretary, read out with a mixture of pity and shame a letter from a midshipman which showed how right Lord Derby had been to stand as an advocate for the feeble defencelessness of China against the overpowering might of Great Britain: 'Dear Mother, don't trouble yourself about me, for I am no more in danger than if I were practising against an old tea-caddy.'

In the Commons, Richard Cobden took up the attack. He had been a friend of Bowring in the past, as he freely admitted, but this present attempt to impose free trade on China by force could never be condoned; nor could the Government's practice of pursuing one policy towards the strong and another towards the weak. As for Bowring's letter in which he asserted that, since Yeh did not know that the *Arrow*'s registration had lapsed this need not be taken into account, why that was the 'most flagitious public document' he had ever seen, an assertion he repeated on the last day of the debate. Lord John Russell, who as Prime Minister had dismissed Palmerston from the Foreign Office in 1851, agreed with Cobden, declaring in an impassioned speech that never would England stand higher in the world's estimation than when it could be said that although 'troublesome and meddlesome officials' had prostituted her arms, 'the House of Commons, representing her people, have indignantly declared that they will be no parties to such injustice'.

Disraeli was in quieter mood, poking gently at the Government's waywardness and quietly regretting that, as Sir John Bowring's categoric opinions were well known before he was appointed to his post, the Prime Minister had not hesitated before allowing him to occupy it. Gladstone, however, as he had been in the opium debate of 1840, was deeply and emotionally involved. Refraining from a personal attack on Bowring—whom his fellow Peelite, Sir James Graham, had characterized as being 'more remarkable for his self-confidence than for the soundness of his judgement'—Gladstone laid the blame squarely on a Government which could contemplate taking up arms in defence of a repugnant trade; for even though the *Arrow* may have been carrying nothing more than rice, it was an undoubted fact that most vessels of her kind were used in the smuggling of opium. In any case, even if it were morally justified, the war had no purpose since the *Arrow* incident had already been closed by Yeh's concessions, and the right of entry into Canton would bring more harm than good. British power, Gladstone concluded, could never be well founded on injustice; and it was the duty of the House of Commons, 'the most ancient and the noblest temple of freedom in the world', to show that it was also 'the temple of that everlasting justice without which freedom itself would be only a name or only a curse to mankind'.

There was no doubt that both in the House of Commons and in the House of Lords the opponents of Palmerston's China policy had the best of the debate. Admittedly, Lord Clarendon was right when he said that the Chinese had shown little inclination to observe the terms of the Treaties signed after the late war; and the Opposition were quite mistaken when they contended, as Cobden did, that the Chinese authorities in every part of the Empire to which the British had access manifested 'the most consistent and earnest desire to carry out the provisions of the Treaties'. It was true, too, that, as Lord Clarendon said, Bowring could not have been expected to wait for instructions to arrive from London before taking action, and that to condemn him now might endanger the dignity and safety of the British residents in China. It was also true, as Lord Palmerston maintained, that the Chinese version of events was inconsistent, that they had at first said they wanted a member of the crew who was the father of a pirate, but later that the pirate himself had been recognized on board by his red turban and a missing front tooth. 'A man who could distinguish in rapidly passing another vessel in a river whether one man of the crew had or had not lost a front tooth,' Palmerston commented, 'would be a valuable addition' to one of the country's sharp-shooting regiments. And it was probably true, as Lord Granville claimed, that if Bowring had not reacted as strongly as he had done to Yeh's provocation, he might have been condemned as hotly for being a Manchester radical careless of his country's honour as he was now being condemned for behaving like a firebrand.

But none of the Government's apologists could gloss over the central weakness of their case: to make an attack on Canton in reaction to an incident which had nothing whatever to do with British claims to right of entry to the city could not possibly be justified. Undeterred by this weakness and uninfluenced by the rhetoric of Lord Derby—who contrived to crowd into his speech, as *The Times* disdainfully put it, more compliments to the Chinese than they had received 'since the days of the French philosophers'—a majority of the House of Lords, including thirteen of the bishops, voted in the Government's favour.

The House of Commons, however, were more impressed by the Opposition's reasoned arguments than by Lord Palmerston's jokes and the Attorney-General's laboured presentation of the Government's legal position. The House divided early in the morning of 4 March. The Government were defeated.[16]

The Queen was appalled. As soon as she heard the result she wrote to the Prime Minister: 'Though prepared for an unfavourable result, the Queen is not the less grieved at the success of evil party motives, spite and a total absence of patriotism. The Queen would be glad if Lord Palmerston would let her know by telegraph at what hour she may expect him this afternoon, in order that she may be at home at the right time.'[17]

Lord Palmerston arrived at Windsor at six o'clock. He was 'looking ill and suffering from a return of the gout,' the Queen noted in her journal, 'but was in excellent pluck.' He told her that the Cabinet had unanimously decided not to resign but to advise a dissolution of Parliament and an appeal to the country. The Queen was deeply relieved. She was in the last weeks of a new pregnancy—her last child, Princess Beatrice, was born the following month—and she was not feeling well herself. As Prince Albert had warned the Cabinet, she was not up to the strain and worry of helping to form a new ministry; moreover, she agreed with Lord Palmerston that the 'country had more confidence in this Government than any other that could be formed', and that the Opposition had displayed the most 'wretched cant and humbug in the debates'.[18]

The Queen was quite right about the feeling in the country. The electorate cared little for the niceties of the matter; they agreed with old Admiral Sir Charles Napier who had bluntly exclaimed in the Commons that he did not know why there was all this fuss about Bowring demanding an apology: 'Good God! There was nothing extraordinary in that. If a man knocked another's hat off and then knocked him down, surely an apology would be required.' The electorate were also quite prepared to accept Palmerston's assessment of Yeh as 'one of the most savage barbarians that ever disgraced a nation', guilty of every crime which could 'degrade and debase human nature'. He and his kind were 'a set of kidnapping, murdering poisoning barbarians', whose characters seemed all the more monstrous when contrasted with the 'amiable qualities' and 'mild disposition' of Sir John Bowring. The country also fully shared Palmerston's indignation that 'an insolent barbarian wielding authority at Canton has violated the British flag, broken the engagements of treaties, offered rewards for the heads of British subjects . . . and planned their distruction by murder, assassination and poisons'.[19]

Most of the newspapers, including *The Times*, supported the voters in these beliefs, as did most of those who did not have the vote but attended election meetings to shout 'What about China?' when the candidates were speaking about some other issue involved in the election.

The Queen was delighted, when the first results began to come in, that the elections appeared to be 'going on so famously'; that Cobden and his friends should have been turned out was 'excellent' news, and 'very striking'. She retired to bed on 2 April happy in the knowledge that the Government had greatly increased its majority, gratified by Lord Palmerston's congratulations that, although Gladstone had been returned unopposed for Oxford University, she had managed to get rid of so many 'bores'.[20] There was little doubt now that a forward policy in China could be vigorously pursued.

14 | 'The Massacre of the Innocents'

> *One of the gunboats got ashore yesterday,*
> *within a stone's throw of the town of Canton,*
> *and the officer had the coolness to call on a*
> *crowd of Chinese, who were on the quays, to*
> *pull her off, which they at once did! Fancy*
> *having to fight such people!* The Earl of Elgin,
> December 1857.

Happily for the Government, the new strong policy in China could be pursued in conjunction with the French. On 29 February 1857, while the House of Commons in London were heatedly debating Commissioner Yeh's provocative conduct in Canton, there occurred in the province of Kwangsi an event that was to arouse the people of Paris to even greater anger. This was the murder of the French missionary, the Abbé Chapdeleine.

Father Auguste Chapdeleine was arrested on 24 February at Silin, a small town in west Kwangsi. He had been living in Kwangsi for three years and had not previously been molested, although his preaching of Christianity in an area infested by Taiping rebels and outside the limits of the Treaty ports had been a cause of some annoyance and concern to the Chinese authorities. On being taken before the magistrate he was savagely beaten and later tortured and decapitated, his head being hung on a tree outside the city where children threw stones at it so that it fell to the ground and was eaten by dogs.

'Nobody seems to know what happened to the body,' the Abbé's superior, Monseigneur Guillemin, wrote. 'Some people say that Father Chapdeleine was buried in the plot set aside for criminals, while others, probably closer to the truth, declare that he was chopped to pieces and thrown among the refuse, where he was eaten up by the many foul animals that fill the streets. And what happened to his heart! . . . His heart was torn out of his chest and, still beating, was placed on a plate, where it was closely and joyously examined by his barbarian and bloodthirsty torturers. Then they chopped it into pieces, fried it in a pan with pig's grease and ate it.'[1]

Other, even more horrific, versions of Father Chapdeleine's death filled column after column in the French press, and loud demands were made all over the country for revenge upon his murderers. The Emperor Napoleon III was far more interested in the unification of Italy than in the misdeeds of Chinese officials, but the French had by the Treaty of Whampoa become the champions of Christianity in China. So cruel a murder of a Christian missionary, who was at the same time a French citizen, could not be ignored. The military alliance which had brought victory in the Crimea was once more formed, and orders were given for the organization of an expeditionary force. Jean-Baptiste-Louis, Baron Gros, an experienced diplomat who had represented his country in Mexico and South America, had helped to compose Anglo-Greek differences in Athens and to redraw the Franco-Spanish frontier, was appointed the Emperor's *Commissaire-extraordinaire* in China with instructions to cooperate with Queen Victoria's plenipotentiary, Lord Elgin.

* * *

James Bruce, Earl of Elgin, was the son of the 7th Earl who had brought back at great personal expense the marble friezes from the neglected Parthenon. Although he was only forty-five in 1857, he had already had a most distinguished career from which he had retired to the pleasures of his country house in Scotland. Unlike his father, who was sent to Harrow and St Andrews, James was educated at Eton and Christ Church, proving himself a young man of superior intelligence, pleasant manner and forthright opinions. On inheriting his father's title and an estate sadly diminished by the losses sustained in the transfer of the Elgin Marbles from Athens to the British Museum, Lord Elgin asked for a Government appointment and was made Governor of Jamaica in 1842. So well did he fill the post that in 1846 he was granted the Governor-Generalship of

Canada. Once again he occupied a difficult diplomatic appointment with distinction, and soon after his return in 1854 he was offered a seat in the Cabinet as Chancellor of the Duchy of Lancaster.

This he declined; but when Palmerston offered him an appointment in China as demanding as those he had so successfully filled in Jamaica and Canada, he accepted immediately, although he was suspicious of politicians and did not underestimate the difficulties that might arise in his dealings with them.

His instructions were to proceed to Hong Kong, from there to sail north to the mouth of the Peiho river, to make contact with the authorities in the province of Chihli, to ask for compensation for losses incurred and injuries suffered during the recent disturbances at Canton and to obtain undertakings that the Treaties would in future be observed. He was also to procure permission for an English ambassador either to live permanently in Peking or to make occasional visits there, and for the Superintendent of Trade to communicate directly with the 'high officers at the Chinese capital'. Finally, he was to use his best endeavours to persuade the Chinese to open other ports to trade, in addition to the five opened as a result of the late war. He was to use force only if necessary, and then with all due regard to the safety of the Chinese people and of Chinese property.[2] The force to be placed at his disposal was to be only half the size of that asked for by Sir John Bowring, as Canton was not to be occupied unless future events there made this essential. Several gunboats, however, were to be despatched to the support of Admiral Seymour, and further troops would be sent out if required. Moreover, although the American Navy was not to be employed in support of the British action, the President's new representative in China, a lawyer from Pennsylvania, William B. Reed, had been instructed to be otherwise cooperative. It was hoped that this cooperation would be freely and willingly given, for, despite their Government's declared belief that 'peaceful contact' and 'commerce itself' were more likely to open China to the rest of the world than force, the Americans at Canton had recently responded to an attack on one of their corvettes as it sailed up to Canton by heavily bombarding the forts in the Pearl River. Finally, even if the

Americans were not prepared to fight, the French now certainly were.

Lord Elgin had good cause to hope, therefore, when he set sail at the end of April 1857 that his mission would prove successful. Certainly, as he recorded in his journal, he was 'more and more determined' to do all he could to make it so. He enjoyed the first few days of his voyage out. He paid a short visit to Malta, and 'how beautiful' he thought it was with its 'narrow streets, gorgeous churches, and impregnable fortifications'. He was regally entertained in Alexandria and Cairo; and he had an interesting ride across the desert to Suez, first of all in a coupé placed in front of the railway engine so that he should be given the best possible view, and then, from where the uncompleted railway line came to an end, 'in a carriage as capacious and commodious as a London town coach'.[3]

But towards the end of May, as the steamship in which he was travelling approached Ceylon, he began to feel less sanguine, for the more he read of the blue-books and papers with which he had been furnished, 'the more embarrassing the question' with which he had to deal appeared to him. Also, he was beginning to feel homesick in the stifling heat; and he confessed to his wife—she was his second wife: the first had died soon after being shipwrecked on her way to Jamaica—that his eyes filled with tears when he thought of her and of the children. She had not wanted him to accept the appointment, but had written to say that she would 'not in the world dissuade' him if his conscience and feelings told him to say yes: 'God bless you my own darling. I promise you to do my best not to distress you.' On his birthday—the same day of the year as his father's—Elgin felt miserable as he looked at the 'inhospitable sea' and dreamed about the smiling countenances with which he would have been surrounded at home 'and the joyous laugh when papa, with affected surprise, detected the present wrapped up carefully in a paper parcel on the breakfast table'.[4]

Then, on his arrival at Ceylon on 26 May, to depress him still further, there came 'bad news from India'. At first he hoped that 'this news, if confirmed, might provide him with a justification for pressing matters with vigour in China and so hastening the period' at which he might expect to see his family again. But when the news was confirmed it was far graver than had at first been supposed. There had been 'a most serious mutiny in the Bengal army'; the whole edifice of British rule in India was threatened with destruction. Lord Elgin felt obliged to accede to a request from Lord Canning, his contemporary at Christ Church and now Governor-General of India, that the regiments on their way to Hong Kong should be diverted to Calcutta to quell the Munity.[5]

By the time Elgin reached Hong Kong on 3 July, therefore, he had no troops with which to undertake his mission; and without troops, so he was immediately informed upon landing, he could expect to do nothing. For the belief at Canton, shared alike by Sir John Bowring, the merchants, and Admiral Seymour, was that before any satisfactory arrangements could be made with the Chinese, Canton must be captured.

Sir John Bowring was emphatic on the point; and he had no doubt at all that its capture could easily be effected. Indeed, he was convinced that there was a strong party in Canton 'longing to come to terms', that 'Yeh's position had already crumbled and the smallest push was required to bring him down'. For this reason he could not view Elgin's appointment as his superior without regret, since credit for the imminent success would be given to Elgin rather than to himself. 'A great success attends him, I doubt not,' he told Lord Clarendon, adding with more than a hint of self-pity. 'For this and much more will I labour whoever shall reap the glory. I am getting old now, and there has been much trampling on my bald bare head, but I trust before I die to see the great purpose accomplished for which I wish to live, and for which I hope Providence may have spared me through many, many troubles.'[6]

When Bowring 'very profusely' and in an 'excited manner' assured Elgin of his unfailing support in similar terms, expatiating at great length on the policies that had been pursued and ought to be pursued in future, Elgin could not forbear ending the discussion rather coldly: 'I thanked him and told him that if the matter ended well all who had been concerned would get credit and vice versa.'[7]

Sir John Bowring soon became a severe trial to Lord Elgin's not unlimited patience. Rather than expose himself to Bowring's seemingly endless series of monologues, arguments, remonstrations and reprobations, by becoming his guest at the Governor's residence, Elgin chose to remain aboard his flagship, the frigate *Shannon*, hot and stuffy as she was.

Elgin got on better at first with Admiral Seymour, a more ponderous, less talkative man than Bowring, a sailor since the age of eleven when he had joined his father's ship. A man of experience and sound common sense, Seymour assured Elgin that, of course, he would escort him to the mouth of the Peiho river in accordance with the Government's instructions—that is, if Lord Elgin was determined to follow them, but in his view they were quite unrealistic. To leave Canton would seem to the Chinese an admission that they had the upper hand there, and that they could continue to deny the foreigners the rights guaranteed to them by treaty. Worse than this, a diplomatic failure at Chihli might well result in a war far more extensive, costly and disruptive than the quick engagement necessary to bring Yeh and the Cantonese to their senses, a war that might extend to the other ports at which trade was at the moment peacefully continuing. Seymour, in fact, as Elgin told his wife, was 'strong on the point' that Canton was 'the only place where we ought to fight'. Having listened to his arguments and the 'more incoherent' ones of Bowring, Elgin concluded that there was a fixed idea in Hong Kong that 'nothing ought to be done till there [had] been a general massacre at Canton'.[8]

But, even had he been convinced by the arguments and prepared to ignore the Government's instructions, Elgin did not have enough men to attack Canton until the regiments arrived from India. He could not act without the French; and de Bourboulon, considerably put out to learn that he had been superseded by Baron Gros, declined to give any orders or undertake any responsibility in the matter until the Baron arrived. Nor was there any chance of the Baron arriving for some time. He was a man with a strong distaste for either hurry or discomfort and had refused to make the desert crossing that Elgin had made, choosing instead to make a leisurely sea voyage round the Cape.

Elgin explained his dilemma to his wife: 'I found myself at Hong-Kong, without troops and without competent representatives of our allies (America and France) to concert with; doomed either to *aborder* the Court of Pekin alone, without the power of acting vigorously if I met a repulse, or to spend three months at Hong-Kong doing nothing . . . except to lose my prestige by becoming the subject of Hong-Kong Gossip . . . and proclaiming to the whole world that I am waiting for the Frenchman; i.e. that England can do nothing without France.' A way out of his dilemma had come in a letter from India where the Mutiny was more serious than ever, and where the three hundred marines he still had under his control and the crew of the *Shannon* might therefore come in useful as a Naval Brigade. So here he was, aboard H.M.S. *Shannon* on 19 July, he went on, 'actually on my way to Calcutta! to *Calcutta*! . . . Will you think me mad? or what will your view of my proceedings be?'[9]

Lord Canning at least was pleased to see him again and proved 'very friendly', though Elgin did not see much of him, so pre-occupied with the Mutiny was he, working from 'five or six in the morning till dinner-time'.[10] Elgin, on the contrary, had virtually nothing to do, and was relieved beyond measure when he heard towards the end of August that the Government were sending 1,500 marines to China to replace the troops he had given to Canning.

In Calcutta he had been constantly irritated by the 'rather crude notions respecting the Chinese expedition' that prevailed there. The popular belief seemed to be that 'by some lucky chance a large military force was despatched from England this spring to these Eastern Seas, and that the India Government [had] conferred a great favour upon [it] by providing something for it to do'.[11] Now, at last, he could get the Chinese expedition on the move.

But when he arrived back at Hong Kong on 20 September, he found that Baron Gros had still not arrived, that many of the troops who were there were sick, that there was no news yet of the marines that had been promised him, that the experts considered it was now too late in the season anyway to risk ships in the uncertain waters of

North China, and that Bowring and the merchants were still clamouring for an attack upon Canton. He himself, recovering from a fever which had shaken his nerves so badly that he could hardly write, was as deeply depressed as he had ever been since leaving England. The weather was foul; he found it difficult to sleep; and he felt that, because of the Indian Mutiny, the Government had dropped him 'like a hot potatoe' and left him to 'wallow in the mire'.[12] On hearing reports of all this, Commissioner Yeh at Canton noted with satisfaction, 'Elgin passes day after day at Hong Kong, stamping his foot and sighing'.[13]

Then on 18 October, the clouds lifted, and Elgin was able to write in his journal: 'The instructions brought by the last mail give me much greater latitude of action; in fact, untie my hands altogether.' Lord Clarendon had sent him a despatch authorizing him to make an attack on Canton should he not yet have been able to move north.

Two days before, Baron Gros had arrived at last. Initially he had disapproved of an attack upon Canton, but after discussing the matter with Lord Elgin he began to change his mind. Then, four hours with Bowring left him so exhausted that, as Elgin put it, 'he was ready to make almost any concession rather than entertain another assault of rhetoric'. So it was settled that if Yeh did not give way to the allied demands, Canton should be bombarded and captured.

The agreement, though deeply gratifying to the Hong Kong merchants, did little to smooth Lord Elgin's troubled relations with Sir John Bowring who continued to argue, explain and condemn as tirelessly as ever, maintaining that the capture of Canton could easily be effected by a naval brigade and that the troops that had come out to support Elgin should all be sent back to England forthwith. Bowring even went so far as to write to Canning to say that no more troops were required. When Elgin heard of the letter, he felt obliged to speak to him 'pretty plainly and the way he dodged and insinuated revealed [more than he] had before seen of the man's character'.[14] Later Elgin learned that while he was in Calcutta, contrary to his direct orders, Bowring had 'intimated that he was ready to receive communications from Yeh. It [was] impossible to put the slightest trust in' the man.[15]

Bowring was by no means the only difficult personality with whom Elgin had to contend. 'Though some are certainly more so than others,' he confided to his journal, 'we are all more or less insane.'[16] The American Minister, Reed, a 'good enough sort of man', in Elgin's opinion, if sadly inexperienced, was almost inclined to agree with him. He informed the Secretary of State in Washington that there was 'a great irritability' among all the British. 'They are fretful not only at their dependence on the French, without whom they could not take a step in advance, but by their inability to involve the U.S. in their unworthy quarrel. For such, as it now stands, I confess it seems to us.'[17]

Elgin himself could not but agree that the *Arrow* case, which was the indirect cause of his being in Hong Kong at all, was a 'wretched' one and a 'scandal to us'; while the 'utter want of judgement evinced by the whole party, Sir John Bowring, Seymour and Parkes' the year before 'much enhanced' his difficulties.[18] Fortunately he had come to like the cultivated, thoughtful, slow-moving Baron Gros despite his 'unsociability'; and he also got on well at first with the Russian Minister in China, Admiral Count Putyatin, who had arrived in Hong Kong in the middle of November having got 'considerably snubbed' when he asked to be received by the Emperor at Peking.

Gros and Elgin agreed on the nature of the proposals to be delivered to Yeh—'mild proposals', in Elgin's opinion—asking for recognition of the right of entry into Canton and for compensation for losses incurred during the riots at the factories and elsewhere. So moderate, indeed, were the proposals, Elgin believed, that if they had been accepted he would have been 'torn to pieces by all who were ravening' for vengeance. But as it happened Yeh turned out to be Elgin's 'fast friend'; nothing 'would induce him to be saved'.

His reply to the ultimatum was wordy but uncompromising; it advised Elgin to emulate the policy of Sir George Bonham who had given up England's demands to enter Canton and had been rewarded with his investiture as a Knight Commander of the Order of the Bath. It would obviously be in Lord Elgin's interests to imitate

Sir G. Bonham. All through, Elgin complained, the letter was 'sheer twaddle'.[19]

On 20 December, Elgin got into a gunboat and went up the Pearl River as far as the Barrier Forts which the Americans had bombarded the winter before. Since everything was so quiet he determined to go on and 'actually steamed past the city of Canton, along the whole front, within pistol-shot of the town'. He confessed that he had 'never felt so ashamed' of himself in his life to think that, upon his orders, a bombardment would soon be opened up on a town which was evidently quite unprepared to make any resistance. He noticed with apprehension that the day upon which the allied commanders had told him that they would be ready to open the attack was marked on his calendar as 'The Massacre of the Innocents'.[20]

A line of English men-of-war had approached the town on 15 December without any opposition being offered, and were now anchored in front of it. 'The ships are surrounded by boats filled chiefly by women, who pick up orange-peel and offal, and everything that is thrown overboard,' Elgin wrote to his wife. 'One of the gunboats got ashore yesterday, within a stone's throw of the town of Canton, and the officer had the coolness to call on a crowd of Chinese, who were on the quays, to pull her off, which they at once did! Fancy having to fight such people!'[21]

Elgin's private secretary, Laurence Oliphant, was astonished by their apparent indifference to all the warlike preparations being made by the foreigners. Only a few of the river people showed the least interest in the idea of self-preservation, Oliphant wrote, 'and every now and then I was startled by seeing a two-storied mansion with verandahs and tiled roof, which appeared to be the last house of a street, deliberately detach itself from its neighbours, and float complacently down the stream to some secure aquatic retreat.'[22]

The foreigners launched their attack on the morning of 28 December. The ships began throwing shells into the town at six o'clock 'without almost any reply', except from a few guns that lobbed their shot 'in distant cabbage-gardens' or 'into unoffending trees in the rear' and from rockets, barbed like arrows, that thudded about and fizzed for a moment in the grass.[23]

'I hate the whole thing so much,' Elgin said, 'that I cannot trust myself to write about it.'[24] In fact, the number of civilians killed during the twenty-seven hours of bombardment was probably about two hundred. Rather more than twice this number of Chinese soldiers were killed or wounded in the subsequent fighting, but there was nothing like the massacre that Elgin had feared. The armies landed with very little difficulty and had soon surrounded the town. Early next morning ladders were carried to the walls and the French and English soldiers clambered up them 'like bees, holding on to one another's legs and nearly pulling' each other down in the eager scramble. By evening the allies had captured the whole length of the wall and had occupied the surrounding heights. The entire operation had cost the allied armies the lives of no more than eight British and two Frenchmen.

After going ashore with Baron Gros on New Year's Day 1858 and looking down through the pouring rain upon the narrow streets and chimneyless roofs of the town from the top of the hill where the British had established their headquarters, Elgin expressed his concern at what might happen once orders were given for the troops to occupy it. 'There is a word called "loot",' he noted in his journal, a Hindu word the British soldiers had picked up in India, 'which gives, unfortunately a venial character to what would, in common English, be styled robbery. . . . *Looting* was practised to a great extent, I suspect, even by persons in high position, during the last Chinese War, and people are apt to think that they are defrauded of a right when the privilege of robbing is put under restraint. Add to this, that there is no flogging in the French army, so that it is impossible to punish men committing this class of offences.' Nor was it possible, until some sort of authority had been formed, to undertake the responsibility of bringing order back to the town and to prevent the pillaging that was being openly carried on by gangs of Chinese criminals. Yet, as Elgin lamented, 'these incomprehensible Chinese', although they had made no defence, did not come forward to capitulate.[25]

'These curious, stolid, imperturbable people seem determined simply to ignore our presence here, and to wait till we are pleased to go away,' wrote *The Times* correspondent, Wingrove Cooke. 'Yeh lives much as usual. He cut off four hundred Chinese heads the other morning, and stuck them up in the south of the city. Our leaders seem to be puzzled by the tenacious, childlike, helpless obstinacy—the passive resistance—of their enemy.'[26]

After waiting vainly for a week for an offer of surrender, it was decided to send patrols into the town to fetch the leaders out. The patrols entered by way of the Avenue of Benevolence and Love and within a few hours had captured both the Manchu commander of the garrison and Yeh's deputy, Pih-kuei, the Governor of Kwang-tung. But of Yeh himself there was no sign. There were rumours that he had fled from Canton and that he had killed himself; but Harry Parkes, who had accompanied the patrols as interpreter, felt sure that he was still within the walls and set off at the head of a hundred sailors in search of him. With the help of a Chinese student who acted as guide, Parkes eventually tracked his quarry down 'in a third-rate *yamen*, which appeared closed and deserted. The doors were forced open and the blue jackets were all over the place in a moment. . . . The house was full of hastily packed baggage. Mandarins were running about—yes, *running* about; and at last one came forward and delivered himself up as Yeh. It was a fine act of devotion but . . . the man was not fat enough and was at once pushed aside, and, hurrying on, [Parkes] at last spied a very fat man contemplating the achievement of getting over the wall at the extreme rear of the yamen.'[27] 'The old brute took his capture very coolly,' according to an English Commissariat officer, 'and it is said only asked to be allowed to make water.'[28]

Yeh—'an uninteresting Monster' in Lord Elgin's opinion[29]—was carried away under guard and placed aboard the *Inflexible*. At first he was 'rather bumptious', but an artist attached to Elgin's staff said that he became 'very civil and *piano*' once aboard the British steamer to whose captain he remarked that if it were not an indiscreet question he would like to know if it was intended that he should be executed. On being assured that it was not, he made himself comfortable and settled down to enjoy what food and drink the steamer's galley could offer him. Since his continued presence in the

Pearl River was considered a hindrance to the full acceptance by the Chinese of a new government in the town, he was shipped off to Calcutta where in less than two years he died.[30]

The new government comprised Pih-kuei as Governor and a commission of three Europeans: Harry Parkes, Captain Martineau des Chenez, a French officer who also spoke Chinese, and a British colonel in the Marines. The commission was to have the authority to approve or amend all proclamations issued by the Governor and to deal with all cases in which foreigners were involved. The arrangement proved satisfactory. The Chinese, grateful for being protected from further looting by patrols of allied police, and accepting the impartiality of the commission which ordered the flogging of any offenders, settled down to the resumption of their normal life. Shops reopened, trade recovered, tubs of live fish, sea chestnuts and bamboo shoots were brought out once more into the streets, gambling began again, cooking stoves were re-erected and the meat hissed and spluttered on the heated iron.[31]

'One of our amusements at Canton was to go down to the city and poke about the shops,' wrote John Robertson Pughe of the Bengal Staff Corps. 'The principal street was called the "Street of Love and Benevolence". The shops were well arranged and set out. One of the beliefs of the Chinese was that it brought them bad luck to refuse the first offer made them on each day; so that if you wished to buy anything very cheap your plan was to go out very early in the morning so as to be a first customer. One of our amusements was to go for a picnic by boat to one of the large tea gardens in the vicinity of Canton. On one occasion we went to the country house of Howqua, the great tea merchant. The garden was laid out exactly after the design of the old Willow Pattern plates. There were small bridges over minute streams, and every here and there a small pagoda. The trees were cut out in the most fantastic shapes. We always took our own food with us. It was amusing to see the Chinese coolies, after our repast was over, finishing up the remains. The debris was put into a large salad bowl and all mixed up together, sweets and savouries, tea, beer etc., and this mess was eaten to the last grain of rice and seemed to afford immense enjoyment.'[32] Foreigners could walk about unmolested 'without the slightest sign of resistance or animosity,' reported Rutherford Alcock, now returned to his duties at Canton, 'whereas before no foreigner could pass the gates, or even walk in the suburbs or outskirts without suffering insult and contumely from the very children'.[33] Indeed, the people of Canton were very submissive', according to Laurence Oliphant, 'always standing when an Englishman passes, and removing their hats out of deference to our prejudices upon the subject'.[34] They showed particular respect to the imposing figure of Lord Elgin, although he walked about the town with little ceremony. One day John Robertson Pughe caught sight of him 'walking along dressed in an old shooting coat and only attended by an Aide de Camp and a couple of orderlies. The tea merchant was quite horrorstruck at his appearance, and on his asking if that was really our "number one mandarin" and being told it was, he said, "How can he so fashion do?"'[35]

Life soon became more agreeable for foreigners at Hong Kong as well. At the beginning of February it was still 'dangerous to walk any distance from the town unless armed'[36], and several attempts were made to rob and murder Europeans when alone. But a fortnight later, after the Chinese new year, foreigners began to feel safe again, to walk out into the country and to accept invitations from Chinese merchants. H. C. Lewis, an army commissary, accepted one, 'longing to have some regular Chinese chow', though he fully expected it would make him sick for a week afterwards.

At the door of his host's house, he and his fellow guests were greeted by a lot of singing girls who entertained them for an hour with music—'holy moses such a jargon of sounds . . . such an infernal row'. They then sat down on 'very uncomfortable seats without any backs' for the chow-chow; they had birds' nest soup ('really very good'), sharks' fins, crabs, and 'about twenty other dishes one after the other as fast as possible'. The girls would not eat anything, and, as Lewis complained, 'would hardly look at us but kept their eyes fixed on their fans, except for just a moment when taking wine with you . . . but they would not always condescend to swallow the wine but spit it out again on the floor behind. . . . A lot of English dishes then made their appearance, out of compliment to us, I suppose. Roast mutton, Pigeon Pie, and as a winder up Plum Pudding. The desert was in the European style with Sherry & Port and Coffee. This was the conclusion of the business except that some of the fellows took it into their heads to smoke opium.'[37]

Although the return to normal was generally welcomed at Canton and Hong Kong, the policy of appeasement did not suit everyone. It did not suit Harry Parkes for one. Indeed, Parkes, who had soon established himself as the dominant member of the allied commission, thought that Lord Elgin's policy was 'disconcerting'.

'The Canton people appear completely perplexed,' he confided to the Permanent Under Secretary for Foreign Affairs in London. 'That a city should be captured and then at once given back into the hands of its former Government is a circumstance wholly without precedence in their annals, and they scarcely know how to regard the fact. I doubt whether they consider it as a mark of strength on our part.' To his brother-in-law he admitted that he did not consider Elgin 'a *great man*. . . . Conciliation, mildness, etc., etc., is with him the order of the day.'[38]

Conciliation and mildness were not Parkes's way; nor were they the way of most of the merchants and officials in Hong Kong where, as Elgin wryly noted in his diary, 'the thirst for blood [was] not yet slaked among the meek Christians of that locality', those 'over-bearing, arrogant and vindictive' fellow countrymen of his who, no doubt, were 'revelling in the prospect of the insolences' in which they had a fancy to indulge in Canton.[39] Nor were they the way of *The Times* which attacked Elgin and Gros for their 'strange and overweening modesty'.

Influenced by these arguments, Lord Clarendon wrote to Elgin reprovingly of the 'rather too much respect' that had been paid to 'that barbarian Yeh' and to Pih-kuei (known in London as Pickwick). But Elgin was not to be induced by any 'human power . . . to accept the office of oppressor of the feeble'. He resented the criticisms, refusing to be deflected by such men as Parkes from following a policy which the American Minister congratulated him upon as being a 'great success' due to his 'gentle and discreet counsels'.[40]

Lord Elgin did not greatly care for Parkes. He agreed, as he told his wife, that he exerted himself with 'considerable effect' and was 'really very clever'; but he was 'exceedingly overbearing in his manner to the Chinese' and too much inclined to display his 'infinite wrath' when things went wrong.[41]

Nor did Elgin have much sympathy for those Hong Kong merchants who supposed that trade with China would be vastly increased once force had been used to obtain a new treaty removing all obstacles in the way of trade. He realized that many of them—that Bowring, too, for that matter—sincerely believed that this opening of China to the manufactured goods of the West would be as beneficial to the Chinese as it would be to the merchants themselves and that it must, therefore, be forced upon them, poor ignorant creatures, even against their will. Yet Elgin doubted that this was a valid argument. He believed that the Chinese were closer to the truth when they protested that they had no need of foreign goods, that they took a limited amount because they wanted to export tea, silk and porcelain, and that that limit could not be much expanded.

Elgin disagreed also with the Protestant missionaries who were demanding that a new treaty should allow them the same freedom as the Treaty of Whampoa allowed the Catholic French, that they should be granted permission to travel freely in the interior and that toleration and special privileges should be given to their Chinese converts. In his reply to the missionaries Lord Elgin insisted that while it was 'most right and fitting that Chinamen espousing Christianity should not be persecuted', it was most wrong that they should be tempted hypocritically to profess Christianity in order to obtain exceptional advantages.

So it was in an atmosphere of growing criticism from the missionaries and the merchants, as well as from his subordinates, that Lord Elgin awaited a reply to a reasonable letter which, with the agreement of the French, Russian and American Ministers, he had written to Peking asking for a responsible representative of the Chinese Government to meet him at Shanghai to discuss the possibility of a new treaty. Having despatched the letter he sailed north for Shanghai to await a reply to it there. The reply, which did not reach him until the end of March, was equally polite but wholly un-satisfactory: Lord Elgin should not have ignored the principle, 'ever religiously adhered to' by officials of the Celestial Empire in Peking that there could be no intercourse between them and foreigners; he should have applied to Yeh's successor, the newly appointed Imperial Commissioner at Canton.

*   *   *

Elgin had enjoyed his voyage north from Canton to Shanghai where he had hoped to negotiate a treaty which would bring his mission to an end and enable him 'to hurry home'. The weather was fine, the winds fair; it was 'a very pleasant break'. He had called at several ports on his way, finding the Chinese people pleasant and friendly everywhere. Admittedly he had not liked the atmosphere at Swatow where the foreign merchants were chiefly engaged in the iniquitous coolie trade which 'consisted in kidnapping wretched coolies, putting them on board ships where all the horrors of the slave trade [were] reproduced, and sending them on specious promises to such places as Cuba'. But at Foochow, a more beautiful place than any other he had seen in China, 'with the exception perhaps' of the 'most charming island' of Chusan, the people were 'perfectly civil'. On Chusan they seemed 'really to like' foreigners; at Chapu they were 'civil as usual' and made no difficulties, although this was not a Treaty Port so the ship had no right to land there. At Ningpo, where he walked about with 'Mr Meadows, the author', who was vice-consul there, the people were 'more amiable than at any other place' he had visited.[42]

At Shanghai, however, his hopes were dashed by the rebuff from Peking. He regarded it as a sign that he must follow Lord Claren-don's original instructions and move further north towards the mouth of the Peiho river, the gateway to Tientsin and the capital. There the allies might be able to force the Chinese Government to begin negotiations by concentrating a fleet of gunboats which could intercept the junks taking rice to Peking and which could, if the Emperor's officials still remained obdurate, enter the Peiho river.

Protecting the mouth of the river were a series of forts on either bank by the small town of Taku, and a bar five miles out to sea

which deep draught warships could not cross. It was essential, therefore, to assemble a sizeable fleet of gunboats of a draught shallow
enough for them to get over the bar and to sail up the winding river.
Orders were accordingly given to Admiral Seymour to muster the
necessary craft.

Seymour's gunboats were already occupied patrolling the Pearl
River and the Canton estuary, and it was some time before he had
succeeded in overhauling those in need of repair and bringing them
all up to the Gulf of Chihli where, in stormy seas and under a grey
and misty sky, Lord Elgin impatiently awaited their arrival. Warned
by Count Putyatin, who knew North China well, that he must get
the business settled by the end of May as, after that, it would be too
hot for the European troops to carry on operations, Lord Elgin grew
more and more impatient with each passing day. By the middle of
April he still had only one gunboat capable of crossing the bar, and
was damning the naval commanders with uncommon virulence in
his diary. Seymour was a 'perfect driveller', 'so headless an associ-
ate', his second-in-command, Captain Nicolson was 'an old woman',
the commodore, 'a regular sot . . . so drunk at the assault of Canton
that he could hardly support himself'. Seymour 'must be in his
dotage', wrote Elgin on 24 April. 'It is stupidity beyond anything I
ever met with. . . . Even after receiving my letters telling him that
I had taken all the ships I could get and come north, he has done
nothing to support me. Nay, he has actually left all his steamers behind him waiting for mail, and doing odd jobs of all kinds. I did not
complain to him because I have found out that it is perfectly useless.
He never seems to understand either what is said or written. It is
very hard . . . I should be made the victim of such folly.'[43]

By 29 April Elgin felt himself to be in the most humiliating
position in which he had ever been placed in his whole career. The
French flag was represented by two gunboats *'within the bar of the
Peiho river*—that of England by two despatch boats *aground on top
of it.* Gros has a very small force—but he has a man with a head to
command it . . .; what a business it will be if the French get the
whole credit of these operations'.

It was not, in fact, until 19 May that the British had gathered a force sufficiently strong to attack the forts; and by then the long delay had enabled the Chinese to extend and reinforce them and to get eighty-seven guns into position along the ramparts. During the intervening weeks, Baron Gros and Elgin made a last attempt to negotiate, but the Governor-General of Chihli, who offered himself as the person with whom the foreigners must deal, did not have authority to conclude a treaty without reference to Peking, and the two Ministers decided that this would inevitably entail a prolonged and ultimately futile series of talks.

So, watched by the Russian and American Ministers, who had arrived in the Gulf as neutral observers willing to act as intermediaries and determined to share in any benefits the French and British might win, the attack began.

At ten o'clock in the morning of 20 May six gunboats rapidly approached the forts under a heavy fire. But although the poor fellows in the forts 'stood at their guns and fired away pretty steadily', in Lord Elgin's words, it was of very little consequence for they hardly ever hit their targets. As soon as the allied landing parties went ashore upstream from the forts, Elgin's private secretary saw the Chinese, who had not adequately prepared themselves for an attack from the rear, abandoning the forts in panic 'and scattering in all directions'.

'We have hardly had any loss, I believe,' Elgin wrote home. There were, in fact, five British killed and seventeen wounded, one of the British soldiers killed being shot by one of his comrades as he pranced about in some Chinese clothes he had discovered in a deserted fort. 'But the French, who blundered a good deal with their gunboats, and then contrived to get blown up by setting fire to a powder magazine [in one of the occupied forts] have suffered pretty severely' by losing sixty-one men wounded and six killed. Most of these losses were quite unnecessary; the Chinese had 'no notion of directing their firearms' and were 'without tactics and discipline'. Lord Elgin would 'venture to say that twenty-four determined men, with revolvers and a sufficient number of cartridges, might walk through China from one end to the other'.[44]

* * *

With the fall of Taku all Chinese opposition collapsed. Baron Gros and Lord Elgin, preceded by the two admirals, sailed up the river towards Tientsin, watched by the riverside villagers whose grandparents had gazed with such curiosity upon the progress of Lord Macartney. Some of them ran towards the river's edge to greet the foreigners as conquerors. 'Hail, O King! Be thou our Emperor,' they shouted. 'Come thou and reign over us.'[45]

'I do not think that these poor poor timorous people have any notion of resisting,' wrote Elgin in his diary on 27 May after pacing the deck looking at 'the dancing waves sparkling under a bright full moon', feeling more content than he had done for weeks; 'I only trust that they may make up their minds to concede what is requisite at once, and enable us all to have done with it.'

He had made up his mind to act the role at Tientsin 'of "the uncontrollably fierce barbarian"'. The part he confessed was 'disgusting' to him, yet he believed that the 'stupid' Chinese 'never yield anything except under the influence of fear. It is necessary therefore to make them feel that one is in earnest, and that they have nothing for it but to give way.'[46]

Elgin took on the appearance of the 'fierce barbarian' at his first meeting with the two senior mandarins who had been deputed to conduct the negotiations. He left for the Temple of Oceanic Influences where the discussions were to take place accompanied by a guard of 150 marines, a band of the Royal Navy and all his 'suite in chairs, *tambour battant*'; and he marched into the flower-bedecked courtyard, where refreshments had been set out on tables shaded from the blazing sun, with the air of a conqueror. He told the Emperor's plenipotentiaries that he had consented to have this interview merely in order that his powers might be compared with theirs, at which one of them brought out a letter wrapped in a sheet of yellow paper, standing up as he did so and raising the paper reverentially over his head before unfolding it.

When this document had been translated to him, Lord Elgin also rose, affecting to be dissatisfied with it and with the delegates' lack of a seal of office. He would need time to consider the position further, he said, before negotiations began; and he left the temple, brusquely declining all offers of refreshments. He could not but feel sorry for the two mandarins whom he was treating so rudely. One of them, with his big nose and square, solid face reminded Elgin's secretary of Oliver Cromwell; the other was a 'venerable man of placid and benevolent expression, with a countenance full of intelligence, though his eye was somewhat dimmed and his hand palsied from extreme age'.[47] They both made great efforts to induce Elgin to sit down again. 'But I acted the part of the "uncontrollably fierce" to perfection,' Elgin prided himself, 'and set off for my abode. I had hardly reached it when I received two cards from my poor mandarins, thanking me for having gone so far to meet them.'[48]

Thereafter Elgin took no further direct part in the negotiations, leaving their conduct to his younger brother, Frederick Bruce, who had come out to China as the Secretary of the mission, to Thomas Wade, one of its interpreters, and to Horatio Lay, a young man employed by the Chinese Customs whose hectoring, bullying manner towards the mandarins seemed to Elgin the best way to deal with them. Others found Lay's methods profoundly embarrassing and distressing. The American, Reed, interceded with Elgin on the mandarins' behalf and the Russian, Putyatin, asked Gros to see what he could do to persuade the British not to allow the young man to be so overbearing. But Elgin would have none of these criticisms of Lay; his own distaste for the methods employed made his defence of them all the more heated. He was convinced that he was acting, and allowing Lay to act, in the best interests not only of his country but of China, too. 'Though I have been forced to act almost brutally,' he wrote when the negotiations were over, 'I am China's friend in all this.' The American and Russian Ministers were 'sneaking scoundrels' to criticize his methods; while they pretended to support the Chinese they were, in fact, behaving as their worst enemies.[49]

Both these Ministers, as well as Baron Gros, were conducting separate negotiations; and certainly Count Putyatin was not being honest with the British about them. He had already been in touch with Chinese representatives before the Anglo-French fleet entered the Peiho River, and, while advising the allies to take this strong action, had at the same time been promising that, if her claims were met, Russia would help China to 'destroy the British and French'.[50] Russia's claims *were* met and a treaty with China was signed on 13 June shortly before news reached Tientsin that, a few weeks before, far away to the north in Eastern Siberia, Russian warships had bombarded Aigun and forced the Manchu plenipotentiary there to sign a treaty recognizing Russia's right to long-disputed lands in the region of the Amur river. It was here, a hundred years later, that the Russians and Chinese were to fight each other in the snow along the banks of the Ussuri.

By their Tientsin treaty the Russians gained the right to send an Ambassador on occasional visits to Peking, and to enjoy the same rights as other foreigners at the five existing Treaty Ports as well as to have access to two other ports, one on Formosa, the other on Hainan. The treaty also included a clause recognizing Russia's right to any further benefits which the other nations might subsequently obtain for themselves.

Five days after the signing of the Russian treaty, the Americans signed a similar one; and five days after that the French had also come to terms. Baron Gros, however, did not want to sign until the British were also ready to do so; and the British seemed as far from agreement as ever. They were insisting—and rudely insisting—on Chinese agreement to their merchants being allowed to travel freely outside the Treaty Ports and to their Ambassador not merely visiting Peking on occasions, but actually living there. In effect they were attempting to force the Emperor to receive in his capital the representative of a foreign power whose sovereign he would therefore by implication recognize as his equal; to do something, in fact, that he had never done before, something entirely repugnant to Chinese ways of thought.

Determined as the Chinese were not to have a British Ambassador living permanently in Peking—and once the right was conceded to the British, the other nations involved, the Russians, French and Americans, would invoke their treaties to demand the same privilege—Lord Elgin was quite as determined to compel the Chinese to agree to it, understanding well enough that, when a foreign minister was established at Peking, the Manchus would find it increasingly difficult to maintain the fiction that the Emperor was superior to all the other rulers of the world.

He accordingly instructed his brother, Frederick, to tell the Imperial Commissioners that he was 'indignant beyond all expression', and that unless they agreed to all his conditions he would 'consider negotiations at an end, go to Pekin and demand a great deal more'. The Chinese gave way; the Treaty of Tientsin was signed on 26 June 1858.

In addition to the two most hotly contested clauses, the British now gained the opening of ten more ports to trade, ranging from Manchuria to Formosa and including four towns on the Yangtze as far west as Hankow. British naval vessels were to have right of access to all these towns. Disputes between British subjects were to be dealt with by British officials; if Chinese subjects were involved the case would be heard by a mixed court comprising a Chinese magistrate and a British consul. The freedom of missionary activity was guaranteed; and an indemnity of four million dollars was to be paid for the losses incurred at Canton and for the expenses of the expedition.[51]

Details of new tariffs and other commercial details were left to be decided later at Shanghai. But although these were matters of relatively minor importance, the same two high-ranking mandarins who had conducted the negotiations at Tientsin arrived at Shanghai to settle them; and it soon became apparent that they had not come to discuss details of trade but to reopen the far more controversial matter of foreign ambassadors living in Peking. They explained that it would be 'an injury to China in many more ways than they could express. In the present critical and troubled state of [the] country this incident would generate . . . a loss of respect for the Government in the eyes of the people.'[52]

Convinced as he still was that the point was a fundamental one affecting the whole future relationship between China and the West, knowing that if he gave way his toleration would be represented as a great victory for Chinese diplomacy, an indication that for all the contents of the Treaty of Tientsin nothing had really changed, Elgin nevertheless felt that to continue unyielding was unreasonable. He feared that to carry the point might, indeed, undermine the authority of the Empire which British interests were now concerned in supporting, whereas to make the concession might lead to a better understanding between China and Britain in the future. Also, there was the feeling that an ambassador living in Peking so far from the protection of his country's ships would be dangerously exposed in times of unrest. This was one reason why Baron Gros had never favoured the idea, why Lord Malmesbury, the new Foreign Secretary in the Tory Government which had now replaced Palmerston's, considered that 'Peking would be a rat trap for the envoy if the Chinese meant mischief'.[53] So Elgin gave way. The right remained a right in the Treaty, but, as formerly with British entry into Canton, it was not immediately insisted upon.

The decision satisfied the new Government in London. So, to a lesser extent, did the news that Elgin and the Imperial Commissioners at Shanghai had agreed on the legalization of the opium trade. There were bound to be strong reservations about this; but, as Reed reported to Washington, explaining his reasons for disagreeing with the American Government's policy of trying to get the trade suppressed, 'Most honest men concur that nominal prohibition is in point of fact encouragement, and that the only remaining chance of restraint is making the drug dutiable and placing it under direct custom house control'.[54] Certainly it could not be denied that it was virtually impossible to suppress the traffic which had been increasing in volume year by year. In 1857 well over 60,000 chests were imported from India, mostly in British ships and mainly through the offices of the two leading British firms in Hong Kong, Jardine & Matheson and Dent & Co. If the British ever succeeded in stopping their own people from engaging in the trade, it would, it was felt, merely be carried on by the Americans. If a tariff of eight per cent were fixed for opium, which was three per cent higher than that fixed for most other goods, the imports of the drug would be unlikely to increase, while the beneficiaries would be the Chinese government rather than the Chinese officials into whose hands the bribes had formerly passed. The Chinese Commissioners readily agreed to the suggestion of legalization.[55]

*   *   *

After visiting Peking and then sailing down the Yangtze as far as Hankow, passing the Taiping-held city of Nanking, Lord Elgin returned home well satisfied with the results of his mission, happy in the knowledge that his brother, Frederick, had been appointed the first British Minister in China and would be able to finish the work which he had himself so satisfactorily begun.

15 | At the Taku Forts

*It is supreme nonsense to talk as if we were
bound to the Chinese by the same rules which
regulate international relations in Europe.*
The Duke of Argyll, July 1859.

On 18 June 1859, the anniversary of the day upon which the
Americans had signed their treaty with the Chinese at Tientsin,
J. E. Ward, Reed's successor as the United States representative in
China, was on board a frigate in the Gulf of Chihli. He had arrived
there with the intention of going up the Peiho to Peking to deliver a
letter to the Emperor from President Buchanan and to exchange
ratifications of the American Treaty. With him in the Gulf were the
British Minister, Frederick Bruce, and the French Minister, de
Bourboulon. Apart from the frigate in which Ward and his staff
were accommodated, the only other American vessels in sight were
two small steamers. The British mission was accompanied by a
battleship, two frigates and thirteen gunboats, the French by two
warships, a naval force which would have been considerably aug-
mented had not the Far East squadron been involved in operations
along the coast of Vietnam.

For the British and French had thought it prudent to be prepared
for trouble in their attempts to get their treaties ratified in Peking,
as agreed at Tientsin the year before, and they had come ready to
enforce their rights.

There were well-supported rumours in Hong Kong that a firmer
policy with the West had been decided upon in Peking; and Bruce
had been reliably informed by an official of the Chinese Customs
that the Taku forts had been repaired and strengthened, and that a
powerful army was massed in Chihli in support of them.

Now that they had arrived at the mouth of the Peiho once again,
the British could see for themselves that the forts had indeed been

prepared and that the entrance to the river was blocked by sunken hulks, chains, spikes and bamboo booms. Admiral Sir James Hope, Seymour's successor as the British naval commander, went ashore with a small landing party to demand that the obstacles be removed. He was informed that they had been placed there by members of the local militia as a defence against the Taiping rebels and that they could on no account be dismantled. So, with the agreement of de Bourboulon, Bruce gave an ultimatum to the Chinese that unless the passage were cleared he would give orders for it to be forced.

An hour or so before the attack was due to begin, Bruce received a letter from Heng-fu, Viceroy of Chihli, inviting him to land a few miles further north at Pehtang where arrangements would be made for his conveyance by road to Peking. But Lord Malmesbury had instructed Bruce to sail up the Peiho in imposing style, not to go to the capital by cart: 'The Admiral in charge of Her Majesty's naval forces in China has been directed to send up with you to the mouth of the Peiho a sufficient naval force, and unless any unforeseen circumstances should appear to make another arrangement more advisable, it would seem desirable that you should reach Tientsin in a British ship of war.'[1]

Bruce did not consider that merely because the river was blocked he was justified in agreeing to the Viceroy's request that he should go round to Peking by what Palmerston was later to term the 'back door'. If he left all his warships behind him in the Gulf, he could not hope to exert the same sort of pressure in Peking that his brother had been able to do by bringing them up to Tientsin; there was no telling what sort of indignities he would be subjected to or into what disadvantageous a position he would be placed. In any case, he was eight miles out to sea when the Viceroy's letter was received; and there was no time to stop Hope carrying out the attack he had been ordered to make as soon as the ultimatum expired.

The Admiral began his attack in the early afternoon, standing himself in one of the leading gunboats, the *Plover*. He was so confident of an early victory that he had taken trouble neither to devise a careful plan of operations nor to discover the strength of the enemy opposition.

The ships under his command reached the outer barrier of iron stakes without mishap and began to open up a passage through them without interference from the guns of the silent forts; but when the leading gunboats passed the barrier there was a sudden roar as the Chinese guns opened fire, pouring shot amidst the tightly packed gunboats in the water below them.

'What could we do against such a fearful number of guns?' complained a midshipman in one of the 'poor little gunboats, enclosed in such a small space'.[2] There was only one course that could be taken, and that was to retreat as quickly as possible. Numerous sailors had already been killed; most of the gunboats had been damaged; in the Admiral's boat all but nine of the crew had been hit, Hope himself in the thigh. By six o'clock, when the fire from the forts had at last begun to slacken, there were only five gunboats still in action. Hope had transferred his flag to the *Opossum* and had been hurled to the deck by the collapse of the mainstay, hurting himself so painfully that he fainted. But despite the crippling damage done to the British fleet and the failure of their guns to silence the Chinese forts, it was decided by Hope's second-in-command to press on and capture them before nightfall. Landing parties scrambled ashore across the mudflats, which the receding tide had exposed along the shore, sinking deep into the soft slime and struggling to reach the walls of the forts through a heavy fire.

Unable to contain himself as he watched the fight aboard the United States steamer *Toeywan*, incapable of standing idly by while British sailors and marines were being so mercilessly treated, the American naval commander, Commodore Josiah Tatnall, decided to ignore his country's neutrality and enter the action. 'No, sir,' he is said to have exclaimed in his Southern accent, 'No, sir, old Tatnall isn't that kind, sir! This is the cause of humanity!' He could not just watch while white men were being butchered; for, as he added, giving new fame to an ancient maxim, 'blood is thicker than water'. He issued orders for his ships to tow up the British reserves, to help in getting away their wounded, and he set off himself in his barge to the ship where Admiral Hope lay wounded.[3]

The Commodore's impetuous action was much appreciated by

Hope—it was also later officially approved by the United States Secretary of the Navy—but it could do nothing to alter the outcome of the battle. Early next morning, when the last exhausted survivor of the landing parties had retreated across the mud to the water's edge, the British with the loss of eighty-nine men killed and 345 wounded had suffered a serious and humiliating defeat, a humiliation shared in only a small degree by the French whose lack of boats had saved them from losses any worse than four men killed and ten wounded. Although ten of the gunboats were found not to be too badly damaged to be cobbled and put back into service, there could be no question of any further attempt upon the forts until a far larger force had been assembled.

All kinds of excuses were found to explain the disaster: the crafty Chinese had lured the British towards the guns of the Taku forts with the deliberate intention of destroying them there rather than ratify the Tientsin Treaty; the guns had been fired not by Chinamen at all but by trained artillerymen whose fur hats and cropped skulls clearly identified them as Russians determined to be revenged upon the French and British for their defeat in the Crimean War; the Mongol military commander in Chihli, Seng-ko-lin-ch'in, was identified as an Irish adventurer, Sam Collinson, a well-known Anglophobe who had once served in the Royal Marines.

The rash tactics of Admiral Hope, however, came in for little criticism. He was a brave man who had remained at his post though badly wounded; he may have been a little impetuous, perhaps, but he was a hero. 'If we would keep up the old tone in our Navy,' *The Times* declared, 'we must hold it through good and through evil fortune as a maxim that it is not want of success but want of audacity that can alone ever be imputed as a disgrace to an English admiral.' As the scornful London correspondent of the New York *Daily Tribune*, Karl Marx, was later to remark, the whole debate about the responsibility for the sad affair 'evaporated in grotesque compliments showered . . . on the head of Admiral Hope for having so gloriously buried the British forces in the mud'.[4]

Frederick Bruce was to be less generously treated; but for the time being he could derive some satisfaction from the fact that the

American representative, who had accepted the Chinese invitation to travel overland to Peking by way of Pehtang, had become involved in the undignified wrangling over the kotow that had bedevilled the mission of Lord Amherst. Ward had been kept waiting for three weeks in Pehtang where the Viceroy of Chihli had urged him to go back to the mouth of the Peiho and induce the British and French Ministers to go with him by the overland route; and then, after Bruce's attempt to force the river passage had resulted in the repulse of the British fleet, Ward had been provided with one of those closed, unsprung carts that had driven Henry Ellis almost frantic with discomfort and irritation on his journey to Peking in 1816.

On his arrival in Peking, Ward was told that the letter from President Buchanan to the Emperor would have to be delivered in person, and that on the occasion of its delivery the American must of course perform the usual ceremonies observed at the Chinese Court. Ward protested: America was a republic; he did not even so much as bend his knee to his own President; he knelt 'only to God and woman!'

Well then, as a particular favour, he might dispense with part of the ceremony, kneeling once only and bringing his head to the ground but three times. He replied in writing that he 'would enter the presence of His Majesty with head uncovered and bowing low . . . retire by walking backwards. . . .' Very well, but would he bow low enough to touch the ground with his fingers? No, he would not. The tiresome negotiations continued and eventually broke down. The letter was given to a mandarin for onward transmission and the American treaty was ratified not in Peking but at Pehtang.[5]

Better to have no contact with the Chinese at all than submit to the nonsense 'practised on the Yankee Minister who was sent to Peking, caged in a van like one of Wombwell's wild beasts', exclaimed the Duke of Argyll, expressing a common opinion when the news of all this reached England. 'It is supreme nonsense to talk as if we were bound to the Chinese by the same rules which regulate international relations in Europe.'[6]

The newspapers took up the theme, urging that the 'perfidious hordes' of China should be taught such a lesson that 'the name of

European' would thereafter be a 'passport of fear throughout the land'; there 'must be no faltering while the blood of our murdered soldiers' remained unavenged.[7]

There was no doubt that this was the mood of the people as well as of the Press, but the new Government were at first inclined to be more cautious. Neither Lord John Russell—now Foreign Secretary and a man who had said in the House two and a half years before that the war against China 'ought never to have been begun'—nor Gladstone, the Chancellor of the Exchequer, was hot for punishment. Nor was Lord Elgin who, on his return from China, had been given a seat in the Cabinet as Postmaster General and who, with a firsthand knowledge of China that none of his colleagues possessed, was frequently appealed to for advice. Elgin thought that Admiral Hope had 'acted like a madman' and was distressed to have to admit that he thought his brother, Frederick, had been misled into making a serious mistake.

'The general notion is that if we use the bludgeon freely enough,' he wrote to the First Lord of the Admiralty, 'we can do anything in China. I hold the opposite view so strongly that I must give expression to it at whatever cost to myself.'[8] Even the Prime Minister was hesitant, far from being as clear cut in his views as he had formerly been. 'We must I think resent this outrage in some way or other,' Palmerston wrote vaguely to Edmund Hammond, the Permanent Under-Secretary at the Foreign Office, but he was not sure what could be done. 'To make an attack on Peking would be an operation of great magnitude.'[9]

Hammond himself, however, was convinced that strong action must be taken; and so was Lord Clarendon to whom Lord John Russell appealed for advice. Clarendon was convinced that 'to attempt to evade the real difficulty of avenging our honour would only make matters worse'. Hammond was equally convinced—and to Elgin's annoyance told him bluntly—that the decision to yield on the matter of a permanent Ambassador in Peking had been proved in the result to be 'perfectly wrong', for in making that concession Elgin had 'encouraged the Chinese to believe they could obtain more, and was therefore responsible for all that had now happened'.[10]

Under pressure from Hammond and those who shared his views, feelings in the Cabinet began to harden; and most remaining doubts were finally resolved when it became known that the Emperor Napoleon III was determined at all costs to send a large force to China to avenge the honour of France. It was unthinkable that France should be allowed to step in alone where England feared to tread, that she should be allowed to gain a position in China that would threaten Britain's dominance there. Besides, Gladstone, Lord John Russell and Palmerston were all intensely concerned about the unification of Italy which Napoleon III had tried to accelerate by his invasion of the Austrian provinces of North Italy the year before. An alliance with France against China would serve to weaken the anti-French feeling in the country—which had recently been reawakened by absurdly persistent rumours that Napoleon III now planned an invasion of England—and would, therefore, also serve the interest of Italian liberals.

But although a British expedition was decided upon, there still remained disagreement as to what its precise purpose should be. Lord Elgin was as anxious as ever to prevent the Chinese Emperor being humiliated to such an extent that his influence over his people was seriously impaired, for in that case China would be thrown into confusion and Britain's lucrative trade with her would be imperilled.

Mistakenly believing that to intercept the junks which carried the Emperor's tributes of rice to Peking would be to starve out the capital, Elgin suggested a tight blockade should be imposed upon the Peiho river. The Government agreed and instructed Frederick Bruce, whose conduct at Taku had been grudgingly approved, to put the blockade into effect if the Chinese did not submit within thirty days to an ultimatum demanding an apology, an indemnity, and the ratification of the Treaty of Tientsin. At the same time an expeditionary force at least as large as that of the French must be sent out, in case the ultimatum were to be rejected and the blockade to fail. Lord Elgin was to go out, too, and in company with Baron Gros—as reluctant to leave the restaurants of Paris as Elgin was to abandon once more the pleasures of family life in Scotland—he was to make a dignified entry into Peking and to insist on an honourable reception. Elgin sailed in April, arriving at Shanghai on 28 June aboard the steamship *Ferooz*, feeling that he must be the 'greatest fool that the world ever saw' to have become involved once more in Chinese affairs.[11]

*   *   *

The greater part of the British expeditionary force of about eleven thousand British and Indian troops, together with a French army seven thousand strong, had moved up to Shanghai from Hong Kong in May; for the Chinese had disdainfully rejected the ultimatum, instructing Frederick Bruce not to be so disrespectful and impertinent in his language should he have occasion in the future to address a petition to Peking.

While in Kwangtung the allied troops had been stationed opposite Hong Kong on the peninsula of Kowloon which the astute Harry Parkes had leased for them at a rent of £160 a year; this obviated any unpleasantness there might have been with the French had Lord Elgin exercised the authority which the British Government had given him and annexed the peninsula by force. The weeks that they had spent in Kwangtung had enabled the allied officers to recruit a corps of coolies which was to prove of considerable help to the armies in the forthcoming campaign. The recruits were offered two suits of clothes, generous rations and the, for them, extremely high pay of £1 17s 6d a week. These inducements, according to one British officer, attracted at first only the riff-raff of the area, as a rumour had spread that the coolies were to be used as cannon fodder and pushed into the front line to receive the brunt of the battle. But eventually when suspicions of the foreigners' motives had died down, when the clothes, the money and the rations had proved irresistibly tempting, and the ban against the smoking of opium, which many of the coolies could not do without, had been lifted, a large force was enrolled. Each man, content enough to be enrolled in the foreign army to serve against the almost equally foreign Manchus of the north, was provided with a uniform jacket on which, fore and aft, was stamped his number and the number of his company within a black circular line, together with a conical bamboo hat with C.C.C.—denoting Chinese Coolie Corps—painted on its front. By the time the allies moved north from Hong Kong on their way to Shanghai, the C.C.C. was by no means the undisciplined rabble that its early critics had foreseen.[12]

On their arrival at Shanghai the allied officers were confirmed in their belief that service in China had little to recommend it. The voyage north had been tedious, the coastline was 'uninteresting' and the country inland, what little one could see of it, looked 'barren'. The small houses in the coastal villages appeared to be poor hovels of stone and mud and straw with roofs of millet stalks; some of them had a few hollihocks growing in front of their doors, but most were surrounded by a walled yard in which there could occasionally be seen a fowl pecking about in the mud or a pig ambling through the gate.

Lieutenant-Colonel Garnet Wolseley, the Deputy-Assistant Quartermaster-General, agreed that the island of Chusan, which the army occupied on its way north as a useful bargaining counter in the future negotiations, was pleasant enough; but the depressing inhabitants of its squalid town, Tinghai, were in pitiable contrast to the fisherfolk of the China Sea, a hardy people, 'inured from childhood to maritime occupations, ever ready to act as pirates when opportunities presented themselves'. The inhabitants of Tinghai displayed no such hardihood. Most of them with memories of the foreign troops' behaviour in 1840 in mind had fled into the country at the allies' approach. Those few who remained seemed all to be old, ugly, or beggars, the beggars obtruding their sores and self-inflicted disabilities and accepting the money thrown to them as a matter of right.

The monks in the temples of Chusan seemed to Wolseley scarcely preferable to the beggars. 'Their clothing was of a dirty dull grey, which corresponded well with the colour of their shaven crowns, lending them, doubtless, a very solemn air, but also adding to the general filthy effect of their appearance.' The monks invited the British visitors—who strolled round the temple, knocking the gongs and bells with their umbrellas and walking sticks, staring at priests meditating in fixed stillness, sniffing distastefully at the joss-sticks and the oily smoke from the numerous red tallow candles—to stay for a meal after a visit to their abbot. The abbot received them most courteously, taking off his hat out of deference to their usages; but the boiling tea he gave them was 'of what old women in England would consider very weak nature', while the meal the monks afterwards provided consisted of rice and dried, salted cabbage, 'a very coarse, rank-looking vegetable', served up in a 'bowl of the commonest description of earthenware'.

Apart from being poor hosts, the monks were useless as informants, 'for, besides being an ignorant class, they spoke a peculiar patois, which those of [the] party who spoke Chinese could understand but imperfectly'. Poor and ignorant as the monks were, however, the coolies who worked in the fields around the temple were far more so, being 'miserably clad and extremely dirty'. One had not shaved his skull. He was asked if he were a Taiping rebel. No, he answered, 'he only allowed his hair to grow because he could not afford to shave it. He was evidently skilled in the arts of begging, as he at once prostrated himself, . . . saying, "Ye are gods; I will worship you".'

Wolseley liked Shanghai little better than Tinghai. Its narrow and ill-paved, dirty and smelly streets were full of beggars; its walls hung with cages filled with the heads of rebels and pirates. The town provided but 'one racket court, no club, a stiflingly hot room surrounded by bookshelves called by the inhabitants a library, a dismal-looking race course enclosed by deep and unwholesome-looking ditches'. One could take a walk in the tea gardens, but there the rockeries, high arched bridges and dirty ponds were hardly to be admired. One could walk across the bridges onto one of the islands, but there the peepshows, fortune-tellers, jugglers, tea shops and restaurants were scarcely likely to impress those who had savoured the delights of Cremorne Gardens in London. One might go for a stroll in the country, but there the strong-smelling manure in the ploughed fields, whose flat expanses were broken only by coffins laid upon the earth and the rows of stunted willows and sallows overhanging the slimy creeks, made such an expedition less than inviting. Shanghai, in fact, was 'one of the dullest places under heaven'; nothing except a desire to grow rich could possibly induce anyone to remain there.[13]

In that summer of 1860 Shanghai was peculiarly unwelcoming, for the Taiping rebels had taken Soochow and were reported to be advancing eastwards down the Yangtze River. Many Chinese merchants were preparing to flee from the town; the shops were closed; the trading junks had gone from their anchorage; the streets were full of homeless refugees. In his anxiety the Governor of Kiangsu asked for help against the rebels from the allied commanders; but although the French commander felt disposed to mount an attack against the Taipings, the British argued that it was not their duty to interfere in the internal disputes of the country.

*   *   *

The French commander was General Cousin de Montauban, a capable but irascible officer, quick to take offence and determined not to accept any orders, either from the British, though their army was so much larger than his own, or, indeed, from Baron Gros. The British commander, Sir James Hope Grant, was a far more easygoing man whose popularity with the troops he had commanded during the Indian Mutiny was remarked upon by Lord Elgin. 'Hope Grant seems very much liked,' Elgin told his wife. 'It can hardly be otherwise, for there is a quiet simplicity and kindliness about his manner which, in a man so highly placed, must be most winning. I am particularly struck by the grin of delight with which the men of a regiment of Sikhs who were with him at Lucknow, greet him whenever they meet him. I observed on this to him, and he said, "Oh, we were always good friends. I used to visit them when they were sick, poor fellows."'[14]

Hope Grant had served in China before, having been appointed to the staff of one of Lord Gough's brigade commanders, Lord Saltoun, an appointment given to him, so it was rumoured, mainly because of his expertise as a cellist, a musician required by Lord Saltoun, who was himself an ardent violinist. It was said, indeed, of the inarticulate Hope Grant, who could neither read a map nor tell the points of the compass, that he was a better performer on the cello than on the field of battle, and that he knew the Bible a good deal more intimately than the works of von Clausewitz. He was nevertheless esteemed perfectly capable of getting the army that Her Majesty's government had entrusted to his care inside the walls of Peking, an operation which, in Colonel Wolseley's opinion, no other general in the British army could hope to do more satisfactorily. Certainly, as Lord Elgin remarked, everyone liked Hope Grant, contrasting his affability, the friendly expression on his bewhiskered, sunburned face, the homely Scottish accent, with the brusqueness of Admiral Hope who was notorious for never returning the salute of a military officer.[15]

Before Lord Elgin's arrival at Shanghai the military commanders had already met to discuss their plan of operations. It had been decided that something more subtle was required than the brutal tactics adopted against the Taku forts the year before. This time the forts would be taken from the rear, the British landing to the north of them at Pehtang, the French to the south, and both armies moving round upon Taku in a pincer movement. When the time came, however, the French discovered that to get ashore south of the forts would entail a march of two miles across mud flats; and it was therefore agreed that both armies would land together at Pehtang.

* * *

At nine o'clock on the morning of 1 August 1860, the landing at Pehtang began. The sea was calm and settled, and although the rain fell in sudden torrents through gusts of a strong wind, the Taku forts could clearly be seen three miles off on the port quarter, 'looking sullen and threatening', to a young officer, Robert Swinhoe, 'but giving no other sign of life than a Tartar flag which waved from the largest battery'. All the embrasures were masked and no troops were visible, though on the causeway that led inland from the forts across the marshy ground to the town of Taku behind them, a picket of Tartar cavalry could be seen; and beyond the walls of Taku there were several inhabitants hurrying off to safety and two mandarins in sedan chairs protected by a mounted escort.

The allied soldiers clambered out of the boats and jumped on to the mud, sinking in it almost up to their waists. Firmer land, above which gulls and curlews and small terns could be seen circling round brackish pools, mounds of salt and clusters of conical-shaped tombs, lay three quarters of a mile in front of them; the soft and sticky mud stretched out of sight on either side.

Their orders had been to land 'with three days' cooked provisions, fifty-six rounds ammunition, greatcoats, canteens, water-bottles full, and haversacks'. They were to wear 'cloth trousers, summer frocks, worsted socks and wicker helmets'; but Brigadier-General Sutton, commander of the troops that were the first to land and known to them all as 'Blaspheming Billy', showed his contempt for such instructions by taking off his trousers, boots and socks, tying them to the scabbard of his sword and slinging them over his shoulder. 'Picture a somewhat fierce and ugly bandy-legged little man thus accoutred in a big white helmet, clothed in a dirty jacket of red serge, below which a very short slate-coloured shirt extended a few inches, cursing and swearing loudly "all round" at everybody and everything as he led his brigade through the hateful mire.'[16]

Fortunately the Pehtang forts, though mined, were unoccupied and the landing was not opposed. By nightfall the allies were safely ashore, and the next day the small town of Pehtang surrendered. It was immediately occupied by the two armies, the French taking one side, the British the other, a matter much to be regretted, in General Hope Grant's opinion, for the plunder and robbing committed by the French was a very bad example to his own men; the French officers appeared 'not to try to stop it'.

Within a few minutes of the allied occupation of the town, the air was rent with the 'continued squeaking of expiring pigs', and French soldiers could be seen dashing all over the town with shovels and pickaxes, chasing the animals in and out of houses and down the muddy streets, wandering into the British half of the town to see what they could find there. According to Colonel Wolseley they found that the British soldiers had already been put to hard work, 'either at repairing the roads, making wharves, carrying water, or landing stores, whilst the French strolled about with their hands in their pockets, gaping at our working parties, or looking in wonder at our huge dragoons, as they and their horses landed, until their energies were roused by the appearance of some old sow coming round a corner, when pursuit was immediately commenced'.

One good reason for this foraging by the French, Wolseley said, was that they were supposed to have with them on landing six days' provisions, more than any man could or would carry. He might have kept his biscuit but he would not carry about with him six days' supply of salt meat which went bad and smelled horribly after the first two or three days and was therefore invariably thrown away. 'The Frenchman was thus obliged to go pig-hunting or actually fishing, to keep himself alive, a system of supply which relieved their commisariat of much difficulty. Our men, on the other hand, landed with only three days' provisions, including the rations for the day on which they landed, and on the fourth, regular supplies of food and drink were issued to them.'[17]

Robert Swinhoe felt sorry for the 'poor French soldiers' who were compelled by this system of supply 'to search the streets and ditches for pigs, which not lasting many days, they were then obliged to have recourse to the dogs and cats of the village. It was a common sight to see several Frenchmen at a time chasing the dogs on the mud beyond the forts, whither the poor animals had sought their last refuge'.[18]

Nor was it only food that the French soldiers plundered. For some time after the occupation of Pehtang they, and Chinese coolies, were 'constantly to be met with, big sticks in hand, rushing into the houses and ransacking right and left. What articles they did not want to carry away they ruthlessly destroyed' or threw into the streets, which were soon littered with broken pottery and furniture, torn books and pictures. They appeared at the doors of the houses dressed in Chinese women's clothes, fanning themselves, or roamed about the streets in all varieties of Chinese silks.[19] 'Such scenes of desolate ransacked houses made one shudder at the idea of our cottage homes of England ever being visited by a foreign foe,' wrote an officer of the King's Dragoon Guards. 'They caused many a fervent wish to rise in our hearts that our own favourite land may ever be spared from such scenes of desolation.'[20]

Although French officers complained that the British and Indians were quite as bad as their own men were, or even worse—'the English are our master,' wrote Armand Lucy, 'they have an ancient reputation; you cannot find so much as a nail in places where they have been'[21]—the strong injunctions against pillaging, and the savage flogging of offenders, did ensure that the British soldiers were less commonly found looting than the French whose example they would otherwise have certainly followed. Yet severe as the injunctions and punishments were, looting by British troops was by no means unusual. If they were prevented from widespread plundering within the town, they did succeed in robbing the inhabitants who tried to escape from it with their possessions. Many, if not most, of the town's inhabitants had already fled, as they had done from Tinghai. A few had committed suicide, the rest were eventually imprisoned within a pen after a French soldier died foaming at the mouth, it being supposed that they had contrived to poison the water supply. But in the early days of the occupation they were still to be found scurrying belatedly out of Pehtang along the causeway that led southwards to the town of Sinho and the Peiho river.

Robert Swinhoe recorded how these pitiable inhabitants, forced by the allied soldiers to lay open the bundles which they were endeavouring to carry off to safety, collected outside the town on the mud flats begging for food. 'With these poor houseless beings we used occasionally to go and converse,' he said, 'and give them any assistance in our power; and, in return, they would sometimes bring apples and peaches by way of thanks-giving for our attention.'

They pleaded with the British officers to be allowed back to collect those provisions in their houses which they had left behind and which would not be to the foreigners' taste, such as pickled vegetables and salted fish. 'Gathering a number together,' Swinhoe wrote, 'I bade them follow me. I led them to a house where I knew numbers of jars of salt fish were stored in the courtyard. As I passed down a narrow street with all this tagrag and bobtail at my heels, a soldier appeared on a house-top with a spear in his hand. "Stand clear, sir," he cried out to me, "until I dig this into the blackguards." I cautioned him not to be so mad; and taking these men into a house, made each fill his bag with salt fish. It was stinking stuff, and the sight of it was enough to make one feel sick; but with what avidity these poor wretches dived into the jars with their naked arms, and threw the mess into their bags! I was then obliged to walk with them till they got clear of the village again.'[22]

The allies could scarcely contain their impatience to be clear of it themselves. It was at the best of times the 'vilest place in the world', decided the British chaplain, the Rev. R. J. L. M'Ghee. Only a few of the houses and the temples were tiled, the rest of the buildings were of mud, chopped straw and thatch, the deeply sunken, narrow streets outside them filled with drainage and refuse. By the time the occupying forces had been there a week, it reminded those who had served in the Crimean War of Balaclava.[23]

The landing place, a medical officer recorded in his diary, could 'be compared only to a swamp, to say that it is ankle-deep in mud does not express its state. Officers and men are going about without shoes, trousers rolled up to their knees. . . . Heaped in masses are lying all sorts of military stores and munitions of war, amongst which figure prominently guns and their carriages, pontoons, ammunition wagons, casks, kegs, scaling-ladders, wheel-barrows, pick-axes, shovels. . . . The bank of the river hereabouts is strewed with matting, broken crockery, and other debris thrown out of the houses to make room for the stores. The town bears unmistakable evidence of the destructive character of a military occupation, especially in the French quarter, where attempts have been made to lessen the depth of mud by macadamizing the streets with bricks procured by pulling down portions of the houses.'[24]

For a week it rained almost continuously, and the sticky, slippery mud that covered everything, the shortage of boats and the lack of a usable jetty made it impossible to unload the stores, the cavalry horses and the heavy guns quickly enough for a general advance towards Sinho and Taku before 12 August. An armed reconnaissance towards Sinho by two thousand men had been attempted on 3 August and had been abandoned when it was discovered that the causeway was strongly defended.

The advance on the 12th was carried out on two fronts. The

First British Division, under Sir John Michel, moved forward with the French Army along the causeway, the Second British Division, commanded by Sir Robert Napier, down a track through the mud flats to the north of it.

'It was a fearful trudge for the unfortunate troops across that mud,' an officer recalled, 'numbers kept dropping out in the line of march and rested for awhile on the side of some grave-mound; others, especially the Punjaubees [the Punjab Native Infantry], finding their boots an impediment, preferred throwing them away, and tucking up their trowsers, pushed boldly on. The appearance of languor throughout the line was distressing. The gun-carriages sank so deeply in the slush that great fears began to be entertained of their ever getting on. . . . It was likewise painful to see the cavalry horses [many of whom sank up to their girths in morasses] struggling on knee-deep with their heavily accoutred burdens. The morass seemed interminable; but a travel of some four miles brought us to harder ground, and in sight of a long line of Tartar cavalry drawn up to oppose our advance.'[25]

To the advancing troops the Tartars seemed, in the strange light, to be of an enormous size, 'magnified by the mirage into giant-warriors on giant steeds'. They firmly stood their ground as the British brought up their new Armstrong guns and opened fire at a range of less than a mile. 'Shell after shell broke over their heads, but the [Tartars] remained unflinching for some minutes, closing up instantaneously the gaps that were made in their order by the murderous shells, bravely discharging their wretched gingalls without the slightest effect.'[26]

When the British and Indian cavalry charged, however, the fight was very soon over, for the little Tartar ponies were knocked over in a matter of minutes by the heavy chargers of the Sikhs and Dragoons who cut up the helpless riders with savage pleasure, afterwards recalling with satisfaction the numbers they had 'bagged' as though their enemies were animals.[27]

By the evening of that day the town of Sinho at the end of the causeway was in allied hands. Numerous of its inhabitants had committed suicide, including the family of a mandarin whom Colonel

Schmitz of the French army found waving a fan to prevent the flies from settling on the blood of his cut throat. His womenfolk struggled in their death agony and his children moved about the floor, their faces 'smirched with blood like those of babies eating jam'.[28]

The next day, 14 August, the neighbouring village of Tangku was also taken without difficulty. The Taku forts now lay less than two miles away, open to attack from the rear.

But another six days passed before the attack was made. While supplies were brought up to Sinho, while guns and ammunition were dragged to the front, while the Engineers built roads and threw bridges over the ditches and canals, the people of Tangku were subjected to the same violence as those of Pehtang had been. Numbers of French soldiers rushed down the streets with bayonets fixed, breaking down doors on either side, ransacking houses; Chinese coolies followed them, raping what girls they could find; British soldiers took what they could when their officers were not looking.

General Napier set aside a series of hovels for the reception of the villagers and here hundreds of men and women and children were collected, some of them wounded by a large Chinese gun that fired occasional shots into the village from Taku, most of them on their knees in supplication, and all of them in tears.

Lord Elgin laid the blame for the people's suffering entirely on the French. 'This dreadful alliance,' he wrote, 'what will it not have cost us before we are done with it? The French by their exactions and misconduct have already stirred to resistance the peaceful population of China. They are cautious enough when armed enemies, even Chinese, are in question—but indisputably valorous against defenceless villagers and little-footed women.' The sooner the campaign was finished and the alliance ended the better.[29]

Already there had been strong differences of opinion between the allied commanders. Before he had met him, General Hope Grant was assured that de Montauban was 'a great Turk';[30] now that he knew him he was convinced of the fact. Although an easygoing man, Hope Grant had been deeply offended by his colleague's affectations of superiority as a general, his arrogant independence; and he had

been profoundly irritated—making few allowances for the difficulties of supply for the French army which had no base comparable
to that of the British in India—by his tiresome slowness. Now there
was renewed trouble between the two men as to the best method of
attacking the Taku forts.

There were four of these forts, two on the northern bank of the
Peiho, two across the river on the southern bank. It was Hope
Grant's plan to capture the nearer of the two northern forts. Being
the furthest from the river mouth, this fort was the least strongly
defended, and once taken from the enemy it would command the
other three. This plan, in de Montauban's opinion, was 'completely
useless': a far more sensible operation would be to cross the river to
the southern bank, attack the enemy's positions there and so prevent
his troops from escaping towards Peking. But, Hope Grant argued,
this would stretch the supply lines dangerously and expose them to
attack by Tartar cavalry. In any case, the main object was to take the
forts, the capture or destruction of their garrisons was of secondary
importance. De Montauban grudgingly gave way, composing a
memorandum which would make it clear in Paris that in the event
of failure he could not be held responsible for the plan of attack.[31]

The attack began at daybreak on 21 August with a heavy artillery
bombardment which sent the wild fowl whirling away across the
swampy saltmarsh and caused a thunderous explosion in the northern fort as a shell blew up the powder magazine, covering the
crenellated walls in clouds of thick smoke. The allies hoped that they
had silenced the garrison; but when the smoke cleared the Chinese
guns opened up again, and it was obvious that the first real battle of
the war was about to be fought.

The rear gate of the fort was blocked by rows of strong timbers,
the whole of its rear face protected by barriers of sharp pointed
bamboo stakes, planted as thickly as stubble, by iron crows' feet, and
by dykes filled with water. Pontoons had been made to lay across
these dykes; and when the allied assault was launched at seven
o'clock in the morning the Chinese coolies in the French service
dashed forward with them. An English officer watching them had
'never seen men under fire behave with greater coolness, or perform

their allotted work in a more matter-of-fact way'. Another was astonished by their 'remarkable steadiness and alacrity'. A third, who had seen them in the earlier engagements turning over the bodies of the Chinese dead, pointing and giggling at the distorted or empty faces, thought that they actually 'enjoyed the fun'; they were 'mostly thieves and pirates hardened to blood', and they shouted with pleasure at every well aimed shot whether it killed a Chinese or an allied soldier.

On this occasion when the pontoons proved inadequate for getting across the ditches, they jumped into the water, holding scaling ladders above their heads, so that the soldiers could scramble across by trampling over them. The British, who were prevented from laying their pontoons by the matchlock fire from the fort, either jumped headlong into the water and splashed through it, half swimming, half walking, or they availed themselves of the improvised bridges provided by the coolies.[32]

All the time the Chinese in the forts kept up their fire on the enemy below, hurling round shot from their cannon and handfuls of slugs from their primitive gingalls, shooting bolts from their crossbows, discharging flights of arrows, and dropping pots filled with lime, bits of masonry and cannon balls onto those who had managed to reach the bottom of the walls.

Despite this barrage the French succeeded in getting three or four ladders up to the wall; but as soon as they raised them up and began to climb to the top, the Chinese seized them and pushed them away, sending both ladders and men hurtling back into the mud at the foot of the wall, to the delight of the laughing coolies who had risked their lives to get them there.

At length one French soldier—maintaining his balance on a ladder which was being rigorously shaken by a Chinese soldier who had caught the top of it in his bow—contrived to leap over the parapet waving the tricolour. Almost immediately he was shot through the heart; but as he fell, a lieutenant of the 44th (East Essex) Regiment, a lieutenant and a private of the 67th (South Hampshire) Regiment and a young ensign, carrying the Queen's Colour of the 67th, clambered over the parapet after him. The Chinese continued to

fight inside the work; but as more and more French and British
soldiers poured over the walls, jabbing and slashing at the Chinese
troops with their swords and bayonets, resistance ceased. The
mandarin in command, who had stayed to fight to the end, was shot
by an officer of marines; and the allied colours flew freely in the
wind as the sky, clear and bright in the early morning, now clouded
over and the rain poured blindingly down.

Piles of corpses lay around the overturned guns and broken gun-
carriages, some of them, in Robert Swinhoe's words 'most fearfully
lacerated'. He thought it astonishing how they had managed to
stand so long, but he 'observed, in more instances than one, that the
unfortunate creatures had been tied to the guns by the legs'. This
seemed incredible, but 'several officers' besides himself saw the
'poor victims lying dead or dying thus tied'.

Colonel Wolseley thought it more likely that there had been no
earlier surrender because the 'peculiar nature of the defences of the
forts' made it almost as difficult for the Chinese to retreat from
them as it had been for the allies to get into them. It may also have
been that the Chinese had been 'to the last so confident of victory
from the strength of the place and our former defeat, that they
never even contemplated retreating'.

But whatever reasons they found for their determined resistance,
all the allied officers agreed that the Chinese had fought with
notable spirit and that for once their leaders had shown themselves
worthy of their soldiers' courage. The mandarin who had been
killed inside the captured fort had clearly 'encouraged by his
presence and example all who were inside'.

Seng-ko-lin-ch'in himself had received an imperial rescript to the
effect that it would be wasteful to risk his person, on whom the State
relied, 'in combat with ugly Barbarians';[33] and, in obedience to this
advice, he had ridden off to Peking with a guard of Manchu horse-
men. His abandoned headquarters were found to be 'tastefully furnished and fitted up with sofas and cushions'. They contained good
maps, detailed plans of each of the forts and a cane-bottomed chair
taken from one of the gunboats which his cannon had destroyed in
his earlier and more successful encounter with the allied forces.

'Along the walls, immediately above his sleeping place, there was a long description, illustrated with quaint-looking pictures, of a proposed plan for annihilating the Barbarians, should they ever attempt a march upon Peking. The plan consisted in placing large quantities of combustibles and explosive mixtures upon bulls, and covering them over with a sort of umbrella like clothing: these were to be brought in front of our army, having crackers or other fireworks attached to their tails, under the terrifying influence of which the animals were supposed to rush in upon us, the combustibles then exploding, to the utter confusion and destruction of the assembled army.'[34]

With the departure of Seng-ko-lin-ch'in all Chinese opposition in the area came to an end. The other northern fort was taken without further loss by the French two hours after the capture of the first. The next day, both the forts on the far side of the Peiho were surrendered and, while the obstacles at the mouth of the river were pulled up and towed away or sunk, the bodies of the dead were thrown into a large shallow pit, after Signor Beato, an Italian photographer who had attached himself to the expedition, had taken their likenesses, begging the soldiers not to move the 'deada mansa' until he had finished. 'They were brought in by ropes attached to their heads or heels, according as they had lain most conveniently. A couple of soldiers harnessed thereto dragged them in through the mud, as merrily, to all appearance, as if they were engaged at a harvest home. Dead dogs and cats were thrown into the same pit amidst laughter and jokes.'[35]

No less than six Victoria Crosses were awarded for acts of gallantry during the storming of the Taku forts which had cost the British army the loss of seventeen men dead and 184 wounded, the French seventeen dead and 141 wounded, compared with Chinese losses estimated at between 1,200 and 1,500. It was held to be an action worthy of the best traditions of both armies, and one, in view of its important prizes, that had been cheaply won. There was a feeling that the war was as good as over. Colonel Wolseley told his mother that it was certainly so. Captain Mackintosh of the 44th wrote to tell his wife that he would be home before Christmas; and Lord Elgin, though he 'did not like to be too confident', assured his family that he did not think his homecoming would be long delayed now and that many things were more improbable than that he should be eating his Christmas dinner in Scotland.[37]

* * *

Elgin sailed up the Peiho towards Tientsin, in the wake of Admiral Hope's gunboats, meeting with no resistance, and arrived there on 25 August. The 'indefatigable Parkes', as Elgin referred to him, was already there, having obtained a written capitulation of the Taku forts and organized a committee of supply in Tientsin. Parkes shared Lord Elgin's confidence, believing, as he told his wife, that he did 'not now expect to hear another gun fired'.

'I am very cheerful,' he went on to assure her contentedly. 'By the next mail I trust I shall write you that we have seen the interior of Peking . . . the climate is really very fine: very hot in the middle of the day, but cold enough at night for a blanket. I wear blue flannel all day, and though much exposed to the sun, have not suffered from it at all. It is a very different sun to that of the south of China. Now we have reached Tientsin we have lots of luxury—fine beef, particularly fine mutton, and fruit and vegetables that make one's mouth water.'[38]

While the troops enjoyed this fine mutton at only threepence a pound and became so partial to the ice which the hawkers sold about the camp that they would not drink their grog without it, while de Montauban began to issue coloured scarves to the soldiers who were to form the French contingent of the Ambassadors' escort for their entry into Peking, Parkes discussed with the Imperial Commissioners the terms of the Chinese surrender. At first matters seemed to be 'going on well,' Parkes thought. 'The Convention was agreed to by the Commissioners and ready for signature. At the eleventh hour we found (as usual to Chinese negotiators) that they had been deceiving us.'[39] They had no authority to sign.

More firmly convinced than ever that 'a little more bullying' would be necessary before 'this stupid Government' was brought 'up to the mark', Elgin determined—and Gros agreed—that the allied armies must be got nearer to Peking to make it 'come to its senses'. The delay, Elgin comforted himself, had been to the allies' advantage rather than to that of the Chinese: 'My idiotical Chinamen . . . have gone on negotiating with me just long enough to enable Grant to bring all his army up to this point. Here we are, then, with our base established in the heart of the country, in a capital climate, with abundance around us, our army in excellent health, and these stupid people give me a snub, which obliges me to break with them.'[40] So, as he told his wife on 8 September, he was 'at war again!'

The armies moved slowly north. It was 'a very nice ride', Elgin thought, through crops of millet fourteen feet high, with the enemy nowhere to be seen. About twenty miles above Tientsin he was handed a letter, jointly signed by Tsai-yüan, Prince I, cousin of the Emperor, and by the President of the Board of War. It informed him that there had been a mistake at Tientsin, that the Commissioners there had misunderstood their orders, and that they themselves were leaving for Tientsin to sign the Convention. 'Of course,' Lord Elgin recorded in his journal, he could not agree to this; he must stick by his programme and 'decline to have anything to say to them' until he had reached Tungchow. But when the Chinese wrote again, suggesting as a compromise that the allies should halt short of Tungchow, at Ho-se-wu, he agreed to the suggestion and sent Parkes ahead to try once more to come to terms with them.

He had quite altered his opinion of Parkes. No longer did he consider him an irresponsible firebrand; he was, on the contrary, '*the* man of the situation'; it was not only that no one except Horatio Lay could speak Chinese as well as he did, but his 'cunning, courage and ability' combined to make him one of the most remarkable men that Elgin had ever met.[41]

At Tungchow, Parkes and his colleague, Thomas Wade, soon reached agreement with the Chinese, who readily submitted to the allied demand that the two foreign Ambassadors should be admitted to Peking with an escort of two thousand men to ratify the Treaty of Tientsin; they assured the British delegates that they spoke in the Emperor's name and that their signatures were as binding as his.

The only outstanding points were the site of the camp that the allies should occupy in the meantime, and the question whether Elgin should be granted an audience with the Emperor in order to hand over the letter he had for him from Queen Victoria. Neither of these points seemed of primary importance to the allies; and both Parkes and Wade on their return to the army were 'thoroughly satisfied' that Prince I, 'a tall dignified man with an intelligent countenance, though a somewhat unpleasant eye', was 'at last bona fide in his offer to surrender'.

Yet when Parkes went back to Tungchow to settle the outstanding questions, he found Prince I quite adamant that in no circumstances whatever could the Emperor grant an audience to Lord Elgin. It appeared that 'a convenient law of the realm, invented for the occasion, compelled his Majesty to go to his hunting-lodge that season'. The Prince's demeanour, brusque yet apprehensive, was quite different from what it had been the first, promising day of the negotiations; and Wade felt sure that now the warlike counsels of Seng-ko-lin-ch'in had prevailed at Court.[42]

* * *

Wade was fully justified in his belief. Seng-ko-lin-ch'in had himself advised the timid and dissolute Emperor to leave Peking, to go north and to leave the defence of the capital in the hands of his soldiers untroubled by problems of the Son of Heaven's safety. Other mandarins had advised the Emperor to stay in Peking; to leave it could not but cause widespread consternation in the city. The Emperor, for his part, had characteristically suggested that he should march out of Peking as though he intended to take personal command of his armies, but then ride away to the safety of his palace at Jehol. In the end, he hurriedly went north without even this pretence at resistance.[43]

Seng-ko-lin-ch'in, however, was determined to resist. He was not unduly concerned with honouring his word to Barbarians whose own honour had been besmirched, and whose evil designs proved by their presence in the metropolitan province of Chihli. They would not enter Peking if he could possibly prevent them.

16 | The Burning of the Palace

*Never did a Division march with a better will
to perform a more just and loudly called for
act of retribution, upon an imperious, treacherous and cruel power.* The Rev. R. J. L.
M'Ghee, October 1860.

With Parkes in Tungchow on the evening of 17 September were
several men who had accompanied him as colleagues in the negotiations, as observers or as members of his escort. There was Lieutenant Anderson, commander of a mounted escort of dragoons and
Sikhs; there was Lieutenant-Colonel C. P. Beauchamp Walker,
the Assistant Quartermaster-General of the cavalry brigade; there
was Thomas Bowlby, correspondent of *The Times*; and there were
two diplomats, Henry Loch, Lord Elgin's private secretary, and de
Normann, an attaché on Frederick Bruce's staff, a promising young
man who had come up from Shanghai to gain experience.

Early on the morning of 18 September, Parkes, Loch and Colonel
Walker, with an escort of dragoons and Sikhs, rode back towards the
allied lines to report that, although they had agreed with the
Chinese a site for the allied camp, they had still not been able to
settle the matter of Lord Elgin's audience with the Emperor.

On approaching the ground that had been agreed upon the night
before as a suitable place for the camp, Parkes was appalled to find
that it was occupied by 'a considerable force of Chinese troops, while
other bodies could be seen approaching from other directions'. It was
immediately clear that Seng-ko-lin-ch'in was preparing his army
for battle.

Leaving Henry Loch and two Sikhs to try to get through the
Tartar cavalry screen to Hope Grant's headquarters with an urgent
warning not to move forward into what was evidently an ambush,

and asking Colonel Walker to stay where he was with five dragoons and observe the Chinese movements for as long as he could, Parkes galloped back into Tungchow to 'look out for the Commissioners and see if they would immediately direct the withdrawal of these troops'.

When Parkes arrived in Tungchow, where the rest of his party were out shopping not knowing yet that anything was wrong, Prince I told him bluntly that the Commissioners would certainly not order the troops to retire, that the question of the audience with the Emperor had not been settled and, therefore, peace had not been settled upon either. Prince I told him this 'in such a tone' that Parkes soon saw that the quicker he withdrew himself from the Commissioners the better, 'as they were surrounded by a host of men whose manner was very different to that of previous occasions'.

So Parkes hurried off to look for de Normann and Bowlby, to warn them that this was no time for shopping. Before he found them he came across Henry Loch who, accompanied by Captain Brabazon of the Royal Artillery, had obtained permission from the British headquarters to go back through the Chinese lines to Tungchow to see what he could do to help his friend Parkes get out of the town.

Loch told Parkes that Hope Grant was just about to launch an attack on the Chinese, who were now edging round both his flanks, and that if they did not make a run for it immediately they might never be able to do so. At that moment Bowlby and de Normann appeared, and Parkes, having collected all his party together at last, was able to gallop off.

'We had a good six miles to go,' he wrote to his wife afterwards, 'and the whole Chinese army between us and our people; but I relied upon our flag of truce carrying us through, if we could only get out before the battle began. We rode hard, and had only about half a mile more to go to place us in safety, when we got amongst the masses of the Chinese troops . . . who levelled their pieces and would have fired, had not an officer, who galloped up simultaneously, persuaded them to desist. In quicker time than it takes me to write, we were surrounded by them, and when I called out for the officer I wanted to see, I was pointed to a fat fellow on horseback some distance off on the other side of a creek, and told to dismount and cross over to him.'

Before Parkes had reached him 'a greater man appeared, even Sankolinsin himself, the Chinese Commander-in-Chief'. As Parkes approached Seng-ko-lin-ch'in, he was seized by his attendants and hurled down before him because he 'had not instantly obeyed their order to kneel'. Loch and a Sikh who was by his side were treated in the same way.

Then Seng-ko-lin-ch'in, 'in a very forbidding tone', demanded of Parkes why he had not settled the audience question the day before, and when Parkes denied that he had authority to do so, cried 'Listen! You can talk reason. . . . You say that you do not direct these military movements; but I know your name, and that you instigate all the evils that your people commit. You have also used bold language in the presence of [Prince I], and it is time that foreigners should be taught respect for Chinese nobles and ministers.'

Parkes, Loch and the Sikh were bundled into a cart with two French soldiers who had recently been captured, and Seng-ko-lin-ch'in angrily ordered that they should be taken away to Prince I. Bowlby, de Normann and the rest were put in other carts and carried off to Yüan-ming Yüan. Parkes murmured to Loch, as though his friend could have any doubt of the fact, 'I fear we are prisoners'.[1]

*   *   *

At the very moment that Parkes, carrying the flag of truce, had ridden full tilt 'amongst the masses of the Chinese troops', the allied guns had opened their barrage. The cannonade was immediately followed by persistent cavalry attacks that charged the dense ranks of Tartars, now numbering about twenty thousand men, 'over and over again'.

'Through and through them' the charges went, Wolseley said, 'bowling them over like ninepins, until all had retired leaving all their guns in our possession amounting to over seventy in number. We pursued them through the town of Chanchiawan, and took a number of their camps which we consigned to the flames. . . . There were considerable quantities of powder in almost every tent, so that when the tents were set on fire, the numerous explosions filled the air with volumes of smoke, which shot up in tall graceful columns every moment whilst the work of destruction was going on.'[2]

It was not only the Tartar camps which were destroyed at Chang-chia-wan. As a punishment for the treachery of the Chinese leaders, the town was given over to loot. No steps were taken to prevent either pillaging or vandalism 'as the town was a capture in war, and hence [considered by the military traditions of the time] lawful booty'.[3] For two days the plunder continued; pawnbrokers' shops, distinguished by their gold and green signboards in the shape of dragons' heads, were broken open and their contents pulled out into the street where crowds of poor people from the surrounding villages eagerly helped themselves to the larger articles, bedding and furniture, for which the allied soldiers had no use. The doors of a warehouse were smashed down and its stores, mostly comprising five million pounds of tea, were hurled outside. Private houses were entered and all that they contained was pocketed, pulled out or destroyed. Shops were ransacked and the goods that the looters did not fancy were thrown into the air and against the crumbling, moss-grown walls of the town. One 'rare old house,' Robert Swinhoe reported, 'with its exquisite carvings and hangings, and its rooms filled with curiosities too big to carry away, was completely ransacked and destroyed internally, the roof and walls merely being left'. Dresses, hats and shoes, fans, beads and hair-combs littered the streets 'and coolies and niggers vied with each other in gay and fantastic apparel. Some hairy old Sikh, attired in feminine costume, would stroke his beard and strut in long boots before the admiring eyes of his surrounding comrades.'[4]

With as much of their loot as they could carry with them, the armies moved forward, outflanking Tungchow and making their way towards the Yangliang canal which led from the Peiho river into Peking. There were two bridges over the canal, a wooden bridge in the line of the British advance on the left, a stone and marble bridge at Pa-li-ch'iao on the right in front of the French. The Pa-li-ch'iao bridge, as Montauban was soon to discover, was strongly defended by large numbers of Tartar cavalry, separated by groups of infantry, and by a number of batteries of artillery half concealed amongst the tall trees and the tombs of mandarins.

The Tartar cavalry advanced towards the French in silence, controlled by huge yellow banners with black inscriptions which were waved up and down and from side to side by their commanders. They approached to within fifty yards of the French skirmishing line, swayed a little in the face of a brisk fire, then straightened and wheeled to the right. Another body skilfully manoeuvred round the other flank of the French, who were in danger now of being trapped in a well executed pincer movement. But the aim of the Chinese gunners was wildly inaccurate, and while their shells flew harmlessly over the heads of the enemy, de Montauban's guns opened up with rockets that exploded under the bellies of the Tartar horses with devastating effect. The Chinese infantry came forward to the rescue of the cavalry, but the French guns continued to pour forth such a barrage of shells and rockets, Count d'Hérisson, de Montauban's secretary, said, 'that we could see deep furrows opening within the enemy's dense masses of men and horses. The attack gradually turned into a retreat, and the cavalry fell back toward the bridge, though not without closing its ranks. At that very moment, Montauban ordered the sounding of the charge, and the whole French army rushed towards the bridge, which was defended by ten cannon manned just as badly as the rest of the enemy artillery. Their shells, too, flew over our heads. . . . It was like fighting in a dream: we kept advancing, firing and killing the enemy, yet no one, or hardly anyone, was hurt in our own ranks.' The crew of the ten cannon defending the bridge were all killed at their posts. Finally, the last man still standing, a gigantic Tartar, flag-bearer to the enemy general, who stood to the end fast at his post amidst the corpses, was knocked to the ground, his dismembered arm still clutching the pole of his banner.[5]

In this well-conducted and successful operation—in honour of which General de Montauban chose the name Palikao for the title of nobility which was later conferred upon him—the French troops suffered trifling losses; the Chinese left a thousand dead on the field.

*　　*　　*

'Exterminating the Yüeh Bandits.' A battle scene depicting Imperial forces fighting the Taiping rebels (known to the Manchu government as Yüeh bandits) in the 1850's. On the right is the city of Chinkiang, occupied by the governor of Kiangsu; and on the left is Yangchow, defended by the rebels

Above: Interior of the North Fort at Taku after its capture by the British, August 1860. *Right:* Prince Kung, the Emperor's brother, negotiator of the 1860 Treaties of Peking with the British, French and Russians

ord Elgin's entrance into Peking on 24 October 1860 to sign the Convention of Peking, s seen from the top of the Anting gate overlooking the Tartar city

Lord Elgin signing the Treaty of Tientsin, 26 June 1858

Above: Costumes of Mandarins and Imperial soldiers at the time of the Taiping Rebellion. *Right:* Li Hung-chang (1823-1901), Governor of Kiangsu, at the time of the Taiping Rebellion.

Below: Costumes of Taiping officials and soldiers. *Right:* Lieutenant-Colonel Charles George Gordon in 1863

Above: Cartoon from the Chinese periodical *Jen-ching hua-pao*. The train bears the caption, 'The repayment of foreign debts endangers the life and property of the people'. The bridge (the foundation and economy of the state) is being sabotaged by foreigners who will plunge it into the water named 'The whirlpool of power'. *Below:* Cartoon from *Jen-ching hua-pao*. The caption reads 'those who are being protected from ferocious animals (oppressive mandarins), the sentiment being that their 'protector' will prove an even worse menace to the people

大清國當今慈禧端佑康頤昭豫莊誠壽恭欽獻崇熙聖母皇太后

Tz'u-hsi, the Empress Dowager sitting beneath a banderol upon which is written a grandiose description of her numerous virtues and accomplishments. It is dated 1903; she was then 68

The Emperor Kuang-hsü (1872–1907), nephew of Tz'u-hsi, the Empress Dowager

Assault by German and Austrian troops on the Taku forts, 25 September 1900

Sir Claude MacDonald (1852–1915), British Minister in Peking at the time of the Boxer Rising

Field-Marshal Count von Waldersee entering Peking by the Ha Ta Men gate accompanied by the commanders of the other allied forces

Sun Yat-sen (1867–1925), elected President of the Chinese Republic, 29 December 191

Lord Elgin, who was with the army, saw all the allied operations that day, and gave it as his opinion that 'considering that the Tartars are so wretchedly armed and led, they did pretty well. We are now,' he added, 'about six miles from Peking, but I believe the generals will not move for a week.'

They were waiting for the siege guns to come up by river from Tientsin, for they feared that without these guns there was no possibility of storming the forty-foot high walls of Peking, behind which Parkes and the other allied captives were known to be imprisoned. Prince Kung, younger brother of the Emperor, who was now conducting the negotiations on Hsien-feng's behalf, offered to release the prisoners if the army and fleet would withdraw from Peking and retire altogether from the country. In reply to this 'cool' demand made to an army 'in excellent health, abundantly supplied and which in five actions with the enemy [had] lost some twenty killed', Lord Elgin replied that, unless the prisoners were returned to the camp within three days and an undertaking given that the Treaty of Tientsin would be ratified, Peking would be assaulted. It was a cruelly difficult decision for Elgin and Gros to have to make; but they felt that they could not abandon the entire expedition for the sake of the lives of the few men in Peking. Moreover, as Elgin later explained, had he given way to Prince Kung's demand the Chinese in future would think that all they had to do to gain their ends was to kidnap one or two foreign officials.[6]

On 5 October, the siege-train having at last arrived from Tientsin, the armies began to move cautiously forward again, the French on the left, the British on the right. In the difficult country, cut up by brickfields and kilns, tombs and walled gardens, traversed by narrow, sunken roads, the two armies lost contact with each other, and the British, held up for some hours by Tartar cavalry, failed to reach the rendezvous at the Summer Palace of Yüan-ming Yüan suggested by Hope Grant for the night of 6 October. When the British vanguard did arrive there on the morning of the 7th they found that the French army, 'officers and men, seemed to have been seized with a temporary insanity; in body and soul they were absorbed in one pursuit, which was plunder, plunder'.

The evening before, they had brushed aside the few eunuchs who had been able to steel themselves to offer some sort of resistance at the gates, and had poured inside the grounds. De Montauban claimed in his *Souvenirs* that 'after having visited apartments of indescribable splendour', he 'had sentries posted everywhere and ordered two captains to make sure that no one entered the palace, and that everything in it be kept intact until the arrival of the British commander-in-chief'.

But the sight of those numerous, beautifully ornamented garden houses, the halls with their gilt doors and porcelain tiles glittering in the sun, the ornate gateways and clock-houses, temples and pavilions, all full of treasures and all undefended, was too much for the French troops. Prompted, so Count d'Hérisson said, by the fear that the Cantonese coolies and the local peasants, who were advancing across the park with ladders, straw cords and wicks, would either 'filch everything or burn everything' in the palace buildings, they fell upon the treasure themselves. Silver clocks and rosewood tables, enamel screens and porcelain vases, peacocks' feathers and precious jewels, crackle-ware bowls, crystal chandeliers and gilt looking-glasses, books, pictures, snuff-boxes, silk robes and fans, jewelled music boxes, alarm clocks and mechanical toys, the accumulated treasures of centuries, were soon being carried in armfuls from the buildings, tipped into wagons or piled in broken pieces on the paths. What could not be carried off was smashed with clubs and rifle butts, what could not be torn from the walls or ceilings was shot to pieces.

Officers and men alike could be seen with their heads and hands knocking together as they scrambled for treasure in the same box, tore state robes from gilded cupboards, pulled out armfuls of *soieries, bijoux, porcelains, bronzes, sculptures, trésors enfin*. '*Je ne crois pas qu'on ait vu chose pareille,*' one of them told his father, '*depuis le sac de Rome par les barbares.*'

'Being a mere spectator', Count d'Hérisson 'deeply enjoyed this strange and unforgettable vision'. 'It all looked [to him] like a giant ant-hill half crushed under the foot of a passer-by, with its panic-stricken black workers fleeing in every direction carrying a grain, a larva, an egg, or a straw between their mandibles. Some soldiers had buried their heads in the red-lacquered chests of the Empress, others were half-hidden among heaps of embroidered fabrics and silkware, still others were filling their pockets, shirts and kepis with rubies, sapphires, pearls and pieces of crystal.' A large majority of them, d'Hérisson said, were 'grown children' who were 'mainly tempted in the midst of all this unbelievable accumulation of wealth' by the extraordinary variety and number of mechanical toys and clocks, so that the whole area was 'one continuous symphony' with monkeys beating cymbals, rabbits rolling drums, birds singing, toy soldiers playing cornets and bagpipes, clocks chiming, some four thousand musical boxes simultaneously tinkling their several tunes, and every now and then all this noise was 'drowned out by the easily amused soldiers roaring with laughter'.

Jewellery of incalculable value was found in drawers which were soon cracked open with bayonets. One officer found a string of pearls, each pearl the size of a marble, which he later sold in Hong Kong for the absurdly low price of £3,000. No attempt had been made by the Chinese Court to take the most precious objects away, or even to hide them. In the Emperor's bedroom, his hat was found lying on his bed, his pipes on a table beside it, a silk handkerchief and 'sundry writings in the vermilion pencil about the Barbarians' under his pillow.

When the British arrived they found the ground covered with lanterns and masks, broken boxes and wrapping paper, smashed porcelain, yellow cushions embroidered with the five-clawed dragon, Louis XV clocks smashed to pieces for the sake of their jewels, silks and clothing of all kinds. 'The men [were still running] hither and thither in search of further plunder, most of them . . . being decked out in the most ridiculous-looking costumes they could find. . . . Some had dressed themselves in the richly-embroidered gowns of women, and almost all had substituted the turned-up Mandarin hat for their ordinary forage cap. . . . One of the regiments was supposed to be parading; but although their fall in was sounded over and over again, I do not believe there was an average of ten men a company present.'

De Montauban 'kept on repeating that looting was strictly

prohibited,' an English officer recorded, 'and he would not allow it, although his officers were doing it without any reserve before his own eyes. He told the Brigadier that nothing should be touched until Sir Hope Grant arrived. Just as we were walking out of the chief gateway an officer accosted the General and informed him that they had caught a Chinese stealing a pair of old shoes out of the imperial grounds. "Bring him here!" said the indignant General. "Have we not said that looting is strictly forbidden?" The prisoner came forward trembling, and the gallant General exhausted his wrath with his cane about the shoulders of this luckless scapegoat.'

When Lord Elgin arrived, de Montauban came up 'full of protestations. He had prevented *looting* in order that all the plunder might be divided between the armies, etc. etc.' He proposed that the spoils should be equally divided between the two armies, saw to it that Elgin himself received one of the Emperor's green jade batons, and that when a hoard of 800,000 francs worth of gold and silver ingots was discovered, the English got half. But, as Elgin could see, despite de Montauban's protestations, there was no possibility of there being any equal division of the spoils or any stop to the looting which was still proceeding apace.

'There was not a room that I saw,' Elgin wrote, 'in which half the things had not been taken away or broken to pieces. . . . Plundering and devastating a place like this is bad enough, but what is much worse is the waste and breakage. . . . French soldiers were destroying in every way the most beautiful silks, breaking the jade ornaments and porcelain. War is a hateful business. . . . The more one sees of it, the more one detests it. . . . I tried to get a regiment of ours sent to guard the place, but it is difficult to get things done by system in such a case.'

In fact, many of the British officers themselves were behaving 'in a most unbecoming manner', as one of them admitted, showing that they were quite as avaricious as the French, that had they arrived at the Summer Palace first its finest treasures might have filled their baggage instead of that of their allies. They forced all the Chinese looters to drop their bundles, to hand over what was best in them and to carry the items selected back to camp for them. As soon as they arrived in the palace grounds, they and their men 'made a general rush' towards the buildings. 'Most of our men realized some hundreds of pounds worth,' a dragoon officer wrote in his diary. 'We obtained many valuable articles, fully compensating us for past fatigues. . . . The gold was in such quantity we could not believe it was genuine so threw most of it away, a bad job for ourselves.'

According to Count d'Hérisson this was a mistake more often made by Frenchmen than the British. The British, indeed, he said, were far more methodical in the looting than his own countrymen, going about it in a highly organized manner. They 'moved in by squads, as if on fatigue duty, carrying bags, and were commanded by non-commissioned officers who, incredible as it sounds (yet strictly true), had brought jewellers' touchstones with them'.

One of their chaplains would have joined in, too, and taken one of the temple idols if 'that lazy syce' of his had been there to carry it off for him; but as it was it proved too heavy and he left it on the temple's marble floor where his companion had thrown it down to see if he could smash it.[7] Another chaplain cut short the Sunday service to ride over to the palace from which he returned with a mule cart piled high with loot. The next Sunday he preached an 'admirable sermon against covetousness'.[8]

To placate the private soldiers in the British army, only a few of whom—mostly Sikhs and dragoons—had managed to join in the looting, Hope Grant ordered the officers to hand over everything that they had taken from the Summer Palace. The loot was then to be auctioned and the proceeds of the sale distributed throughout the army.

Many small articles were held back, no doubt; but by the first day of the sale the hall of the lama temple in which the auction was held was packed with jade, inlaid jars, silks and immense piles of furs—sable, astrakhan, sea-otter and ermine. The proceeds of the sale—123,000 dollars—were divided into three parts, one-third for the officers, two-thirds for the non-commissioned officers and men. The Commander-in-Chief renounced his share, and his two brigade commanders followed his example. The men received seventeen dollars (about £4) each.

Most French soldiers were far more fortunate. As Baron Gros later admitted in a letter to Paris, 'One Corps commander is said to have in his baggage pearls and diamonds worth more than 800,000 francs. Tientsin at this moment presents the distressing sight of soldiers selling at every cross roads, rolls of silk, jewels, jade, vases, and thousands of precious objects coming from Yüan-ming Yüan worth at least thirty million francs.'[9]

*　　*　　*

On the day that Hope Grant ordered the auction to be held, Harry Parkes and Henry Loch, with a Sikh trooper of Probyn's Horse, l'Escayrac de Lauture, the head of a French scientific commission, and four French soldiers, arrived in the British camp. They had a dreadful story to tell.

After being questioned by Seng-ko-lin-ch'in, Parkes was thrown onto his knees before another mandarin and submitted to a further examination in the middle of which his interrogator suddenly stood up and left the room. A squad of soldiers then entered with drawn swords, bound up Parkes with tight cords, bound Loch, the Sikh and the two French soldiers as well, and ran them all out of the house in the way that Chinese prisoners were hurried out to execution. They were then thrown into a cart and carried off to Peking where they were put into separate prisons. 'Poor Parkes suffered much in mind and body,' wrote Loch, 'and yet maintained outwardly an appearance of calm indifference to all that could be done to him.' So, too, did the Sikh; when Loch told him to keep his spirits and not to be frightened, the sowar replied, 'Fear! I do not fear. If I do not die today, I may tomorrow, and I am past sixty.'

For four days Parkes was kept in a prison 'with some seventy wild-looking felons, foul and diseased'. His hands had swollen to twice their normal size because of the tight cords round his wrists; and, although these cords were later removed, they were immediately replaced by iron fetters that secured him by a chain to a beam in the ceiling. At twelve o'clock on the first night he was taken before the Board of Inquisitors and, while soldiers twisted his ears and pulled his hair, underwent another long interrogation, part of which he afterwards recorded:

INQUISITORS: 'State the name of your head man.'
ANSWER: 'Which one do you mean—the Ambassador, General or Admiral?'
INQUISITORS (angrily): 'You have no such functionaries. Don't presume to use such titles.'
Here the torturers suited their action to the tone of the Mandarins, by pulling simultaneously at my hair, ears, etc.
INQUISITORS: 'Now give the name of your head man.'
ANSWER: 'Which one?'
INQUISITORS: 'The head of your soldiers.'
ANSWER (in English): 'Lieutenant-General Sir Hope Grant.'
INQUISITORS: 'What?'
ANSWER (in English): 'Lieutenant-General Sir Hope Grant.'
INQUISITORS: 'Say something that we can understand.'
ANSWER: 'I am obliged to use the English terms, as you will not let me give you these in Chinese.'
They attempted to write down, in Chinese characters, the sound of 'Lieutenant-General Sir Hope Grant', but not succeeding, they asked the name of another head man.
ANSWER (in English): 'Ambassador Extraordinary the Earl of Elgin.'
Finding it equally impossible to write this down in Chinese, or to get on with the examination, they told me I might revert to Chinese names and titles, and I then gave them those of the Ambassador and the Commander-in-Chief. . . .

The interrogation continued painfully and unprofitably for some time until the exasperated inquisitors ordered that Parkes be sent back to prison where they visited him from time to time to upbraid him for his disgraceful conduct and his obstinacy in not ordering the foreign armies to withdraw. His fellow convicts, however, were kind and considerate, 'interested', so he said, 'in any description I gave them of foreign countries. They were seldom disrespectful, addressed me by my title, and often avoided putting me to inconvenience when it was in their power to do so. Most of them were men of the lowest class, and the gravest order of offenders—as murderers, burglars, etc.'
Eventually, convinced that Parkes could help in restoring peace,

Prince Kung ordered that he should be transferred to a more comfortable cell and then to a temple where Henry Loch, who was allowed to go there with him, was amused to notice that pasted to one of the chairs was a piece of paper marked, 'Returned to store, after being supplied for the use of the American tribute-bearer, Ward.'

Both in his cell and at the temple, Parkes received regular visits from one of the Imperial Commissioners, Heng-ch'i, whom he had met at Tungchow and previously at Canton. Heng-ch'i tried to persuade him to write to Lord Elgin asking him to call a halt to the hostilities. After being allowed a bath and a meal—for whose forty-eight dishes, sent in from a nearby restaurant, they could in their weakness summon little appetite—Parkes and Loch agreed to write the letter, but Loch managed to scribble in Hindustani beneath his signature that it was written under compulsion. 'As it was in Chinese the information was hardly necessary,' commented Elgin when he received it. 'It said that *they two* were well treated, complimented Prince Kung, and asked for some clothes. We have heard nothing about the others who are missing.'

Amongst the clothes which were sent and were allowed to be accepted was an embroidered handkerchief. On it Loch discovered, almost invisibly worked around the embroidery, a sentence in Hindustani, minutely stitched, which informed the two prisoners that the allies would begin their bombardment in three days time, and asked them for the exact location of their place of imprisonment. Since Heng-ch'i had warned them, 'the first shot of the bombardment will be the signal for your execution', they derived cold comfort from this intelligence; nor were they much consoled when they received a letter from Thomas Wade, the interpreter, assuring them that if any harm befell them Peking would be 'burnt from one end to the other'. So, allaying their apprehension with frequent games of backgammon on a board they had made themselves, and drinking cups of a tea specially grown for the Emperor, Parkes and Loch awaited death while praying for deliverance.

On 5 October Heng-ch'i told them that they would be executed that evening since there seemed no possibility now of coming to terms with the foreigners. Three days later, however, when news had come in of the allied advance from Pa-li-ch'iao and of the occupation of the Summer Palace, the two prisoners were told that Prince Kung had decided on their release.

'It is impossible to describe our feelings,' wrote Loch, remembering that afternoon of 8 October when he and Parkes were put into a cart, saw the temple gate open, and a path being cleared through the crowds outside in the street by an escort wielding whips. 'Our hopes were raised—and yet we felt how much still lay between us and safety. . . . It seemed as if we should never reach the city gate; at last we had a good view of the heavy doors, which, with a sinking feeling, we saw were closed, but then within thirty yards they were thrown open, and we heard the heavy bang of their being shut behind us with a sensation of intense relief. The outer gate was opened, and closed, in the same manner, and we found ourselves once more outside the walls of Peking and in the open country.'[10]

As soon as they caught sight of the first English sentry, both he and Parkes jumped out of the cart and ran towards him. They had 'behaved very well under circumstances of great danger', Lord Elgin commended them; and they seemed to be 'in good health notwithstanding the hardships they [had] gone through'. But although the stoical Sikh and five of the French captives had also returned safely, Elgin felt 'great concern that nothing certain as yet' was known of the other prisoners who had been taken on 18 September.

His concern for these prisoners was well justified; within a week he learned that several of them were dead. In depositions taken by their commanding officer, Captain Fane, the Sikhs spoke of their treatment, how they had been forced to lie on their backs with their feet and hands tied together, how their limbs had become dark and tumid because of the tightness of their bonds, how maggots had got into their lacerated flesh, how they had been left out in the open at night and their captors had poured water on their cords to make them tighter still until their fingers had swollen and burst; how dung and dirt had been crammed down their throats when they had asked for food. Some of them had died in agony. 'At the end of three days irons were put on our necks, wrists and ankles,' one of the survivors deposed, 'and about 4 o'clock on the fourth day we were taken away in carts. There were eight of us, three Frenchmen, four Sikhs and myself [Mahomed Whan of Fane's Horse]. One Frenchman died upon the road—he was wounded by a sword on the head. . . . A Frenchman died after we had been in the gaol eight or nine days and [a Sikh] about three or four days after that. They both died from maggots eating into their flesh. The Chinese prisoners were very kind to us, they cleansed and washed our wounds and gave us what they had to eat.'[11]

Bowlby of *The Times* was also dead, and so were young de Normann and Lieutenant Anderson. Bowlby's body had been partially eaten by pigs. The body of Captain Brabazon was never found, but it was believed that, with a French abbé, he had been decapitated at Pa-li-ch'iao. The captured coolies had been buried up to their necks in the ground and left for dogs to eat their heads.

These were atrocious crimes, Lord Elgin wrote in horror when he learned the details of them, 'and, not for vengeance but for future security ought to be severely dealt with'.[12] He pondered long on what form that retaliation should take. There were those in the allied camp, Baron Gros reported to Paris, who would like to burn Peking to the ground and 'torture every Chinese mandarin'.[13] Elgin would have liked to have totally crushed the Chinese army; but the 'want of energy at headquarters', the agonizing slowness and caution of Hope Grant, made it more likely that, if that were to be attempted, the allies would have followed Seng-ko-lin-ch'in's men 'round the walls of Peking till Doomsday without catching them'. Now, he could not very well act against Peking because an ultimatum had been sent demanding the handing over of the Anting gate by noon on 13 October if the city were not to be harmed.

After tiresome negotiations, Prince Kung agreed to the allied terms for its surrender.[14] Elgin felt that if he demanded that the mandarins responsible for the cruelty to the prisoners should be given up to him for punishment, he would get not mandarins at all but scapegoats.[15] He rejected proposals for a large indemnity on the grounds that it would be impossible to collect. So having, to the best of his judgement, 'examined the question in all its bearings', and being unable to reconcile it with his 'sense of duty' to suffer the crimes which had been committed to remain unavenged, he 'came to the conclusion that the destruction of [the Imperial Palace at Yüan-ming Yüan] was the least objectionable of the several courses open' to him. Its architectural features made no such appeal to him as they had done to his grandparents, *chinoiserie* having long since gone out of fashion in Britain. It was here that Bowlby, de Normann and the others had been tortured; this was the Emperor's 'favourite residence, and its destruction could not fail to be a blow to his pride as well as to his feelings'. Moreover, the 'punishment was one which would fall, not on the people but exclusively on the Emperor whose direct responsibility' for the crimes committed was well established. 'As almost all the valuables had already been taken from the palace,' Lord Elgin concluded his despatch of 25 October, 'the army would go there, not to pillage, but to mark, by a solemn act of retribution, the horror and indignation with which we were inspired by the perpetration of a great crime.'[16]

A week before this despatch was written, on 18 October, a cold, bright day, with a strong wind blowing across the plain from the snow-covered mountains, the First Division marched into the Imperial park to burn its buildings 'and all imperial property within a circuit of several miles'. The French had refused to join their allies in this *vandalisme*. 'I must keep you in touch with the situation, certainly very serious, in which we are, and of the delicate position in which I am placed, *vis-à-vis* my English colleague,' Baron Gros had reported to the Foreign Minister in Paris. 'He wants to go too far, torch in hand, to follow a course on which I cannot and will not accompany him.'[17] Baron Gros did not accompany him; but his objections seemed less than convincing coming from a man who had suggested that the Imperial Palace in Peking should be destroyed if Prince Kung did not agree to the allied terms, and who implied in a letter to Montauban that if Yüan-ming Yüan were to be destroyed by the British alone the French could be represented as having played the *beau rôle* in the eyes of both Europe and China.[18]

If the objections of some Frenchmen could be interpreted as hypocritical, their allies' approval of Lord Elgin's ruthless order seemed more than a little self-righteous. Harry Parkes expressed the opinion that Elgin had come to the proper decision 'in determining to raze to the ground the Emperor's Summer Palace' since, obviously, either that or the Peking palace had to be made 'a monumental ruin of', and Yüan-ming Yüan was 'the proper one of the two'. Also, 'to have burnt Peking would have been simply wicked, as the people of the city, who would in that case be the sufferers, had done us no harm'.[19]

To the chaplain, M'Ghee, a man who believed wholeheartedly in the expedition from the first, 'knowing that Civilization and Christianity could reach the people of China only through the medium of western commerce', it seemed that a division never marched 'with a better will to perform a more just and loudly called for act of retribution, upon an imperious, treacherous, and cruel power'.[20] Most English officers agreed with him; and even those who shared the regrets of the young Engineer, Charles George Gordon, to whose duty it fell to supervise the burning of some of the buildings, were satisfied that Elgin's decision had been justified.

For two days the work of destruction continued, covering the whole area with dense clouds of black and heavy smoke which were carried by a north-west wind over Peking itself where showers of burnt embers fell into the streets.

'The world around looked dark with shadow,' Wolseley wrote. 'By the evening of 19th October, the Summer Palace had ceased to exist, and in their immediate vicinity, the very face of nature seemed changed: some blackened gables and piles of burnt timbers alone indicating where the royal palaces had stood. In many places inflammable pine trees near the buildings had been consumed with them, leaving nothing but their charred trunks to mark the site.'[21]

*   *   *

A Chinese diarist living in Peking watched the 'vast columns of smoke rising to the north west' and was given to understand that 'the Barbarians had entered the Summer Palace, and after plundering it . . . had set fire to the buildings. Their excuse for this abominable behaviour is that their troops got out of hand, and had

committed the incendiarism.' For days now, the diarist recorded, the
inhabitants had been leaving the city in their thousands. Early on
the morning of 22 September 'His Sacred Majesty, attended by all
his concubines, the Princes, Ministers and Dukes, and all the
officers of the Household' had left Peking 'in a desperate rout and
disorder unspeakable, affording a spectacle that gave the impression
that hordes of Barbarians were already in close pursuit'. Three
weeks later news had been received that 'the Sacred Chariot had
reached Jehol in safety' and that His Majesty, 'greatly alarmed, had
issued a Decree expressing regret for his failure to commit suicide
on the approach of the invaders'. With the exception of those entrusted with the duty of negotiating, there were by then 'no other
officials remaining in the city'. [22]

Lord Elgin's triumphant procession entered Peking by the Anting
gate on the afternoon of 24 October. The gate had been surrendered
a few minutes before the allies' ultimatum was due to expire at midday on the 13th, and Sir Robert Napier's 2nd Division, followed by
the French, had immediately entered the city to occupy the walls.
These were now manned by strong reserves of troops, and three guns
were placed beside the gate ready to give warning to the 1st
Division to leave camp and march into Peking should there be any
trouble.

The 2nd Division—'horribly disappointed' to find that Peking
was just an ordinary, dirty city like any other—lined the route of the
procession, which extended for three and a half miles from the gate
to the Hall of Ceremonies, and provided an escort of a hundred
cavalry and four hundred infantry. It was a fine day; the sun shone
and the wind had dropped. Preceded by two regimental bands, by
various officers in full dress uniform and General Hope Grant and
his staff, Lord Elgin was carried through Peking in a large sedan
chair by sixteen coolies in scarlet livery.

The chair, 'hung about with long streaming tassels of many
colours after the most approved Chinese fashion', was put down at
the edge of the carpet spread on the floor of the Hall, and as Elgin
stepped out Prince Kung came forward to meet him, 'making a stiff
bow,' an observer noticed, 'and shaking his own hands vigorously,

after the ordinary manner of Chinese etiquette. . . . Upon reaching their respective chairs, it was of great importance that both should sit down exactly at the same moment; a fact which was most satisfactorily accomplished. . . . Prince Kung looked round upon the assembled "Barbarians" almost with a scowl; but this supercilious expression may have partly resulted from his most strangely set eyes. . . . He looked a boy, as well as a gentleman, amongst the crowd of bilious, bloated, small-pock-marked, and hideous-looking faces of the mandarins who surrounded him. A very young man, unless of royal birth, seldom holds any great office of importance in China; and as rank is to be had either by purchase or competitive examination, it is frequently enjoyed by the very commonest of the people.'[23]

Hope Grant thought that Kung was not so much supercilious as 'overpowered with fear'. When he had come up to greet Lord Elgin and closed his hands in front of his face, Elgin had 'returned him a proud contemptuous look, and merely bowed slightly, which must have made the blood run cold in poor Kung's veins'. His discomfiture was further increased by the energetic efforts of the indefatigable Italian photographer, Beato, who was manipulating his cumbersome apparatus at the Hall door. Kung 'looked up in a state of terror, pale as death,' Hope Grant wrote, 'and with his eyes turned first to Elgin and then to me, expecting every moment to have his head blown off by the infernal machine opposite him—which really looked like a sort of mortar, ready to disgorge its terrible contents into his devoted body. It was explained to him that no such evil design was intended, and his anxious pale face brightened up when he was told that his portrait was being taken. The treaty was signed, and the whole business went off satisfactorily, except as regards Signor Beato's picture, which was an utter failure, owing to want of proper light.'[24]

The Convention of Peking—the French treaty was signed the day after the British—confirmed and extended the provisions of the Tientsin treaties. The indemnities were increased to eight million dollars for each ally; Tientsin was added to the list of ports to be opened to foreign trade; Kowloon was ceded to Britain; confiscated

Catholic churches and chapels were to be restored and the Church allowed to buy land and build places of worship throughout the Empire; Chinese labourers were allowed to be recruited for work abroad; the representatives of Western powers were to be allowed to live in Peking.[23]

The British representative was to be Frederick Bruce; and Lord Elgin, living in the palace of Prince I, waited in Peking until his brother arrived so that he could introduce him to Prince Kung as a person of high authority. He was also concerned to choose a suitably imposing palace for the British legation. By 10 November these duties had been performed, and Elgin left Peking. Early in the New Year he sailed for England, persuaded that his work had been well done.

The Government agreed, so Lord Russell assured him, that his conduct had been worthy of 'full approbation', and that the Convention concluded with Prince Kung was 'entirely satisfactory'. The war had not been popular in England, but now that it was over there was cause for much rejoicing. The burning of the Summer Palace was regretted in some quarters; but, if few felt able to go so far as Lord Palmerston who professed himself to be 'quite enchanted' by it and only wished that it had been possible to present Sen-ko-lin-ch'in's head to the Emperor on a charger,[26] it was usually approved of as a sad necessity.

In China it was scarcely to be expected that it could be considered as anything other than barbaric. The feelings of revulsion aroused by it were in no sense diminished by the behaviour of the occupying forces left behind in China after the signing of the Peking Convention. Scarcely a week passed throughout the winter of 1860–61 without some unpleasant incident involving British troops. The snowballing of elderly and stately Chinese was no doubt properly considered a venial offence; perhaps British officers were right to suppose that a people used to being knocked out of the way by the large retinues of mandarins did not object as strongly as others might have done to being shoved out of the way by a horse's shoulder, to being given a tap from a riding-cane and a warning 'to look out next time', or to being poked in the jaw by a foreign soldier walking resolutely down the street with a stout stick over his shoulder. The troops had at least the excuse of the extreme cold—in which two men died of exposure, in which the bread was frozen so solid it could only be cut with a saw, and in which the porter ration had to be served out in lumps—for dismantling the insides of any houses they could get into for firewood. But what the intelligent Chinese found difficult to tolerate was the assumption of many English officers that John Bull, as the Rev. R. J. L. M'Ghee characteristically put it, was 'sixteen times as great and as good a fellow' as any mandarin. Nor could he easily tolerate the English soldier's evident belief that all he had to do to make John Chinaman understand him was to talk English in a loud voice. 'The Gaul generally picked up a few Chinese words', according to M'Ghee; but if an Englishman had any at his command he was generally content to insert them into an English commentary: 'I say, my man, there's no use, you see, in your talking to me, because I don't understand your language, but just you listen to what I say to you; if you don't bring lots of "suiah", that is plenty of water; "ming tien", that's tomorrow morning at six o'clock, I'll just knock saucepans out of you, that's all; now "woilo", i.e. go away.'

All too often the Chinese did get saucepans knocked out of them. Dr Rennie reported the case of an English officer who strode into a shop, picked up an article and threw down some money. The shopkeeper, declining to sell for the price offered, put out his hand to take the article back, whereupon the officer knocked him down and walked out of the shop with it tucked under his arm. Dr Rennie also recorded the behaviour of a gunner employed by the military police whom he observed 'sauntering along the streets with a heavy whip in his hand amusing himself with lashing every unfortunate dog that came within his reach, whether they happened to be quietly walking along or sitting at the doors of the shops they belonged to. . . . The man had anything but a good example set him by his betters, dog-spearing on the plain outside the city having been one of the favourite amusements of the officers of the garrison for some time back, the unfortunate animals being hunted down by mounted spearmen until they sank exhausted, when they were subjected to a lingering and painful death, in consequence of the unskilfulness of their tormentors in despatching them with the spear. These dogs are the property of the neighbouring villagers, and the cruel scenes which take place in connection with these hunts, from all accounts, would seem to be but little calculated to dispel from the Chinese mind the term Barbarian.'

Frequently *samsu*, the fiery Chinese spirit not unlike coarse London gin, which could be bought for threepence a pint, was held to blame for the army's acts of indiscipline and thoughtless cruelty. Certainly floggings for drunkenness in the army were very common at this time, and certainly the motive for the murder of a Chinese at Taku was his refusal to supply some soldiers of the 31st Regiment with *samsu*, the sale of which was forbidden by both the army and the Chinese authorities.[27]

But for all the arrogance of some of the officers and the depredations of some of the men, relations between the Chinese people and the army as a whole were not altogether unfriendly. The English did not much care for Peking, its smelly, muddy streets, the 'faded, uncared-for, most dilapidated' buildings in the Tartar city, 'some of them looking as if they might tumble down at any moment and one of which had already done so—it was the Board of Finance'. They did not like the importunate beggars who roamed about, refusing to move on until they had been given alms, relentlessly calling attention to themselves by knocking together pieces of wood. Nor did they like the Tibetan priests who smelled of sheep and were almost as ubiquitous as the beggars. But there was something peculiarly endearing about the ordinary people, so inquisitive, so cheerful, so friendly despite provocation, so ready to laugh at themselves, so inextinguishably good-natured. As Wolseley noted, if the people of North China felt any resentment towards the occupying forces, they very rarely showed it.[28]

The same was not true of the officials of the Empire. To Prince Kung it was quite clear now, so he informed the Emperor in a despatch, that all the Barbarians had 'the nature of brute beasts'; and of all the Barbarians it was the British who were 'the most unruly'.[29] Yet, despite his distaste for the British and his distrust of them, it was the Russians who now worried Prince Kung more. The British were 'merely a threat to the limbs' of the Empire; the Russians 'menaced its very body'.[30]

Kung had been forced to this conclusion by the activities of the Russian envoy, Major-General Ignatiev. For months Ignatiev had been assiduous in his efforts to impress upon the Chinese Court the view that Russia was China's friend, that she was willing to help China in the struggle against the British, and that she was prepared to send military technicians to advise the Chinese army. Prince Kung had not been convinced by Ignatiev's sincerity. The Russian had been too much in Lord Elgin's company—Elgin, indeed, wrote of him, 'we are always very good friends . . . we always seem to agree remarkably'—and although Ignatiev would have the Chinese believe that this was because he was anxious to help bring about a satisfactory conclusion of peace, Kung could not bring himself to trust him. Nor did the Russian occupation of Haishenwei and its re-naming as Vladivostok, 'Master of the East', by Murayev, the Russian Governor-General of Eastern Siberia, improve the relations between them. The Russians were the 'most cunning' of the Bar-barian nations, and rather than risk Ignatiev's making any further trouble in Peking, Kung agreed to his demands for a confirmation of the 1858 Treaty of Aigun which gave the north bank of the Amur to Russia, a ratification of the Treaty of Tientsin which granted her access to the same ports as the other maritime powers, and a new Treaty of Tientsin which handed over to her the disputed Ussuri territory between the Amur River and Vladivostok.

Yet dangerous to China as the grasping Russians were, unruly as the British were, and troublesome as were the French, there was an even greater threat to the country's security, a threat to the Empire within the Empire itself. Prince Kung urged the Emperor to re-member what this greater threat was. Some day soon, he told him, 'we must settle accounts' with the foreigners; but first of all 'we must extirpate the rebels'.[31]

17 | The Last of the Taipings

I hold the Empire in an iron grasp. . . . My
troops are more numerous than the streams.
What have I to fear from the demon Tseng
Kuo-fan? If you are afraid of death then you
will die. Hung Hsiu-ch'uan, the Heavenly
King, to Li Hsiu-ch'eng, the Loyal King,
May 1864.

Among the scores of concubines, eunuchs, princes, dukes, ministers
and officers of the household who accompanied the Emperor in his
hasty and disorderly flight from Peking to Jehol in September 1860
was a young concubine of the first rank, Yehonala, the Yi Concubine. She was twenty-four.

Yehonala was the daughter of a minor Manchu official from the
province of Anhwei, a girl of extraordinary charm, intelligence and
ambition, with a beautifully melodious voice. She had been selected
as a suitable concubine for Hsien-feng by his mother, the Empress
Dowager, who had also picked out from the numerous candidates
presented for her inspection in the Forbidden City, Yehonala's
placid cousin, Sakota. Yehonala had been placed in the third rank of
concubines, Sakota in the second; but although Sakota had become
pregnant first and consequently been raised to the rank of Empress
Consort, it was Yehonala who had pleased the Emperor more, for her
baby was a healthy boy whereas Sakota's was a sickly girl that died.

In honour of her having given the Emperor an heir, Yehonala
was raised to the second rank of concubines in April 1856, and by
1860, though still so young, she was one of the most influential
persons at Court, advising the Emperor on public as well as domestic
matters, particularly upon ways and means of suppressing the
Taiping rebels in the Yangtze Valley where she had been born and
where her early years had been spent.

She had used her influence to try to persuade the Emperor to

289

remain in Peking 'as his presence there could not fail to awe the Barbarians [who would not] spare the city, its shrines and the altars of the Gods once the Sacred Chariot fled and left them unprotected'. The advice was not taken, but the 'Concubine Yi put out a decree in her own name, offering large rewards to any who would slay the Barbarians'.

On 22 August 1861 the Emperor died at Jehol, worn out by his dissipations and overwhelmed by resentment towards the Barbarians for their burning of Yüan-ming Yüan and their forcing of Prince Kung to surrender to their terms. Before his death, he had been persuaded by Prince I and two other Manchus, one an Imperial Prince, the other a senior Minister, to sign a document creating them Joint-Regents and excluding Yehonala from any control in the upbringing of her son, the five-year-old heir to the Empire. But Yehonala refused to be pushed aside. Not content with the title of Empress Dowager, conferred upon her as a consolation on Hsien-feng's death, she induced her cousin, the Empress Consort, to agree to her writing a letter to Prince Kung which would be carried to Peking by a trusted eunuch, An Te-hai. Having despatched the letter, she took advantage of the rule that widows must not travel with the corpses of their husbands, to set out for Peking with the Empress Consort ahead of the main funeral procession. Determined that neither of the Empresses should reach the city alive, the three Joint-Regents gave orders to their military escort to ensure that some fatal accident befell them; but the captain of the late Emperor's bodyguard, a man named Jung-lu, who was said to be Yehonala's secret lover, heard of the plot and took adequate steps to foil it.

Yehonala and Sakota reached Prince Kung in safety; and the Joint-Regents on their later arrival were all arrested. The Minister was decapitated, Prince I and the other Imperial Prince were given the opportunity of hanging themselves which they both obligingly did. The two Empresses were created Regents in their place; Prince Kung was appointed Adviser; and the central Government—a determined woman of twenty-six its dominating influence—could now turn its attention to the suppression of the Taiping rebels.

* * *

One of the new Government's first acts was to appoint Tseng Kuo-fan, the official responsible for the formation of the well-trained Hunan Army in the South, to the supreme military command in the provinces of Kiangsu, Anhwei, Kiangsi and Chekiang. An English officer who met Tseng in the 1860s described him as 'a man of low stature, with a black straggling beard and mustache, a careless dress, and a very ancient hat'.[1] Despite this unprepossessing appearance, however, Tseng was already recognized as one of the most remarkable men in the history of modern China. His Hunan Army had shown its prowess by capturing from the rebels the Yangtze river-port of Anking, south of Nanking; and it was in this area that Tseng Kuo-fan knew that the war against the rebels would be decided, not in the coastal areas of Kiangsu and Chekiang where the French and British might in their own interests be expected to give help to the Government's forces. At Yehonala's request, Tseng recommended two men to act as his subordinates in Kiangsu, the province in which Shanghai was situated, and in Chekiang, the province of Hangchow and Ningpo. He suggested Tso Tsung-t'ang for Chekiang and Li Hung-chang, the artful, ambitious young son of one of his closest friends, for Kiangsu. Both recommendations were immediately accepted; and soon after his appointment Li Hung-chang went to Shanghai to ask the foreigners for assistance in the training and equipment of the army he had quickly formed.[2]

Li was sympathetically received. The foreigners, having come to satisfactory terms with the Manchu Government, were naturally now anxious for it to continue in power and for their new opportunities for trading in North China and the Yangtze Valley to be exploited to the full. Also, now that the importation of opium had been legalized by the additional clauses to the Treaties of Tientsin, it was essential to keep all supply routes open to maintain the ever increasing flow of the drug into the country.

In June 1860, when a Taiping army had captured the city of Soochow less than fifty miles from Shanghai, the French and British had taken it upon themselves to organize the defence of the city to prevent any further advance by the rebels. A force of mercenaries, mainly composed of foreign adventurers who had found their way to the Shanghai waterfront in search of money or excitement, was organized under the leadership of an American, F. T. Ward, a buccaneer with experience of fighting in South America. Ward's mercenaries had achieved an early success by recapturing the Taiping-held town of Sunkiang; but in a counter-attack led by the brilliant rebel commander, Li Hsiu-ch'eng, the Loyal King, the son of a peasant who had emerged as the Taipings' greatest soldier since the murder of Yang Hsiu-ch'ing, Ward's men had been thrown out of Sunkiang with heavy losses. Exultantly, the Taipings chanted their songs of victory:

> *The foreigner is like an eagle*
> *With his yellow hair, hooked nose and green eyes.*
> *Kites and eagles are savage and wild,*
> *But they fear the bow.*
> *Likewise the foreigner fears the red turbanned army.*[3]

Following its defeat at Sunkiang, Ward's force had been re-organized. It had been given the name of the Ever Victorious Army, 'a name to be taken,' in the words of the editor of the British-sponsored *China Mail*, 'not in a literal but in a transcendental and Celestial sense'[4], and its ranks had been filled with Chinese soldiers whose objection to being drilled and commanded by Foreign Devils had been overcome by generous rates of pay. After Ward had been mortally wounded in action against a mud-walled village in September 1862, its command passed into the hands of another American adventurer, Henry Andrea Burgevine, the quarrelsome, heavy-drinking son of a Frenchman who had served as an officer under Napoleon and had subsequently settled in North Carolina. Burgevine led the Ever Victorious Army into action in Kiangsu province, where it acted in cooperation with the army of Tseng's subordinate, Li Hung-chang; while a similar Franco-Chinese force left to operate in Chekiang alongside the forces of Tseng's other subordinate Governor, Tso Tsung-t'ang.

But Burgevine, though a brave commander, was neither liked nor trusted by Li Hung-chang who described him as being 'full of intrigues and stubborn'.[5] Before joining the Ever Victorious Army he had sold arms to the Taipings, and his ferocious temper and callous nature imposed but a fitful discipline upon his troops who were known not merely to loot after a victory but to amuse themselves by blowing up their prisoners. It was Li's hope that he could get Burgevine replaced by an English officer, thus involving Britain more deeply in the Imperial cause. So, with the intention of provoking him into some action for which he might be dismissed, Li ordered Burgevine to march towards Nanking. When Burgevine, recovering from a recent wound, refused to move so far from his base, Li withheld the Ever Victorious Army's pay. The American lost his temper, stormed into the house of the Shanghai banker who acted as the Army's paymaster, slapped the banker across the face, took the money, and was, accordingly, dismissed from his command.

Li's hope that he might be replaced by an English officer was not at first shared by the British Government. It was accepted that British troops, in cooperation with the French, were justified in taking action against the rebels to protect Shanghai and to clear them out of the countryside within an agreed limit of thirty miles of it, leaving Imperial troops to garrison any towns captured from them. But the appointment of a regular officer to the command of such a force as the Ever Victorious Army was 'quite another matter'; and it was with reluctance that permission was granted for a British officer to command the force 'provided he be on halfpay and in the service of the Chinese Government'.

Frederick Bruce's earlier objections had been to some extent overcome by the fact that, when permission was finally granted for an official and permanent appointment, a British officer of outstanding qualities was already in command of the cosmopolitan army on a temporary basis.

This was Major Charles George Gordon, the brisk and wiry Engineer officer who had helped to burn down Yüan-ming Yüan and who had since played a prominent part in the capture of Tsingpo, a rebel stronghold west of Shanghai. Gordon was at this time just thirty years old. An officer of remarkable courage and deep religious sense, he was to demonstrate in his new command astonishing gifts of leadership and organization, and a character at once proud, cantankerous, resolute and touchy. No one who knew him doubted his worth or was surprised to learn that at Woolwich he had lost his chance of a commission in the Royal Artillery through losing his temper with another cadet and hitting him over the head with a hair brush.[6]

Li Hung-chang liked and admired Gordon from the first. He seemed 'more reasonable' than the previous commanders of the Ever Victorious Army; his 'readiness to fight the enemy' was also greater. 'Even if he squanders forty or fifty thousand dollars,' Li reported to Tseng Kuo-fan, 'it will still be worth while.' In later reports Li described Gordon as 'brave, industrious and able'; his 'will and zeal' were 'really praiseworthy'; he had a violent temper, to be sure, but he had managed to bring the Ever Victorious Army under firm control.[7]

'It is a direct blessing from Heaven,' Li believed, 'the coming of this British Gordon. . . . He is superior in manner and bearing to any of the foreigners I have come in contact with, and does not show outwardly that conceit which makes most of them repugnant in my sight. Besides, while he is possessed of a splendid military bearing he is direct and businesslike. Within two hours after his arrival he was inspecting the troops and giving orders; and I could not but rejoice at the manner in which his commands were obeyed.'[8]

Gordon was to be faced by two mutinies and the loss of half his force by desertion before the rebels were defeated; but, within a few months of his taking it over, the Ever Victorious Army was already one of the most successful, well organized and well supplied fighting units in China. It numbered about 3,500 Chinese troops who were paid twice as well as those of the Imperial army and were dressed in brown uniforms with green turbans. Its artillery, equipped with both field and siege guns, was excellent; its cosmopolitan officers— American, German, French, Spanish and Scandinavian—were unruly in garrison but generally reliable in action.

In a series of operations against Taiping strongholds west of Shanghai, the men of the Ever Victorious Army proved their value to the Imperial cause. Using heavily armed gunboats and steamers, commanded by American captains with experience in river navigation, they relieved Changsu on the Yangtze estuary, captured Taitsang, and assisted Li's best general, Ching, in taking Kunshan where the guns of Gordon's paddle-steamer, *Hyson*, massacred hundreds of rebels as they poured out of the west gate in the darkness in a vain effort to reach Soochow.

After the capture of Kunshan, the Ever Victorious Army began to disintegrate. In the days of Ward and Burgevine the officers and men of the force were free to loot, get drunk, smoke opium, and enjoy the concubines captured from the rebel leaders; but although he had no objection to looting—indeed, he frequently quarrelled with Li Hung-chang over the duties assigned to his army when these deprived his men of what he took to be their fair share in opportunities of plunder—Gordon had no taste for women, and did not disguise his contempt for those who failed to live up to the rigid standards of discipline he set. He went into action sprucely turned out, carrying nothing but a rattan cane; and when the action was over he retired alone to his quarters, to his Bible and his work. He expected his men to be on parade, as he would be, at sunrise.

After Taitsang had been taken there had been a short-lived mutiny; and now, when Gordon decided to remove his headquarters from Sungkiang, a town well liked by his men both for its brothels and for the number of dealers prepared to buy loot, there was further trouble. Gordon dealt with it in a characteristic way. Dragging a man he took to be one of the ringleaders out of the ranks, he ordered his bodyguard to shoot him on the spot. He then told the rest that they had one hour in which to submit, otherwise one in five of them would be similarly executed. Within the hour the mutiny was over. But during the next few days more than half his force deserted him; so, giving as his reason the slowness of the Imperialists in meeting his demands for pay, he sent in his resignation.

On learning that Burgevine had gone over to the Taipings, taking with him three hundred European filibusters, an armed steamer and a howitzer, Gordon changed his mind. He withdrew his resignation and, with an army whose numbers had been made up by the enlistment of Taiping prisoners, he marched out to battle once more. He was convinced, as he had said earlier, that he was 'the only stay of the force', taking his small army to help General Ching in the reduction of the Taipings' few remaining strongholds in Kiangsu.

By the end of November 1863 the rebels had been pushed into an ever diminishing area of land around Soochow; and in Soochow itself their leaders were losing heart. For a time the Loyal King, Li Hsiu-ch'eng, was able to maintain the will to resist; but the tone of a letter he wrote to the Heavenly King at the Taiping capital of Nanking shows how desperate the situation had become: 'From this beleaguered place, I indite these lines. Our provisions are exhausted; in the camp, the cooking pots are empty. . . . Corpses are carved to pieces and mothers sell their sons for food. For many days past we have been shouting "Dinner is ready" at meal times so as to deceive the enemy. . . . Our danger is that of the tiger at bay upon the mountain precipice. Your Majesty has founded a new Empire, but its roots are shaken, the branches tremble. Soochow is Your Majesty's lower jaw: if the lips perish, the teeth must speedily decay. As soon as you can force a way through the beleaguering armies, it behoves you to dispatch troops to our assistance. I send these few lines beseeching you to take care of your health. Interrupting the whetting of my spear, I write this message, earnestly praying for your welfare.'[9]

But no troops came; and when the Loyal King escaped through the lines of the encircling armies to Nanking, the other leaders made up their minds to capitulate. Cutting off the head of the only one still determined to resist, they sent it to General Ching. Ching and Gordon both gave undertakings to spare their lives if the town were surrendered.

On 5 December the Imperial forces marched through the eastern gate of the town. Knowing what his troops would do once they got through the gate, Gordon had been pleased to agree that they should be granted extra pay instead of joining in the plunder; and as the Imperialists entered the town, the Ever Victorious Army marched off to Li's headquarters to demand a bonus of two months' pay. Li considered this extortionate, offered one month's pay, and when Gordon went back to Soochow, having refused to attend the forthcoming peace conference with the Taiping leaders, he ordered the

Ever Victorious Army's second-in-command to take it back to Kunshan.

In Soochow, Gordon saw the Taiping leaders being taken away to Li's headquarters for the conference which was held aboard a steamer on the Soochow–Kunshan canal. So far, according to Gordon's own version of these events, all had been quiet in the town; but on a subsequent visit he found to his indignant fury that the Imperial troops had been allowed to get out of hand. They were running wild, looting, raping, murdering all the inhabitants who offered them any resistance.

'The streets were inches deep with clothing,' wrote an officer who accompanied him, 'shops broken into, and looted, many houses on fire, very many dead bodies of rebels, all ages and sexes, some of them half roasted, and numerous pigs feeding on them. Women and children running about the streets, screaming with terror, pursued by straggling parties of Imperial Chinese troops, maddened with lust and excitement, besmirched with blood, who were entering and looting the shops, cutting down with their sharp, bill-hooked-shaped knife every one who came in their way irrespective of age or sex, and firing at random at locked doors and closed windows.'[10]

Gordon's fury became hysterical when the son of one of the Taiping leaders directed him to a creek where his father's headless body and those of eight other rebel commanders, whose lives Gordon and Li had promised to spare, lay in the mud. Gordon picked up one of the heads and stormed off to write a letter to that 'asiatic barbarian' Li Hung-chang, demanding his resignation as Governor of Kiangsu and threatening that unless he did resign he, Gordon, would hand back to the Taipings every town that had been captured from them. He withdrew the Ever Victorious Army from Li's command and threatened to resign himself if Li was not dismissed forthwith.

In reply to this outburst, Li wrote to assure Gordon that he was entirely responsible for the execution of the rebel commanders who had made impossible demands upon him, that no blame could possibly be attached to the meritorious leader of the Ever Victorious Army, and that the executions had been essential if further trouble were to be prevented. Unappeased by these soothing overtures, Gordon marched off to Kunshan, taking the Taiping's head with him. He swore that Li would be arrested and publicly executed for his dastardly treachery, and was determined to obtain the support of the British authorities in Shanghai for the uncompromising line he was taking.

He did gain the support of the new commander of the British forces in China, Major-General Brown who, in an uncomfortable interview with Li, had found the Governor brusque and unapologetic, 'unwilling or unable to offer any exculpation or explanation of his conduct'. But Frederick Bruce was less sympathetic; he was 'inclined to think that Governor Li, in putting these chiefs to death, may have acted in a spirit of revenge for the perfidious massacre of his own men at Taitsang [where Imperialist soldiers had been 'inveigled' into the town during the surrender negotiations and afterwards murdered]. This may have palliated, in the eyes of Governor Li, his breach of faith towards these men. The *lex talionis* is quite in accordance with Chinese maxims.'

Nor did Sir Robert Hart, the influential Inspector of Chinese Customs, think that Gordon had been right to take so strong and un-compromising a line; and he went to Kunshan to use his best endeavours to calm Gordon down. When he arrived Gordon was already in a less indignant mood. He had immediately returned to Li a gift of 10,000 taels which had been sent to him with a covering letter from the Chinese Court; but he was ready to concede that the Governor was perhaps not such a scoundrel as he had at first insisted. He agreed to go with Hart to Li's palace at Soochow and there he agreed to continue in the Chinese service if Li undertook to announce publicly that he alone was responsible for the execution of the Taiping chiefs.

Li readily agreed; and Gordon returned to his army eager to lead it into action once more. He informed Bruce that if he did not do so the war might go on for another six years, but that once *he* took the field there could be little doubt that the rebellion would not last six months longer.[11]

In fact, when the Ever Victorious Army took the field again, the rebellion was almost over. The stronghold of Yesu was taken without much difficulty; Kintan was evacuated by the rebels after Gordon had been wounded in the leg during an unsuccessful attempt to storm it; Tanyang, an important fortress on the Grand Canal that guarded the escape route from Changchow to Nanking, was also abandoned; and Changchow fell on 11 May, leaving Nanking at the mercy of Tseng Kuo-fan's forces which had been slowly but remorselessly closing in on it for the past few years.

The Ever Victorious Army was no longer needed.[12] There were those, indeed, who insisted it had never been needed at all; and certainly its part in the suppression of the Taiping rebellion has in the past been given an undue prominence. *The Times*, for instance, on 15 August 1864, reported that Colonel Gordon, who 'found the richest and most fertile districts of China in the hands of the most savage brigands, cut the rebellion in half, recovered the great cities, isolated and utterly discouraged the fragments of the brigand power and left the marauders nothing but a few tracts of devastated country.' 'The Taeping monster,' declared the *London and China Express*, 'has been crushed by British skill and valour.'[13] Undeniably Gordon's army played an important part in the last stages of the war in the area around Shanghai; but it could not possibly have achieved its successes unaided or held the towns captured from the rebels without the garrisons provided by the Imperialists whose numbers were so vastly greater. Gordon admitted this himself. 'The Imperialists are not so very contemptible,' he wrote in a private letter; 'and it is a mistake to put down everything to the Foreign Forces, the latter are certain [*sic*] give the Imperialists great confidence, and make the Rebels fear, but the Foreign Forces solo would not do much. They could not retain their conquests.'[14]

At Changchow the Imperialist commander had ten times as many troops under his command as Gordon had; at Soochow the Ever Victorious Army numbered less than four thousand men, while the Imperialists had over thirty-five thousand troops in the immediate vicinity. Moreover, although the victories won in Kiangsu were fundamentally of greater consequence than those won by the Franco-Chinese forces in Chekiang where Hangchow surrendered not long after the fall of Soochow, the real battle against the Taipings was being fought by Tseng Kuo-fan in the upper Yangtze area in Anhwei, and around the Heavenly Capital of Nanking itself.

Also, by the time the Ever Victorious Army was formed the Taipings were already in sad decline both militarily and morally. The behaviour of the Imperialists, European mercenaries and sometimes of the regular British and French troops, on capturing a rebel-held town was appalling. Not only at Soochow, but at Changchow and other towns which were given over to loot, men and children were horribly mutilated, women violated and murdered. At Tsing-po, according to a letter in the *Shanghai Recorder* from a well-known merchant, a European trader had held the heads of fourteen women while their throats were sewn up. 'There were many more, but he held the heads of fourteen with his own hands.' The merchant trusted that in the future steps would be taken to 'prevent such atrocities either by our own men or the "disciplined Chinese". . . . The women stated that their throats had been cut by the English, but, upon being asked to identify them, pointed to the French.' At Chelin there had been what the *China Mail* called 'a most indiscriminate carnage on the part of our allies'; and the *Overland Trade Report* confirmed that the French troops behaved 'like fiends, killing indiscriminately men, women and children. Truth demands the confession that British sailors have likewise been guilty of the commission of similar revolting barbarities not only on the Taipings, but on the inoffensive helpless country people'. At the capture of Taitsang, prisoners were tortured with 'the most refined cruelty', reported the *North China Herald*. At Soochow, the creek was 'still (after twenty days' of slaughter) reddish with blood . . . the ground *soaked* with HUMAN BLOOD!'[15] But the Taipings themselves, and the thousands of banditti who joined their ranks for women and plunder, were no more humane.

'You can scarcely conceive the crowds of peasants who come into Shanghai when the rebels are in the neighbourhood,' Gordon told his mother. 'Words could not depict the horrors these people suffer from the rebels, or describe the utter desert they have made of this rich province.'[16]

'The cruelties these Rebels committed were frightful,' Gordon continued in another letter. 'In nearly every village there were from ten to sixty dead, either women frightfully mutilated, old men or small children. . . . If you saw the state of these poor people, the horrible furtive looks of the wretched inhabitants hovering around one's boat, and the knowledge of their nourishment would sicken anyone. They are like wolves, the dead lie where they fall, and are in some cases trodden quite flat by the passers by.'[17]

They murdered their prisoners with as little compunction as the Imperialists did, executed those who showed sympathy with their enemies and brought the areas they controlled to such a pitiable state that cannibalism was common.

In Nanking the decline of the Taipings had been marked for several years. In 1858 Lord Elgin's secretary, Laurence Oliphant, who went to Nanking with Thomas Wade, found the leaders 'men of the worst description. Drunkenness and opium-smoking were prevalent vices . . . the odour of garlic which pervaded [their] undisciplined retainers, their boisterous and noisy manner and filthy aspect, rendered [his] audience by no means agreeable.'[18] In 1860, an English visitor, followed about by crowds of idle people calling out 'Foreign Devil! Foreign Devil!'—in tones, it had to be admitted, of surprise rather than resentment—found the markets poorly stocked, the shops closed, the people more anxious to buy cigars and opium than to talk of their revolution. The drab clothes of the populace were in sad contrast to the bright if tawdry yellow robes of the Kings who wore on their heads 'a ridiculous gilt cardboard tiara cut into fantastic shapes ornamented with flowers and figures of tigers'. No criticism of the regime was permitted: two women were beheaded during the Englishman's visit for speaking ill of the Government. Over the entrance of the huge palace of the Heavenly King, Hung Hsiu-ch'uan, whom all were required to worship, was the legend, 'The Sacred Heavenly Gate Of The True God'.[19]

The Heavenly King had by 1863 lost all touch with reality. While the Imperialists were gaining support by alleviating the land tax in the provinces they occupied, his so-called Government had not merely abandoned all efforts at land reform but had long since acquiesced in plundered property being retained in private hands rather than, as formerly, being taken to the communal Holy Treasury.

So preoccupied was the Heavenly King with his harem, his religious exercises and his reinterpretations of Taiping doctrine, that he appeared to have no idea how close his followers were to defeat, how pitiably his people were suffering. When an attempt was made to bring home to him the realities of the Taiping position, he would answer, as one of his few responsible advisers complained, with some remarks 'totally irrelevant to the main point of view'. When he was told that only the richest people in Nanking could afford to buy food, he gave instructions that the people should subsist on 'sweet dew'. While his defeated, starving troops were retreating towards him, eating grass, the green tips of bamboo and their own dead, he occupied himself with the promulgation of decrees concerning the manner of death to be inflicted upon those who failed to use the term 'Heavenly' in all official documents.

When the Loyal King reached Nanking from Soochow and urged him to abandon the Heavenly Capital which could not possibly hold out much longer, the Heavenly King loftily replied that he had received the commands of God and Jesus to come down and rule the Empire, and that he had nothing to fear since he was 'the sole Lord of ten thousand nations'. 'I hold the Empire, hills and streams in an iron grasp,' he declared; 'and if you do not support me there are those who will. You say, "There are no soldiers." But my troops are more numerous than the streams. What have I to fear from the demon Tseng Kuo-fan? If you are afraid of death then you will die.'[20]

It was not until Tseng's miners were tunnelling towards the city's walls in June 1864 that the Heavenly King at last accepted the fact that the days of the Taipings were over. Crying that he had failed his Heavenly Father and his Brother, Jesus Christ, he appointed his young son his successor and poisoned himself with a dose of gold leaf. He was buried secretly in a corner of the palace garden where several of his wives committed suicide above his grave by hanging themselves in the trees.

On 19 July, after two sorties by the Loyal King had been driven back, an enormous mine exploded beneath the ramparts and the Hunan army rushed into Nanking through the sixty-foot breach. The rebel garrison under the Loyal King's inspired command fought back with ferocious courage; but they were outnumbered and weak with hunger. By nightfall, when the Loyal King escaped with a picked escort and Hung's young heir, the garrison had been slaughtered and the Hunan army had begun a massacre which was to continue for three days.

Tens of thousands of people were decapitated, burned to death in their houses, committed suicide with swords or threw themselves into the Yangtze. The number of dead was over 100,000, Tseng Kuo-fan estimated in a laconic report to the throne. 'The Ch'in-huai creek was filled with bodies. Half of the false kings, chief generals, heavenly generals and other heads were killed in battle, and the other half either drowned themselves in the dykes and ditches or else burned themselves. The whole of them numbered about 3,000 men. . . . [The army] searched through the city for any rebels they could find, and in three days killed over 100,000. . . . Not one surrendered but in many cases gathered together and burned themselves and passed away without repentance.'[21]

The Loyal King was soon captured, for he had given up his fast horse to his young Sovereign who was himself poorly mounted on a 'wretched pony'. Orders came from Peking for him to be taken to the capital where he was to suffer death by a 'slow and ignominious process'; but Tseng Kuo-fan, moved by his captive's bravery, dignity and selflessness, replied that he could not take the risk of sending him through a countryside where his name was so revered, and had him beheaded at once. He sent his head to Peking where it was exhibited upon the spikes of one of the gates.[22]

In celebration of the 'glorious victory' over the Taipings, Yehonala, the Empress Dowager, issued a decree, giving thanks 'to the bountiful protection of Heaven, to the ever-present care of our Ancestors, and to the foresight and wisdom of the Empress Dowager, who, by employing and promoting efficient leaders for their armies' had thus secured cooperation of all the Empire's forces and the 'accomplishment of this great achievement'. The final defeat was due to the generals who had brought about the defeat of these unspeakable traitors, above all to Tseng Kuo-fan upon whom was conferred the title of Senior Guardian of the Throne, a marquessate of the first rank, hereditary in perpetuity, and the decoration of the double-eyed peacock's feather.[23]

The Court had cause for its gratitude towards the generals. A few years before, it had seemed as though the Taipings might bring about the collapse of the declining Manchu dynasty. Now, the suppression of the rebellion, which had devastated immense areas of fertile land and had caused the death of twenty million people, had given the dynasty new strength and hope. Yet there were those who understood that in its moment of triumph the Court had cause to feel alarm as well as gratitude; for the very forces that had been created to crush the rebellion would one day turn upon the dynasty itself.[24]

IV | *Aggressors and Reformers*

18 | Slicing up the Melon

Do not the foreign Powers surround our Empire, committing frequent acts of aggression? Unless we learn and adopt the sources of their strength, our plight cannot be remedied. The Emperor Kuang-hsü, June 1898.

In the early 1870s a French missionary travelling down the Yangtze valley in the province of Szechwan discovered a China that, for all the upheavals of rebellions and wars, had remained virtually unchanged for more than a hundred years. In the riverside towns the dirty, muddy streets were full of workers, soldiers and carriers 'pushing and jostling their way about, while the deafening noise of exploding firecrackers and rockets was heard all around'; fruit merchants were selling oranges and dried figs; barbers were demonstrating their dexterity in plaiting pigtails; jugglers were performing their tricks outside puppet theatres; farmers on their way to market paused to have their fortunes told. Well-to-do ladies toddled along on their small bound feet, leaning on the shoulders of maids, while a few dignified Buddhist monks, draped in their large ashen-grey robes, made their way through the crowd, smelling of musk. Sooner or later gongs would be beaten and the attendants of a mandarin would suddenly appear, clearing a way for their master's palanquin with whips and rattans, and the people would obediently give way bowing their shaven heads in respectful submission.[1]

In these remote places in the upper Yangtze valley, foreigners were still objects of intense curiosity. Indeed, even in the metropolitan province of Chihli, a foreigner could not escape from the persistent inquisitiveness of the Chinese who would peer at him through the holes in the paper windows of his squalid, evil-smelling inn or poke their fingers through the paper to make holes of a more convenient shape and size. Sometimes they would break into the room, and there discuss his appearance—with particular reference to the dimensions of his nose—his likely occupation and his destination. On leaving his inn he would often be followed by a crowd of shouting men and boys who vociferously called attention to this oddity, the Foreign Devil, they had discovered. To escape such 'familiarity most offensive to a sensitive stranger', as one of their calling termed it, missionaries usually wore Chinese dress, fixing a pigtail to the inside of their hats.

Most of these missionaries were deeply distrusted by the mandarins and the ordinary people alike. Their activities in China were supposed to be a cloak for their real intention of spying out the land and enlisting traitors prepared to rise up against their own people when next the foreigners invaded the country. Their religious ceremonies were alleged to include cannibalism, as encouraged by the practice of eating the body and drinking the blood of their god. Their converts, 'secondary devils', were nothing but 'rice Christians' who pretended to accept the doctrines of the new religion as an insurance against starvation in times of famine. And, indeed, in the appalling famines of 1876–79, when between fifteen and twenty million people died in the northern provinces, and famished children wandered about with spears and rusty knives to protect themselves from wolves and from men ready to murder them for what flesh remained on their bones, it was noted that the 'rice Christians' contrived to find food enough.

On occasions resentment against the missionaries, generally condoned and often actively encouraged by the mandarins, broke out into violent rioting. At Tientsin in 1870 rumours flew round the town that the French Sisters of Charity who ran an orphanage there cut out the children's eyes and hearts to make their medicines. Who would collect and preserve unwanted children if not for some evil purpose such as this? After an epidemic broke out in the orphanage and several children died, stones and bricks were hurled at both the Mission and the French Consulate. The cry went up, 'Let's kill all foreigners. . . . Let's hurry and kill them now; it's the right moment: there's no warship on the river.'

On 21 June the Consul was attacked by the mob and had a spear thrust into his side. He appealed for help to the mandarin who had been deputed by the Chinese High Commissioner to guard him; the mandarin shook his head and said, 'It's no business of mine.' Later, close to panic, the Consul opened fire with his revolver on the mob, and tried to shoot the mandarin who jumped behind his servant so that the servant was killed instead. Before the day was out, both the Consul and his Chancellor had also been killed, and sixteen nuns had been hacked to pieces in their mission and then thrown into its flames.[2]

Provided that no unpleasant reprisals were provoked, news of such ferocious outbursts of xenophobia were never unwelcome at Peking. Here, the higher mandarins were engaged on a campaign directed not only against the foreigners themselves—who must at all costs be prevented from enjoying the full benefits of the treaties they had forcibly imposed upon the Empire—but also against those Chinese officials now actively preaching the doctrine that traditional ways of meeting the challenge of the foreigner must be discarded in favour of the methods of the foreigner himself.

As early as 1860 a scholar of Soochow, Feng Kuei-fen—probably the first man to apply to China's problems the term *tzu-ch'iang*, 'self-strengthening'—had proposed that there should be shipyards and arsenals on the Western model in every trading port in China; that 'Westerners should be invited to teach students the spoken and written languages of the various nations', and that, although the books that expounded the doctrine of Jesus were 'generally vulgar, not worth mentioning', Western books 'on mathematics, mechanics, optics, light, chemistry and other subjects' contained 'the best principles of the natural sciences' and should be translated into Chinese. 'According to a general geography by an Englishman,' Feng concluded, 'the territory of our China is eight times larger than that of Russia, ten times that of America, one hundred times that of France, and two hundred times that of England. . . . Yet we have been shamefully humiliated by these four nations in the recent treaties. . . . We must discover means to become their equal.'[3]

Soon after Feng's essays were written, Li Hung-chang, one of those local officials who had been thrown into prominence by his part in quelling the Taiping rebellion as Governor of Kiangsu, took up the theme himself. While cooperating with the foreigners against the Taipings, he had been aboard both British and French warships and had reported to Tseng Kuo-fan that, although the Barbarians were 'too cautious and timid in face of the enemy, in comparison with our own good troops', it had to be admitted that their guns and cannon-balls were 'well constructed'; their weapons 'well served' and their 'detachments well drilled, in all of which China [could] not compete with them'.[4]

Now, in 1864, Li memorialized Peking upon the need to 'acquire the use of modern weapons' and to 'install machinery for making these weapons' in order 'to turn China into a strong country'.

'In China,' Li continued, 'our officials are plunged in the elucidation of classical texts and in the refinement of calligraphy, while our military men are for the most part ignorant dullards. Our education seems quite divorced from utility. When we are at peace we despise foreign inventions as worthless, while if trouble comes our way we exclaim that it is impossible for us to learn how to employ such mysterious contrivances.'[5]

Prince Kung, to whom this memorial was addressed, was sympathetic towards its ideas. He did not believe—nor did Li believe—that there could be any satisfactory alternative to the Confucian theory of the State as the basis of organized society, but good use could nevertheless be made of Western techniques. And this, he argued, had long been recognized: in the seventeenth century Jesuit missionaries had been employed by his ancestors because of their specialized knowledge of iron founding, clockwork and astronomy.

In accordance with Prince Kung's belief that China must follow Japan's example in adopting Western methods in order to survive, a Board of Foreign Affairs had been established at Peking in 1861; a School of Languages in 1862; arsenals and shipyards were built; by 1872 a China Merchants Shipping Company was in existence at Shanghai—a modern cosmopolitan city that provided the Chinese with a taste of the West on their own coastline. By 1880 there was a telegraph office in Tientsin; and the first railway track was laid down in 1881.

Yet these steps towards the Westernization of China were carried out in the face of the most passionate opposition from conservative-minded mandarins. It was not merely that the laying of railway tracks would disturb the *feng-shui*, the spirits controlling the geomantic harmony of the earth, that true education had nothing to do with test tubes and alloys, that it was impossible to forget that the Barbarians had taken up arms and rebelled against the Empire. 'Why is it necessary to learn from Barbarians at all?' Wo-jen, the head of the Hanlin Academy in Peking, who was also the boy Emperor's tutor, demanded to know. 'The Barbarians are our enemies. In 1860 our capital and its suburbs were invaded by them, our ancestral altar was shaken, our Imperial palace was burned, and our officials and people were killed. There had never been such insults during the last two hundred years of our dynasty. How can we forget this enmity and this humiliation even for one single day?'[6]

This prejudice against the Barbarians and against the aping of their ways, which was shared by mandarin and peasant alike, was increased amongst the Manchus by the fear that the demands for reform that had followed the end of the war and the suppression of the Taipings were a threat to their own existence as a ruling caste. Both Chinese and Manchu officials and scholars had cause to feel concerned at the menacing eclipse of the traditional system by which they had so laboriously achieved their distinguished positions. But it was the Manchus in particular whose superiority was being endangered by the rise to authority and influence of those Chinese who had been largely instrumental in crushing the Taipings, and who were now aspiring to posts from which they would have been rigorously excluded in the recent past.

The conservatives could, however, take comfort from the knowledge that they had a powerful ally at Court; for, although Prince Kung was generally on the side of reform, the young Emperor's mother was certainly not; indeed, Empress Dowager was showing herself to be an even more formidable woman than had previously been supposed.

*   *   *

On assuming the Regency with her cousin Sakota, she had taken the title of Tz'u-hsi, 'Kindly, Motherly and Auspicious'. Later she was given the designation Sheng-mu, 'Holy Mother'; and it was as 'Holy Mother', or as 'Old Buddha', that she was to be known for the rest of her long life. Having rapidly established her authority over her co-Regent and all her immediate entourage, she soon showed Prince Kung, her chief minister, that she was determined to dominate him too. An opportunity to do so occurred at an audience in April 1865.

It was the custom for Tz'u-hsi and Sakota to be conducted to the Audience Hall at dawn, the most auspicious time of day for such a journey, in chairs of state, each borne by eight eunuchs with two further eunuchs on either side of them, four eunuchs in front and twelve behind. In the Hall the Empresses sat concealed from view behind a yellow curtain, while those granted an audience knelt before the curtain to answer any questions that Tz'u-hsi might feel disposed to ask them. When the voice behind the screen fell silent, the audience was at an end.

Prince Kung, by whose favour Tz'u-hsi had risen to her present eminence, did not take kindly to this tiresome traditional procedure. He was often known to push his way brusquely past the attendant eunuchs on his way to the Audience Hall, and on occasions to fidget with impatience as he knelt inside it. At one particular audience held in April 1865 he was noticed by one of the attendant eunuchs, who was peering at him round the curtain, to be standing up rather than kneeling. When this gross misdemeanour was reported to Tz'u-hsi, she rose screaming to her feet in simulated terror and ordered the guards, who ran into the Hall to protect her, to escort the Prince from the Palace.

Prince Kung had little doubt that the eunuch responsible for this indignity was An Te-hai who had acted as Tz'u-hsi's messenger during the intrigues that had followed the death of the Emperor Hsien-feng. Certainly An Te-hai had become the Empress's most trusted servant and her constant companion, performing the leading part opposite her in Court entertainments and masques, and even going for trips with her on the Palace lake wearing the Dragon Robe.

Whenever he rode out of the Palace gate, the 'Lord of Nine Thousand Years', as he almost blasphemously styled himself—the Emperor being the Lord of Ten Thousand Years—An Te-hai was accompanied by as magnificent a retinue as attended any mandarin.

In 1869 An Te-hai went too far. Splendidly clothed, and with numerous servants and other eunuchs, he left on a journey down the Grand Canal. This was something no eunuch had done for two hundred years. Ever since the days of the Ming dynasty, when overbearing eunuchs had been the bane of the Court, they had been forbidden, under pain of death, to travel in the provinces. On learning from the Governor of Shantung that An Te-hai had flagrantly broken this rule, Prince Kung immediately seized his opportunity and had him executed. Tz'u-hsi flew into a savage rage when she heard of her Chief Eunuch's death, storming off to the palace of Benevolent Peace to upbraid her cousin, Sakota, for allowing Prince Kung to persuade her to sign the death warrant, swearing that one day she would be revenged upon both of them.

For the moment, however, she was prepared to await a suitable time. She returned to the extravagant pleasures of the Court, and found a suitable replacement for An Te-hai in another eunuch, Li Lien-ying, a former cobbler—a cobbler of extraordinary ugliness, cunning and depravity—who had, so it was said, castrated himself in order to qualify for a life of pleasure and power in the Imperial palace.

Li Lien-ying's power in the palace was soon absolute. The Empress Dowager allowed him to sit in her presence, even on the throne itself, to address remarks to her without first being spoken to himself, and to appropriate the title, Lord of Nine Thousand Years, adopted by his predecessor. In her private apartments he discussed with her the most important matters of state; and when reporting on these discussions to officials he would use the familiar pronoun, *tsa-men*, meaning 'we two'.

It was known that he was cruel, vindictive and avaricious; but it was known too that he was devotedly loyal to his mistress. He was also excellent company, a brilliant raconteur, and a generous, amusing host, capable of exercising over his guests a strangely persuasive charm.[7]

Soon after Li Lien-ying's rise to a position of such influence at Court, in 1873, Tz'u-hsi's regency officially came to an end, and her son, T'ung-chih, assumed nominal control of the Government. But in the Decree that announced this change, doubt was publicly expressed as to its wisdom; for T'ung-chih, now eighteen, had developed, and been encouraged to indulge in, all the licentious tastes and scandalous habits of his father, including an inordinate passion for the small-footed Chinese girls to be enjoyed in the pleasure-houses of Peking. This distressed his mother not at all; but as soon as her son, who obviously disliked her, began to show his determination not to consult her on matters of state, and was incited to ignore her by his spirited young bride, she reacted with characteristic force.

When T'ung-chih was granted the happiness of a visitation of Celestial Flowers—which, in blunter terms, meant that he had contracted smallpox of which he died on 13 January 1875—the Empress Dowager could scarcely be held responsible, though there were those to whisper that the damp towels with which he wiped his lips at mealtimes had previously been brushed across the pustules of a man dying of the disease. Nor when his pregnant widow killed herself so as to follow him to heaven, could Tz'u-hsi be properly blamed for her death, though again there were those who reported that she had urged upon her daughter-in-law the propriety of suicide for one 'so downcast by the death of her husband'. Nor yet when the Empress, Sakota, a woman who described herself in her Valedictory Decree as one of 'naturally robust constitution', died of a mysterious illness was there any real evidence that her demise had been occasioned by some cakes sent to her by her cousin. But there could be little doubt that Tz'u-hsi's fervent determination not to lose any of her influence and power rendered her at least capable of murder; and in her ruthless resolve to foist her little nephew upon the throne as her dead son's successor, she showed a wilful selfishness capable of trampling down all opposition.

This nephew, her unwilling protégé, was the son of her younger sister who had married a brother of Hsien-feng and so had some title to the inheritance; but it was a highly questionable title, opposed by all the Imperial Princes including Prince Kung whose own son, he considered, had a better one. Nevertheless, Tz'u-hsi had her way. At the Council held to nominate the new Emperor, she imposed her will on those entitled to vote by the force of her personality, the fear she inspired, the acuteness of her arguments and casuistry, and the knowledge that she was supported by the powerful Li Hung-chang. 'The high officials were very much afraid of her,' a mandarin who knew her well in later years commented. 'She would ask questions without stopping. There was no end to her talk. She was in the habit of using the four- or two-word sentence form. Classical quotations and proverbs dropped at will from her lips. She understood personal relations and human emotions and the affairs of the world.'[8]

So it was that, in the middle of a bitterly cold January night, her nephew, a child of three, was roused from his sleep, dressed in quilted silk and furs, taken to the Palace in the Imperial yellow palanquin, and, weeping pitiably by now, made to kotow before the corpse of his cousin. The reign of the Emperor Kuang-hsü had begun; and the Regency of the Empress Dowager was restored.

With the death of her former co-Regent, of her son and her daughter-in-law, Tz'u-hsi's climb to power as absolute ruler of China was now prevented only by her chief minister, the detested Prince Kung. He was the only member of the Grand Council with sufficient courage and authority to oppose her. He had been responsible for the death of her Chief Eunuch, An Te-hai, and was now using his influence to discredit An Te-hai's successor, Li Lien-ying, blaming him for what was represented as the extravagance and corruption of her Court. In 1884 Tz'u-hsi decided that she might at last dismiss Prince Kung with impunity. Accusing him of 'nepotism and slothful inefficiency', she deprived him of all his offices.

The opportunity of doing so had been presented to her by the 'critical state of the Country' which was once again at war.

*　　*　　*

This time the enemy was France; yet France was but one of several powers with eyes set hungrily on the border territories of the Empire and on the satellite countries beyond its borders. These satellite

315

countries, or dependencies as Chinese Ministers referred to them, were self-governing, but they all paid homage and tribute to China, the Middle Kingdom. They included the Loochoo Islands, between Japan and Formosa, Burma, Korea and Vietnam; and one by one China lost them.

She lost her influence over Burma to Britain whose armies had already twice invaded the country, for the second time in 1852; she lost her influence over the Loochoo Islands in 1878 when the King of Loochoo was stopped from sending tribute to Peking by Japan; and in 1884 she was in the process of losing her influence over Vietnam to France.

Cochin-China, the southern part of Vietnam, had become a French protectorate in 1862; and with the intention of opening up trade with the south-western provinces of China, in particular with Yunnan, the French had invaded the north of Vietnam and occupied Tonkin in 1874. Nine years later, in 1883, France announced that she had extended her protectorate over the Kingdom of Annam, and, defeating a Chinese army sent into Annam, she forced upon China a new Convention of Tientsin which confirmed France's protectorate over Tonkin.

One of the terms of the Convention of Tientsin provided for the withdrawal of Chinese troops from Tonkin and, on China's failure to fulfil this obligation, a French force was despatched from its camp near Hanoi to occupy Langson on the Tonkin-China border. At the village of Bac-le, in wild and rocky country, this French force was ambushed and forced to retire with heavy losses down the Songt'uong river. As its survivors fell back they passed several rafts drifting downstream. 'On these rafts,' one of the survivors recorded, 'the Chinese had attached the bodies of our soldiers killed at Bac-le. All of them had their helmets sewn to their shoulders, but they were empty: their heads had been cut off.'[9]

News of the humiliating massacre at Bac-le so shocked France that the panic, said a witness, 'was no greater after Waterloo. All seemed to be lost.'[10] As worse reports came in, the Government was forced to resign; and to escape the flood of anger Jules Ferry, the Premier, had to leave the Chamber by a private door.

French pride demanded immediate revenge; and revenge soon came at Foochow. A French fleet bombarded the great naval arsenal and destroyed almost the whole of the Chinese fleet. By the subsequent Second Treaty of Tientsin, signed in June 1885, France's protectorate over both Tonkin and Annam was confirmed. The soldiers of the Third French Republic were securely lodged in Hue, and France's hold over Vietnam was as secure as Britain's over Burma.

* * *

But now an even greater menace to China than either France or Britain was the ever increasing power of Japan whose ambitious and energetic Emperor, Mutsuhito, was determined to end China's suzerainty over the 'Hermit Kingdom' of Korea. He did so in 1894 when, in order to suppress an insurrection in Korea, both Chinese and Japanese troops entered the country and, finding the rebels already defeated, fell upon each other. After a number of decisive Japanese victories a treaty, more humiliating to China than any other yet imposed upon her, was signed at Shimonoseki in April 1895.

Not only was China's suzerainty over Korea ended by this treaty, not only was she forced to pay a huge indemnity, and to open Chungking and three other riverside towns as treaty ports to the Japanese, but she was obliged to cede to Japan the Liaotung Peninsula in southern Manchuria, the Pescadores off the west coast of Formosa and the island of Formosa itself.

The Treaty of Shimonoseki, which established Japan as the dominating power in the Pacific, both alarmed the European powers and increased their own appetites for bigger shares of the Chinese melon now ready, it seemed, to be cut to pieces.

In the hope of recompense for their good offices on China's behalf, Russia, France and Germany combined to persuade Japan to return to China the Liaotung Peninsula in exchange for an indemnity increased from 200 million to 250 million dollars. As a reward for her intervention, Russia obtained the right to build the Trans-Manchurian Railway across the provinces of Heilungkiang and Kirin, linking the Trans-Siberian line to the coast at Vladivostock, and to use this railway, in peace as well as in war, for the transport of troops. Soon after this, Russia also obtained a lease of the Liaotung Peninsula, which she had persuaded Japan to hand back to China, and a right to build another railway to Port Arthur on the Peninsula's southern tip.

While Russia was securing these concessions in the north, France was extending her control over the south with the cession of territory in the province of Yunnan, a lease of the harbour of Kwangchowwan south west of Hong Kong, and of trading and mining rights in Yunnan and the two other southern provinces of Kwangsi and Kwangtung. At the same time Germany, whose authorities in Kiaochow were always ready to send troops into Chinese territory to burn villages on the slightest provocation, now used the murder of two Catholic missionaries as an excuse to move into the province of Shantung, forcing the Chinese to grant a lease of Kiaochow Bay and commercial rights in the hinterland.

Not to be outdone in what had now become a headlong scramble for territory, trading privileges, railway concessions and mining rights, Britain also moved into Shantung, obtaining a lease of the port of Weihaiwei as a counterbalance to Russia's lease of Port Arthur; and to offset the advantages France had obtained by leasing Kwangchowwan, she demanded and was granted further territories in Kwangtung inland from Kowloon.

Of all the leading powers the United States—occupied as she was with the opening up of her own western territories and her merchant marine weakened as a result of the Civil War—alone remained aloof from this slow dismemberment of China, content to obtain the agreement of the European nations that the spheres of influence which they were carving out for themselves did not take on the exclusive nature of colonies. But the United States, while condemning imperialism, was ready to participate in its benefits.[11]

*   *   *

With each fresh military defeat, with each new loss of territory and humiliating treaty, the demands for reform in China grew in force and persuasiveness. To be beaten by Western Barbarians was bad enough; to be degraded by those 'dwarf bandits' from Japan was intolerable. After the disastrous Treaty of Shimonoseki in 1895, the Chinese official who had signed it, the Empress Dowager's powerful supporter, Li Hung-chang, became the most hated man in the Empire: a man whose flesh, so memorialists to the Throne suggested, would make a most satisfactory dinner; a man who, it was later suspected—and the Soviet publication of Tsarist archives has proved the suspicion well founded—accepted a huge bribe in Moscow when the Sino-Russian treaty was being negotiated in 1896.

Even before the Sino-Japanese war, Li was suspected—and again rightly suspected—of misappropriating the large funds that had been allocated to the Chinese navy as a result of its mauling by the French at Foochow. In this the Empress Dowager was deeply implicated. Her inordinate extravagance, and in particular, her lavish expenditure on a new Summer Palace, known as the Hill of a Myriad Longevities, close to the ruins of the Round Bright Garden of Yüan-ming Yüan, had drained the Treasury. On being approached by the Empress's egregious go-between, the eunuch Li Lien-ying, Li Hung-chang obligingly replenished the Imperial Treasury from the Naval funds of which he had been appointed administrator.[12]

For all his unpopularity and the stories of his corruption, Li Hung-chang remained in charge of the Board of Foreign Affairs until September 1898 when the Emperor Kuang-hsü, by then a young man of twenty-six—so 'strange and unusual a man . . . stately, somehow effeminate'[13]—and on the worst possible terms with his aunt, the Empress, found courage enough to dismiss him.

Li's dismissal marked a critical stage in the reform movement which had been rapidly gathering momentum since the Treaty of Shimonoseki. For several years before that a number of Chinese scholars, influenced by Western ideas and Western books, by visits to Shanghai and Hong Kong and, in some cases, by courses in Western universities, had been propagating doctrines that horrified conservatives as much as they gave hope to the intelligent young. These scholars formed societies such as the Anti-Footbinding Society and the Higher Learning Society. They opened schools, published articles in the Chinese Press, and translated Western books. They popularized slogans like 'Chinese culture for the foundation, Western learning for practical application', a maxim coined by Chang Chih-tung, the Viceroy of Hunan and Hopei, whose *Exhortation to Study*, criticizing the rigid formalism of Manchu officialdom, achieved a wide circulation. Another reformer, Yen Fu, who had spent two years in England, thereafter becoming head of the naval school of Tientsin, translated Huxley's *Evolution and Ethics*, which was serialized in a Tientsin journal. He also wrote numerous widely read articles advocating a central overhaul of education. K'ang Yu-wei, a young Confucian scholar from Canton who had studied in Japan and collected a large library of Western books in Shanghai, published a series of influential works on a variety of subjects from the *Renovation of Japan* and the *Decadence of Turkey* to *Peter the Great* and *Constitutional Changes in England*. His best known disciple, Liang Ch'i-ch'ao, one day to achieve an international reputation, urged his readers to look at the fate of those peoples and countries which, turning their backs on change, had insisted on following tradition: at India, for instance, 'now rendered a colony of England'; at Turkey, 'dominated by six large countries which have divided her territory'; at the Muslims in central Asia who had 'observed the old ways without changing' and who were now being devoured by the Russians 'as silkworms eat mulberry leaves'.[14]

Liang Ch'i-ch'ao had once been secretary to the Rev. Timothy Richard, an English missionary who strongly supported the movement for reform and wrote enthusiastically in his memoirs of the impact of translated Christian and secular literature on the Chinese mind. Formerly, he said, such works as were translated were made into soles for Chinese shoes or burned in temple buildings, but 'after the appearance of [Robert] Mackenzie's *History of the Nineteenth Century* [which he himself translated] . . . and other books . . . a great change came over the Chinese bookseller. In one city—Hangchow—there were no less than six pirated editions of the *Nineteenth Century*. . . . Altogether there must have been a million pirated copies in circulation throughout China.'[15]

The excitement and intellectual fervour of the movement did not fail to impress the young Emperor, who was constantly enjoined to save his country by bringing it into the light as Peter the Great and the Emperor Mutsuhito had saved theirs. Ignoring the malignant threats of the Empress Dowager that the time was rapidly approaching when he would have to be taken off the throne as hurriedly as he had been put onto it, he recalled Prince Kung from his retirement and listened attentively to those Court officials who urged him to heed the advice of such reformist scholars as K'ang Yu-wei. The old Prince Kung, wary of the reactions of the Empress Dowager, warned the Emperor not to be too hasty, to read K'ang Yu-wei's works discreetly by all means, but not to receive him at Court. But Prince Kung did not long survive his recall to Peking; and soon after his death, in defiance of his advice, K'ang was granted an audience in June 1898.

'It lasted for two hours,' K'ang recalled. 'Port Arthur had just been taken over by Russia, and the Emperor wore an anxious, careworn expression. . . . He was led in by eunuchs, and took his seat on a dais on a large yellow cushion, with his feet folded beneath him. He sent his attendants away, and we were left alone; but all the time we were conversing his eyes were watching the windows, as if to see that no one was eavesdropping. There was a long table in front of him with two large candlesticks. I knelt at one of the corners of the table. . . . I remained kneeling during the whole of the audience. We conversed in the Mandarin dialect. The Emperor said to me: "Your books are very instructive." I practically repeated what I had said in my memorial about the weakness of China being due to the lack of progress. The Emperor said: "Yes, all these conservative Ministers have ruined me." I said to him, "China is weak now, but it is not yet too late . . ."[16]

Immediately after this interview, as though there were no time to be lost, edict after edict issued from the Emperor's palace proclaiming a new era in the history of China. There were to be reforms in the educational system and in the army and the navy; schools were to be reorganized; banks, chambers of commerce, new Government departments were to be opened; the Press was to be free; there was to be a university at Peking. The traditional examinations were to be modernized; various conservative officials were dismissed and sinecures abolished.

Enthusiastically, the Emperor announced that he would never feel his duty to be fulfilled until all his people had been raised to a condition of peaceful prosperity. 'Moreover,' he continued, 'do not the foreign Powers surround our Empire, committing frequent acts of aggression? Unless we learn and adopt the sources of their strength, our plight cannot be remedied.'17

By now Kuang-hsü's own plight was critical. Appalled by his cataclysmic programme of reform, both conservatives who had never wanted change, and moderates who were frightened by the speed of it, turned to the Empress Dowager on whose sympathy and help they knew they could rely. To forestall any action she might take against him, the Emperor called for help from Yüan Shih-k'ai, a senior army officer who had distinguished himself during the war in Korea and now, as commander of the one modern Westernized army that China then possessed, was presumed to be in favour of the reformers. Yüan came to Peking and, at an audience with the Emperor, agreed to the suggestion that a party of his most reliable troops should surround the Empress Dowager at her Hill of a Myriad Longevities and hold her there.

But Kuang-hsü in his dilemma had chosen the wrong man. Yüan, with little confidence in Kuang-hsü's ultimate success, feared for his own future should he fail. He went to Tientsin, to the house of his friend Jung-lu, the Empress Dowager's former lover—some said her lover still—the man who had saved her from murder on her journey from Jehol thirty-seven years before and who had since risen to positions of power in both state and army. Yüan told Jung-lu what the Emperor had asked him to do. Jung-lu was 'apparently unaffected by the message', merely expressing surprise that the Old Buddha could have been kept in ignorance of the plot; but he immediately left Tientsin, travelling by special train to Peking. He arrived there soon after five o'clock in the evening and went directly to the Lake Palace where he laid before Tz'u-hsi all the details of the plot against her.18

Tz'u-hsi, in a terrifying rage, came down from the Lake Palace and was carried to her nephew's door. The Emperor, roused from sleep by a eunuch and warned of the dreaded woman's approach, 'knew instantly' that he was lost. He 'did not know what to do,' he afterwards confessed. What he did do was to get up, to dress and to throw himself in submission at her feet.[19]

19 | Righteous Harmony Boxing

*If there are Christian converts in your village,
you ought to get rid of them quickly. The
churches which belong to them should be burned
down without exception. Anyone who disobeys
our order by concealing converts will be
burned to death.* A Boxer proclamation, 1900.

The reform movement was over. Kuang-hsü was left to languish in lonely confinement at Ying T'ai, the Ocean Terrace, a four-roomed chalet on the edge of the lake of the Winter Palace; and it was given out in an Abdication Decree that, 'the Emperor being ill', the Empress Dowager had resumed the Regency. For the rest of his life Kuang-hsü lived in abject submission to his aunt, miserable and lonely, talking in so soft a voice, 'light and thin like the hum of a mosquito', that it was difficult to hear what he said.[1] After his relegation to the Ocean Terrace it was announced that an heir apparent to the throne had been appointed; this was P'u Chün, the rampagingly lecherous young son of Prince Tuan.

Prince Tuan was Kuang-hsü's cousin and a grandson of the Emperor Tao-kuang. As an intimate adviser of the Empress, the new President of the Board of Foreign Affairs, and an implacable enemy of the foreigners, he was to play an important part in the extraordinary events which were now to follow. His voice was amongst the most persuasive of those urging upon the Empress the cause and virtues of a secret society whose numbers were growing fast in the province of Shantung, and whose banners proclaimed the exhilarating summons: 'Support the Manchus. Exterminate the Foreigners.'

The members of this society which so excited the imagination of Prince Tuan practised a kind of shadow boxing, Taoist in origin, which was known as *Shen Ch'üan*, Spirit Boxing; *T'ai Chi Ch'üan*,

Supreme Ultimate Boxing; or *I Ho Ch'üan*, Righteous Harmony Boxing. Taking note of their addiction to these exercises, a missionary, writing in the *North China Daily News*, gave them the name by which they became known throughout the world, the Boxers.

For countless centuries secret societies had proliferated and agitated beneath the surface of Chinese life, occasionally breaking out in violence against some overbearing landlord or official. There were the Red Fist Societies and the Big Knives, the Society of Heaven and Earth, the Eight Diagram Sect and the Six Times Sect, the Small Sword Society, the White Lotus, the sect of the Golden Ball and many others of less renown. Most of them had numbered the alien Manchu dynasty amongst their selected enemies; but what distinguished the Boxers from the rest was that with their proclaimed hatred of the foreigner, and of all Chinese who took on foreign ways, went an evident willingness to support the Manchus against the common enemy. They had not originally been prepared to give the dynasty this support. Indeed, in the early days of the movement most of its members were as anti-Manchu as any other secret society; and Boxer chants virulently condemned the 'stupid Manchu Government' which knelt before the foreigner, and the 'wavering Manchu bannermen' who fled before his troops. The words of one popular early Boxer chant were these:

> *Surely Government bannermen*
> *are many; certainly foreign soldiers*
> *a horde; but if each of our people*
> *spits once, they will drown,*
> *bannermen and invaders together.*[2]

Once Prince Tuan was known to be prepared to encourage the Boxers, however, their policy had changed.[3] Their chants omitted all unfavourable references to Manchus, concentrating their hatred upon the Foreign Devils whom all true Boxers strove to kill to 'give face to the Chinese people'.[4]

From both Shantung and Chihli came enthusiastic reports of the prowess of these Boxers. It was not only their ritualistic addiction to the art of pugilism that made them so formidable in a fight; they were subjected to the severest discipline by their commanders who did not allow them to eat meat or drink tea. They were furthermore instructed to avoid contact with women.[5] Also, their rites of initiation, involving incantations, genuflections, stampings, the knocking of the head on the ground and the making of esoteric signs with the hands and fingers, induced spasms, fits and trances that afterwards made the initiate immune to pain and fear and even, it was said, to injury. 'They work themselves into a state of nervous exaltation that suppresses the sensation of pain and the consciousness of danger,' wrote one observer. 'This they achieve by means of deafening shouts, wild contortions, and frenzied antics with lance and sword. The ceremony takes place in the midst of a crowd driven wild by the spectacle. . . . In order to impress the crowds, the initiated pretend to be invulnerable, and they demonstrate their contempt for European arms by ordering some of their confederates to fire upon them with blank cartridges; they drop to the ground, as if hit, and immediately rise to their feet again, holding in their hands the projectiles they had hidden in their clothes.'[6]

On other occasions they invited the bystanders to attack them with swords, and the Governor General of Chihli himself reported that he had witnessed a demonstration in which his soldiers had slashed at a group of initiated Boxers without causing them the least hurt.[7]

These exciting reports were welcomed in Peking and accepted by many of the Empress's advisers and by the Empress herself as certain truth. It seemed to them that in the power of the Boxers might lie the salvation of the dynasty. Already they had been led to suppose that a firm policy against the foreigners would keep them in check far better than the appeasement of Li Hung-chang and Prince Kung. In February 1899 the Italian Government, anxious not to be left out of the scramble for Chinese territory, had demanded Sanmen Bay in the province of Chekiang as a naval base. The demand had been refused, and when the Italians repeated it more firmly the Governor of Chekiang was ordered to resist any further pressure 'immediately and with all might'. He did so with such determination that the Italians were forced to withdraw the claim and to recall their Minister.

The following month, after German troops had burned down two villages and had occupied the town of Jihchao in Shantung as a reprisal for the murder of three German nationals, the Governor of Shantung had been given orders 'not to be intimidated . . . not to accede unendingly to the aggressive demands of the Germans'; and the Germans had withdrawn. By the Spring of 1899 there was a growing feeling in Peking that if only these strong measures had been taken against them in the past the foreigners would have been kept at bay, and that the Boxers, even at this late hour, might be used to terrorize them into retreat.

* * *

It gradually became clear to the foreigners that the Boxer movement, once it had established its credentials as a firm supporter of the Manchu dynasty, would not be suppressed on orders from Peking. When several Boxers were killed in a clash with provincial troops in Shantung, the Governor of the province, the rabidly anti-foreign Yü-hsien, took severe action against the officials responsible. In the face of furious German protests he was dismissed from his post, but the Empress showed him that, in her eyes, he had done nothing to be ashamed of and appointed him to the governorship of the more westerly province of Shansi where he could take action against the Barbarians less hindered by German interference. His successor at Shantung, Yüan Shih-k'ai, the officer who had betrayed Kuang-hsü's plot to the Empress's friend Jung-lu, understood how fatal to the welfare of the dynasty the Boxers might yet prove to be; but when he endeavoured to put an end to their activities in his province he was sharply instructed by Peking to be 'extremely careful'. On 11 January 1900 a decree issued by the Empress Dowager, in which a distinction was made between 'good and evil' secret societies, made it obvious enough to the world at large that in her view the Boxers were a good one.[8] The British, American, French, German and Italian Ministers in Peking sent identical notes to the Board of Foreign Affairs, protesting against this decree and asking that the Boxers should be suppressed. But the Government, strongly resenting this attempt by the foreigners to foist new laws on the Empire to suit their own convenience, declined to give a satisfactory reply.

As the weeks of 1900 went by, the activities of the Boxers increased. They began to extend to foreign missionaries, whom they had sound reasons to hate, the violence that had at first been limited to Chinese Christians.

Repellent enough, in the Boxers' eyes, were the foreign businessmen and overseers whose detested railways would soon be carrying 'fire-carts' and rattling, iron-wheeled wagons all over the country, desecrating burial places, disturbing the spirits of the earth, putting honest carters and porters, trackers and boatmen, muleteers and camel-men out of work. Equally obnoxious were the foreign operators of the chugging steamships on the inland waterways, the foreign mining engineers whose deep shafts upset the *feng-shui* even more than the railway tracks did, the foreign importers grown rich on the sale of opium and piece-goods, the foreign mechanics who put up the wires and the poles for the telegraph companies.

'The iron roads and iron carriages are disturbing the terrestrial dragon and are destroying the earth's beneficial influences,' ran one of the anti-Western tracts distributed by the Boxers' supporters. 'The red liquid which keeps dripping from the iron snake [the rust-coloured rain water that dripped from the telegraph wires] is nothing but the blood of the outraged spirits of the air.'[9]

But evil as were the men who exploited the land and waters and befouled the air of China, far worse were those missionaries who extracted 'the eyes, marrow and heart of the dead in order to make medicines'. 'Whoever drinks a glass of tea at the parsonage is stricken by death,' the people of China were warned: 'the brains burst out of the skull. The drinks offered by these traitors are poisons that corrode your stomach. The unfortunate people attending religious services are being bewitched. As for children received in orphanages, they are killed and their intestines are used to change lead into silver and to make precious remedies.'[10]

Such charges against the missionaries were widely credited, as they had been at Tientsin in 1860. It was impossible for the Chinese to understand the motives that lay behind the opening of orphanages, the care of burdensome children whom nobody wanted. The collection of so many useless and helpless infants—especially when their rate of mortality was bound to be high, when missionaries paid rewards to those who brought waifs and strays to be baptized, thus encouraging criminals to kidnap children—was immediately connected with the superstition that foreigners mutilated children's bodies for the purposes of alchemy and magical potions. Nor was it only the fearful practices of the missionaries that so horrified the Chinese. Their heavy churches weighed down by high steeples were just as much a threat to the spirits of the earth as the mines and railways were; their refusal to allow their converts to contribute to what they condemned as idolatrous rites, to Taoist festivals and to the upkeep of temples placed an unfair and in some places intolerable liability on the rest of the community; their pestering interference in cases between converts and other Chinese often influenced the magistrate's decision in the converts' favour; their encouragement of converts in refusing to kotow before officials was a flaunting of the traditional manners of China; their forcing a man to give up his concubine before being received into their sect caused unnecessary misery and hardship; above all, the insistence of the Roman Catholic Church that their senior clergy in China should have secular rights and privileges, that their bishops should enjoy all the honours of rank accorded to mandarins, caused the deepest offence throughout the Empire.[11]

No words seemed strong enough to castigate the follies and vices of the missionaries; and anti-Christian pamphlets which depicted Christ as a crucified pig, and his worshippers as the most horrendous devils, appeared to their readers as reasonable statements of fact.

'The scandalous conduct of Christians and Barbarians is angering our gods and spirits,' the peasants of China were warned by the Boxers, 'hence the many scourges from which we are now suffering. The dreadful drought afflicting vast areas this year will continue as long as one single Western Devil resides within the Four Seas.'[12]

Notices posted up in the province of Shansi proclaimed: 'The

Catholic and Protestant Churches deceive our gods, destroy our belief in our saints, and disobey the precepts of the Buddha. Hence the present famine and other disasters.'[13]

The Empress Dowager could not be other than happy to have the blame for the recent months of drought, famine, flood and pestilence, the failures of harvests and the plagues of locusts, placed so squarely upon the Western Devils, since it conveniently diverted the people's attention from her own Government's failure to provide any adequate relief. She believed firmly in the Boxers' magical powers. She also realized that if this society were to be suppressed, another, traditionally anti-Manchu society, would arise to take its place. In the hope therefore that she would be able to control its pretensions once its mission in destroying the foreigners had been accomplished, she shut her normally astute mind to the consequences of allowing the Boxers to rampage and murder foreigners without check, refusing to consider that the Boxers' depredations would bring the quarrelling powers together in an alliance which might possibly overthrow her

The 'final defeat' of these foreign powers, the amputation of 'the ruthless hands of the invader', the destruction of China's 'great enemies' were objects that, no matter how urgent the edicts in which their desirability was expressed, China's antiquated, incompetent armies had never been capable of attaining. The Boxers, with their supernatural powers and dedicated spirit, might well achieve them. For a time the Empress even wondered whether these 'Children of China' might perhaps be enlisted in a militia, and her representatives in Chihli and Shantung were asked for their opinions of this scheme. Given an opportunity to express his views, Yüan Shih-k'ai, Governor of Shantung, replied that the Boxers, 'setting fire to houses, kidnapping people, and offering resistance to Government troops', could not be termed other than criminal; 'plundering and killing the common people and stirring up disturbances', they could not be said to be merely anti-Christian. They were 'devoid of any skills'; whenever they had come into conflict with regular troops they had always been beaten.[14]

Yü-lu, Viceroy of Chihli, though a less outspoken man, pointed out that a careful distinction ought to be made between peasants who practised the art of fighting for purposes of self-defence and roving vagabonds who boxed and roamed the streets for personal profit. These men had been arrested by local officials and found lacking any real ability; their leaders were all bad elements; if they were organized into a militia it would hardly be a law-abiding one.[15] But despite his low opinion of them, Yü-lu did not take the vigorous action against them that Yüan Shih-k'ai did in his province; and by the early summer of 1900 the Boxers were slaughtering Chinese converts indiscriminately all over Chihli and Shansi, and urging villagers to join them in their holy war against the foreigner and his religion.

Notices appeared everywhere demanding support on pain of death: 'If there are Christian converts in your village, you ought to get rid of them quickly. The churches which belong to them should be burned down without exception. Anyone who disobeys our order by concealing converts will be burned to death for impeding our programme. . . . Hasten, then, to spread this doctrine far and wide, for if you gain one adherent to the faith your own person will be absolved from all future misfortunes. If you gain five adherents your whole family will be absolved from all evils, and if you gain ten adherents your whole village will be absolved from all calamities. Those who gain no adherents to the cause shall be decapitated. . . .'[16]

These were not idle threats, Wu Yung, a district magistrate said. 'When the Boxers burned churches or houses, they were in the habit of commanding the onlookers, whether men or women, old or young, to kneel around the building and to cry out in a loud voice, "Burn, burn, burn, kill, kill, kill!" The sound of the shouting would shake the heavens. This was to add strength to their barbarities. Those who did not obey were called Secondary Hairy Ones and were immediately chopped to the consistency of a flour sauce.'[17]

Wherever missionaries could be found in North China they suffered the same fate as their congregations. In the province of Shansi, whose Governor was the wildly xenophobic Yü-hsien, two hundred and thirty foreigners, nearly all of them missionaries and their families, were massacred. Ten of them, Swedish missionaries, were killed as a punishment for having brought drought to the province; but most of them were slaughtered for no other given reason than that they were foreign and Christian.

On a single day in the main courtyard of the Governor's *yamen* at Taiyüan, forty-five foreigners were decapitated under the personal direction of Yü-hsien himself. A Chinese Baptist convert who survived described the scene in these words: 'The first to be led forth was Mr Farthing (English Baptist). His wife clung to him, but he gently put her aside, and going in front of the soldiers knelt down without saying a word, and his head was struck off with one blow of the executioner's knife. He was quickly followed by Mr Hoddle and Mr Benyon, Drs Lovitt and Wilson, each of whom was beheaded by one blow of the executioner. Then the Governor, Yü Hsien, grew impatient and told his bodyguard, all of whom carried heavy swords with long handles, to help kill the others. . . . When the men were finished the ladies were taken. Mrs Farthing had hold of the hands of her children who clung to her, but the soldiers parted them, and with one blow beheaded their mother. The executioner beheaded all the children and did it skilfully, needing only one blow, but the soldiers were clumsy, and some of the ladies suffered several cuts before death. Mrs Lovitt was wearing her spectacles and held the hand of her little boy, even when she was killed. She spoke to the people, saying, "We all came to China to bring you the good news of the salvation by Jesus Christ; we have done you no harm, only good, why do you treat us so?" A soldier took off her spectacles before beheading her. . . . When the Protestants had been killed, the Roman Catholics were led forward. The Bishop, an old man with a long white beard, asked the Governor why he was doing this wicked deed. I did not hear the Governor give him any answer, but he drew his sword and cut the Bishop across the face one heavy stroke; blood poured down his white beard, and he was beheaded. . . . The priests and nuns quickly followed him to death. . . . All were surprised at the firmness and quietness of the foreigners, none of whom except two or three of the children cried, or made any noise.'[18]

A few days after this a small group of other missionaries and their wives were found hiding in a cave in the nearby village of

Liu-chia-shan. They were arrested by the Boxers and taken to the local gaol from which they were eventually released with the promise that they would be transported to the coast. 'Arriving at the east gate of the city, the missionaries were dragged from their carts, and stripped of all their clothes. Then both Boxers and soldiers set upon them and literally hacked their heads to pieces. Their bodies were dragged outside the city and left on the banks of a river where they were shamefully treated by the villagers. . . . After the massacre the highest military official went to the mission houses, and then turned the houses over to the soldiers and the people to loot.'[19]

When reporting these events to the Empress Dowager, Yü-hsien said proudly that he had caught the foreigners in a net, 'and allowed neither chicken nor dog to escape'.

'You did splendidly,' Tz'u-hsi commended him, 'in ridding Shansi of this whole brood of Foreign Devils.'[20]

20 | The Siege of the Legations

*La situation est excessivement grave, nous
allons tous mourir ce soir.* Stephen Pichon,
French Minister at Peking, July 1900.

Some months before the massacre at Taiyüan, the Empress Dowager
had broken with precedent and invited the wives of the foreign
diplomats to a reception in the Forbidden City. Her graciousness and
courteous amiability had charmed them all. 'She was bright and
happy,' said Mrs Conger, wife of the American Minister, 'and her
face glowed with goodwill. . . . In simple expressions she welcomed
us, and her actions were full of freedom and warmth. Her Majesty
arose and wished us well. She extended both hands to each lady,
then, touching herself, said with much enthusiastic earnestness,
"One family—all one family."'[1]

It was difficult indeed for most foreigners in Peking to believe that
the beguiling little Empress, who spoke so gently in a beautifully
melodious voice, was not as sincere as she seemed. Certainly Sir
Robert Hart, head of the Chinese Customs Service, a man who had
lived in the country for almost half a century, and by now the
respected doyen of the foreign community, could see little cause for
alarm when the first reports of the Boxers' depredations reached the
capital. Sir Robert loved China and the Chinese people, and refused
to accept that the telegrams reaching the various legations from the
missionaries in the provinces were other than alarmist, or that the
newspapers' stories were less than wilfully exaggerated. Even if
there were to be any trouble in Peking, the foreigners would be protected, as foreigners were undeniably being protected by the governors of the southern provinces of the Empire.

Sir Claude MacDonald, the British Minister, could also see little cause for alarm, though he had been informed that the French Minister had received from the Vicar-Apostolic of Peking an urgent message imploring him to believe that the lives not only of missionaries but of all Europeans were in danger. 'The Boxers' accomplices await them in Peking,' the Monseigneur continued, 'they mean to attack the churches first, then the Legations. For us, in our Cathedral, the date of the attack has actually been fixed.'[2]

The French Legation scarcely stood in need of such a warning. Two days after it was written, on 21 May, Baron d'Anthouard, one of the French Minister's staff, noted in his diary, 'The Boxers are already very numerous in this city, and are said to number several thousand men. . . . You can see them everywhere . . . they distribute handbills, and advocate the massacre of foreigners and the destruction of all religious institutions. They no longer take the trouble to hide, and move about carrying their insignia: a red scarf tied round their heads with the inscription "Fu" (Happiness) on their chest, and red bands round their wrists and ankles.'[3]

At a meeting attended by the various foreign ministers on 20 May, Stephen Pichon, the French Minister, pressed the views and apprehensions of Monseigneur Favier and Baron d'Anthouard on the other members of the Corps Diplomatique. He suggested that in order to induce the Government to outlaw the Boxers, a guard for the Legations should be called up from Tientsin; but he failed to convince them all of their danger. Little had come to his knowledge, Sir Claude MacDonald reported to London, 'to confirm the gloomy anticipations' of Monseigneur Favier. Sir Claude's two little daughters were allowed to leave Peking, accompanied by his sister-in-law and a small guard of marines, to enjoy the relative cool of the British Legation bungalow in the Western Hills.

Before the month was out, however, the children had been bustled back to Peking and what Sir Claude referred to as the 'wholesome calm' of the Legation quarter had been badly shaken. On 28 May the railway station and the houses of the foreign engineers at Fengtai, south of Peking, were attacked and set on fire. The next day the houses of several Europeans further down the line at Ch'anghsintien were also burned, and the telegraph wires were cut. There could be no doubt now that guards were urgently needed in Peking and, belatedly, with unforeseen consequences for the foreigners, they were sent for. By 3 June rather more than four hundred of them, sailors and marines from the foreign warships anchored at the mouth of the Peiho, had arrived in the capital.

Confidence was immediately restored. Sir Claude assured Admiral Sir Edward Seymour, the naval commander, that he did not think matters would become any more complicated, that no more ships would be needed at Taku for the moment, and that the Legations would be 'the last place attacked'.[4]

A week later Sir Claude had been given good cause to change his mind and was sending express demands to Seymour for the landing of troops and an immediate advance on Peking. The situation there was 'hourly becoming more serious'.

The railway line to Tientsin had now been cut; Belgian railway engineers fleeing to Tientsin from Paotingfu had been attacked; two British missionaries had been murdered not far from Peking; and when Sir Claude had protested to the Board of Foreign Affairs about this, one of the members of the Board to whom the protest was delivered was seen to be so unconcerned as to be fast asleep. On 9 June the race course grandstand, only three miles from the walls of Peking, was set alight and a group of Europeans who rode out to inspect the damage were obliged to fire into a threatening crowd. More ominous even than all this, the latest Imperial Edict had made it unequivocally clear that the missionaries and their converts, now flying for their lives towards Peking, could expect no protection from the Government troops.

*   *   *

As soon as he received Sir Claude MacDonald's summons, Admiral Seymour set out by train for Peking with an international force of rather more than five hundred men which, since the British contingent was the largest, he himself commanded. By 13 June he had about fifteen hundred other men under his control. There were, in all, about nine hundred British, five hundred Germans, three hundred Russians, a hundred and fifty French, a hundred Americans and smaller detachments of Japanese, Italians and Austrians. The British officers, looking forward to 'a journey of a few hours', took with them their full dress uniforms.

Four days later the expedition's leading train was still only about thirty miles north of Tientsin. All along the line, stations and water-tanks had been destroyed; sleepers had been burned, buckling the rails; bridges had been made impassable; and on 18 June the wagons of the German detachment were attacked by a powerful force of Chinese.

Previous attacks by Boxers, who ran headlong towards the railway line armed with gingalls, rifles, spears and swords, and calling upon the God of War for protection, had been repulsed without much difficulty and with heavy losses. But the troops who attacked the Germans on the 18th were not Boxers; they were hardy, well-trained Muslim cavalry from the province of Kansu, and they were commanded by the Imperial General, Tung Fu-hsiang, a formidable Kansu warrior who had once been a bandit. Opposed now by Boxers and Imperial troops alike, Seymour was forced to abandon all hope of getting through to Peking with so small a force, many of whom had been wounded and all of whom were running short of ammunition and supplies. He ordered a withdrawal towards Tientsin.

The alliance of Boxers and Imperial troops, officially sanctioned by Peking, had been provoked by the captains of the foreign warships off the Taku Bar who had taken independent and desperate action to keep open the Peiho river and thus save Seymour's force from being cut off, surrounded and destroyed. On the morning of 16 June they had delivered an ultimatum to the Chinese to hand over the Taku forts by two o'clock the next morning; and, on this ultimatum being met by a ferocious fire from the forts, they had replied to the can-nonade. In a short, melodramatic and decisive action their men succeeded not only in silencing and taking the forts, but in boarding and capturing four new German-built destroyers.

On hearing of the foreigners' ultimatum and something of the subsequent events—though not too much of these, since the Viceroy of Chihli followed the tradition of his predecessors, cautiously with-holding the most disturbing reports—the Empress Dowager decided that the time had come to declare war upon all her numerous enemies.

Obedient to her wishes, Imperial troops now joined the Boxers in their attacks upon the foreign settlements in Tientsin, whose hard-pressed defenders fought desperately night and day to keep them out. Some officers and men of H.M.S. *Terrible* who had been at Ladysmith during the Boer War afterwards told Robert Gartside-Tipping of the Bengal Lancers that '*that* was a perfect joke compared to what went on at Tientsin'.[5] They never expected to be able to hold out until the relief forces reached them.

There were two of these forces. One of them was an international force about two thousand strong, composed mainly of British soldiers and marines recently arrived from Hong Kong, and of Russians from Port Arthur. While this force was fighting its way from Taku, Admiral Seymour's expedition was also fighting its way towards Tientsin from the opposite direction, suffering severe casualties, occasionally blinded by duststorms and throughout the day stifled by the appalling heat. On 26 June the two expeditionary forces met in Tientsin where, three days later, a frantic message was received from the hands of a Chinese courier from Peking. It was from Sir Robert Hart and it read, 'Foreign community besieged in the Legations. Situation desperate. MAKE HASTE!!'[6]

*   *   *

Just over a fortnight before, the Chancellor of the Japanese Legation in Peking had gone out one afternoon to the railway station to make enquiries concerning the expected time of arrival of the fifty-four men forming the Japanese contingent of Admiral Seymour's expeditionary force.

Outside the southern gate of the Chinese city he had been dragged from his cart by several Kansu troops who, taking exception to the sight of his oriental features beneath a bowler hat of unmistakably Western design, set about him with their swords. His heart was cut out and despatched to their commander, the former bandit, Tung Fu-hsiang.[7]

He was not the only foreign Minister to be murdered that month.

The death of Baron von Ketteler, the German Minister—'a very passionate and excitable man' in Sir Claude MacDonald's opinion, and in that of the American missionary, Arthur Smith, 'particularly obnoxious to the Chinese'—had already been announced in the European Press several days in advance of its actual occurrence. On 13 June von Ketteler was enraged by an unendurable sight in Legation Street. It was that of a Boxer riding on the shaft of a cart past the very gate of the German Legation, flaunting the red girdle and ribbons of his brotherhood and affecting to sharpen a knife on his boot. Von Ketteler stormed towards him and belaboured the impudent devil with his walking-stick. The man escaped; but another younger Boxer inside the cart was more severely beaten, carried inside the German Legation and there held prisoner.

These two Boxers were the first to be seen in the Legation quarter; but a few hours after they had been dragged from their cart, an immense rabble of their companions came bursting into the Tartar City through the gate by the American Methodist mission, swinging swords and spears above their heads, shouting their fearsome war-cry '*Sha! Sha!* Kill! Kill!', driving the terrified crowds before them, looting shops and houses, cutting down all those whom they suspected of being infected by the Christian religion.

They set fire to missions, to the buildings of the Customs Service, to the houses of the foreign lecturers at the University, and the Roman Catholic East Cathedral inside which a priest and several Chinese Christians were burned alive. The clergy and congregation of the South Cathedral were saved from similar destruction by a band of volunteers, including the Swiss proprietor of the Hôtel de Pékin and his intrepid American wife, who brought them back with twenty-five nuns to the relative safety of the Legations. The South Cathedral itself was burned down immediately after their departure; and the next morning, when a patrol of marines went out to bring in any converts who might have survived the slaughter that had gone on for much of the night around its blazing walls, they came upon fearful sights of 'women and children hacked to pieces, men trussed like fowls, with noses and ears cut off and eyes gouged out'.[8]

For the next few days the looting and slaughter continued until there were so many corpses in the streets that orders had to be given to the Peking Field Force to remove them from the city. Human sacrifices were carried out in blood-spattered temples; shops and business premises were burned to the ground; and the spreading flames soon destroyed the Chien Men, the vast gatehouse whose soaring tiled roofs with their upswept eaves towered above the wall that divided the Chinese from the Tartar City south of the Imperial palace. The Legation guards, and the adventurous Europeans and Americans who joined forces with them, went out into the streets and climbed onto the Legation roofs to shoot down any Boxers or any Chinese they thought might well be Boxers—not too fine a distinction was made between them. When they were out on patrol they took no prisoners; all were shot out of hand.

Up till now, the Imperial troops in Peking had not interfered in the fighting. Indeed, Jung-lu, commanding the Chinese armies in and around the capital, had received orders to protect the Legations; and messages kept arriving from the Board of Foreign Affairs assuring the Ministers that they and their staff were in no danger, that there was no need to send for any more troops from Tientsin. But then at a meeting of the Imperial Council on 17 June a document was introduced which decided the Empress to adopt a more positive policy, a policy that resulted the following day, when the news of the ultimatum delivered at Taku reached Peking, in China's declaration of war upon the Western world.[9] This document purported to be a demand from the foreign powers that the Empress Dowager should abdicate and that Kuang-hsü should be restored to the throne. This 'insolent proposal', as the Empress referred to it, was a forgery; but when a member of the Council found courage to suggest as much, implying that Prince Tuan himself had fabricated it in order to force the Empress's hand against the foreigners, she angrily dismissed him from the Audience Hall. After he had gone 'no one else dared to say anything. She then ordered the promulgation of the Decree, for immediate communication to all parts of the Empire', calling upon the provincial governors to join in the hostilities.[10]

Yüan Shih-k'ai in Shantung and Li Hung-chang in Kwangtung, as well as most of the leading officials in the provinces of Central and South China, ignored the edict;[11] but in Chihli and Shansi it was put into effect. In Peking the Kansu troops of Tung Fu-hsiang rampaged through the streets massacring all those whom they suspected of being spies or 'Secondary Devils'. They 'entered and sacked nearly every house in my neighbourhood', wrote Heng Yi, a visitor to the capital from Kiangsi who was afterwards told that a quarter of a million people lost their lives in Peking that summer; 'I could hear the shrieks of the women and children, whom they were butchering and their shouts, in the Kansu dialect, "Bring out the Secondary Devils!" . . . We collected the whole of the family in one of the main rooms, and told them not to get excited or scream. I had scarcely mustered them when nineteen of the Kansu braves came rushing in. Their swords and clothes were still dripping with blood, as if they had come from a slaughter-house.' Heng Yi got rid of them only by assuring them that none of his family had 'eaten' the foreign religion, and by allowing them to plunder the house.[12]

On 19 June Sir Robert Hart and each of the eleven foreign Ministers received an ultimatum to leave Peking with the Legations' guards within twenty-four hours, and 'to proceed to Tientsin to prevent any unforeseen calamity'.[13]

To the accompanying noise of exploding crackers and rockets in a burning fireworks factory, the Ministers met to discuss this alarming ultimatum in the Spanish Legation. At first the general feeling was that it would be far more dangerous to leave Peking than to remain in it. Moreover, to leave it would certainly mean abandoning not only the survivors of the Boxers' massacre of Chinese converts, who had been streaming in their hundreds into the Legation quarter for the past several days, but also Monseigneur Favier and the French defenders of the Northern Cathedral; this stood hard by the western wall of the Imperial City, which, though it had so far escaped the fate of the South and East Cathedrals, was being ever more closely besieged. As the evening wore on, however, the mood of the meeting began to change. The fierce Baron von Ketteler remained as strong as ever in his refusal to accept the ultimatum; he insisted that they must all hold out in Peking. But the French Minister, Stephen Pichon, and the American, E. H. Conger, thought perhaps it might be better after all to give way, and eventually they carried the other Ministers with them. A compliant answer was returned to the Board of Foreign Affairs, and a request made for an interview with Prince Tuan the next morning at nine o'clock so that the details of the withdrawal might be discussed.

When he heard of the Ministers' decision, Dr G. E. Morrison, *The Times*'s enterprising and courageous correspondent, was appalled. An Australian physician who had led a life of high adventure, Morrison had been largely responsible for organizing the patrols that had brought so many Chinese converts back to the safety of the Legation quarter. Now that he learned they were to be abandoned, he felt he could no longer look his Chinese servant in the face. He felt, so he told Conger, 'ashamed to be a white man'.[14]

Baron von Ketteler was also distraught. By half past nine no answer had been received from the Board of Foreign Affairs in response to the Ministers' request for an appointment at nine o'clock, and this overtaxed the Baron's slender reserves of patience. Banging his fist on a table in the French Legation where the Ministers were now assembled, he shouted, 'I will go and sit there till they do come, if I have to sit there all night'.[15]

Accompanied by one of his staff and two liveried and mounted outriders, he left for the offices of the Board in a hooded sedan chair. He was carried through the streets smoking a cigar, leaning his arms on the front bar of his sedan, 'looking for all the world as if he were going on a picnic'.[16] As he was approaching his destination, a Chinese soldier stepped forward, took aim through the window of the chair and shot him dead.

His assistant managed to escape, though shot through both legs, and struggled back to the Legation quarter where, shortly after his return, a message was received from the Board of Foreign Affairs. In it, regret was expressed 'that the foreign Representatives might have cause for alarm on their way to the Board from the Legations, which would be a subject of regret to the Princes and Ministers'.[17] It was suggested that the meeting with Prince Tuan was not, therefore, advisable, though adequate measures to guard the foreigners on their way to Tientsin would certainly be taken.

The Ministers, adequately warned by von Ketteler's death, had no longer any thought of exposing themselves to danger on the journey to Tientsin, and prepared to defend the Legations against attack. The isolated American Methodist mission was evacuated and its occupants, including seventy-six missionaries together with their families and over a hundred Chinese Christian schoolgirls, were crammed into the chapel of the British Legation; being the largest of the Legations and in a rather less exposed position than the others, it became both the headquarters and the main stores of the defenders. It also became the refuge of scores of European missionaries, of hundreds of Chinese Christians as well as of the staffs of the other Legations, their wives and families. In the outlying Legations —the Belgian, Spanish, Japanese, French, Austrian and Italian to the north of Legation Street, the Dutch, American and German to the south of it—pickets were posted and hasty preparations were made to resist the expected attack.

There were in all just twenty regular officers, 389 men of eight different nationalities and four pieces of light artillery to oppose the thousands of Boxers and Kansu troops that Prince Tuan could throw against them. 'The foreigners,' wrote the Empress Dowager contentedly, 'are like fish in the stew-pan.'[18]

*   *   *

When the siege of the Legations began on 20 June, few of the foreigners believed that it could possibly be of long duration. Admiral Seymour—although already referred to in *The Times* correspondent's diary on 27 June as Admiral See-No-More—would surely arrive with his relief force soon. If, by some unlikely and dreaded mischance, he did not, the Legation guards could not be expected to hold out by themselves for more than one or two days. Indeed, on the first day, the most northerly and the most westerly of the Legations, the Belgian and the Dutch, were abandoned, and both of them were burned down. On the second day, there was what *The Times*'s correspondent called 'a veritable stampede' when the guards of all the other Legations hastily withdrew from their positions and fell back into the British compound. This gave the Chinese the opportunity to burn down the Italian Legation at the eastern end of Legation Street, and to advance as far as Jardine and Matheson's offices in Customs Street. Yet on neither day did the Chinese take advantage of their opportunities. When they could have overrun the position they refrained from doing so; and the foreigners were able to strengthen their defences, reorganize their guards, set up committees, enlist volunteers in what became known as the Carving Knife Brigade, and put the converts to work building barricades, digging trenches and making loopholes.

Gradually the defenders took fresh heart. They had little ammunition, but there was a plentiful supply of water from the wells in the compound and food was abundant. The corn merchants and grocers in Legation Street were well stocked, and the stables in the British Legation were full of ponies. Amongst the five hundred Europeans and Americans in the Legation—mining and railway engineers, lecturers and customs officials, as well as servants and missionaries—there were a number who made no effort to assist in their own protection, proving more of a hindrance than a help to the defenders. The Italian Minister, the elegant Marchese di Salvago Raggi, spent most of the time 'chatting with his wife, a very beautiful woman, in a *chaise longue*'; he never failed to dress for dinner. The Dutch Minister offered his services as a sentry, 'but stated at the same time that he did not know how to shoot and was very short sighted'. The French Minister walked about, gloomy and foreboding, telling everyone who spoke to him, '*La situation est excessivement grave, nous allons tous mourir ce soir*'.[19] One of the Norwegian missionaries went out of his mind, indecently exposed himself to the wife of the Russian Minister, took to wearing a black cassock and a top hat and stood on the top of the wall of the Tartar city, shouting, howling, appealing 'to King Oscar and the whole of the Norwegian royal family to right his wrongs'.[20]

But most of the men and nearly all the women behaved well and kept their nerve. Sir Claude MacDonald, who had been an infantry officer in his youth, assumed responsibility for coordinating the defence, and his tact, cheerfulness and military acumen impressed all his colleagues, though before the end of June he was already looking, 'very ill and worn'.[21] His chief of staff, Captain Strouts of the Royal Marine Light Infantry, was a young officer of exceptional talents, and, after he had been killed, his duties were taken over by Herbert Squiers, the American First Secretary, a man of equal courage and intelligence who had spent many years in the United States Cavalry and whose son, Fargo, clearly enjoyed every minute of the siege.

Under their direction, and often accompanied by the stalwart Dr Morrison of *The Times* and Nigel Oliphant of the Chinese Postal Service, the defenders undertook regular patrols and sorties. On one memorable occasion a small force of Americans, Russians and British assaulted a troublesome bastion on the Tartar Wall, captured it, killed almost thirty of the Chinese who had occupied it, and took numerous rifles and bandoliers of ammunition.[22] The Japanese, commanded by their military attaché, Colonel Sheba, a 'plucky little man' whose dependability became a byword, performed a succession of similarly bold and successful actions.[23]

While the men were fighting, the wives made sandbags out of the Legation's expensive furnishings and silks, 'foreign trouserings out of the tailor's shop, sheets, tablecloths, curtains'. They formed lines with their children, passing buckets, basins, jugs and chamber pots from hand to hand as they helped to put out fires, as when the Hanlin Academy, with its irreplaceable library, was set on fire by the besiegers in the hope that the Legation buildings would burn down too—which they would have done had not the wind changed direction when all seemed lost. Mrs Conger, the American Minister's wife and a convinced Christian Scientist, 'earnestly assured us', wrote one of her companions, 'that it was ourselves, and not the times, that were troublesome and out of tune, and insisted that, while there was an appearance of war-like hostilities, it was really in our own brains. Going further, she assured us that there was no bullet entering the room; it was again but our receptive minds which falsely lead us to believe such to be the case.'[24] All in all, the American President of the Chinese Imperial University decided, Mrs Conger was 'one of the most admirable women' it had been his privilege to know. It was believed that she, like every other woman within the Legation, had made arrangements to shoot herself and the girls within her care if the defences should fail.[25]

Two of the women, the young American wife of the proprietor of the Hôtel de Pékin, and Madame von Rosthorn, wife of the Austrian *Chargé d'Affaires*, fought alongside their husbands. Madame von Rosthorn, whose courage in the opinion of the British Legation's chaplain was 'most astonishing', was wounded while trying to set fire to the Chinese barricades by throwing on them straw dipped in kerosene.[26]

But what really saved the foreigners from being overwhelmed was not so much their spirit, bravery and resource as the apparent reluctance of the Chinese to force the fight to a conclusion. Although they had numerous pieces of artillery in Peking, including new German nine-pounders from the factory of Baron Krupp, they rarely brought them into action. There were, indeed, many occasions when the defences would have collapsed before a determined attack, particularly after the beginning of July, when the defenders were badly weakened by casualties and so short of ammunition that the French bayoneted their prisoners to death to save cartridges. On one particular day, in fact, the Chinese attack was suddenly called off altogether by the sound of horns and bugles blowing from the Imperial City. It was clear that Jung-lu, and those other of the Empress Dowager's more moderate advisers who disapproved of the siege, had not lost all influence over her and that Jung-lu himself, as military commander in Peking, was able to restrain Prince Tuan from the massacre upon which his heart was set.

* * *

When news reached the Court that on 14 July at Tientsin the foreign expeditionary force, reinforced since its relief of the Foreign Settlements there, had stormed the South Gate of the old walled city and, after fierce fighting, had captured it, the arguments of Prince Tuan and the extremists were further weakened. It had already become painfully obvious in the Forbidden City that the Boxers were not the invulnerable fighters they had been supposed to be, and that the provincial governors were flagrantly disobeying the Imperial command for reinforcements; indeed, thirteen of them, on the day that Tientsin fell, went so far as to send a memorial to Peking suggesting that the foreigners should be compensated for their losses and the rebels forcibly suppressed.[27] There could be no mistaking now the unpalatable fact that, even if the Legations were to be taken and their occupants all killed, the combined forces of the most powerful nations in the world would still remain at large in Chihli, united in their call for vengeance.

It was for this reason that Jung-lu, though he had no particular liking nor respect for the foreigners, thought that the siege of the Legations was worse than an outrage; it was 'a piece of stupidity which would be remembered against China for all time'.[28] It was for this reason, also, that on 16 July the firing stopped and negotiations began. Baskets of ice, cartloads of fruit and vegetables arrived at the British Legation, together with messages assuring the foreigners that the 'general ferment' was 'absolutely beyond the control' of the Chinese authorities, and repeating the suggestion that the Legations' staff and guards should 'temporarily retire' to Tientsin.[29]

The truce lasted until 26 July when the extremists, encouraged by the vehement opinions of Li Ping-heng, the violently patriotic Imperial Inspector of the Yangtze Naval Forces—who had arrived that day in Peking, had immediately been granted an audience by the Empress and been appointed Jung-lu's second in command— once more won her over to their side. 'Only when one can fight,' cried Li Ping-heng, 'can one negotiate for peace.'[30]

Yet after the truce, as before it, the Chinese attacks were both infrequent and ineffectual, until, on 13 August, a really determined effort to break down the foreigners' resistance seemed about to be made. Loud cries of '*Sha! Sha!* Kill! Kill!' could be heard on every side; 'every weapon in the Legation was handed out', as the Legation's chaplain said, and 'everyone was prepared for a grand assault'[31]; the noise of firing was so deafening, so Nigel Oliphant wrote in his diary, that the defenders could not hear themselves speak, and the attackers put up notices saying 'Not a dog or a chicken shall escape'[32]. But the effort had been made too late. The relief force had at last arrived beneath the walls of the city.

21 | Retribution

Let all who fall into your hands be at your mercy. Just as the Huns a thousand years ago, under the leadership of Attila, gained a reputation by virtue of which they still live in historical tradition, so may the name of Germany become known in such a manner in China, that no Chinese will ever again dare to look askance at a German. The Kaiser Wilhelm II, July 1900.

The International Relief Force had not left Tientsin until 4 August. There had been a general feeling in July that it would be impossible to collect together sufficient troops to get through to Peking before the Legations were captured. There was, in fact, 'an utter disbelief in the possibility of saving' them, a disbelief which seemed to be confirmed when on 16 July the London *Daily Mail* printed a gruesome story from its correspondent in Shanghai which led to tickets being issued for a memorial service to be held in St Paul's Cathedral 'for the Europeans massacred in Peking'.

When General Gaselee, the commander of the British contingents, arrived in Tientsin on 27 July, however, and persuaded several of his colleagues that speed was essential, hinting that if any of the allies were not ready the rest should set off without them, the lethargy was replaced by a sense of extreme urgency.

Since most of the powers were heavily committed elsewhere—the British in South Africa, the Americans in the Philippines, the French in Vietnam, the Russians in Manchuria—the Relief Force numbered less than 20,000 men, and half of these were Japanese. But, once it had started on 4 August, following the route of the Peiho rather than that of the railway, its progress was triumphant, thanks mainly to the Japanese who bore the main burden of the fighting. There was some opposition at Peitsang, and there was further fighting at Yangtsun; yet, in spite of the suffocating heat, the dearth of drinkable water, and the problems of communications, the Force pushed its way past the Chinese defenders so quickly that the Japanese, American, British and Russian contingents had all reached Chang-chia-wan by 11 August. By now the smaller German, Italian and Austrian contingents had got left behind through lack of adequate transport, and the exhausted Tonkinese troops under French command had fallen out of the race altogether; but the rest hurried on, spurred by the thought that the more their strength was reduced the larger would be the share of the survivors' loot.

Tungchow was captured—and thoroughly looted—on 12 August; and two days later, the Relief Force, including once again some French troops forced back into the race by the indomitable General Frey, was advancing towards the eastern gate of Peking. One by one the gates fell, the Russians and Japanese having the fiercest fights, the British walking through a hole in the Hsia Kuo Men without any trouble at all. At half past two General Gaselee, smiling broadly and with tears in his eyes, was standing in the compound of the British Legation shaking hands with those whose freedom he had helped secure. Catching sight of a little American girl, a missionary's daughter, he went up to her and asked her how old she was. 'When I told him eight years old,' she wrote later, 'he stooped down and kissed me for the sake, he said, of his little girl at home.'[1]

To some of Gaselee's companions the scene seemed strangely unreal. These people could surely not have been reduced to any pitiable extremities? Sixty-six foreigners had been killed, it was true, and over 150 wounded, and the Chinese converts had gone hungry towards the end, reduced to eating the bark and leaves from the trees in the Legation grounds; many of their babies had died. But the white people who had been saved, compared with the sweating dusty troops who had saved them, looked as though they might as well have been at a garden party. On General Gaselee's first appearance amongst them, they had greeted him with 'most hysterical enthusiasm', Nigel Oliphant said;[2] but this had soon subsided. 'They had speckless linen on; some of the non-fighting men wore starched shirts with extra high glazed collars, fancy flannel suits, and vari-coloured ties.'³ Beyond the lines of defence were grim reminders of the battle that had been fought, skulls picked clean by dogs, the dead bodies of the scavenger dogs themselves, 'pathetic wisps of pigtails half covered with rubbish, broken rifles, rusted swords, heaps of brass cartridges'.⁴ Yet within the compound all seemed calm, even relaxed. A few women cried as they patted the faces of the relieving troops, but a naval officer serving as International Provost Marshal was assured that, while 'the Relief People were tired, hot dirty and almost done up, the Legation people looked fresh, and by no means done up and all the ladies were quite "got up"!'⁵

A mile away to the north-west the defenders of the Northern Cathedral who, without benefit of any truce, had been keeping the Chinese at bay throughout the whole eight weeks of the siege, could present no such spruce appearance. There were nearly 3,500 Christians inside the Cathedral, including about a hundred Europeans, mostly French. There had been almost nothing for them to eat since 10 August other than the leaves and roots in the grounds of the Cathedral compound. They had suffered far worse than the people in the British Legation who, in their own predicament, seem to have put them out of mind.⁶ They had had to contend with mines exploding in the compound as well as small arms and artillery fire. The gallant and inspiring young leader of their small garrison of forty sailors, Paul Henry, had died from a shot through the neck on 30 July; and on 12 August five of the surviving sailors and a hundred Chinese were killed when a huge charge exploded beneath a building used as a children's nursery. But the besiegers never made the attack that had so long been expected; and on 16 August the Cathedral was relieved.

*   *   *

Already the looting of Peking had begun. Soldiers and civilians alike, officers and officials together with their servants, women as well as men, wandered about the capital looking for valuable or interesting articles that the Kansu troops, the Boxers and the ordinary criminals of the district, had failed to prize or to notice. Over half the houses were deserted since many families had been murdered and many others had fled from the city, so there was much still to be found; and there were few foreigners of any nationality who did not devote themselves, as, according to one British officer, even Lady Mac-Donald did, 'most earnestly to looting'.[7]

Russian troops robbed people in the streets. Americans, Japanese and Germans climbed over the walls of the Forbidden City to plunder the Imperial treasures, ripping open coffers and tumbling their contents on to the floor in what Pierre Loti described as 'streams of glass, cascades of enamel, ivory and porcelain. . . . Everything was in the most indescribable disorder.' The British, who were not officially allowed to possess private loot, sent out regular foraging parties under the command of officers and brought back 'quantities of silks, furs, china, silver plate and ornaments of all kinds' which were sold by public auction every evening.

In a vain effort to protect themselves, Chinese householders and shopkeepers put up homemade flags proclaiming themselves the dutiful subjects of one or other of the allied powers, or displayed notices begging for consideration and mercy. Some of these notices were written by Chinese who knew a little English and bore some such legend as 'MOST NOBLE GREAT MAN SIR I HOPE YOU WILL NOT KILL US. WE ARE ALL GOOD MEN HERE.' Others were provided by the looters themselves and gave the sardonic injunction, 'NO FURTHER LOOTING PERMITTED. THIS SHOP IS CLEANED OUT.' One shopkeeper stuck to his door a placard covered with a lot of completely unintelligible characters, and on being asked what they meant replied that he did not know; he had copied them off a Japanese matchbox.

To escape the depredators hundreds of Chinese women and girls committed suicide by throwing themselves down wells, 'because they were afraid of the troops, especially of the black troops'; and hundreds of their husbands and fathers were ruined. An English employee of the Chinese Customs Service, who had himself looted with untiring fervour, was moved to pity by the story of a distinguished scholar of the Hanlin Academy who was reduced to selling little cakes down the side-alleys to save his few remaining relations from starvation.⁸

* * *

Having summoned Li Hung-chang, now nearly eighty, to come to Peking and, in conjunction with Prince Ch'ing, conduct the peace negotiations, the Empress Dowager left the Forbidden City dressed in the blue cotton clothes of a peasant, her hair brushed and knotted in the Chinese manner, her long finger nails, of which she was so proud, cut off. She ordered Kuang-hsü to accompany her, together with Prince Tuan's son, P'u Chün, the profligate heir apparent. Not wanting to draw attention to a large caravan, she informed the Emperor's concubines that there would be no room for them in the travelling carts and they must stay behind. One of them, the Pearl Concubine, the Emperor's favourite in less troubled days, pleaded on her knees not to be separated from him. But the Empress Dowager was 'in no mood for argument', the Comptroller of her Household recorded in his diary. 'Without a moment's hesitation she shouted to the eunuchs on duty, "Throw this wretched minion down the well!" At this the Emperor, who was greatly grieved, fell on his knees in supplication, but the Empress angrily bade him desist, saying that this was no time for bandying words. "Let her die at once," she said . . . So the eunuchs took the Pearl Concubine and cast her down the large well which is just outside the Ning Shou Palace. Then to the Emperor, who stood trembling with grief and wrath, she said, "Get into your cart and hang up the screen, so that you will not be recognized." (He was wearing a long gown of black gauze and black cloth trousers.)'⁹

Tz'u-hsi left Peking by the Gate of the Victory of Virtue, ordering the carters to drive their hardest to the Summer Palace, announcing that she was going out 'on a tour of inspection'. She left the Summer Palace and by way of Kalgan entered the province of Shansi, eventually establishing her court at Sian, the capital of the neighbouring province of Shensi. Here she ordered messages to be despatched to all viceroys and governors commanding them to send her tribute. She looked very young and well, wrote one official who had carried tribute to Sian from Kiangsu. 'One would not put her age at more than forty, whereas she is really sixty-four.'10

In Sian, her temporary capital, Her Majesty set about refashioning her legend and creating a highly idiosyncratic version of the recent past. She saw to it that all the Decrees and Edicts in which she had spoken favourably of the Boxers were expunged from the records; she ensured that the Emperor issued a Penitential Decree taking to himself all blame that might otherwise be attached to herself; she made certain that the gifts of fruit and vegetables to the occupants of the British Legation during the siege were given due prominence and attributed to her bounty; she excused her failure to commit suicide in the presence of the tutelary deities of the dynasty by condemning the officiousness of her Ministers who forcibly led her away 'from that place where bullets fell like rain and where the enemy's guns gathered thick as forest trees'; she granted posthumous honours to the Pearl Concubine whose exemplary courage had led her to drown herself 'when unable to catch up the Court on its departure' from Peking; and, since Prince Tuan was to be held principally responsible for the Government's errors, his oafish son, the heir apparent, was instructed to petition for his own disinheritance and disgrace.11

Prince Tuan himself was exiled to Turkestan, and, in compliance with the foreigners' demands, those prominent officials who had shared his views were also punished. Yu-hsien, the Governor responsible for the butchery of the missionaries at Taiyüan, failed to take the Empress's hint that 'the price of coffins was rising', and was decapitated. Ying-nien, the Vice-President of the Censorate, was more cooperative and choked himself to death by swallowing mud. Li Ping-heng, the Inspector General of the Yangtze Naval Forces, whose arrival in Peking had resulted in the ending of the truce and the execution of several moderate Ministers, had already poisoned himself on the day Tungchow fell but was posthumously degraded. Tung Fu-hsiang, the Kansu general, would also have been executed rather than dismissed had he not been the popular commander of a formidable army; nearly a hundred lesser officials, who enjoyed no such protection, were executed for crimes committed against the foreigner.

The foreign powers, however, were not satisfied merely with the punishment of the malefactors. The Russians, who were less concerned than the other powers with the fate of missionaries, and had reaped much benefit from the Boxer rising, which had given them an excuse to tighten and extend their hold over Manchuria, were inclined to be conciliatory.[12] The Americans, for less calculating reasons, were also in favour of a moderate attitude towards reparations.[13] It was the commander of the American troops in Peking, General Chaffee, a gruff, tough veteran of the Indian Wars, who had, on his own responsibility, launched an attack on the Imperial City; but after several men had been killed in storming the gates, the attack had been suddenly called off in accordance with a decision taken at a conference of the other commanders-in-chief, and the action was strongly at variance with the Americans' usually lenient policy. The Americans, indeed, in the sour view of Field Marshal Count von Waldersee, seemed to desire that nobody should 'get anything out of China'.[14]

Von Waldersee was determined that Germany, for her part, should get something out of China even if it were only to be glory and retribution for the murder of von Ketteler. He had been appointed to the command of a strong German expeditionary force which had been exhorted by the Kaiser to model its behaviour on that of the Huns so that the name of Germany should become known 'in such a manner in China that no Chinese [would] ever again dare to look askance at a German'.[15]

Von Waldersee arrived in Peking too late for the Victory March, during which the few German soldiers of the International Relief Force—who had themselves arrived too late to take part in the final assault—goose-stepped down the streets, sweating profusely in the heat, to the unconcealed amusement of the onlookers. But as soon as he did arrive at the beginning of October, he urged that the Allied Force, of which he was grudgingly appointed Commander-in-Chief, should pursue the Court to Sian. When he was dissuaded from so drastic a course, he settled for a series of punitive expeditions which, so General Chaffee calculated, resulted in the deaths of 'fifteen harmless coolies and labourers, including not a few women and children', for each single genuine Boxer.[16] Yet what worried von Waldersee was the allies' 'slackness with the Chinese'. This was a commonly held opinion. A young English interpreter agreed that 'an idiotic spirit of mercy' pervaded everyone;[17] and an American Doctor of Divinity from the Chinese Imperial University, on hearing of a punitive raid into the city of Paoting during which its walls were broken down, some of its public buildings destroyed and its highest officials condemned to death, wrote that it deserved 'to be sown with salt' and that the capital of the neighbouring province of Shansi ought to be treated in the same way.[18]

The terms imposed upon China for the outburst of wild patriotism in the northern provinces, though not as hard as many would have liked, were severe enough. The indemnity was fixed at no less a sum than 450 million dollars, though the American Minister had proposed it ought to have been fixed at a sum that China could afford to pay and then distributed amongst the powers in accordance with their actual expenses and losses. The Taku forts were to be demolished; foreign troops were to have the right to be stationed between Tientsin and Peking; an official Legation quarter was to be assigned to the foreigners in Peking and to be garrisoned by foreign troops; China was to import no more armaments; officials failing to repress anti-foreign outbreaks were to be dismissed immediately and never re-employed; and to punish the official classes for their supposed responsibility, the state examinations were to be suspended for five years in all the places where outrages against foreigners had taken place.[19]

Ten days after the treaty was signed, on 17 September 1901, the international garrison left Peking. But considerable numbers of foreign troops remained elsewhere in China to quarrel intermittently amongst themselves, to blame each other for the looting and raping that had taken place during their recent operations; to grow bored and to catch syphilis. The French quarrelled with the Germans about their opposing rights to the instruments in the Imperial observatory, which the French claimed on the grounds that they had been made in France and presented to the Emperor K'ang-hsi by Louis XIV, and which the Germans claimed because the Observatory was in the German sector of Peking. The Russians quarrelled with the British over the former having operational control of railways which were the property of the latter. Each nation blamed the other for the terrible outrages that had been committed, for the looting that had taken place everywhere 'from the sea right up to Peking', for the disgraceful plundering of Tientsin which had been picked 'clean as a bone'. According to both G. E. Morrison and Pierre Loti the Russians were the worst offenders, though the Japanese and Germans ran them very close.

A letter to his sister from a British officer in the Indian Medical Service, Lieutenant A. L. MacGilchrist, presents a revealing picture of the sad lack of harmony in the combined expeditionary force. General Gaselee was 'too good-natured to cope with foreigners' so it was left to his Chief of Staff, General Barrow, to 'boss our show', and an unpopular show it was. 'At Tientsin,' MacGilchrist wrote, 'all British officers go about with revolvers in case of being attacked by French or German soldiers. . . . Lately seven French soldiers attacked a British officer quite alone and unarmed as he was going home from the club one night. The Americans, Japs and ourselves have been great friends all through. The best of it is that both French and Germans get the worst of it in all fights even with Indian coolies. German discipline and military tactics are subjects of ridicule among British officers.'[20]

Bad as the Russians were 'and, it must be added, the Japs' who did 'a good deal of murder', the International Provost Marshal told his wife, confirming MacGilchrist's account of the dissensions in the allied armies, 'they are not so cowardly and brutal as the French . . . the French have incurred everyone's contempt. They are always the . . . first to grab, to loot, to stick their filthy flag over everything. . . . Their cruelties are fiendish. Major Luke told me that two of his Marines fainted at the sight of some of the devilish things done by the French. . . . If all the things which have happened could only be published in the newspapers, there would be a pretty kettle of fish. The correspondents, ours at any rate, have had the strictest orders not to send home anything calculated to disturb the "friendly relations"!!!! between the Allied Nations. Nearly everybody has fired into an ally! The French fired into the Americans, the Russians and Japanese exchanged volleys, a cavalry patrol of ours did the same with some Cossacks, a Russian battery fired into the Americans, who accused our people of doing it and altogether there have been "proceedings". . . . An American Colonel, a friend of mine, and a Virginian gentleman, up here for intelligence and observation purposes, said, "Two lessons have been learnt by everyone, viz. respect for the Japanese and contempt for the French." And so it is. The French are an insolent, ill disciplined, ill dressed, disorderly, cowardly crowd and are all thieves and liars.'[21]

Robert Gartside-Tipping of the Bengal Lancers agreed with him. 'The Americans, Japs and ourselves all pal very much,' he wrote home. 'The Japs are far the best as soldiers. Everything in their army is well done. They are not barbarous or cruel. They are very good to us and help us in every possible way they can. The Russians too are civil, but a bit crafty; their soldiers are stolid, heavy good-humoured sleepy sort of chaps without an atom of dash and no sort of smartness. They are barbarous, but not absolutely cruel. But the French are beneath contempt—not possessing a single soldier-like quality. They are barbarous and cruel to a degree. Of course, we did not see any of their best troops. None have come out.'[22]

Pierre Loti, however, reported that the French behaved better than the soldiers of any other nationality. 'Everywhere I went,' he wrote, 'I noticed how good and almost brotherly they were towards the most humble Chinese.'[23]

MacGilchrist informed his sister that the monks in Peking were no more to be trusted than the French in Tientsin. On entering a temple during a sight-seeing tour of Peking, he was careful to make the deeply groaning monks walk in front of him and his party 'in case they might attack us from behind'.

The monks had cause enough for their dislike of the foreigners, it had to be admitted, as by now had most of the other residents of Peking whose property and persons had been treated so wantonly. It was well known amongst them that the military commanders and diplomats had helped themselves to various objects that caught their fancy when being shown round the Imperial Palaces by the eunuchs after the Victory Parade, and that they had shown as little respect for the sacred places of the Forbidden City as the roughest soldier. MacGilchrist himself pitched his tent in the Temple of Heaven and, on a tour of the Forbidden City, threw himself down for a rest on the Empress's bed, as B. L. Simpson of the Chinese Customs Service had done, thinking it the most peaceful act of vandalism he could commit in 'repayment for certain discomforts occasioned by this old lady's whims during eight weeks of rifle-fire'. 'Delighted by the little detail' of the old lady's 'magnificent silver *pot de chambre*' hidden modestly in one corner, Simpson lay on the bed, smoking one of her Russian cigarettes, eating a pot of her sweet and fragrant rose-leaf preserve.[24]

* * *

With peace restored and the foreigner returned to his former eminence in Peking, poets lamented the failure of the uprising and attacked the fawning servility of those Chinese who so meekly accepted their degradation:

> *Last year we called him the Foreign Devil,*
> *Now we call him 'Mr Foreigner, Sir'.*
> *We weep over the departed but smile when a new wife takes*
> * her place.*
> *Ah, the affairs of the world are like the turning of a wheel:*
> *When 'Sir' goes out of the door,*
> *Even old Mr Wang gets out of his way,*
> *For fear he should get a taste of the foreigner's whip.*
> *When 'Sir' buys something*
> *There's no question of haggling over the price*
> *Lest the police in the street intervene on his behalf.*
> *When he comes to your house*
> *Your wife and daughter are both at his disposal,*
> *And he even has the nerve to thank you for your hospitality.*
> *When he goes home, drunk,*
> *You escort him, all smiles.*
> *'If you have time, come again tomorrow, a little earlier'.*
> *If he utters a word*
> *It is accorded the respect of an Imperial decree . . .*[25]

Most objectionable of all sycophants in the poet's opinion, was the Christian convert.

The Christian convert, the Christian convert,
Strides around the capital so arrogant.
Last year he could not bear the knives of the Boxers,
Now he is like a tiger come down from the mountains. . . .
If one word is out of order the convert rages,
Give him a little money and he is all smiles.
The convert's scorching breath can devour people.
He wants to be the foreigner's tame rabbit.
The daughters of high officials escort him at banquets.
The daughters-in-law of Ministers act as his go-between. . . .
Alas! Oh, for more knives like the Boxers
To deal with the Chinese Christian converts![26]

22 | The Society of Sworn Confederates

China is the China of the Chinese. The Government of China should be in the hands of the Chinese. After driving out the Tartars we must restore our national state. Sun Yat-sen, 1905.

The Empress Dowager, comforted by reports of the Allies' differences and jealousies and by the knowledge that they had excused her personally from any punishment, decided to return to Peking. She left Sian at the end of October 1901, and as she was borne along in her yellow sedan chair, escorted by squadrons of cavalry and long lines of officials, preceded by trumpeters and surrounded by banners and flags, her journey back to her capital assumed the dignity of a triumphal progress.

A party of foreigners stood on the walls of Peking to watch her pass through them, she having graciously waived that rule which forbade them to cast their eyes upon her in the streets of the capital. She caught sight of them as she alighted from her chair, and, though her eunuchs would have had her hurry on, she paused to return their gaze, 'continuing to stand between two of her ladies who held her up under the arms on either side,' as an Italian midshipman looking down at her recorded, 'not because she needed any support but because such is the custom in China'.

Then suddenly she made a gesture that, coming after the splendid sight of the brilliant pageant of riders, palanquins, uniforms and fluttering banners, made the onlookers immediately forget all their resentment against a woman they knew responsible for so much bloodshed. In quick movements of extraordinary grace and charm she, still looking up, lifted her closed hands under chin and made a series of little bows. The foreigners, to whom this gesture was addressed, suddenly felt 'that the return of the Court to Peking was a turning-point in history'.[1] They answered the Empress, who, so her First Lady-in-Waiting said, 'always hated foreigners', with a spontaneous burst of applause.[2]

*　　*　　*

If it deserved a less dramatic description than a turning-point in history, the return of the Court to Peking was certainly an event that transformed the life of the *Corps Diplomatique*. Receptions for the diplomats and their wives and daughters became both frequent and magnificent. The Empress Dowager in the exercise of her extraordinary charm made it seem utterly incredible that 'this friendly little woman with the brown face of a kindly Italian peasant,' as Lady Susan Townley described her, 'was the mysterious and powerful autocrat who had deliberately debased and degraded the unfortunate Emperor sitting beside her; the fiend who had egged on the Boxers to nameless outrages'.[3]

If the evidence of Princess Der Ling is to be believed, she herself thought that her support of the Boxers was the 'only mistake' she had ever made in her life. She had never dreamed that the movement would end with such serious results for China. Nevertheless, she went on, 'Do you know, I have often thought that I am the most clever woman that ever lived, and others cannot compare with me. Although I have heard much about Queen Victoria [a picture of whom she often inspected with interest] and read a part of her life which someone has translated into Chinese, still I don't think her life was half so interesting and eventful as mine. My life is not finished yet and no one knows what is going to happen in the future.'[4]

But what she herself knew must happen in the future, if the Manchu dynasty were to survive, was the granting of certain concessions to Chinese susceptibilities, certain reforms. As an early step, the prohibition of intermarriage between Manchu and Chinese was abolished. Later, after lengthy discussions with Yüan Shih-k'ai, who since the deaths of Li Hung-chang in 1901 and of Jung-lu in 1903 had become her most influential adviser, decrees were issued placing Chinese and Manchu officials on terms of equality, revising the Empire's legal code, reorganizing the army under foreign instructors, and arranging for the payment of the fees of Chinese students at Japanese, American and European universities.

The reform movement was much accelerated and encouraged after 1905 when Russia, after a series of defeats at the hands of modernized and Westernized Japan, was forced to abandon its rights in Southern Manchuria, to give up the Liaotung Peninsula with Port Arthur and Dairen, to cede the southern part of the island of Sakhalin and to recognize Japan's interest in Korea.

To many observers in the Western world, Admiral Togo's victories at Port Arthur and in the Straits of Tushima, like the Japanese army's victories on land, seemed a fearful portent that boded ill for the world in the twentieth century; but to the Chinese reformers this new triumph of the formerly despised 'dwarf bandits' was a powerful stimulus. More and more students flocked to study in Japan where Liang Ch'i-ch'ao, who had played a leading part in the reform movement that had led to the deposition of the Emperor Kuang-hsü in 1898, had been living ever since his escape from the Empress Dowager's wrath, and where numerous secret societies were dedicated to the concept of a new China.

Liang Ch'i-ch'ao himself advocated the reform of the dynasty along constitutional lines; but his moderate opinions were no longer acceptable to the younger generation of reformers who saw in violent revolution the only hope for the future. One of these was a young man of peasant stock from the province of Kwangtung, a convert to Protestant Christianity. After leaving his mission school, he had qualified as a doctor in Hong Kong and had gone to Japan in the summer of 1905, a few weeks after Togo's final victory over the Baltic Fleet. His name was Sun Yat-sen.

He was thirty-nine in 1905 but looked considerably younger. To a Western journalist he appeared more Japanese than Chinese, with his closely cropped hair, and his rather large head with high cheekbones. His countenance was 'extraordinarily impassive . . . impenetrable and strong', and behind it one felt 'the presence of an unusually self-possessed mind, as well as of a very strong character steeled against adversity'.[5]

In 1894, after a memorial he had written to Li Hung-chang on the need for qualified men in Government service had been disdainfully rejected, Sun Yat-sen had formed the Revive China Society, and the next year had made an attempt to carry out that revival by organizing an armed rebellion in Canton. The attempt failed and Sun was forced into exile. He spent three months in America, then sailed to England where a lecturer at the medical school in Hong Kong was now living. This former teacher befriended him, found him lodgings, and entertained him almost daily at his house. 'One day at luncheon,' Sun recalled, 'he alluded to the Chinese Legation being in the neighbourhood and jokingly suggested that I might go round and call there; whereat his wife remarked, "You had better not. Don't go near it; they'll catch you and ship you off to China." We all enjoyed a good laugh over the remark.'

But one Sunday morning soon afterwards, Sun was walking towards the doctor's house, 'hoping to be on time to go to church with him and his family'. A Chinese approached him 'in a surreptitious manner from behind', engaged him in conversation and, with the help of another Chinese, 'half-jokingly, half persistently compelled' him to enter his lodgings for a smoke and a chat. The lodgings turned out to be part of the Chinese Legation where, as a prisoner, Sun eventually learned that he was to be shipped back to China for decapitation. He managed, however, to get a message out to his friend, the doctor, who created such a disturbance in the Press and at the Foreign Office that he was released.[6]

He returned to Japan, his prestige so much enhanced by the publicity, that he became the acknowledged leader of the Chinese revolutionaries there, the head of all the secret societies whose members he persuaded to join together in one single group, the T'ung-meng-hui, the 'Society of Sworn Confederates'.

The aims of this Society went far beyond those of Liang Ch'i-ch'ao, K'ang Yu-wei and the reformers of the 1890s. They were crystallized as Three People's Principles: the principle of nationality, a principle that covered the elimination of the Manchus; the principle of the People's Livelihood—the reformation of land ownership; and the principle of the People's Authority, that was to say the establishment of a republic.

'The Chinese have come to realize,' Sun Yat-sen told a journalist in 1907, 'that their country's woes stem from the Court and the Mandarins much more than the Europeans. It was always the Mandarins who provoked anti-foreign riots, in order to divert the wrath of a people dissatisfied with the administration. Above all, we are anti-Manchu, because this usurping dynasty has brought about our national decline.' Sun could not work with reformers who were monarchist and pro-Manchu, he insisted; the Court was quite insincere in its reforms and in any event wholly unable to keep its promises. It would have to be swept away.[7]

*   *   *

A few months after this interview was given, the Emperor Kuang-hsü went to the Empress Dowager's palace to make his daily obeisance to her for the last time. He was thirty-eight and he was dying. As he tottered into the throne-hall, his head drooping and his legs trembling, the eunuchs who were supporting him noticed with astonishment that there were tears on his old aunt's painted cheeks. In past years the ceremony had always been performed in complete silence; but this time the Empress spoke. 'You need not kneel,' she said.

'I will kneel,' he replied. 'It is for the last time.'[8]

On 14 November he died. The Empress Dowager was blamed, of course, for his death. He died in agony, Princess Der Ling said, and it was the detestable eunuch, Li Lien-ying, who had poisoned him on instructions from his mistress. The eunuch had discovered, so her story went, that he was to be beheaded in accordance with the Emperor's instructions immediately upon the Empress Dowager's death, and he had reported this to her knowing how outraged she would be to hear that her sickly nephew, who should have killed himself honourably in 1898 when his plot to imprison her had failed, had had the audacity to suggest that he would outlive her.[9]

As it happened he almost did outlive her; for during his illness she too fell ill. She caught a cold on her seventy-third birthday while taking part—in her favourite role as Goddess of Mercy—in one of those Court entertainments that so delighted her. Simultaneously she contracted dysentery after eating, with her usual appetite, a dish of crab apples and clotted cream during the course of a picnic on the lake that had concluded her birthday's festivities. She seemed to have recovered on the day of her nephew's death, but at her midday meal the next morning she had a seizure. She died at three o'clock in the afternoon of 15 November, with her face to the south, the correct position for a dying sovereign, having issued her valedictory decree in the name of Tz'u-hsi, Empress Grand Dowager, the Loving-hearted and Fortunate, Upright and Aiding, Happy and Careful, Bright and Pleasant, Earnest and True, Longlived and Serious, Reverent and Good, Exalted and Brilliant.

'Her mouth remained fixedly open', according to those who stood by her bed, though she remained conscious almost to the end, and this was interpreted as a sign that her spirit was 'unwilling to leave the body and take its departure for the place of the Nine Springs'.[10]

At least she was comforted to know that she had been able to arrange for the ultimate power in the State to be transferred to her niece, Kuang-hsü's widow, the new Empress Dowager, and thus to be kept in her family.

The new Emperor was the two-year-old P'u Yi. His father, Prince Ch'un, the Emperor Hsien-feng's brother, was appointed Regent. On all matters of importance, however, the Regent was required to consult the new Empress Dowager. But Prince Ch'un paid as little attention to this requirement as he could. A man of erratic, though usually reactionary opinions, he was determined to do all he could to block any further advance to constitutionalism or reform; and was equally determined to restore the power of the Ch'ing dynasty he represented. He dismissed the influential Yüan Shih-k'ai, who had become far too presumptuous for a mere Chinese, from the vice-royalty of Chihli; he appointed his Manchu brothers to important positions; and he ensured that the programme of limited constitutional reform that the late Empress had begun to initiate was stultified. Under increasing pressure he did give way to the demands that the government of the Empire should be by cabinet; but when the names of the thirteen members of the cabinet were eventually announced, in May 1911, it was discovered that ten of them were Manchus and six were Imperial Princes.[11]

Sun Yat-sen made the most of the opportunities the reactionaries of the Court were presenting to him. He increased month by month the numbers of his followers—who from 1908 included Chiang Kai-shek—and pointed to China's growing economic problems and poverty as the result of the Court's political incompetence and corruption.

On 9 October 1911 the expected outburst came, though it came by accident. There was that day a thunderous explosion in a house at Hankow in the province of Hupei. The police investigated its cause, finding not only a secret arsenal but a list of Chinese revolutionaries, many of whose names were those of officers of the garrison. Forced prematurely into action, the revolutionaries led their followers into the streets on the night of 10 October. The Manchu viceroy fled; a military government of Hupei was set up and declared its independence of Peking. Soon, encouraged by Hupei's success, other provinces flared into revolt, and provincial governments were established in all but three of them. At the beginning of December, Nanking was captured by the rebels; and on Christmas Day, Sun Yat-sen, who was in Denver, Colorado, when the revolution began, landed at Shanghai. On 29 December 1911 he was elected President of a Chinese Republic.

Yet *The Times* took leave to doubt that, with the establishment of a republic, the modern history of China had at last begun, or, indeed, that any fundamental change had taken place at all. It thought it unlikely that 'a form of government so utterly alien to Oriental conceptions and to Oriental traditions as a Republic can be substituted for a monarchy in a nation of four hundred millions of men whom Kings with semi-divine attributes have ruled since the first dim twilight of history'.[12]

What at least was certain was that the Chinese, after centuries of seclusion, had been pushed by circumstances and by force into unwanted contacts with the Western world and that they looked forward to the day, whether under President or Emperor, when they would be strong enough to break off those contacts, to proclaim with impunity, 'China for the Chinese and out with the foreigners!'

As Sir Robert Hart foretold, the Boxers of the future would be 'armed, drilled, disciplined, and animated by patriotic—if mistaken —motives'; they would 'make residence in China impossible for foreigners'; they would 'take back from foreigners everything foreigners have taken from them and pay off old grudges with interest'. 'They will carry', he prophesied, 'the Chinese flag and Chinese armies into many a place that even fancy will not suggest today, thus preparing for the future, upheavals and disasters never even dreamt of.'[13]

Notes and References

Bibliographical details are not repeated for works cited under Sources

PART I: AMBASSADORS BEARING TRIBUTE

CHAPTER 1: *Barbarians from the Western Ocean* (pages 1–26)

1. Descriptions of the gardens at Jehol (Cheng de) are given in the *Memoirs of Father Ripa* (Naples, 1832, trs. Fortunato Praudi, 1855) and *Macartney's Journal*, 124, 134–6. See also Sven Hedin, *Jehol, City of Emperors* (Kegan Paul, 1932).
2. *Macartney's Journal*, 117.
3. *Ibid.*, 115–18.
4. The Ming Emperor Wan-li (1573–1620) had been supplied with roughly faithful maps of the world by Jesuit missionaries, but in drawing the best known of these, which appeared as a frontispiece to *Yüeh-ling Kuang-i* (1602), Matteo Ricci employed a contrivance to gain the good graces of the Chinese who were 'very angry', so Father Nicholas Trigault, Ricci's contemporary, wrote in his *De l'Expédition Chrétienne*, 'when they find our geographers putting their Empire in a corner of the extreme east. They believe that the sky is round but the earth square and that China is situated in the midst of it. . . . Father Ricci, therefore, brought the Empire into the centre of his map, to their great satisfaction' (Abbé Huc, *Christianity in China, Tartary, etc.*, quoted by Hughes, xv).

   Since Ming times the Chinese had lost their former interest in foreign countries, and maps of them instead of improving in accuracy had become cruder and more fanciful. As late as the middle of the nineteenth century the American missionary, Dr Charles Taylor, saw maps of the world in Chinese schools that represented the United States, Africa, and various European countries as insignificant islands dotted about the great expanse of the Middle Kingdom; on some maps the inhabitants of these outlandish places were shown as having only one eye or with holes through their stomachs so that they could be carried about on poles (*Five Years in China*, 212–13).
5. *Huang Ch'ing chih-kung t'u*, an illustrated eighteenth-century work on the tribute nations, quoted by Wolfgang Franke, 94.
6. *Hai-lu*, ('A Maritime Record'), a late eighteenth-century account written down by a scholar, of a Chinese sailor's memoirs of his travels in foreign ships, quoted by Wolfgang Franke, 94–5.

7. Wang Hsi-ch'i, *Hsiao-fang hu-chai yü-ti ts'ung-ch'ao*, trs. Franz Schurmann and quoted by Schurmann and Schell, i, 115–19, who say that the book was probably written in the late 1830s.

8. The Emperors of China were known, not by their personal name, but by the title given to their reign at the time of their accession. Ch'ien-lung's personal name was Hung-li; and he is sometimes, therefore, referred to as Hung-li, the Ch'ien-lung Emperor. A possible rendering of the sense of the words Ch'ien-lung is 'Lasting Glory'.

9. Harold H. Kahn, 'The Education of a Prince: The Emperor Learns his Roles' in *Approaches to Modern Chinese History*, ed. Feuerwerker *et al.*, 19–20.

10. Quoted by Costin, 11.

11. The demand for such Chinese goods had reached its peak in England in the 1750s when the passion for *Chinoiserie* affected not only the design of furniture and ornaments, but even bridges and park railings. Gentlemen went so far as to dress up on festive occasions in flowered and bedragoned mandarin robes; and ladies endeavoured to procure little Chinese boys as pets or pages. See Hugh Honour, *Chinoiserie: The Vision of Cathay* (J. Murray, 1961) and Dawson, *The Chinese Chameleon*.

   The fashion was given further encouragement by one of the leading English architects of his time, Sir William Chambers who, as a young man, had worked in Canton for the Swedish East India Company. His *Designs for Chinese Buildings etc.*, was published in 1757 and his *Dissertation on Oriental Gardening* in 1772. The temples and pagodas he designed for the Princess Dowager of Wales at Kew Palace between 1757 and 1762 were not universally admired, and he himself did not persist in his *Chinoiserie*. See H. M. Colvin, *A Biographical Dictionary of English Architects*. (J. Murray, 1954, 132). But the Chinese taste, said to have entirely eclipsed the Gothic mode in the 1750s, still had many cultivated admirers at the time of Lord Macartney's mission, and did not entirely go out of fashion until the Early Victorian Age.

12. *Macartney's Journal*, 65; Staunton, i, 410.

13. *Macartney's Journal*, 66–7; Barrow, 65.

14. *Macartney's Journal*, 71; Barrow 66–7.

15. Chou was probably Ch'iao Jen-chieh, a civil official from Tientsin who later became Judicial Commissioner of Chihli. Cranmer-Byng's appendix to *Macartney's Journal*, 328–31.

16. *Macartney's Journal*, 216, 217.

17. Wang, identified by Cranmer-Byng as Wang Wen-hsiung, had distinguished himself fighting in Burma; he was killed during a campaign against rebels in Shensi province in 1800. Cranmer-Byng's appendix to *Macartney's Journal*, 325–8.

18. *Macartney's Journal*, 71–2; Barrow, 69–73.

19. Staunton, ii, 2–3; *Macartney's Journal*, 72–3; Barrow, 75.

20. *Macartney's Journal*, 74.

21. Staunton, ii, 17.

22. 'A man of distinction travelling by Water,' Sir Erasmus Gower explained, 'is always known by the Flags the Junk wears, and all the Vessels that he passes Salute him with beating on an Instrument called the Gong, and sounding a Trumpet' (MS Journal of H.M.S. *Lion*).

23. *Macartney's Journal*, 74–6, 77.

24. *Ibid.*, 88; Barrow, 68–9.

25. *Macartney's Journal*, 78, 85. Cheng-jui, who was over eighty when he died in 1815, was later appointed Grand Minister of the Imperial Household.

26. The painful custom of binding the feet began about the tenth century A.D. Although supposed to have been originally adopted as a means of preventing women wandering too far away from their men, the practice seems to have persisted more for aesthetic and erotic reasons. Manchu women were forbidden to adopt it, and from time to time new statutes had to be promulgated repeating the ban since, feeling themselves to be less elegant and attractive than Chinese women, they would have liked to ignore it and sometimes did ignore it. The Manchu Emperors were not allowed to have Chinese queens or concubines and it was said to be their passion for small feet that induced both the Emperors Hsien-feng and T'ung-chih to frequent the brothels of Peking outside the walls of the Forbidden City.

Foot-binding seems to have had little effect on the mobility of Chinese women. Lord Macartney concluded that the peasant women he saw running about with such agility along the banks of the Peiho had not had their feet bound. 'It is said, indeed, that this practice, especially among the lower sort, is now less frequent in the northern provinces than in the others.' (*Journal*, 74). But other observers did not think that Chinese women were incommoded by having such tiny feet. 'They stump about with great apparent ease,' wrote Dr Duncan McPherson who had much to say on the subject; 'but I cannot agree with those who say it adds gracefulness to their gait. They reminded me, when first I saw them, of a boy walking on stilts.' (*McPherson*, 41).

27. Barrow, 69–73, 143; Staunton, ii, 40.

28. Barrow, 77. In the middle of the next century European visitors to Tientsin castigated the dirtiness of the population in even stronger terms. In Laurence Oliphant's opinion, 'filth, nakedness and itch were their prevailing characteristics'. The poorest of the men wore a piece of mat or tattered matting thrown over their shoulders: 'decency was ignored' (Laurence Oliphant, 399).

29. *Macartney's Journal*, 225.

30. Anderson, 26, 27, 32; Staunton, ii, 5.

31. Barrow, 85.

32. Anderson, 88.

33. Staunton, ii, 46.

34. Barrow, 84; *Macartney's Journal*, 87.

35. *Macartney's Journal*, 87.

36. *Ibid.*, 84–6.

37. Staunton, ii, 114–15; Barrow, 88–90; *Macartney's Journal*, 89–92; Anderson, 44–9.
38. Staunton, ii, 115–25; Barrow, 91–9; Anderson, 52–61; *Macartney's Journal*, 92, 156–8.
39. *Macartney's Journal*, 95–6.
40. *Ibid.*, 97, 114.
41. Anderson, 61.
42. Staunton, ii, 162; *Macartney's Journal*, 104.
43. *Macartney's Journal*, 106–14, 116–17.
44. *Ibid.*, 90, 98, 99–100.
45. Cranmer-Byng, 'Lord Macartney's Embassy to Peking in 1793, from Official Chinese Documents', *Journal of Oriental Studies*, iv, nos 1 and 2, 1957–8 (Hong Kong, 1961), 145.
46. *Macartney's Journal*, 119.
47. Cranmer-Byng, 'Lord Macartney's Embassy . . .', 156–8.
48. *Macartney's Journal*, 222. Two generations later a medical officer in the British Army in China described how in the streets, 'every few yards', you could see men saluting each other. 'Nothing can exceed their politeness. They first make a profound bow, at the same time clasping their hands and lowering them towards their knees. As they raise themselves from the bow profound, they shake their clasped hands, towards one another, accompanying the movement by several short bows' (D. F. Rennie, *British Arms in North China* (1864), 243–4).

CHAPTER 2: *The Son of Heaven* (pages 27–42)

1. *Macartney's Journal*, 221–2, 108.
2. Loewe, 150–61.
3. The colours and markings of the buttons, in order of seniority, were 1. smooth red, 2. engraved red, 3. transparent blue, 4. opaque blue, 5. crystal, 6. white, 7. smooth gold, 8. engraved gold. A ninth rank was added later. Imperial princes wore a larger, amethyst button; and Imperial clansmen—those who could claim descent from the founder of the Dynasty—were entitled to the distinction of a yellow girdle. High officials who had performed especially meritorious services were granted the right to wear a peacock's feather in their hats as well as a button.
4. For concise accounts of the Chinese system of Government see Fairbank, *The United States and China*, 1959; Fairbank and Teng Ssu-yü, *Ch'ing Administration* 1960; Loewe, *Imperial China*, 1966.
5. Wu Ching-tzu *Ju-lin wai-shih* (*An Unofficial History of the Literati*) (Foreign Language Press, Peking, 1957), quoted by Schurmann and Schell, ii, 85–98.
6. 'The population of China, which was presumably in the neighbourhood of 150,000,000 around 1700 or shortly after, probably increased to 275,000,000 in 1779 and 313,000,000 in 1794' (Ping-ti Ho, *Studies in the Population of China, 1368–1953*, Harvard University Press, 1959, 270). At the time of the fall of the Empire in 1911 the population had

risen to an estimated 374 million. A census in 1953 revealed an increase to 590 million; and it is now supposed that there are over 760 million people on the mainland of China, a quarter of the world's population (Nagel, 54).

7. Régis-Evariste Huc, *The Chinese Empire* (1855), quoted Schurmann and Schell, i, 29.

8. *Ibid.*, quoted Schurmann and Schell, i, 27–8.

9. Buddhism, which originated in India in the sixth or fifth century B.C., penetrated into China by way of the silk route. There were Buddhist communities in China by the 1st century A.D. and Buddhist ceremonies were being performed in the palace of the Emperor Huan (147–168 A.D.) in the second century A.D.

10. Macartney was given this account of the Emperor's daily routine (recorded on p. 201 of the *Journal*) by Wang and Chou.

11. Only Manchu girls could aspire to the position of an Emperor's concubine.

12. *Macartney's Journal*, 122; Anderson, 80.

13. Staunton, ii, 227.

14. *Ibid.*, ii, 228; *Macartney's Journal*, 127.

15. *Macartney's Journal*, 124; Staunton, ii, 229–38.

16. *Macartney's Journal*, 125–6, 271.

17. Staunton, ii, 255.

18. *Ibid.*, ii, 261–4; *Macartney's Journal*, 131, 136–41.

19. Dr Gillan's *Observations on the State of Medicine, Surgery and Chemistry in China*, attached to *Macartney's Journal*, 283. Disdainful as they usually were of the foreigners' accomplishments, the Chinese did recognize the skill of their doctors. 'The Barbarians are very good doctors,' recorded a Shanghai diarist, who had good cause to dislike foreigners generally, during the Opium War of 1842. 'A certain man called Chang who lives by the Northern Gate was beaten up by one of the black devils [Indian troops] so badly that his eyes nearly came out of their sockets. His father complained to one of the white devils who, in his strange twittering tongue, explained the matter to his party. Then one of the foreigners smeared some medical preparation over Chang's eyes, put water on the pupils and massaged them without causing the least pain. In no time at all they were cured' (Ts'ao Sheng, *I-huan pei ch'ang chi* in the *Shang-hai chang-ku ts'ung-shu*, leaf 27b).

20. *Macartney's Journal*, 127.

21. *Ibid.*, 127–8.

22. Full details of Macartney's instructions are to be found in Earl H. Pritchard, *The Crucial Years of Anglo Chinese Relations, 1750–1800* Research Studies of the State College of Washington, iv, nos. 3–4 (1936).

23. Barrow, 107–8.

24. Anderson, 58. For a detailed account of Yüan-ming Yüan see Hope Danby, *The Garden of Perfect Brightness* (1950).

25. Staunton, ii, 115.

26. Barrow, 148, 159, 168–70, 194–5, 218–9, 221–2, 332–3, 421–2, 495.

CHAPTER 3: *Failure of a Mission* (pp. 43–53)

1. Staunton, ii, 320–2.
2. *Ibid.*, 323.
3. *Macartney's Journal*, 147–50, 155–6.
4. *Ibid.*, 156; Staunton, ii, 342–3.
5. *Macartney's Journal*, 163–6, 169–75.
6. Staunton, ii, 428.
7. Anderson, 32–3; Staunton, ii, 74–5.
8. Barrow, 509–11, Staunton, ii, 403.
9. Barrow, 148, 161, 162–4, 166–7, 564.
10. *Ibid.*, 167.
11. *Ibid.*, 161–4, 489–9, 490.
12. *Dr Gillan's Observations on the State of Medicine, Surgery and Chemistry in China*, attached to *Macartney's Journal*, 287–8.
13. Barrow, 192–3.
14. *Macartney's Journal*, 176–7, 178, 185.
15. *Ibid.*, 164.
16. Barrow, 603.
17. *Ibid.*, 591–3.
18. Staunton, ii, 583.
19. W. J. Proudfoot, *Biographical Memoir of James Dinwiddie*, LLD (1868), 26. In the years to come Europeans were to be constantly exasperated by this real or pretended lack of interest in Western inventions. Towards the middle of the nineteenth century a Chinese harbour pilot infuriated a British captain by his indifference to the marvels of a modern tug. Surely, the captain demanded at length, the pilot had never seen anything like it before? Oh, yes, the pilot loftily replied, 'we had just such vessels in the old days but gave them up as unprofitable'. (Yorke MS, 190).
20. *Ibid.*, 53.
21. Staunton, ii, 165.
22. Swinhoe, 331.
23. Appendix C to *Macartney's Journal*, 336–41.
24. *Macartney's Journal*, 219.

CHAPTER 4: *Lord Amherst and the Kotow* (pp. 54–69)

1. Cranmer-Byng, introduction to *Macartney's Journal*, 32.
2. *Authentic Account of the Dutch East India Company etc.*, passim; J. J. L. Duyvendak, 'The Last Dutch Embassy to the Chinese Court (1794–5)', *T'oung Pao*, xxxiv (1938); Barrow 8–11, 13, 210–17; Wells Williams, ii, 439.
3. Soothill, 103.
4. Grantham, *A Manchu Monarch*, 56.
5. Soothill, 98.
6. *Ibid.*, 97.

7. Ellis, 59.
8. William Fanshawe Martin, MS Journal (Punctuation supplied).
9. Ellis, 74.
10. *Ibid.*, 87, 107; Amherst, MS Journal.
11. Amherst, MS Journal; Ellis, 72.
12. Amherst, MS Journal.
13. Martin, MS Journal.
14. Ellis, 91; Amherst, MS Journal.
15. Amherst, MS Journal.
16. Ellis, 147–9.
17. *Ibid.*, 176–83; Amherst, MS Journal; Grantham, 177–82.
18. Ellis, 186, 190, 191.
19. *Ibid.*, 74, 81, 82, 85–6, 102–4, 137–8, 333–4, 382, 388.
20. Martin, MS Journal.
21. *Ibid.*
22. Quoted in Grantham, 190–1.
23. Ellis, 301.
24. Amherst, MS Journal; Ellis, 420–1.
25. Quoted in Soothill, 103.
26. *A Delicate Inquiry into the Embassies to China and a Legitimate Conclusion* (1818), 14, 24. 'The beginning of the nineteenth century,' Raymond Dawson writes, 'saw a striking change in the European attitude towards China. This was no sudden general change of attitude: praise was certainly not universal before 1800 nor was contempt universal afterwards. . . . But it was certainly about this time that the tide of China's popularity in Europe began to run out. This was partly due to the fact that both the sinophilism of the Enlightenment and the taste for Chinoiserie had lost their impetus. . . . There was also a more positive factor, which may be regarded as primarily responsible for this change of attitude. This was the rise of British power, and the feeling of superiority which went with industrial progress at home and expansion of territory overseas. . . . At the heart of this new attitude, providing its ideological justification, was Protestant Christianity which now made its first appearance in China. . . . The early Protestant missionaries looked upon China —and wrote about China—"primarily as a country of heathens who lacked the light of God and must be rescued from eternal damnation"' (Dawson, *The Chinese Chameleon*, 132–4).
27. Martin, MS Journal.
28. Li Chien-nung, 18.

PART II: TRADERS IN FOREIGN DIRT

CHAPTER 5: *Merchants and Mandarins* (pp. 73–89)

1. Chang Hsin-pao, 8; Collis (2), 52–6; Hunter, 22–3; Morse (2), i, 70, 72; Davis (1), ii, 24–5.
2. Collis (2), 45, 49; Davis (1), ii, 25–6.

3. Hwuy-Ung, *A Chinaman's Opinion of Us and of His Own Country* (trs. J. A. Makepeace, 1927): 9, 23–5, quoted by Pelissier, 44–5.

4. Downing, iii, 80–6.

5. Yorke MS, 38 quoting R. B. Forbes.

6. Greenberg, 67.

7. Hunter, 36–7; Collins (2), 57–8, 64–8; Morse (2), i, 67–8.

8. Hunter, 40.

9. Collis (2), 47–8; Hunter, 14; Downing, iii, 239, 261, 267.

10. Downing, iii, 227–31; Collis (2), 23, 49–50.

11. Adolphe Barrot, 'Un Voyage en Chine' in *Revue des Deux Mondes*, 1 Nov. 1839, quoted by Pelissier, 39; Morse (2), ii, 69.

12. Hunter, 119–20.

13. *Ibid.*, 30–1.

14. *Ibid.*, 82.

15. Yorke MS 23. George Chinnery claimed that he had chosen to live in Macao because of its proximity to Canton, where no women were ever allowed. He had had the misfortune to marry a wife whom he described as 'the ugliest woman I ever saw in my life'. Whenever his wife threatened to join him in Macao he fled to Canton, exclaiming once on his arrival there, 'Now I am all right. What a kind providence is this Chinese Government that it forbids the softer sex from coming and bothering us. What an admirable arrangement, is it not?' (*Jardine, Matheson & Company*, 8.)

16. Collis (2), 22, 24, 26–7, 28–9; Morse (2), i, 43–5; Hunter, 81.

17. Kuo, 29; Collis (2), 30–3.

18. Chang Hsin-pao, 30–1; Soothill, 113–15.

19. MS letters of Robert Morrison.

20. Morse (2), i, 82, 90–1; McAleavy, 44; Pelissier, 52–3; Collis (2), 37, 69–71, 309.

21. Chang Hsin-pao, 55.

22. *Ibid.*, 19.

23. Waley, 26; Morse (2), i, 205–11.

24. Hunter, 67–70.

25. Yorke MS, 105–24; Collis (2), 78–81.

26. Quoted by Stanley Lane-Poole in *Sir Harry Parkes in China* (1901), 41. Professor Lane-Poole himself wrote that Gützlaff's 'specious manner and intolerable assumption of omniscience procured him the epithet of a "humbug"; he was always posing as a genius and those who knew him best put the least faith in him. He was not a man to be universally trusted. Nevertheless his was a strong and original character . . . certainly very impressive to his juniors.' One of these juniors, a young English army officer, thought him 'very clever, and a pleasant companion' (*The Last Year in China to the Peace of Nanking by a Field Officer*, 1843, 103).

27. Waley, 223–8.

28. K. F. A. Gützlaff, *Three Voyages*, quoted by Collis (2), 82.

29. Greenberg, 136–41; Collis (2), 86.

Notes and References

CHAPTER 6: *The Napier Fizzle* (pp. 90–102)

1. Collis (2), 112.
2. *A Delicate Inquiry into the Embassies to China and a Legitimate Conclusion* (1818), 14.
3. Chang Hsin-pao, 12; Morse (2), i, 106.
4. Quoted by Collis (2), 108.
5. Collis (2), 98. The Prussian missionary, Karl Gützlaff, posthumously published in English in 1852 a life of this ambivalent Emperor: *Taou-Kwang, Late Emperor of China with Memoirs of the Court of Peking*.
6. Costin, 21; Morse (2), i, 119–21; Collis (2), 121–2, 124.
7. Chang Hsin-pao, 57.
8. *Ibid.*
9. Kuo, 20; Morse (2), i, 123–4; Collis (2), 129–32.
10. Morse (2), i, 125.
11. 'In transliterating foreign names,' Morse explains, 'the Chinese shrink from dignifying them by using characters which should have a pleasing meaning or should simulate a Chinese, i.e., a truly civilized name.' The characters selected by Dr Morrison, the interpreter, to represent the sound of Lord Napier's name were not acceptable to the Chinese who 'chose others which, if to be translated, would mean "laboriously vile"—much as if the name of the statesman Li Hung-chang were called in English "Lie hung in chains", as an alternative to translating it "Mr Great-Elegance Plum". . . . This Chinese practice is not, perhaps, a direct insult, but it illustrates the national tendency to belittle the foreigner and to treat him as outside the pale of civilization' (Morse (2), i, 126–7).
12. Morse (2), i, 127.
13. Collis (2), 137.
14. *Ibid.*, 142.
15. Chang Hsin-pao, 56.
16. Morse (2), i, 132–3; Collis (2), 148–54.
17. Collis (2), 155.
18. *Ibid.*, 156.
19. Morse (2), i, 134–5.
20. Chang Hsin-pao, 55; Collis (2), 158–9.
21. Morse (2), i, 135–6.
22. Chang Hsin-pao, 56–7; Collis (2), 162–3; Holt, 56.
23. Chang Hsin-pao, 57.
24. Collis (2), 166; Morse (2), i, 136.
25. Chang Hsin-pao, 58–60.
26. Yorke MS, 213–9; Collis (2), 170–4; Morse (2), i, 137–8.
27. Chang Hsin-pao, 61.
28. Costin, 26.
29. Chang Hsin-pao, 83.

CHAPTER 7: *The Offence of Captain Elliot* (pp. 103–110)

1. Chang Hsin-pao, 63.

2. Costin, 34.
3. Chang Hsin-pao, 69–70; Morse (2), i, 155; Kuo, 46–7.
4. Chang Hsin-pao, 70; Morse (2), i, 156; Collis (2), 206.
5. Chang Hsin-pao, 72.
6. *Ibid.*, 72; Morse (2), i, 157.
7. Chang Hsin-pao, 73.
8. Morse (2), i, 169; Collis (2), 196–7.
9. Hunter, 73–7, 143; Kuo, 107.
10. Collis (2), 202.
11. *Ibid.*, 206–9; Morse (2), i, 193, 199; Chang Hsin-pao, 106.
12. Chang Hsin-pao, 15. In the opinion of John Quincy Adams opium was 'a mere incident to the dispute, but no more the cause of war than the throwing overboard of the tea in Boston harbour was the cause of the North American revolution . . . the cause of the war is the kotow' (quoted by Soothill, 132). The cause of the war might equally well have been attributed to the quarrel over rights of jurisdiction, the extra-territoriality issue.
13. Waley, 12.

CHAPTER 8: *The Opium Destroyed* (pp. 111–126)

1. Chang Hsin-pao, 89–93; Morse (2), i, 186–91; McAleavy, 45–6.
2. Chang Hsin-pao, 120.
3. Hunter, 136.
4. Bingham, ii, 64. For Lin Tse-hsü's biography see Hummel, i, 511–14. See also *The Chinese Repository*, xv, May 1846, no. 5, and xv, Sept. 1846, no. 7.
5. Waley, 15–20.
6. Hunter, 137.
7. Tsiang Ting-fu, *Chung-kuo chin tai-shih* (Hong Kong, 1955), trs. Schell, Schurmann and Schell, 128; an earlier Chinese authority, P. C. Kuo, describes him as 'one of the shrewdest economists of his time'.
8. *Ya-p'ien chan-cheng tzu-liao ts'ung-k'an*, trs. Waley, 29–31.
9. As late as 1851 it was still widely believed in China that the Western nations could not live without Chinese rhubarb and tea. 'The foreigners from the West,' it was authoritatively stated, 'are naturally fond of milk, and cream; indulgence in these luxuries induces costiveness, when there is nothing but rhubarb and tea that will clear their system and restore their spirits. If once deprived of these articles they are immediately laid up with sickness. . . . If we cut off the trade of the Barbarians, turbulence and disorder will ensue in their own countries' (*North-China Herald*, 15 March 1851, quoted by Morse (2), i, 132, note 34).
10. Costin, 61.
11. Hunter, 143.
12. Chang Hsin-pao, 165.
13. Collis (2), 229.
14. Waley, 39.

15. Kuo, 118–19.
16. Waley, 50.
17. *Canton Press*, 20 July 1839.
18. Collis (2), 232.
19. By the time he left Canton, Lin had changed his mind about British warships as about other products of European and American technology. 'We have received great injury from opium;' he wrote, 'but should we not, on the other hand reap great advantage from the superior skill of foreigners? Both the French and Americans brought artisans to Canton who could construct ships; should we not employ European seamen to teach us sailing, as we formerly did European astronomers' (Davis (2), i, 320). See also Kuo, 131.
20. Harley Farnsworth MacNair, *Modern Chinese History, Selected Readings* (Shanghai, 1923), 136; Schurmann and Schell, 140.
21. Collis (2), 241.
22. Waley, 55.

CHAPTER 9: *The Flag Insulted* (pp. 127–143)

1. Waley, 55–6.
2. *Ibid.*, 61–2.
3. Quoted by Collis, 244.
4. Waley, 65.
5. *Ibid.*, 68–9.
6. Quoted by Chang Hsin-pao, 203.
7. Waley, 70, 72.
8. Chang Hsin-pao, 185.
9. Collis (2), 255.
10. Morse (2), i, 245–6; Collis (2), 257–8; Kuo, 128.
11. Before communications were transformed by the now imminent introduction of the steamship on oceanic routes, British officials in Canton often had to wait up to eight months for their despatches to be answered, even when replies were sent immediately from London. Due to the excellent Chinese relay system, however, the authorities in Canton could expect answers from Peking in about six weeks. Couriers were capable of covering 250 miles a day. In 1793 Lord Macartney's valet saw one of them galloping through Chihli, the little bells attached to the basket of letters on his back announcing his approach to the next post-house (Anderson, 101). For details of the system see Fairbank and Teng Ssu-yü, *Ch'ing Administration*, 3–12.
12. Collis (2), 259–60; Bernard, i, 257–64.
13. Hunter, 80.
14. Chang Hsin-pao, 94.
15. *The Rupture with China and its causes including the Opium Question by a Resident in China* (1840), 6, 8.
16. Responsible medical opinion was unanimously in agreement with Dr Dowding. A characteristic view is that of Dr W. H. Medhurst, a physician

and missionary who spent many years in China, quoted in *The Rise and Progress of British Opium Smuggling. Five Letters Addressed to the Earl of Shaftesbury by Major-General R. Alexander, Madras Army* (1856): 'Those who have not seen the effects of smoking in the Eastern World can hardly form any conception of its injurious results on the health, energies, and lives of those who indulge in it. . . . The debilitating of the constitution, and the shortening of life, are sure to follow in a few years after the practice has been commenced.' Millions of Chinese, nevertheless, contrived to smoke opium in moderation—as the Empress Dowager, Tz'u-hsi, did—without any apparent ill effects.

17. *Chinese Repository*, vol. 7, 108.
18. Fairbank and Teng Ssu-yü (1), 24–7; *Chinese Repository*, vol. 8, 321.
19. James Matheson, *The Present Position and Prospects of the British Trade with China* (1836) 15, 60.
20. *Hansard's Parliamentary Debates*, 3rd series, liii (1840), 669–835, 846–995. There is a good resumé in Collis (2), 273–86.

CHAPTER 10: *The Empire at War* (pp. 144–161)

1. Waley, 98–103; Morse (2), i, 263–4; *Chinese Repository*, July, 1840; McAleavy, 48; Collis (2), 289, 293–5.
2. The full text of this long letter is given in Morse (2), i, Appendix A, 621–6.
3. Bingham, i, 201–3.
4. Jocelyn, 45–6.
5. Gingalls were a type of musket fired from a wooden tripod.
6. Jocelyn, 49–58.
7. Bingham, i, 329–32.
8. Jocelyn, 61.
9. *Chinese Repository*, quoted by Waley, 109–10.
10. MS Letters of Colonel Wyndham Baker.
11. Bingham, ii, 29.
12. Waley, 113, 115, 117, 123; Chang Hsin-pao, 212.
13. Collis (2), 295–6.
14. Chiang T'ing-fu, *Chung-kuo chin-tai shih* (Hong Kong, 1954), quoted by McAleavy, 49–50.
15. Chiang T'ing-fu, quoted by Schurmann and Schell, 133.
16. Yorke MS, 331; Collis (2), 297.
17. Bernard, ii, 327–44.
18. Davis (2), i, 177. On Chusan, in the 49th and 26th Regiments alone, 380 men died in hospital between 13 July and 31 December 1840. F. Loraine Petre, *The Royal Berkshire Regiment*, i, 121; see also Bernard, i, 234, who says most of the trouble was caused by the Chinese spirit, *Samsu*. Others attributed the casualties to the 'positively unwholesome' tea which the soldiers also drank in large quantities. (Yorke MS, 372.)
19. Kuo, 145.
20. Ch'i-shan was restored to office at the end of the Opium War. He died

in 1854. Lin Tse-hsü was recalled from exile in 1845, and in October 1850 he was appointed High Commissioner to suppress a rebellion in Kwangsi. He died, aged sixty-seven, on his way to take up the appointment.

A film about him has recently been made in China. The film opens with a shot of Chinese coolies struggling up a flight of stone steps from the Canton wharf. Their limbs are frail as matchsticks, yet they carry on their shoulders enormously heavy chests. Although carrying sticks to support themselves, they reel and stagger as they struggle step by step to make their painful ascent, muttering weakly to themselves, 'Ai-ya! Ai-ya!' The chests bear the printed legend: 'The United East India Company'. The narrator of the film comments: 'The dumping of opium in China by the English poisoned the lives of thousands upon thousands of our Chinese people.' The script of the film was published in Shanghai in 1961.

21. *Letters of Queen Victoria*, i, 261.
22. Quoted by Costin, 89.
23. For the full text of Elliot's letter of dismissal see Morse (2), i, Appendix G, 641–3.
24. McAleavy, 53. On the capture of the forts, the British soldiers found them full of female dress placed there for a similar purpose. Mackenzie, 77.
25. Bingham, ii, 191–2; Murray, 54.
26. McPherson, 105.
27. Morse (2), i, 281–3; Mackenzie, 95; Bernard, ii, 15.
28. Bernard, ii, 25–30.
29. Murray, 27–30.
30. McAleavy, 53.
31. Tai Yi, *Chung-kuo chin-tai shih-kao* (Peking, 1958), quoted by McAleavy, 53.
32. *Chinese Repository*, x, 340, 535; Selby, 32.
33. Holt, 128–9.
34. Bernard, ii, 30–3.
35. McAleavy, 53.

CHAPTER 11: *The Empire in Defeat* (pp. 162–179)

1. Palmerston's instructions to Pottinger are given in Morse (2), i, Appendices K and L, 655–61.
2. *The Last Year in China . . . by a Field Officer* (1843). Pottinger 'is one of the best men to conduct this operation,' Colonel Wyndham Baker confirmed. 'We feel sanguine that this time the public will not be disappointed.' MS Letters of Colonel Wyndham Baker.
3. Pottinger to Palmerston, 30 October 1841, quoted by Costin, 97.
4. MS Journal of Assistant Surgeon C. Pine.
5. MS Letters of Colonel Wyndham Baker.
6. *Ibid.*
7. Bingham, i, 285–90; *Chinese Repository*, September 1841.

8. Rait, 235; Holt, 139. The Government had fallen by the time Pottinger's despatch arrived, and instead of going to Palmerston it went to the milder Lord Aberdeen who noted in the margin, 'The worst proposal I have seen from Mr Pottinger. . . . It ought not to pass unnoticed.'
9. Rait, 261.
10. Murray, 73–4.
11. Waley, 163–4.
12. *Ya-p'ien chan-cheng wen-hsüeh chi*, 24, trans. Waley, 230–1.
13. *Ya-p'ien chan-cheng tzu-liao ts'ung-k'an* (Shanghai, 1955), trans. Waley, 158, 159, 165.
14. McAleavy, 53.
15. Murray, 98–101.
16. *Ibid.*, 99.
17. Waley, 171.
18. Ouchterlony, 239–40.
19. Murray, 107–8.
20. *The Last Year in China . . . by a Field Officer* (1843), 136–7.
21. Murray, 110.
22. *Ibid.*, 140–2.
23. Ouchterlony, 238.
24. Murray, 145–6.
25. Selby, 43; Rait, 282.
26. *Ibid.*
27. The poet, Chu Shih-yün, quoted by Waley, 211.
28. Ts'ao Sheng, *I-huan pei ch'ang chi*, leaf 31b–32a.
29. Ts'ao Sheng, leaf 24b.
30. Ts'ao Sheng, leaf 28a.
31. Li Chien-nung, 41.
32. Lane-Poole, 26.
33. Teng Ssu-yü, *Chang Hsi*, 36–43.
34. Quoted by Holt, 150.
35. The boy was Harry Parkes, nephew of Karl Gützlaff, who is introduced to the reader on page 87. Lane-Poole, 27–8.
36. Teng Ssu-yü, *Chang, Hsi*, 75.
37. Granville G. Loch, 186.
38. Teng Ssu-yü, *Chang Hsi*, 86; Lane-Poole, 33.
39. Full details of the treaty may be found in Morse (2), i, 298–302. See also *Chinese Repository*, xiii, 438.
40. Nye, 48–50; Teng Ssu-yü, *Chang Hsi*, 69–70.
41. Li Chien-nung, 41–2; Cordier, *Histoire des Relations de la Chine*, i, 15. Modern Chinese Communist historians see the Treaty of Nanking as marking a new era in Chinese history. 'As a result of the war, China's independent power was lost. The doors were opened, territorial integrity was shattered and authority compromised, opening the way for invasion by the imperialist powers, political invasion, economic invasion and military invasion. The opening of the treaty ports gave them the chance to divide up the country between them and provided the circumstances

in which modern Japanese imperialism could engulf our country. On the other hand it made for an unprecedented and drastic transformation of Chinese society. . . . It placed China, hitherto pursuing a policy of isolationism and self-sufficiency, onto the contemporary international stage. In fact it made it the main character on that stage' (Chiang Chien-fu, *Chung-kuo-chin pai-nien shih chiao-ch'eng* (1945).

PART III: REBELS AND INNOCENTS

CHAPTER 12: '*The True Lord of China*' (pp. 183–201)

1. Caleb Cushing, the American negotiator of the Treaty of Wang-hsia, afterwards said, as Attorney-General of the United States, 'I entered China with the formed *general* conviction that the United States ought not to concede to any foreign state, under any circumstances, jurisdiction over the life and liberty of a citizen of the United States, unless the foreign state be of our own family of nations, in a word, a Christian state' (Fishel, 11–12).
2. McAleavy, 57–9; Li Chien-nung, 49–52; Michael and Chang Chung-li, 6–7, 10–18.
3. Meadows, 112.
4. Cheng, 3; Michael and Chang Chung-li; McAleavy, 60–1; Wolfgang Franke, *Das Jahrhundert der Chinesischen Revolution* (Munchen, 1958); trs. Schurmann and quoted in Schurmann and Schell, 170–2.
5. Cheng, 8–12.
6. Michael and Chang Chung-li, 25–36; McAleavy, 66–8.
7. Meadows, 149–50.
8. Callery and Yvan, *L'insurrection en Chine depuis son origine jusquà le prise de Nankin* (Paris, 1853), 50, quoted by Pelissier, 100.
9. Lo Ehr-Kang, *T'ai-p'ing t'ien-kuo shih-Kang* (Shanghai, 1938), quoted by McAleavy, 71.
10. Quoted by Meadows, 155–7.
11. Michael and Chang Chung-li, 45–6, 62; McAleavy, 69; Pelissier, 96–8; Le Chien-nung, 53; Hughes, 21; Morse (2), i, 450–2.
12. Michael and Chang Chung-li, 74.
13. Meadows, 258–60.
14. Costin, 161.
15. Rev. Père Brouillon, S. J. *Mémoire sur l'état actuel de la mission du Kiang-nan, 1842–5*, (Paris, 1855), 404–8, quoted by Pelissier, 113.
16. *Ibid.*, quoted by Pelissier, 117–19.
17. Meadows, 314–5.
18. Michael and Chang Chung-li, 75.
19. Li Chien-nung, 66; McAleavy, 73–7.
20. Michael and Chang Chung-li, 26–7, 77.
21. McAleavy, 77–82.
22. Taylor, 360.
23. Quoted by Callery and Yvan, and by Pelissier, 108–9.

24. Arthur Evans Moule, *Half a Century in China, Recollections and Observations* (1911), 55–7, 59, quoted by Pelissier, 111–12.
25. Quoted by Li Chien-nung.

CHAPTER 13: *The* Arrow *Affair* (pp. 202–215)

1. Quoted by Hurd, 35. Hong Kong, Lieutenant C. A. Newman of the King's Dragoon Guards later confirmed, was 'the fearfullest hole in the world, for I might say it is inhabited by a den of thieves; for instance, if anyone were walking down a street with a medal on his brest they would come and snatch it off, and of course it was of no use running after them for they had such clever hiding places that it would take a very cute fellow to find them—in fact, the richest man in the place was nothing but a convict. I was never in such a place before and never wish to go into another like it.' (Autograph Diary of Charles Alfred Newman, 1860.)
2. Costin, 120.
3. Teng Ssu-yü and Fairbank (2), 36.
4. Hurd, 18–19; Morse (2), i, 411–13.
5. Quoted by Hurd, 20.
6. *Ibid.*, 33.
7. Elgin MSS., Journal entry for 8 November.
8. Lane-Poole, 57–9; Hurd, 16.
9. Hurd 17; Morse (2), i, 422; Lane-Poole, 148–9.
10. Li Chien-nung, 83; Morse (2), i, 422.
11. Hurd, 28.
12. Quoted by Costin, 211.
13. Oliphant, 7.
14. Hurd, 37.
15. Costin, 149.
16. *Hansard's Parliamentary Debates*, 3rd series, cxliv (1857), 1155–1243, 1307–1485, 1495–1688, 1725–1850. Hurd gives a good summary, 53–70.
17. Brian Connell, *Regina v. Palmerston: The Correspondence between Queen Victoria and her Foreign and Prime Minister, 1837–1865*, 212.
18. *Ibid.*, 213.
19. Palmerston's election address at Tiverton, quoted by Hurd, 76.
20. Elizabeth Longford, *Victoria RI* (Weidenfeld & Nicolson, 1964), 278.

CHAPTER 14: '*The Massacre of the Innocents*' (pp. 216–240)

1. Quoted by Cordier (2), 20, and by Pelissier, 128–30.
2. For Elgin's instructions see Morse (2), i, 487–8; for Baron Gros's similar instructions, Cordier (2), 145.
3. Elgin *Letters*, 179–81.
4. *Ibid.*, 183, 196; Hurd, 82.
5. *Ibid.*, 184.
6. Hurd, 100.
7. Elgin MSS, journal, 4 July; Hurd, 103.

8. Elgin MSS, journal 3 and 4 July; *Letters*, 193.
9. Elgin MSS, journal, 31 July; *Letters*, 194-5.
10. Elgin MSS, journal, 11 August.
11. Hurd, 107.
12. Elgin MSS, journal, 14 August and 13 October.
13. Elgin, *Correspondence*, 221.
14. Elgin MSS, journal, 22 November.
15. *Ibid.*, 9 December.
16. *Ibid.*, 18 November.
17. Hurd, 113.
18. Elgin MSS, journal, 15 December.
19. Elgin, *Letters*, 207, 212.
20. *Ibid.*, 213.
21. *Ibid.*
22. Oliphant, 113.
23. *Ibid.*, 126, 127.
24. Elgin, *Letters*, 214.
25. Elgin MSS, journal, 2 January; *Letters*, 215. The Barbarians seemed quite as incomprehensible to the Chinese as the Chinese did to the foreigner. A phrase frequently found in Chinese documents of this time is '*i-ch'ing p'o-ts'e*', 'the Barbarian nature cannot be fathomed'. Fairbank (5), 177.
26. G. Wingrove Cooke, *The Times's Special Correspondence from China* (1859), 355.
27. *Ibid.*, 341-2.
28. Autograph Journal of Deputy Assistant Commissary General H. C. Lewis, 15 April 1857–30 October 1858.
29. Elgin MSS, journal, 22 February.
30. Lane-Poole, 171-2; *Letters and Journals*, 217.
31. Oliphant, 165.
32. MS Autobiography of Major-General John Robertson Pughe.
33. Quoted by Lane-Poole, 174.
34. Oliphant, 157.
35. MS Autobiography of Major-General John Robertson Pughe.
36. Autograph Journal of Deputy Assistant Commissary General H. C. Lewis.
37. *Ibid.*
38. Lane-Poole, 177, 178.
39. Elgin MSS, journal, 20 January. The overbearing arrogance of so many British merchants and officials in the East is one of Elgin's recurring themes. From India he had felt compelled to write to his wife, 'I have seldom from man or woman since I came to the East heard a sentence which was reconcilable with the hypothesis that Christianity had ever come into the world. Detestation, contempt, ferocity, vengeance, whether Chinamen or Indians be the object. There are some three or four hundred servants in this house. When one passes by their *salaaming* one feels a little awkward. But the feeling soon wears off, and one moves

among them with perfect indifference, treating them, not as dogs, because in that case one would whistle to them and pat them, but as machines, with which one can have no communion or sympathy' (Journal entry for 21 August).

Previous complaints about the behaviour of the British in China had been made by both Sir Henry Pottinger and Sir John Francis Davis. Pottinger was convinced during the Opium War that it would prove to be, 'in the new era opening in this quarter of the world', 'a far more difficult undertaking to control than to protect British subjects', and that the 'Head British Authority in China' would have to be invested with extraordinary powers to keep in order 'so many turbulent spirits'. Davis wrote home from Hong Kong in similar terms in November 1846, after an Englishman, who had been guilty of numerous similar acts, had kicked over the stall of a Chinese trader and refused to pay the fine the Consul had imposed upon him. His refusal to pay, though he readily acknowledged his behaviour, was vehemently supported by the other English traders. The Chief Justice in Hong Kong, a habitual drunkard according to Davis, quashed the man's sentence on a point of form and made comments liable to increase violence against the Chinese. 'I am not the first who has been compelled to remark,' Davis reported to London, 'that it is more difficult to deal with our own countrymen than with the Chinese government.' (Costin, 102, 128.)

40. Elgin, *Letters*, 221–2; Hurd, 128.
41. Elgin, *Letters*, 219, 220.
42. *Ibid.*, 226, 229, 230, 232, 233, 237. Thomas Taylor Meadows, 'though crotchety on some points' was 'an agreeable and clever man'. (Elgin MSS, journal entry, 18 March.)
43. Elgin MSS, journal, 3, 19, 24 and 28 April.
44. Elgin, *Letters*, 246–8; Oliphant, 275, 297, 303; Hurd, 147–8.
45. Oliphant, 307.
46. Elgin MSS, journal, 5 June.
47. Oliphant, 343.
48. Elgin, *Letters*, 252.
49. *Ibid.*, 254; Elgin MSS, journal, 29 June.
50. McAleavy, 93.
51. Li Chien-nung, 84–6. For details of the Tientsin treaties see Morse (2), i, 477, 525–9.
52. Hurd, 166.
53. *Ibid.*, 167.
54. *Ibid.*, 176; Morse (2), i, 552–4.
55. Morse (2), i, 554.

CHAPTER 15: *At the Taku Forts* (pp. 241–265)

1. Quoted by Hurd, 180.
2. John Fisher, afterwards Admiral of the Fleet Lord Fisher, quoted by Holt, 243.

3. Holt, 245; de Chassiron, 250.
4. Quoted by Holt, 249; Selby, 60–1; Morse, i, 577–9. Letters of Sir James Hope (Ramsden Collection).
5. Hurd, 185–6; Morse (2), i, 580. 'It was so like the Yankees,' Sir James Hope commented in a private letter to the Duke of Somerset, First Lord of the Admiralty. 'They wanted to go in at the *Front Door* with us if we had succeeded in opening it, but as we did not do so, they have very quickly gone in at the *Back Door*.' (Ramdsen Collection.)
6. Hurd, 194.
7. *Ibid.*, 190.
8. *Ibid.*, 198.
9. *Ibid.*, 190.
10. *Ibid.*, 195.
11. Elgin, *Letters*, 331; Morison, 253–6. The military and naval commanders, however, were very pleased to see Elgin. 'I had a most satisfactory interview with him,' Sir James Hope told the Duke of Somerset, 'and am delighted to find that all his views are decided and for prompt action. I think he will be of much service to us in moving on our French allies.' (Ramsden Collection.)
12. Swinhoe, 2, 3, 27; Rennie, 15.
13. Wolseley, 32, 35, 42–7, 52, 59, 60–7.
14. Elgin, *Letters*, 335.
15. M'Ghee, 35.
16. Wolseley, 89.
17. *Ibid.*, 95.
18. Swinhoe, 75.
19. *Ibid.*, 64–5.
20. Newman, MS Diary.
21. Armand Lucy, *Lettres intimes* quoted by Hurd, 211.
22. Swinhoe, 64–5, 68.
23. M'Ghee, 85; Swinhoe, 62; Wolseley, 92–3.
24. Rennie, 77–8.
25. Swinhoe, 84–5; Newman MS Diary; Hope Grant, 65.
26. Swinhoe, 87.
27. Fisher, 391–2.
28. d'Hérisson, 173–4; Lehman, 91.
29. Quoted by Hurd, 211.
30. Selby, 68.
31. *Ibid.*, 74–5.
32. MS. Letters of F. Parry; Swinhoe, 139; Wolseley, 134; Rennie, 122–3.
33. McAleavy, 98.
34. Wolseley, 135–8, 149; Swinhoe, 105; Rennie, 21–8; Selby, 75–6; Holt, 264–6; Hurd, 214–5.
35. Rennie, 126.
36. *The Times*, 3 November 1860.
37. Elgin, *Letters*, 347.
38. Lane-Poole, 227–8.

39. *Ibid.*, 229.
40. Elgin, *Letters*, 350.
41. *Ibid.*, 353.
42. Lane-Poole, 232–3.
43. Hurd, 218–9.

CHAPTER 16: *The Burning of the Palace* (pp. 266–288)

1. H. B. Loch, 131–65; Lane-Poole, 233–9.
2. Wolseley, 180; Lehman, 103.
3. Rennie, 243.
4. Swinhoe, 245; Rennie, 216; Wolseley, 182–3.
5. D'Hérisson, 277–85; Pelissier, 136–40; Maspero, 135.
6. Elgin, *Letters*, 358; Elgin MSS, journal, 27 September.
7. M'Ghee, 212–3; Rennie, 227; Wolseley, 223–38; Hurd, 226–8; Cordier, (3), 353; Maspero, 136; Montauban, 310–17; d'Hérisson, 327–50; Pelissier, 141–5; Elgin, *Letters*, 361–2; Elgin MSS, journal, 7 October, Newman MS Diary. The loot from the Yüan-ming Yüan included scores of 'very pretty little dogs' which it was a capital offence for anyone outside the Imperial family to keep. Most of the dogs had been thrown down a well to prevent them from falling into the foreigners' hands; but so many survived that they were taken away in cartloads. They fetched 'a great sum of money in this country,' Lieutenant Newman said. One of them, a Pekingese Lion Dog called 'Looty', was presented to Queen Victoria.
8. 'Journal of an officer of the 67th Regiment during the North China Campaign of 1860', *The Royal United Service Magazine* xviii (Feb. 1874), 65, quoted by Lehman, 107–8.
9. Gros to Thouvenel, 17 November 1860, quoted by Costin, 336. Elgin told Lord John Russell that gossip had it that Montauban himself had made more money by the looting than anyone, so much, in fact, that he wanted to get home as quickly as possible to enjoy it. 'The French army, well represented by General Montauban is literally gorged with loot—gold, silver, precious stones, enamels, everything to an enormous extent,' Lord John Hay told Sir James Hope. 'They have had enough and wish to be off—They do not care what happens, their pride has been satisfied and as for the treatment of their countrymen they think it only the fortune of war.' (Ramsden Collection.)
10. H. B. Loch, 165–237; Lane-Poole, 239–48.
11. Newman, MS Diary.
12. Elgin, *Letters*, 365.
13. Gros to Thouvenel 19 October 1860, quoted by Costin, 333.
14. 'The French marched a regiment into Peking with much theatrical effect, bands playing, etc.,' Lord John Hay reported to Sir James Hope. 'The crowds of Chinese forming a sea of bald heads shining in the sun swaying backwards and forwards was most curious. Numbers of police with their whips incessantly struck all within reach over their heads, the

front rank catching it over their legs in addition, this and the bayonets of the French, kept curiosity at last within bounds.' (The Ramsden Collection.)

15. 'How to get a hold of the Culprits is the main difficulty, 'Lord John Hay also thought. 'Sankolitsin is one himself and even amidst this wreck of authority, he is one possessed of much power.' (The Ramsden Collection.)

16. Elgin, *Letters*, 366; *Correspondence respecting China, 1859–60*, 216.

17. Gros to Thouvenel, 19 October 1860, quoted by Costin, 333.

18. Hurd, 235–6. 'My worthy friend Baron Gros,' Lord Elgin told the Duke of Somerset, 'was suddenly taken with a fit of tenderness for the existing Chinese dynasty, a fit brought on, in fact, I think, by the exhortations of some Jesuits whom he has got about him and who tell him that by professing sympathy with it and antipathy to the rebels who are iconoclastically inclined he may do a good stroke of business in Churches and establish a Roman Catholic influence all over China.' (Ramsden Collection.)

19. Lane-Poole, 251.

20. M'Ghee, 258, 109.

21. Wolseley, 278–9.

22. Bland and Backhouse (1), 10–20.

23. Wolseley, 292, 293–7; Swinhoe, 345.

24. Knollys, 208–10.

25. Morse (2), i, 614–16; Cordier, *Relations de la Chine*, i, 40–96; de Chassiron, 281–96.

26. Palmerston to Russell, 26 December 1860, quoted by Costin, 337; Hurd, 237.

27. Rennie, 204–5, 207–9, 224, 229, 235; M'Ghee, 298, 300, 350.

28. Wolseley, 308, 311–12, 314–18; Swinhoe 353; Rennie 242.

29. Wu Hsiang-hsiang, *O-ti ch'in-lüeh Chung-kuo shih* (Taipeh, 1954), 30, quoted by McAleavy, 100.

30. *Ibid.*

31. *Ibid.*

CHAPTER 17: *The Last of the Taipings* (pp. 289–304)

1. The description is C. G. Gordon's, Wilson, 293. Another foreigner commented, 'Tseng dresses in the poorest clothes and keeps no state.' As a young man he had, so he confessed in his diary, enjoyed 'opium, women and improper talk'; in his early middle age, he gave up opium entirely yet 'continued to censure himself for lapses on the other two counts'. But throughout his life he kept his personal expenses remarkably low and criticized himself severely for every lapse into what he believed to be self-indulgence (Wright, (1), 73–4). For Tseng's biography see Hummell, *Eminent Chinese of the Ch'ing Period*, ii, 751–5. Austere as he was, Tseng was a delightful companion. 'He liked to tell amusing stories,' Li Hung-chang said of him, remembering the time he had spent working under him as a young man. 'While everyone was laughing heartily, he himself would not even smile, but would sit quietly and

stroke his beard with his fingers. We dared not laugh and yet we could not help laughing.' (Wu Yung, 246.)

2. For Li Hung-chang's biography see Hummell, *Eminent Chinese of the Ch'ing Period*, i, 464–71. A man of great tact and insinuating charm, he was much liked by Europeans who considered him 'an enlightened friend of progress' and enjoyed his friendly company. See Martin, 123. The French journalist, Pierre Loti, described him as 'colossal in height, with projecting cheekbones beneath small eyes—tiny eyes, lively and searching. He is an exaggerated type of Mongol with a certain beauty even so, and *l'air grand seigneur* even though his fur gown is worn and stained.' (Loti, 260.)

3. *T'ai-p'ing t'ien kuo ko-yao chuan-shu chi*, 41.
4. Wilson, 123.
5. Cheng, 107.
6. Nutting, 7.
7. Cheng, 107, 108, 111, 112, 130, 134.
8. J. O. P. Bland, *Li Hung-Chang* (1917), 48, quoted by Pelissier, 154.
9. Bland and Backhouse (2), 424–5, quoted by Pelissier, 155.
10. *Events in the Taeping Rebellion*, 493–4.
11. Cheng, 126–7, 130; Nutting, 46–64; Selby, 131–5.
12. 'The Imperialists do not want me to go [to Nanking],' Gordon petulantly told a friend. 'They feel sure of taking it in time & feel a sort of shame to let us go & capture this city before which they have been so long.' (Autograph Letters of C. G. Gordon, 18 April 1864.)
13. *London and China Express*, 10 October 1864, quoted by Gregory, 152.
14. Autograph Letters of C. G. Gordon.
15. Quoted by Lin le, ii, 517, 612, 613, 722.
16. *Events in the Taeping Rebellion*, 183.
17. Autograph Letters of C. G. Gordon.
18. Oliphant.
19. Wolseley, 336–51.
20. Wilson, 318–20.
21. Michael and Chang Chung-li, 174.
22. In Gordon's opinion the Loyal King was 'the most talented and enterprising leader the Rebels had. He had been in more engagements than any other Rebel leader. His presence with the Taipings was equal to a reinforcement of 5,000 men. He was the only Rebel chief whose death was to be regretted, the others . . . were a set of Bandit chiefs' (Autograph Letters of C. G. Gordon).
23. Bland and Backhouse (2), 61–2.
24. McAleavy, 117.

PART IV: AGGRESSORS AND REFORMERS

CHAPTER 18: *Slicing up the Melon* (pp. 307–323)

1. Lucien Vigneron, *Deux ans au Se-Tchouan* (Paris, 1881), quoted by Pelissier, 169–70.

2. Baron de Huebner, *Promenade autour du Monde* (Paris, 1873), quoted by Pelissier, 175–7.

3. Teng Ssu-yü and Fairbank (2), 50–4.

4. Cheng, 109–10.

5. Chiang T'ing-fu, *Chung-kuo chin-tai shih* (Hong Kong, 1954), quoted by McAleavy, 116; Teng Ssu-yü and Fairbank, 70.

6. Teng Ssu-yü and Fairbank (2), 76–7.

7. Bland and Backhouse (1), 95–6; Der Ling (1), 20, 162.

8. Wu Yung, 179.

9. Capitaine Lecomte, *Guet-apens de Bac-Lé* (Paris, 1890), quoted by Pelissier, 190.

10. Jacques Bainville, *The French Republic 1870–1935* (Cape, 1936), 93.

11. 'The contradictory elements in our China policy,' the American scholar, John K. Fairbank, has written, 'can be understood only if we remember that until the early 1920s our interests in China were junior to those of Britain, under whose leadership they had grown up. This allowed us the luxury of constantly denouncing British imperialism while steadily participating in its benefits. . . . Viewed cynically, the doctrine of China's integrity has been a device to prevent other powers, for example, Russia, from taking over areas of China and excluding us from them. But the independence of China has also appealed to Americans as a matter of political justice. It fits the doctrine of the self-determination and sovereignty of weaker nations, which constitutes one of our major political sentiments.' Fairbank (4), 313, 322.

12. McAleavy, 147.

13. Der Ling (1), 321. The Princess claimed to enjoy Kuang-hsü's friend-ship, 'as far as anyone was able to'.

14. Quoted by Teng Ssu-yü and Fairbank (2), 156.

15. In his introduction to this history, Timothy Richard asked, 'What is the cause of the foreign wars, indemnities, and repeated humiliations suffered by China during the last sixty years?' And he answered the question by saying that 'God was breaking down the barriers between all nations by railways, steamers, and telegraphs, in order that we should all live in peace and happiness as brethren in one family; but the Man-chus, by continual obstruction, were determined from the first to prevent this intercourse.' For a discussion of Mackenzie's book which became 'the main source of information about Europe for the leaders of the Reform Movement, including the Emperor himself', see Purcell, 114–16. The im-portance of China's development of modern railways and telegraphs was emphasized in many letters to and from Li Hung-chang. Kuo Sung-tao, the head of the Chinese Legation in London, for example, wrote to him to say that there was 'a Mr [George] Stephenson here who says that all countries are building more railroads. He particularly and indefatigably advises China to do this with dispatch. . . . The critics merely say that wherever the machines of foreigners reach, the local geomantic harmony is injured. This is a great error. Railways and telegraph lines are always

built on level ground following the state roads. There is nothing to dig up or to destroy.' (Teng Ssu-yü and Fairbank, 101.)

16. Mrs Archibald Little, *Intimate China: The Chinese as I have seen Them* (1899), 576–83, quoted by Pelissier, 207–10; Teng Ssu-yü and Fairbank (2), 177–9.
17. Bland and Backhouse, (1), 175–6.
18. *Ibid.*, 206.
19. Kuang-hsü never forgave Yuan Shih-k'ai for this betrayal, and his hatred of him became obsessional. Towards the end of his life he would spend hours drawing big pictures of tortoises—symbols of infamy in China because of their supposed homosexual proclivities—and, having written the name Yuan Shih-k'ai on their backs, sticking them on the wall and shooting arrows at them. Then he would cut the drawings into pieces with a pair of scissors and 'throw them into the air like a swarm of butterflies. . . . He did this almost every day as though it were a task he must perform.' (Wu Yung, 178.)

CHAPTER 19: *Righteous Harmony Boxing* (pp. 324–333)

1. Wu Yung, 179.
2. *Poems of Revolt*, translated by Rewi Alley (New World Press, Peking, 1962).
3. Wen Ch'ing, 297; Purcell, 131. In his book *China and the Occident* (1927), G. Nye Steiger propounded the theory that the Boxers were not a religious sect or secret society at all, but a legal militia raised in accordance with decrees of the Empress Dowager in 1898. This theory has been effectively disposed of by Chester C. Tan, 36–43, and by Victor Purcell, 181–8, 216–8.
4. *Poems of Revolt*.
5. Purcell, 235.
6. D'Anthouard, *Les Boxeurs* (Paris, 1902), 17–22, quoted by Pelissier, 217–18.
7. The Rev. Roland Allen, chaplain at the British Legation in Peking, was told by many missionaries that 'the influence which the Boxer superstition exercised over the minds of local officials, country gentry and village headmen was appalling. Men who could talk quietly and reasonably about every other subject, the moment the Boxers were mentioned raved like lunatics, and professed unswerving faith in the most childish and incredible stories about their supernatural powers.' (Allen, 25.)
8. For the text of this important decree see Tan, 60–1.
9. Quoted by Pelissier, 218.
10. *Ibid.* The more common charge that mission schools were instruments of denationalization was scarcely deniable. 'The children were taught, not as Chinese children preparing to share in the life of the Chinese race,' wrote the American, Nathaniel Peffer, of his own country's mission schools, 'but as American schoolchildren. Of literature, the Chinese children learned English literature. Of history, they learned American

history. . . . And it is not too much of a caricature to say that thousands of Chinese children grew to the age of sixteen without any clear knowledge that there had ever existed on this planet more than three men worthy of emulation: Christ, George Washington and Abraham Lincoln.' (Quoted by J. O. P. Bland, *China: The Pity of It*, 84.)

11. Purcell, 121–38; Tan 35; Wu Yung, 34.
12. Pelissier, 218.
13. Purcell, 122.
14. Tan, 63.
15. *Ibid.*, 62.
16. Quoted by Fleming, 35.
17. Wu Yung, 76–7.
18. A. H. Smith, ii, 614–5.
19. *Ibid.*, ii, 633–5.
20. Fleming, 236. An Imperial decree, printed in Chien Po-tsan, *I Ho T'uan*, vol. 1, ordered foreign missionaries to leave China for their own countries. Yu-hsien's reasons for ordering the execution were that the missionaries had refused to leave and were plotting against China. See Tan, 258–9.

CHAPTER 20: *The Siege of the Legations* (pp. 334–347)

1. Conger, quoted by Haldane, 164. From the Chinese viewpoint these encounters apparently did not seem so pleasant. 'It was quite common,' the Empress's First Lady-in-Waiting said, 'for the foreign ladies to comment loudly upon the richness of dress of Court ladies, and ladies-in-waiting, speculate on the probable price paid, and even to finger the rich materials, ignoring wearers as of no account, while talking about the clothing in voluble asides to friends who were just as interested, just as curious, and just as inexpressibly rude.' (Der Ling, *Old Buddha*, 231.)
2. Fleming, 64.
3. Baron d'Anthouard, quoted by Pelissier, 217.
4. MacDonald Papers, quoted by Fleming, 70.
5. MS Letters of Robert Francis Gartside-Tipping.
6. Fleming, 132.
7. A coloured print, afterwards 'extensively circulated in Shanghai and elsewhere', represented the Japanese Chancellor's murder 'not as the act of a mob, but as an execution by court martial, with Boxers drawn up in one file and soldiers in another; the whole presided over by General Jung, a high commander of the Imperial forces' (Martin, 110).
8. G. E. Morrison, quoted by Fleming, 95.
9. Tan, 75.
10. Haldane, 193; Fleming, 97; Purcell, 251.
11. Tan, 78–9.
12. Bland and Backhouse (2), 453–4.
13. *Ibid.*, 93–4; Purcell, 251; Fleming, 101.
14. Fleming, 105; Tan, 75; Purcell, 251.

15. Fleming, 106.
16. Weale, 67.
17. Fleming, 109; Hart, 19.
18. Fleming, 113.
19. Polly Condit Smith, quoted by Fleming, 146.
20. Fleming, 151.
21. Autograph diary of G. E. Morrison, entry for 28 June. The Prime Minister, Lord Salisbury, professed himself to be not so much impressed by MacDonald's conduct: he 'should have packed his carpet-bag at once and taken to his heels, not stuck to his post; the first duty of a diplomatist is to run' (*Life with Queen Victoria: Marie Mallet's Letters from Court 1887–1901*, ed. Victor Mallet, Murray, 1968).
22. Nigel Oliphant, 78–86.
23. Autograph diary of G. E. Morrison; Hart, 41. B. L. Simpson of the Chinese Customs Service, who wrote *Indiscreet Letters from Peking* under the pseudonym of B. L. Putnam Weale, pays several compliments to Colonel Sheba though he is strongly critical of almost everyone else concerned in the defence.
24. Mary Hooker, quoted by Fleming, 148.
25. Martin, 88, 116.
26. Allen, 157.
27. Tan, 95, 97.
28. Fleming, 228; Tan, 113–14.
29. Tan, 102, 103, 113.
30. Tan, 105.
31. Allen, 268.
32. Nigel Oliphant, 167.

CHAPTER 21: *Retribution* (pp. 348–359)

1. Mateer, 396.
2. Nigel Oliphant, 168.
3. Quoted by Fleming, 207.
4. Weale, 195, 204.
5. Charles Leonard, 'A "Boxer" Letter', *The Philatelist*, January 1969.
6. Weale, 92.
7. Fleming, 243.
8. Loti, 84; Allen, 282, 283, 284; Weale, 252, 254, 294.
9. Bland and Backhouse (1), 300–1. Doubts have been cast on the authenticity of this diary which was found by Sir Edmund Backhouse in Ching-shan's looted study in August 1900 and which is now in the British Museum. Sir Edmund Backhouse remained convinced of its authenticity up to the time of his death and, though it evidently contains some forgeries and parts of it seem to be based on other documents including the journal of Wang Wen-shao, Viceroy of Chihli, it expresses 'in masterly fashion', as Professor J. J. L. Duyvendak said, 'the atmosphere of those days'. There seems little doubt that the account of the Empress's flight from Peking

and the drowning of the Pearl Concubine is generally accurate. For a discussion of the diary see Purcell, Appendix A, 272–84.

10. Quoted by Haldane, 217–18.
11. Haldane, 221–3; Tan, 136–8.
12. When news of the Boxer uprising reached St Petersburg, General Kuropatkin, the Minister of War, made the often quoted remark, 'I am very glad. This will give us an excuse for seizing Manchuria. We will then turn Manchuria into a second Bokhara' (Count Witte, *Memoirs,* New York, 1921, 109).
13. Clements, 177–202.
14. Quoted by Fleming, 250.
15. Langer, ii, 699.
16. Fleming, 253.
17. *Ibid.*, 242.
18. Martin, 140.
19. For the full text of the Peace Protocol of 7 September 1901 see Clements; Appendix LLL, 213–22, Tan, 223.
20. Printed in the *Journal of the Society for Army Historical Research,* xlvi, no. 186.
21. Autograph letter of Captain Edward Bayly, R.N. 9 September 1900.
22. MS Letters of Robert Gartside-Tipping.
22. Loti, 11.
23. Weale, 269.
24. Yen-shi chiu-t'u, *Hsin-jen chih wen hsin yüeh-fu,* reprinted in *Keng-tzu shih-pien wen-hsüeh chih,* 15.
25. Yen-shi chiu-t'u, *ibid.*

CHAPTER 22: *The Society of Sworn Confederates* (pp. 360–367)

1. Don Rodolfo Borghese, in Varè, 260–1.
2. Der Ling, 225; Fleming, 257–61; Bland and Backhouse, *China under the Empress Dowager,* 402–3.
3. Quoted by Johnston, 69; Haldane, 240.
4. Der Ling (1), 356.
5. Jean Rodes, *La Chine nouvelle* (Paris, 1910), 291–4, quoted by Pelissier, 245.
6. Sun Yat-sen, *Kidnapped in London: Being the story of my capture by . . . the Chinese Legation,* London (1912), 30–6.
7. Jean Rodes, *La Chine nouvelle,* 291–4, quoted by Pelissier, 246–7.
8. R. F. Johnston, *Twilight in the Forbidden City,* 74.
9. Der Ling, *Old Buddha,* 310–16.
10. Bland and Backhouse, (1), 467; Haldane, 249, 257–60.
11. McAleavy, 180.
12. Quoted by McAleavy, 186.
13. Hart, 54–5.

Sources

MANUSCRIPT

The Autobiography of Major-General John Robertson Pughe
The diaries of:
  Deputy Assistant Commissary General H. C. Lewis
  William Fanshawe Martin (Vol. cxi of the Martin Papers, British Museum)
  G. E. Morrison
  Charles Alfred Newman
  William Pitt, Earl Amherst of Arracan
  Major-General Guy Rotton
Documents relating to William Wilberforce Harris Greathed
The Elgin Manuscripts
Sir Erasmus Gower, 'The Journal of H.M.S. *Lion* to China'
The personal papers of Sir Francis Wood (The Hickleton Papers)
The Journal, Letters and Papers of Assistant Surgeon C. Pine
Letters of:
  Colonel Wyndham Baker
  Captain Edward Bayly, R.N.
  James Dundas Crawford
  Robert Francis Gartside-Tipping
  General C. G. Gordon
  Lord John Hay
  Sir James Hope
  Vice Admiral Sir Augustus L. Kuper
  Francis Joseph Parry
The Notebook of Captain P. S. Lumsden
The Papers of Edward Adolphus Seymour, 12th Duke of Somerset (the Ramsden Collection)
G. J. Yorke, 'The Princely House, A Manuscript History of The Early Years of Jardine, Matheson & Co. in China'

PRINTED

Works marked with an asterisk have
not been translated from the Chinese
ALLEN, REV. ROLAND. *The Siege of the Peking Legations* (1901)
ANDERSON, AENEAS. *An Accurate Account of Lord Macartney's Embassy to China* (1795)

Sources

Authentic Account of the Embassy of the Dutch East-India Company to the Court of China in the years 1794 and 1795 taken from the Journal of André Everard Van Braam

BANNO, MASATAKA. *China and the West 1858–1861* (Harvard University. Press, 1964)

BARROW, JOHN. *Travels in China* (2nd edition, 1806)

BERNARD, W. D. *Narrative of the Voyages and Services of the Nemesis from 1840 to 1843, and of the Combined Naval and Military Operations in China* (2 vols, 1844)

BINGHAM, COMMANDER J. ELLIOT, R.N. *Narrative of the Expedition to China* (2 vols, 1842)

BLAND, J. O. P. *Li Hung-chang* (1917)

BLAND, J. O. P. and E. BACKHOUSE. (1) *China under the Empress Dowager. Being the History of the Life and Times of Tzu Hsi. Compiled from State Papers and the Private Diary of the Comptroller of her Household* (1911)

    (2) *Annals and Memoirs of the Court of Peking* (1914)

BLAKE, CLAGETTE. *Charles Elliot, R.N. 1801–75* (Cleaver-Hume, 1959)

BOWRING, J. B. *Autobiographical Recollections* (1877)

Canton Miscellany

CHANG, CH'IEN-FU. *Chung-kuo chin pai-nien shih chiao-ch'eng* (Textbook of Chinese history of the last century, Hong Kong, 1949)

CHANG, CHUNG-LI. See MICHAEL

CHANG, HSIN-PAO. *Commissioner Lin and the Opium War* (Harvard University Press, 1964)

CHASSIRON, BARON CHARLES DE. *Notes sur le Japon, la Chine et l'Inde* (Paris, 1861)

CH'EN, GIDEON. *Lin Tse-hsü, Pioneer Promoter of the Adoption of Western Means of Maritime Defence in China* (Peiping, 1934)

CH'EN, JEROME. *Yüan Shih K'ai, 1859–1916* (Allen & Unwin, 1961)

CHENG, J. C. *Chinese Sources for the Taiping Rebellion 1850–64* (Hong Kong University Press, 1963)

*CHIANG, T'ING-FU. *Chin-tai Chung-kuo wai-chiao shih tzu-liao chi-yao* (Selected Materials on Modern Chinese Diplomatic History, Hong Kong, 1954)

*CHIEN, PO-TSAN, and others (eds.). *I-ho-t'uan tzu-liao ts'ung-k'an* (Source materials of the Boxer War, 4 vols., Shanghai, 1951)

The Chinese Repository, ed. E. C. Bridgman and S. Wells Williams (20 vols., 1833–51)

Ch'ing shih kao (Draft History of the Ch'ing Dynasty, Peiping, 1928)

Ch'ing-tai ch'ou-pani-wu shih-mo (The Complete Account of the Management of Barbarian Affairs under the Ch'ing Dynasty, Peiping, 1930)

Ch'ing Tao-kuang ch'ao liu-chung mi-tsou (Secret Memorials to the Imperial Court during the Reign of Tao-kuang, 1931)

Ch'ing Te-tsung shih-lu (True Records of the Kuang-hsü period of the Ch'ing Dynasty, Changchun, 1937)

CLEMENTS, PAUL H. *The Boxer Rebellion: a political and diplomatic review* (New York, 1915)

COLLIS, MAURICE. (1) *The Great Within* (Faber, 1941)
(2) *Foreign Mud* (Faber, 1946)

CONGER, SARAH PIKE. *Letters from China* (1909)

CORDIER, HENRI. (1) *Histoire des relations de la Chine avec les Puissances Occidentales* (3 vols., 1901–2)
(2) *L'Expédition de Chine de 1857–8* (1905)
(3) *L'Expédition de Chine de 1860* (1906)

COSTIN, W. C. *Great Britain and China, 1833–1860* (Clarendon Press, Oxford, 1937)

CRANMER-BYNG, J. L. *An Embassy to China: Being the Journal Kept by Lord Macartney during his Embassy to the Emperor Ch'ien-lung, 1793–1794* (Longmans, 1962)

Crisis in the Opium Trade: Being an Account of the Proceedings of the Chinese Government (Canton, 1839)

CUNYNGHAME, ARTHUR. *An Aide-de-Camp's Recollections of Service in China* (2 vols., 1844)

DANBY, HOPE. *The Garden of Perfect Brightness* (Williams & Norgate, 1950)

DAVIS, SIR JOHN FRANCIS. (1) *Sketches of China* (2 vols., 1841)
(2) *China During the War and Since the Peace* (2 vols., 1852)
(3) *China: A General Description of that Empire and its Inhabitants* (1857)

DAWSON, RAYMOND. *The Chinese Chameleon: An Analysis of European Conceptions of Chinese Civilization* (Oxford University Press, 1967)

Delicate Enquiry into the Embassies to China and a Legitimate Conclusion (1818)

DER LING, PRINCESS. (1) *Two Years in the Forbidden City* (Shanghai, 1911)
(2) *Old Buddha* (N.Y., Dodd, Mead, 1929)

Diary of a Journey Overland through the Maritime Provinces of China (1822)

DOWNING, C. TOOGOOD. *The Fan-Qui in China in 1836–7* (3 vols., 1838)

ELGIN, 8TH EARL OF. (1) *Correspondence relative to the Earl of Elgin's Special Missions to China and Japan* (1859)
(2) *Letters and Journals of James, Eighth Earl of Elgin*, ed. Theodore Walrond (1872)

ELLIS, HENRY. *Journal of the Proceedings of the Late Embassy to China* (1817)

Eminent Chinese of the Ch'ing Period, see HUMMEL

Events in the Taeping Rebellion: Being Reprints of MSS copied by General Gordon in his own handwriting with monograph introduction and notes by A. Egmont Hake (1891)

FAIRBANK, JOHN K. (1) 'The Manchu appeasement policy of 1843', *Journal of the American Oriental Society*, lix, no. 4 (1939)

(2) 'Chinese diplomacy and the Treaty of Nanking, 1842', *Journal of Modern History*, xii, no. 1 (March, 1940)

(3) *Trade and Diplomacy on the China Coast* (Harvard University Press, 1953)

(4) *The United States and China* (Harvard University Press, 1948)

FAIRBANK, JOHN K. with TENG, SSU-YÜ. (1) *China's Response to the West: a documentary survey, 1839–1923* (Harvard University Press, 1954)

(2) *Ch'ing Administration: three studies* (Harvard University Press, 1960)

FEUERWERKER, ALBERT, MURPHEY, RHOADS and WRIGHT, MARY C. eds. *Approaches to Modern Chinese History* (University of California Press, 1967)

FISHBOURNE, E. G. *Impressions of China and the Present Revolution* (1855)

FISHEL, WESLEY R. *The End of Extraterritoriality in China* (University of California Press, 1952)

FISHER, LT. COL. [ARTHUR A'COURT]. *Personal Narrative of Three Years Service in China* (1863)

FITZGERALD, C. P. *The Chinese View of Their Place in the World* (Oxford University Press, 1964)

FLEMING, PETER. *The Siege at Peking* (Hart-Davis, 1959, and Readers Union, 1960)

FORBES, ROBERT R. *Remarks on China and the China Trade* (Boston, 1844)

FORTESCUE, SIR JOHN. *A History of the British Army*, vols. xii–xiii (1927, 1930)

FOX, GRACE. *British Admirals and Chinese Pirates 1832–1869* (Kegan Paul Trench & Trubner, 1940)

FRANKE, WOLFGANG. *China and the West* (Trs. R. A. Wilson, Basil Blackwell, 1967)

FRY, WILLIAM STORRS. *Facts and Evidence Relating to the Opium Trade with China* (1840)

GRANT, HOPE, with KNOLLYS, H. *Incidents in the China War of 1860* (1875)

GRANTHAM, A. E. *A Manchu Monarch: an interpretation of Chia Ch'ing* (Allen & Unwin, 1934)

GREENBERG, MICHAEL. *British Trade and the Opening of China* (Cambridge University Press, 1951)

GREGORY, J. S. *Great Britain and the Taipings* (Routledge & Kegan Paul, 1969)

GROS, BARON. *Négociations entre France et la Chine en 1860* (1863)

GUTZLAFF, CHARLES [Karl Gützlaff]. (1) *China Opened* (1838)

(2) *The Life of Taou-Kwang, Late Emperor of China with Memoirs of the Court of Peking* (1852)

HAHN, EMILY. *China Only Yesterday* (Weidenfeld & Nicolson, 1963)

HAIL, WILLIAM JAMES. *Tseng Kuo-fan and the Suppression of the Taiping Rebellion* (Yale University Press, 1927)

HALDANE, CHARLOTTE. *The Last Great Empress of China* (Constable, 1965)

HARFELDT, L. *Opinions Chinoises sur les Barbares d'Occident* (1909)

HART, SIR ROBERT. '*These from the Land of Sinim*' (1901)

HÉRISSON, COMTE DE. *Journal d'un Interprète en Chine* (Paris, 1886)

HOLT, EDGAR. *The Opium Wars in China* (Putnam, 1964)

HOOKER, MARY. *Behind the Scenes in Peking* (1910)

*HSIA, HSIEH-NO. *Chung hsi chi shih* (A Chronicle of Sino-Western Relations, 1860)

HUC, RÉGIS-EVARISTE. *The Chinese Empire* (1855)

HUGHES, E. R. *The Invasion of China by the Western World* (2nd edn., ed. R. S. Dawson, A. & C. Black, 1968)

HUMMEL, ARTHUR W. *Eminent Chinese of the Ch'ing Period, 1644–1912* (2 vols., Washington, 1943–4)

HUNTER, WILLIAM C. *Fan Kwae at Canton Before Treaty Days, 1825–1844* (Shanghai, 1911)

HURD, DOUGLAS. *The Arrow War: an Anglo-Chinese confusion* (Collins, 1967)

I-ho-t'uan tang-an shih-liao (Source materials in dispatches relating to the Boxers, 2 vols., Peking, 1959)

Jardine, Matheson & Co. An Historical Sketch (Privately printed by Jardine, Matheson & Co. Ltd. n.d.)

JOCELYN, [ROBERT] VISCOUNT. *Six Months with the Chinese Expedition* (1841)

JOHNSTON, REGINALD F. *Twilight in the Forbidden City* (Gollancz, 1934)

KEETON, G. W. *The Development of Extraterritoriality in China* (Longmans, 1928)

Keng-tzu Chi-shih (Records of 1900, Peking, 1959)

KIEFFER, MARTIN. see PELISSIER

KIERNAN, V. G. *The Lords of Human Kind* (Weidenfeld & Nicolson, 1969)

KNOLLYS, COLONEL H. ed. *Life of General Sir John Hope Grant* (1894)

KUO, PING-CHIA. *A Critical Study of the First Anglo-Chinese War, with Documents* (Shanghai, 1935)

LANE-POOLE, STANLEY. *Sir Harry Parkes in China* (1901)

LANGER, WILLIAM L. *The Diplomacy of Imperialism, 1890–1902* (2 vols., N.Y., Knopf, 1935)

Last Year in China to the Peace of Nanking by a Field Officer, The (1843)

LEAVENWORTH, CHARLES S. *The Arrow War with China* (1901)

LE FEVOUR, EDWARD. *Western Enterprise in Late Ch'ing China: A selective Survey of Jardine, Matheson & Co's operations 1842–1895* (Harvard East Asian Monographs)

LEHMAN, JOSEPH. *All Sir Garnet: A Life of Field Marshal Lord Wolseley* (Cape, 1964)

LEVENSON, JOSEPH, R. *Liang Ch'i-ch'ao and the Mind of Modern China* (Harvard University Press, 1953)

Sources

LI, CHIEN-NUNG (trans. and ed. by Ssu-yü Teng and Jeremy Ingalls). *The Political History of China, 1840–1928* (Van Nostrand, 1956)

LINDSAY, H. HAMILTON. *Is the War with China a Just one?* (1840)

LIN-LE (A. F. LINDLEY). *Ti-ping Tien-kwoh: The History of the Ti-ping Revolution* (1866)

LOCH, G. GRANVILLE. *The Closing Events of the Campaign in China* (1843)

LOCH, H. B. *Personal Narrative of Occurrences during Lord Elgin's Second Embassy to China* (1869)

*LO, ERH-KANG. *T'ai-p'ing T'ien-kuo Ko-ming Chan-cheng shih* (A History of the Revolutionary War of the Taipings, 1949)

LOEWE, MICHAEL. *Imperial China: The Historical Background to the Modern Age* (Allen & Unwin, 1966)

LOTI, PIERRE. *Les Derniers Jours de Pékin* (1901)

LUCY, ARMAND. *Lettres intimes sur la Campagne de Chine en 1860* (1861)

Macartney's Journal, see CRANMER-BYNG

MCALEAVY, HENRY. *The Modern History of China* (Weidenfeld & Nicolson, 1967)

M'GHEE, THE REV. R. J. L. *How We Got to Peking: a narrative of the campaign in China of 1860* (1862)

MACKENZIE, KEITH STEWART. *Narrative of the Second Campaign in China* (1842)

MCPHERSON, DUNCAN, M. D. *Two Years in China. Narrative of the Chinese Expedition* (1842)

MARTIN, W. A. P. *The Siege in Peking* (1900)

MASON, MARY GERTRUDE. *Western Concepts of China and the Chinese 1840–76* (1939)

MASPERO, H. *La Chine Antique*, (Paris, 1927)

MATEER, ADA HAVEN. *Siege Days* (1903)

MATHESON, JAMES. *The Present Position and Prospects of the British Trade with China* (1836)

MEADOWS, THOMAS TAYLOR. *The Chinese and Their Rebellions* (1856)

MICHAEL, FRANZ H. (in collaboration with CHANG, CHUNG-LI. *The Taiping Rebellion: history and documents*, vol. i (University of Washington Press, 1966)

MICHIE, ALEXANDER. *The Englishman in China during the Victorian Era as illustrated in the Career of Sir Rutherford Alcock* (1900)

MOGES, MARQUIS DE. *Recollections of Baron Gros's Embassy to China* (1860)

MONTAUBAN, GÉNÉRAL COUSIN DE. *L'Expédition de Chine de 1860* (Paris, 1932)

MORISON, J. L. *The Eighth Earl of Elgin* (Hodder & Stoughton, 1928)

MORRISON, ELIZA. *Memoirs of the Life and Labours of Robert Morrison* (2 vols., 1839)

MORRISON, G. E. *An Australian in China* (1895)

MORSE, HOSEA BALLOU. (1) *The Trade and Administration of the Chinese Empire* (1908)

(2) *The International Relations of The Chinese Empire*, vol. 1, *1834–1860*, vol. ii, *1861–1893* (1910, 1918)

(3) *Chronicles of The East India Company Trading to China, 1635–1834* (5 vols., Oxford University Press, 1926)

MOULE, ARTHUR EVANS. *Half a Century in China* (1911)

MURPHEY, RHOADS, see FEUERWERKER

MURRAY, LT. ALEXANDER. *Doings in China* (1843)

Nagel's Encyclopedia-Guide: China (Geneva, 1968)

New Quarrel in China, The (1859)

NUTTING, ANTHONY. *Gordon, Martyr and Misfit* (Constable, 1966)

NYE, GIDEON JNR. *The Opium Question and the Northern Campaigns* (Canton, 1875)

OLIPHANT, LAURENCE. *Narrative of the Earl of Elgin's Mission to China and Japan* (2 vols., 1860)

OLIPHANT, NIGEL. *A Diary of the Siege of the Legations in Peking* (1901)

OUCHTERLONY, JOHN. *The Chinese War: An Account of all the Operations of the British Forces from the Commencement to the Treaty of Nanking* (1844)

PARKER, E. H. (1) *China's Intercourse with Europe* (Shanghai, 1890)

(2) *Chinese Account of the Opium War* (Shanghai, 1888)

PELISSIER, ROGER. *The Awakening of China, 1793–1949*, ed. and trans. by Martin Kieffer (Secker & Warburg, 1963)

PICHON, STEPHEN. *Dans La Bataille* (1908)

PRATT, SIR JOHN T. *War and Politics in China* (Cape, 1943)

PRITCHARD, EARL H. (1) *Anglo-Chinese Relations during the Seventeenth and Eighteenth Centuries* (1919)

(2) *The Crucial Years of Early Anglo-Chinese Relations, 1750–1800* (1936)

PROUDFOOT, W. J. *Biographical Memoir of James Dinwiddie, LLD* (1868)

PURCELL, VICTOR. *The Boxer Uprising: A Background Study* (Cambridge University Press, 1963)

RAIT, ROBERT S. *The Life and Campaigns of Hugh, First Viscount Gough* (2 vols., 1903)

RENNIE, D. F. *The British Arms in North China and Japan* (1864)

RICHARD, REV. TIMOTHY. *Forty-five Years in China* (1916)

Rise and Progress of British Opium Smuggling. Five letters addressed to the Earl of Shaftesbury by Major-General R. Alexander, Madras Army, The (1856)

Rupture with China and its Causes including the Opium Question by a Resident in China, The (1840)

SCHURMANN, FRANZ, with SCHELL, ORVILLE. *China Readings, vol. i: Imperial China* (Random House, 1967; Penguin Books, 1967)

SELBY, JOHN. *The Paper Dragon: An Account of the China Wars* (Arthur Barker, 1968)

SERGEANT, PHILIP, W. *The Great Empress Dowager of China* (1910)

Sources

*SHANG, YÜEH. *Chung kuo Li Shih Kang-yao* (An Outline of Chinese History, Peking, 1954)

SHUCK, J. LEWIS. *Portfolio Chinese: Or a Collection of Authentic Chinese State Papers* (Macao, 1840)

SMITH, ARTHUR H. *China in Convulsion* (2 vols., 1901)

Some Pros and Cons of the Opium Question (1840)

SOOTHILL, W. E. *China and the West* (Oxford University Press, 1925)

SPENCE, JONATHAN. *The China Helpers* (Bodley Head, 1969)

STAUNTON, SIR GEORGE. *An Authentic Account of an Embassy from the King of Great Britain to the Emperor of China* (2 vols., 1798)

STAUNTON, G. T. *Memoirs* (1856)

STEIGER, G. NYE. *China and the Occident* (1927)

SUN, YAT-SEN. *Kidnapped in London: Being the Story of my Capture by . . . the Chinese Legation, London* (1897)

SWINHOE, ROBERT. *Narrative of the North China Campaign of 1860* (1861)

SWISHER, EARL. *China's Management of the American Barbarians* (1951)

* *Ta-Ch'ing li-ch'ao shih-lu* (The True Records of the Successive Reigns of the Ch'ing Dynasty, 1937)

* *T'ai-p'ing t'ien kuo ko-yao chuan-shu chi* (Songs and Reminiscences of the Taipings collected orally, Nanking, 1960)

TAIT, THE REV. W. *The Opium Trade: An Appeal to the British Nation Against It* (1858)

*TAI, YI. *Chung-kuo chin-tai shih-kao* (Peking, 1958)

TAN, CHESTER, C. *The Boxer Catastrophe* (Columbia University Press, 1955)

TAYLOR, CHARLES. *Five Years in China* (1860)

TENG, SSU-YÜ, with FAIRBANK, JOHN K. (1) *Chang Hsi and the Treaty of Nanking* (University of Chicago Press, 1944)
(2) *China's Response to the West: A Documentary Survey, 1839–1923* (Harvard University Press, 1954)
(3) *Ch'ing Administration: Three Studies* (Harvard University Press, 1960)

THOMSON, H. C. *China and the Powers* (1902)

Treaties, Conventions, etc. between China and Foreign States (Shanghai, 1917)

*TS'AO, CHENG. *I-huan pei ch'ang chi* (The catastrophes and troubles caused by the Barbarians) in the *Shang-hai chang-ku ts'ung-shu* (Collection of Historical Records of the City of Shanghai) (Shanghai, 1935)

VAN BRAAM, see *Authentic Account of the Embassy of the Dutch East India Company, etc.*

VARÈ, DANIEL. *The Last Empress* (N.Y., Doubleday, Doran 1938)

WALDERSEE, ALFRED COUNT VON. *A Field-Marshal's Memoirs* (1924)

WALEY, ARTHUR. *The Opium War through Chinese Eyes* (Allen & Unwin, 1958)

WALKER, GENERAL SIR C. P. G. *Days of a Soldier's Life: Letters Written During Active Service in the Chinese War* (1894)

WEALE, B. L. PUTNAM [B. L. SIMPSON]. *Indiscreet Letters from Peking* (n.d.)

WEHRLE, EDMUND S. *Britain, China and the Antimissionary Riots, 1891–1900* (University of Minnesota Press, 1966)

*WEI YUAN. *Sheng Wu Chi* (Description of the Military Operations) (1842)

WEN, CH'ING. *The Chinese Crisis from Within* (1901)

WILLIAMS, F. W., ed. *The Journal of S. Wells Williams* (Shanghai, 1911)

WILLIAMS, S. WELLS. *The Middle Kingdom* (rev. edn, 2 vols., 1883)

WILSON, ANDREW. *The 'Ever-Victorious Army': A History of the Chinese Campaign under Lt. Col. C. G. Gordon and of the Suppression of the Taiping Rebellion* (1868)

WINGROVE COOKE, G. *China: 'The Times' Special Correspondence in the Years 1857–8* (1858)

WOLSELEY, G. J. *Narrative of the War with China in 1860* (1862)

WOODCOCK, GEORGE. *The British in the Far East* (Weidenfeld & Nicolson, 1969)

WRIGHT, MARY CLABAUGH, ed. (also see FEUERWERKER). (1) *The Last Stand of Chinese Conservatism: The T'ung Chih Restoration, 1861–74* (Stanford University Press, 1957)

  (2) *China in Revolution: The First Phase* (Yale University Press, 1969)

WU, YUNG. *The Flight of an Empress. . . . Transcribed and Edited by Ida Pruitt* (Faber, 1937)

*YEN-SHIH CHIU-T'U. *Hsin-jen chih wen hsin yüeh-fu* (New Poems heard during the years 1901–2) reprinted in *Keng-tzu shih-pien wen-hsüeh chih* (Literature of the Boxer Rising) (Peking, 1959)

*YÜN, YÜ-TING. *Ch'ung-ling ch'uan hsin-lu* (A True Record of the crisis in the reign of Emperor Kuang-hsü) (Shanghai, 1926)

Index

About the Author

Christopher Hibbert was born in Leicestershire in 1924, and was educated at Radley and Oriel College, Oxford. He served as an infantry officer in the war, was twice wounded, and was awarded the M.C. He has rapidly established himself as a leading historian combining a concern for careful scholarship with what Raymond Mortimer has described as a 'correct, lucid, and pleasing style.' In 1962 he won the Heinemann Award for Literature. He is married, with three children, and lives in Henley-on-Thames.